THE
FABULOUS
FANTASY FILMS

THE FABULOUS FANTASY FILMS

by

Jeff Rovin

SOUTH BRUNSWICK AND NEW YORK: A. S. BARNES AND COMPANY
LONDON: THOMAS YOSELOFF LTD

A. S. Barnes and Co., Inc.
Cranbury, New Jersey 08512

Magdalen House
136-148 Tooley Street
London SE1 2TT, England

Library of Congress Cataloging in Publication Data

Rovin, Jeff.
　The fabulous fantasy films.

　Filmography: p.
　Includes index.
　1. Fantastic films—History and criticism.
I. Title.
PN1995.9.F36R6　　1976　　791.43′0909′15　　76-10876
ISBN 0-498-01803-2

PRINTED IN THE UNITED STATES OF AMERICA

to
my parents
who still regard
most of these movies
as junk.

CONTENTS

Preface 9

Introduction

1. The Ghost 15
2. Angels and Death 25
3. Witchcraft and Voodoo 35
4. The Devil 44
5. The Vampire 56
6. The Werewolf 71
7. The Mummy 82
8. The Monster 90
9. The Dinosaur 101
10. The Giant Monster 112

11. Mythology 139
12. Fantastic Science 172
13. Incredible Lands 184
14. Magic and Beyond 199
15. Fantasy Animation 207
16. Fantasy Film Anthologies 222
17. Television 230

Appendix 1 Cast and Credits of 500
Fantasy Films 236

Appendix 2 Interviews 255

Notes 260

Index 263

PREFACE

The over five-hundred films in this book are limited, by and large, to those that received substantial play in Great Britain and the United States.

Assembling the wide variety of fresh, new stills and information would not have been possible without the help of the following: Ricou Browning, Mary Corliss of the Museum of Modern Art, Brad Franklin, Ray Harryhausen, William Castle, George Pal, Dick Siegel, Tom A. Jones of Walt Disney Productions, Vic Ghidalia of ABC, Michael Silver of CBS, Christopher Lee, Roger Corman, Tony Randall, Robert Wise, and Paula Klaw at *Movie Star News*.

INTRODUCTION

What do King Kong, Judy Garland, Ebeneezer Scrooge, and Willy Wonka's Human Blueberry have in common? The answer, of course, is that they are all a part of the vast playground known as the fantasy film.

By its very definition, the term "fantasy" implies man's imagination unrestrained. That's exactly what you'll find within these pages. Motion pictures in which the situations are far removed from the realm of reason or possibility.

Of necessity, this shuts out such classic genre films as *Frankenstein, 2001: A Space Odyssey,* and *Metropolis.* Man is already transplanting human limbs and organs, building space stations, and subjecting his world to the hazards of dictatorship. Here, then, are motion pictures that showcase the supernatural, mythology, or incredible creatures and events. The decision to include such borderline "horror" or "science fiction" efforts as *Dracula* and *The Wolfman* or *Godzilla* and *Barbarella* was based on the relative void between plausible reality and the situations depicted in these films.

Care has also been taken to avoid pictures like *Things to Come* or the *Flash Gordon* serials, where the emphasis is on science fiction gadgetry. Though it was logic and rational hardware that put men on the moon, it is pure fantasy that takes him always one step beyond. And that is our destination. A world where the irrational reins and common sense is tossed to the wind. A universe of demons and fairy tales, of giants and, yes, human blueberries. The kingdom of *The Fabulous Fantasy Films.*

THE
FABULOUS
FANTASY FILMS

1
THE GHOST

The world of spirits and specters is perhaps the most gripping of all filmed fantasy. With roots in the hazy periphery of man's senses, it is a motif that plays on our inherent fear of the unknown, of a world just beyond life.

Throughout film history, the spirit world has been used by moviemakers as a vehicle for comedy, horror, or allegory. Let's look at these categorical efforts starting with those that are set in the perennial favorite, the haunted house.

Until the trend-setting motion picture *The Uninvited* (1944), haunted houses and their spectral inhabitants were not taken seriously by filmmakers. Producers felt that audiences would laugh at ghosts and find them ludicrous. Thus, they limited the spectrum of these films to light-hearted romps and bizarre comedies such as *The Ghost Goes West* (1936) in which a Scottish castle and its resident spirit are transported to Long Island; *Topper* (1937), *Topper Takes a Trip* (1939), and *Topper Returns* (1941) wherein a family of ghosts is denied eternal sleep until it has done good deeds on earth; *Ghost Breakers* (1940) with Bob Hope and Paulette Goddard lost in a Cuban mansion replete with zombies and specters; the surprisingly well-made *Hold That Ghost* (1941) in which Abbott and Costello are forced by a storm to hole up in a haunted mansion; *Ghost Catchers* with comedians Olson and Johnson in a haunted house; and even a vehicle for Charles Laughton, who got into the spirit of things as *The Canterville Ghost* (1944), a cowardly seventeenth-century spook who is unable to rest until his descendent, Robert Young, has performed some great and heroic deed. During this period there were also very tentative stabs at serious ghost films: *Earthbound* (1940), for example, featured Warner Baxter as a ghost who helps his wife get a confession from the woman who shot him. It wasn't until *The Uninvited*, however, that a ghost picture received the publicity of a "legitimate" film. Not that there weren't doubts as to its commercialism. Paramount Pictures took the precaution of billing it not as film of the supernatural, but as *the story of a love that is out of this world*. Fortunately, the public was ready to take its ghosts seriously.

Based on a novel by Dorothy Macardle, *The Uninvited* is the story of Roderick Fitzgerald (Ray Milland) and his sister Pamela (Ruth Hussey) who rent a home in England, on the Cornish Coast, and soon discover that all is not well with the place. Strange musical sounds are heard from out of nowhere; there is the odor of flowers in closed rooms and the feel of something unearthly in the air. The newcomers are convinced that this is the work of a ghost. Accordingly, a young medium (Gail Russell) is called in to exorcise the spirit, whom we learn is her mother. Before leaving the residence, the deceased appears at the top of a stairway as an indistinct blob of ectoplasm.

Unlike ghost films that follow, in which the spirit's existence is often left to the discretion of the audience, there is no doubt as to the legitimacy of the lurking entity in *The Uninvited*. While this blatancy tends to destroy the mystery, it also evokes a nervous respect for the world beyond. In the reality of *The Uninvited*, the things that go bump in

An extremely rare drawing done by Norman McLeod. McLeod, who directed the first two Topper films, always drew thumbnail sketches in the margins of his script. These served as a guide for whatever scene he was about to shoot. Although he did not direct *Topper Returns*, he did this marginal sketch for friend Roy Del Ruth. Roy evidently liked what he saw, for . . .

. . .this is how the scene looked in the film. Shown are Eddie "Rochester" Anderson, Gail Richards, and Roland Young.

the night are actually there! The picture did well enough to inspire a sequel, *The Unseen* (1945), with Miss Russell as the haunted rather than the hunter. Unlike the first film, this effort was a critical and commercial failure.

The years after *The Uninvited* saw reworkings, both good and bad, of the theme. The immediate releases were *Halfway House* (1944), starring Mervyn Johns and daughter Glynis as ghosts whose hotel causes visitors to relive the year-gone-by; *A Place of One's Own* (1944) in which a guest at an old couple's inn is possessed by the spirit of a murdered girl; and *Blithe Spirit* (1945), based on a play by Noel Coward and featuring Margaret Rutherford as a medium who summons forth the spirits of writer Charles Condomime's (Rex Harrison) first and second wives. In a lighter vein, Abbott and Costello had their second ghostly escapade in *The Time of Their Lives* (1946). Costello and Marjorie Reynolds starred as American colonists killed as traitors by their countrymen. They haunt a home visited by Abbott and others and cannot be set free until the newcomers find a letter from George Washington that proves the spirits' innocence.

Rex Harrison made his second fantasy film appearance as the spirit of sea captain Daniel Gregg in *The Ghost and Mrs. Muir* (1947). He haunts his old home, which has been rented by Lucy Muir (Gene

Tierney) at the turn of the century. The couple falls in love, and after her death they walk off into the clouds. The film was remade in 1955 as *Stranger in the Night* with Joan Fontaine and Michael Wilding. Of a less romantic mold, *Things Happen at Night* (1951) . . . such as a young girl's possession by an evil ghost; a year later Dean Martin and Jerry Lewis were *Scared Stiff* on a Caribbean island. Equally standard slapstick-and-spirit fare was the talking mule *Francis in the Haunted House* (1955).

Bob Hope and Willie Best in *Ghost Breakers*.

Rex Harrison as the spiritual sea captain in *The Ghost and Mrs. Muir.*

The Headless Ghost and consort.

Carol Ohmart is visited by the skeleton under screen-husband Vincent Price's control in *House on Haunted Hill.*

Dean Jones and Peter Ustinov in *Blackbeard's Ghost.* (c) Walt Disney Productions.

As the fifties progressed, ghost films sacrificed mood for shock. Movies of the "old" school like *The Headless Ghost* (1958), who haunted a castle in search of the mystic potion that would grant him eternal peace, and the noble bent of *The Invisible Creature* (1959), a ghost who used his powers to prevent murder in an English mansion, were tame when compared to *House on Haunted Hill* or *Thirteen Ghosts*, both by filmmaker William Castle. The first film, made in 1959, had Vincent Price playing host to guests in his haunted mansion. The ghosts, though a trick, were enough to scare Price's wife, her lover, and the audience to death. *Thirteen Ghosts* (1960) was another very strange entry, this one filmed in *Illusiono*. The once-only process employed gimmick glasses, which allowed a viewer to see or not to see the denizens of the haunted house. These specters, as advertised, were *The Screaming Woman, The Clutching Hands, The Floating Head, Emilio The Mad Butcher, His Wife, Her Lover, The Executioner, The Hanging Woman, The Lion and the Headless Tamer, The Rotting Dr. Zorba*, and *?*. The question mark meant that one of the stars would die and become ghost number thirteen. *Thirteen Ghosts* also marked the return to fantasy of Margaret Hamilton, the witch in *Wizard of Oz* (1939), as Elaine Zacharides, housekeeper of the haunted mansion inherited by paleontologist Cyrus Zorba (Donald Woods) from his eccentric uncle. Even Walt Disney got into the ghosting act, albeit some years later, with *Blackbeard's Ghost* (1967), starring Peter Ustinov as a pirate's poltergeist invisible to all but Dean Jones.

Laying aside the gimmicks and fluff, perhaps the most effective film of this genre was *The Innocents* (1961), based on a five-act play by William Archibald, which, itself, was based on the 1897 novella *Turn of the Screw* by Henry James. *The Innocents* are two children, Miles (Martin Stephens) and Flora (Pamela Franklin) who live in a British countryside estate. A governess, Miss Giddens (Deborah Kerr),

Martin Stephens and Pamela Franklin in a delicate scene from *The Innocents.*

A more macabre scene from *The Innocents*, just before the death of Martin Stephens. Pictured is Deborah Kerr.

Clayton *(The Great Gatsby)* performed his own job admirably by pulling superb performances from his cast, especially Miss Kerr as the ever-building paranoid, and Megs Jenkins as the housekeeper who grows increasingly irate with Miss Giddens.

Although *The Innocents* was a box-office disappointment, this did not deter director Robert Wise *(Sound of Music, West Side Story)* from undertaking a ghost story of his own in *The Haunting* (1963). Wise, no stranger to the fantastic, having directed *Day the Earth Stood Still* (1951) with spaceman Michael Rennie, and Boris Karloff's grave-robbing foray as *The Body Snatcher* (1945), chose Shirley Jackson's novel *The Haunting of Hill House* as the vehicle for his attempt to offer scientific rationale for ghosts.

The Haunting represents a mature and topical

is hired by the children's uncle to watch after them. She joins the housekeeper Mrs. Grose (Megs Jenkins) in this charge, and soon thereafter the hauntings begin, but only in the eyes of Miss Giddens. Curtains billow when there is no breeze, strange whisperings can be heard, and there is a definite evil afoot. The governess comes to believe that the spirits of her predecessor, Miss Jessel, and the girl's lover, Quint, are haunting the mansion, trying to possess the children. She resolves to save the youngsters, but her efforts at exorcism backfire, leaving Miles dead and Flora a raving lunatic.

We are fairly certain, as the moodily photographed black-and-white film concludes, that the ghosts were simply imagined by our heroine. They do not materialize on screen until Miss Giddens sees their portraits—and only then in brief long-shots. Too, there is a pervading reference made to Miss Giddens' sexual inhibitions, and the lovers' own fulfillment may have been what was haunting the governess. In this respect, the film offers a more subjective viewpoint than the James original where a similar explanation for the spirits is suggested, but the reader is free to view them as visitors from the beyond. The film leaves us no such leeway.

Although purists argue against the filmmakers having meddled with the original, *The Innocents* is an excellent movie, frightening in its power of psychosexual suggestion as opposed to being, like *The Uninvited*, a ghost story with real ghosts. Scenarist Truman Capote is largely responsible for the Freudian implications, while director Jack

The original ad-art for *The Haunting*.

approach to its subject matter. A mansion in New England is the playground for psychic investigators Dr. John Markway (Richard Johnson), Eleanor (Julie Harris), and Theodora (Claire Bloom). The research trio is joined by Mrs. Markway (Lois Maxwell) and the young man who is to inherit the haunted house (Russ Tamblyn). The team has come to determine what, if any, extrasensory forces goven the place, a mansion built a century before by a man who was destined never to inhabit its Victorian halls. Shortly after getting married, his bride's carriage ran into a large tree on the estate and she was killed. Since that time, many have died in Hill House.

No sooner have the five researchers arrived when seemingly supernatural events begin. The psychic Eleanor's name appears inexplicably in the dust; the home rattles and shakes. Similar to *The Innocents* in rationale if not in timbre, Markway attributes these events not to spirits but to the force-of-mind personifications of the middle-aged virgin Eleanor's sexual frustrations. When the film has run its course, and the poor woman can take no more of this "haunting," she panics, drives off, and dies when her car crashes into the same tree that killed her predecessor a century before.

Through the use of distorted perspective, bizarre lenses, and excellent special effects, Wise, on the one hand, succeeds in evoking a cold, chilling feel for the unearthly events. Paradoxically, he dilutes his achievement by tying the pulsing terror of the house to Eleanor. Unlike *The Innocents*, which offers only its sexual vantage point, *The Haunting* attempts to straddle the supernatural, the scientific, and the libido. In covering all his bases, Wise spreads thin his loyalties to one or the other. The result is a well-made but indecisive film.

The most recent resurrection of this theme has been *The Legend of Hell House* (1973), written for the screen by Richard Matheson *(The Incredible Shrinking Man, I Am Legend)* from his own novel. Exposition tells us, right away, that Hell House is, in fact, inhabited by the ghost of its former owner, a millionaire by the name of Belasco.[1] As in *The Haunting*, a research team, consisting of a para-psychologist (Clive Revill), his wife (Gayle Hunnicutt), and two mediums (Roddy McDowall and Pamela Franklin), arrives to contact Belasco's spirit. They are well-prepared to seek him out with the mind and hordes of electromagnetic equipment as well. The ghost is eventually exposed and, in a

rousing climax, McDowall exorcises the specter.

The film features sturdy performances, especially by McDowall, and the more-permissive era in which the picture was made led to a proper exploitation of the sexual undercurrents that are clearly a generic part of the supernatural. For example, Belasco's seduction of Miss Franklin is remarkably well done, although through suggestion alone, since he appears to her in the form of a cat.

The only real letdown in *The Legend of Hell House* is the unveiling of Belasco's terrible secret, the reason for which the ghost has remained ensconced in his mansion: Belasco was only five feet tall and wore artificial legs. This denouement is comical in view of what has gone before, and serves to erase the picture's powerful hold on its audiences.

Haunted houses have not been filmmakers' only doorway between our world and the next. Many films feature ghosts out in the open. Charles Middleton, who would gain fame as Ming the Merciless in the Flash Gordon serials, was *The Strangler of the Swamp* (1945), the ghost of a man executed for a crime he did not commit. Middleton returns to kill those who were responsible for his death and is stopped short of slaughtering even their relatives with the intercession of Maria (Rosemary La-Planche). Her love for a would-be victim softens the spirit and he returns to his grave. However, not all ghosts were creatures of evil. *Portrait of Jennie* (1949), for example, is one of the most sensitive films ever made, and a ghost story unlike any other.

Based on a novel by Robert Nathan, *Portrait of Jennie* stars Joseph Cotton as artist Eben Adams, a man who has been unable to earn little more than the money he needs to survive. As a result, both his spirit and work fall to ruin. On a wintertime walk through New York's Central Park, he finds a little girl named Jennie Appleton playing hopscotch. Eben is struck by her charm and, when he returns home, sketches the girl from memory. He sells the drawing to a gallery and is told to do further studies of the girl, perhaps a portrait in oil.

Eben meets Jennie several times during the next year, but on each occasion she has grown much older than the normal passage of time would have allowed. Too, she speaks of places and events that belong to the past, referring to them as if they were topical. Slowly, by questioning people that Jennie has mentioned, Eben learns that she had lived and died over a generation before. Through some mystic quirk, she is reliving portions of her life, which,

Jennifer Jones and Joseph Cotten meet in Central Park
in *Portrait of Jennie*.

Eben realizes, must culminate in her drowning at Cape Cod. He meets her there and tries to prevent her death. Hurrying along the seashore in a mad effort to cheat destiny, the pair is caught in a hurricane and engulfed by a monstrous wave. Only Eben survives, left with the memory of a girl who was reborn to find life and love in his arms.

Portrait of Jennie cost $4,000,000 to make and won an Oscar for its spectacular storm sequence, which alone required a $250,000 expenditure. Billed as *The most tender and yet terrifying love story ever told*, it was a critical and commercial failure. Subsequent releases in 1950, under the banner *Tidal Wave*, and a second time in 1956 with the original title failed to recoup the losses. The film was maligned unjustly by critics who were expecting a work of somewhat more thematic sophistication.

Melodramatic love stories are one thing. Using fantasy to show how love and its pursuit are eternal is quite another. Audiences who had been used to such light-hearted films as *Ghost and Mrs. Muir* were unprepared for *Jennie's* intensity and found its allegory most confusing.

Pandora and the Flying Dutchman (1951) returned to the more safe and standard fantasy of the Victorian Romance. Ava Gardner is the lonely woman on whom Dutch sailor James Mason comes calling. Mason has been doomed to roam the seas for eternity, or until someone gives up their life for his freedom. Naturally, Miss Gardner comes to the rescue. It's a touching little film highlighted by a pair of marvelous performances.

A different type of ghostly love was on display in *Curse of the Cat People* (1946), directed by Robert

Wise and produced under the aegis of forties' horror-master Val Lewton. *Curse of the Cat People* features Ann Carter as Aimee, a six-year-old girl whose dead and insane mother Irena (Simone Simon) returns to fill her daughter's lonely life with companionship. Aimee's father Oliver (Kent Smith) and her stepmother (Jane Randolph) try to rid her of these "delusions," and the little girl runs away from home. When she's rescued, her father comes to realize that Aimee needs his friendship and pretends to see Irena. The film ends on a note of hope, and we recognize, somewhat sadly, that the girl will soon have no further need for her fantasies.

Curse of the Cat People was a sequel to the hugely profitable *The Cat People* (1942) in which Miss Simon was heir to a curse that turned her into a ferocious black leopard (see chapter 6). Director Wise instilled this followup film with delicate, scintillating images and does not shy from letting the viewer see and hear Irena as she and her daughter play. The love that is manifest in Aimee's fantasies leaves us with a warm heart but cold hands: there is still the icy chill of its subject matter. In this respect, the film is less objective and sterile than *The Haunting*. Of course, the picture does have its moments of horror. Aimee's one tangible friend is an old woman who lives in a shadowed house down the street. The mysterious lady tells Aimee the story of the *Headless Horseman*, and the young girl's imagination builds this tale to the point of reality. She comes to believe that the infamous rider is lurking in the dark, galloping ever closer, ready to

sweep her within his black cloak and carry her off. The nightmarish "appearances" of the horseman, realized on screen with only sound and suggestion, occur when Aimee awakens late at night and again when she is lost in the woods while running away from home.

If *Curse of the Cat People* represents ghostly devotion, then *Tormented* (1960) is the flip side of the coin, hate from beyond the grave. *Tormented* was science fiction filmmaker Bert I. Gordon's *(The Amazing Colossal Man, Attack of the Fifty Foot Woman)* first excursion into the supernatural. Richard Carlson portrays a pianist who murders his mistress by pushing her from atop a lighthouse. Her dander incurred, the girl returns to haunt the man as a floating head, a gust of wind, a strangling hand, or crawling lengths of seaweed. Eventually, Carlson falls to his death and his body is found tangled with that of his restless lover. The film is quite effective, and made doubly so because Gordon doesn't try to *explain* ghosts. He simply tells us that this ghost is real and carries on from there. The result is a gripping, surprisingly original work.

Gordon returned to ghostings in 1968 with *Picture Mommy Dead* wherein a girl is haunted by visions of her dead mother. The film has a fine cast, including Don Ameche, Martha Heyer, and Bert's perennial star, his daughter Susan, but is hardly as frightening as Gordon's earlier spooking.

Of a more classical sort are the various adaptations of Charles Dickens' *A Christmas Carol*, featuring any number of strange ghosts. The story tells of the transformation of Ebeneezer Scrooge from miser to philanthropist. This is accomplished

Young Ann Carter hears the approach of the Headless Horseman after running away from home. From *Curse of the Cat People*.

Richard Carlson pushes his mistress from a lighthouse in *Tormented* . . .

. . .and she returns to haunt him.

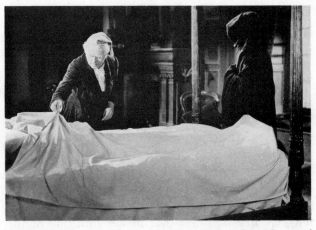

Reginald Owen is shown his corpse by the Ghost of Christmas Yet-to-Come in *A Christmas Carol*.

by showing him his past misdeeds and a hellish future. Scrooge's hosts for the presentation are a trio of ghosts: the spirits of Christmas Past, Present, and Future, with the specter of Ebeneezer's business partner Jacob Marley making a guest appearance.

The story has been twice filmed with live actors, was an Oscar-winning cartoon from the Richard Williams studio of England (1971), and was even an animated comedy with Mr. Magoo as Scrooge. Despite these various incarnations, the finest version remains the 1971 musical *Scrooge*, featuring the brilliant Albert Finney as the title character. It was a

Albert Finney is shown his grave by the Ghost of Christmas Yet-to-Come in *Scrooge*.

part he won over Rex Harrison and Richard Harris, and a role held before by two very difficult acts to follow: Reginald Marsh in 1938 and Alistair Sim in 1953.

Scrooge was made to cash in on the overwhelming success of *Oliver,* even to the point of economically reusing many of the 1968's films exterior sets. No matter. What goes on inside them is pure magic. Alec Guinness gives a virtuoso performance as Marley's ghost, an apparition that sits where there is no chair and rises to the ceiling when enraged. Without the aide of special effects, Guinness carries himself with an airy lightness that makes him one of the most convincing ghosts in screen history.

Lashed to Marley's incorporeal form is a weighty strongbox and interminable length of chain. "I forged this in life," he explains, "by misdeeds to my fellow men. Now I can never be free of it."

"But why do you walk the earth?" Scrooge asks. Herein is the theme of Dickens' story.

"Sooner or later, the spirit of every man must travel among his fellow men. If it does not choose to do so freely during his life, then it is condemned to do so after his death." As if to emphasize the plight of such souls, Marley takes Scrooge on a flight over London to gaze upon the hundreds of airborne specters wandering in limbo. It's a marvelous scene, although the flavor is more Halloween than Christmas.

When the pair returns to Scrooge's room, Marley leaves and Dame Edith Evans arrives, the Ghost of Christmas Past. She is followed by a portly, wine-guzzling Kenneth More as the Ghost of Christmas Present, and finally by the Ghost of Christmas Yet-to-come, an awesome figure in black. He shows Scrooge the future, then sends him to hell. There, Ebeneezer is tormented by Marley and given his own ponderous chain. Miraculously, the miser awakens and finds himself in bed. He promises the world, in song, "I'll begin again!"

The music by Leslie Bricusse *(Dr. Dolittle)* spawned the Oscar-nominated show-stopper *Thank You Very Much,* and the film, released theatrically an incredible three years running, is now an annual Christmas-week favorite on television.

2
ANGELS AND DEATH

The border between ghosts and their kindred souls, the angels, is a fine one. More often than not, ghosts are out to commit mayhem and murder. Angels, on the other hand, are almost always good. Thus, in an angel film, we realize that what's coming is not intended to scare us, but to illustrate, through allegory, some very human aspect of a character's persona: undying love, a last chance to redeem one's soul, a worthy mortal helped by heavenly officers, etc.

Beyond Tomorrow (1940) was one of the first angel films, a picture wherein three spirits journey from above to spend Christmas with the down-and-out Richard Carlson and Jean Parker. The two fall in love and the angels are no longer needed. The following year, prizefighter Robert Montgomery did not get heavenly help with equal felicity. Due to its unique plot and stellar cast, *Here Comes Mr. Jordan* is perhaps one of the most popular angel films. The aforementioned boxer has been called to the pearly gates before his time. Since his own body has been cremated, Montgomery is given the only remains available, those of a drowned man. Claude Rains portrays the angel Mr. Jordan, who helps Montgomery through the complications fostered by his new life. It's all great entertainment and does not fall to exploiting the more gimmicky aspects of the genre, such as magic. A year later, *I Married an Angel* was unveiled, the last film ever made by the team of Jeanette MacDonald and Nelson Eddy. Based on a Rodgers and Hart musical, the picture had Eddy in love with a girl whom he dreams is really an angel. The film was heavy-handed and not commercially successful.

The ghostly Spencer Tracy helps pilot Van Johnson in a mission during *A Guy Named Joe*.

The distinguished Spencer Tracy got his wings in *A Guy Named Joe* (1943) as an angel who lent a helping hand to World War II flyer Van Johnson. He even went so far as to selflessly set him up with his former girlfriend. A popular film, it inspired others that appeared in 1945. In *The Horn Blows at Midnight*, Jack Benny dreams he is Gabriel come to earth to destroy it with a blast of his horn. *That's The Spirit* featured Jack Oakie as an angel who returns to the mortal sphere to explain to his wife (Peggy Ryan) the reasons for everything good and bad he did during his life. In *Stairway to Heaven*, David Niven is an RAF squadron leader who, during a World War II battle, bails from his plane without a parachute and is killed. In heaven, he argues for his life and is returned to earth on the

Jack Benny confronts the heavenly orchestra whose performance will destroy the earth in *The Horn Blows at Midnight*.

Signing in for heaven in *Stairway to Heaven*.

strength of a woman's love. Finally, there came the least-impressive effort of that grouping, *Angel Comes to Brooklyn*, wherein Charles Kemper is a beneficent spirit who helps put on a Broadway show.

The following year saw new and interesting plays on the old themes. Fred Astaire was a con artist in *Yolanda and the Thief*, pretending to be the guardian angel of wealthy and innocent Lucille Bremer that he might abscond with her fortune. Happily, the actual protective spirit (Leon Ames) comes along to rescue Miss Bremer. A more routine but interesting film was *Cockeyed Miracle*, in which Frank Morgan returned to earth that he might make reparation for a fiscal error he committed in life.

Henry Travers was filmland's next angel in *It's a Wonderful Life* (1946), based on Philip van Doren Stern's story *The Greatest Gift*. Under Frank Capra's sensitive direction, the film features James Stewart as businessman George Bailey who, facing bankruptcy, starts wondering why he had ever been born. The angel Clarence descends from above and shows him what his small town would be like had he never been born. The picture is ultimately a comment on the value of life and the importance of one man in the scheme of things. This dignity of the individual is a favorite theme of Capra's, and one he examines at greater length in *Lost Horizon* Unfortunately, a trio of angel films released the following year were not quite as deep.

Although technically not an angel, Rita Hayworth came *Down to Earth* as Terpischore, the

David Niven demands that Cary Grant prove his superhuman powers by walking through a locked door in *The Bishop's Wife*.

Goddess of Dance, to add choreographic life to Larry Parks' uninspired musical play. In *Heaven Only Knows*, the archangel Michael (Robert Cummings) visits a small western town to resolve the problem of a mean and irresponsible gambler who was born without a soul. Lastly, a celebrated actor who donned halo and wings was Cary Grant as the angel Dudley in *The Bishop's Wife*. Grant's mission was to help clergyman David Niven and his wife Loretta Young with their Christmas drive to raise money for a new church.

Several years passed before the next heavenly fodder, *Bad Lord Byron* (1949) wherein Dennis Price must face a heavenly court before passing to the afterlife. The trial reviews Byron's life and the film becomes a romantic biography of the British poet. A delightful film followed hard-upon, *For Heaven's Sake* (1950), based on the stories *Windy* and *May We Come In?* by Harry and Dorothy Seegall. Clifton Webb and Edmund Gwenn are angels who work their magic on earth to see that a pair of babies are born, despite problems between their respective parents. It's whimsical fun given surprising depth by the excellent performances of Webb, Gwenn, and youthful Tommy Retik and Gigi Perreau as the unborn children who are innocent but cogent observers to their parents' problems.

Angels in the Outfield were discovered in 1951, spiritual forces who lift the Pittsburgh Pirates from the cellar to a championship season. Only an orphan (Donna Corcoran) can see them, of course. More concerned with the human race than a pennant race was Dick Powell, the star of *You Never Can Tell* (1951). In his previous life, Powell had been a dog who was poisoned. Appearing before the lion-god of animal heaven, the murdered mongrel asks that he be returned to earth as a human detective in order to find his killer. Powell's wish is granted, and the spirit of a horse (Joyce Holden) goes with him in the guise of a secretary. It's all grand fun, unpretentious and quite clever. Five years later, a less enjoyable fantasy found Diane Cilento who, short on cash, became *The Angel Who Pawned Her Harp*. Based on the novel by Charles Terrot, the title character gets involved with the problems of the pawnbroker and his helpers. The film was sincere but trivial, and made to appear even more so by the release that same year of Hollywood's overwhelming fantasy musical extravaganza, *Carousel*.

Carousel is based on the successful Rodgers and

Gordon MacRae on the heaven set in *Carousel*.

Hammerstein musical and stars Gordon MacRae as Billy Bigelow, an angel who's been dead, when we meet him, for fifteen years. He's standing on a cloud, polishing heaven's stars, when he decides to invoke an option he turned down a decade and a half before: to return to earth for one day. Billy visits the office of his boss to vie for passage. The overseer is reluctant to grant his permission and asks why the angel has changed his mind. Billy, dressed in his sailor's suit, tells his life story. The bottom line is that his daughter has grown up an outcast because her father was killed while robbing a man. The heavenly foreman ponders Billy's motives and gives him one day's leave. The angel descends to give his teenage girl a star and, through it, inspiration.

Carousel is overflowing with sentiment that was contrived to soften even the toughest of moviegoers. By the time the famous *You'll Never Walk Alone* finale rolls around, and Billy returns to Heaven, there isn't a dry eye in the house. The fantasy element is, again, a light and colorful framework for the meat of the story, how carnival barker Billy quits his job, marries a girl, and sponges off her for the rest of his brief life. The performances are generally saccharin, used as window dressing for the ultra widescreen Camera 55 images.[2]

After *Carousel*, screen angels were a poorly represented lot, marked only by an occasional film such as *Two Thousand Years Later* (1968) with a Roman soldier sent by the god Mercury to warn the earth of its coming destruction. Unfortunately, our resurrected hero falls prey to fast-talking con men, the very types from whom he's trying to save us. Walt Disney took a different view of things as his studio put Harry Morgan in charge of Fred Mac-Murray's life for *Charley and the Angel* (1972).

Fortunately for fans of filmed fantasy, not all moviemakers viewed eternity as an airy, fun place in which to be. Death and the human soul were also represented as respectively fearful and fragile commodities, still used allegorically, but not to be taken lightly.

Outward Bound (1930) and *Between Two Worlds* (1944) are original and remake, both similar in style and pacing, and both quite good. They are the story of a handful of people on an ocean liner going from where to where, or even how it got there, no one knows. The passengers begin to quarrel and bicker among themselves until slowly dawns the truth: they have all died and this is a boat sailing to eternity. Unlike *Carousel* where heaven is gaily lit and tinsel-lined, this afterworld is oppressive and alien. Yet, the cold misty setting serves to give the tale only its peripheral atmosphere. The eerie flavor is built not so much on what is seen, but what is said. The passengers act not like vacationers on a cruise, but like scoundrels on trial, each one judging the other while selfishly defending his own life and accomplishments. Based on the play by Sutton Vane, the excellent Leslie Howard and Helen Chandler (Mina in Lugosi's *Dracula*) leads in *Outward Bound* were assumed by John Garfield and Eleanor Parker in *Between Two Worlds*. Would that all remakes had such powerful credentials, a case in point being our next film *Death Takes A Holiday* (1934). As in the play by Alberto Casella called *La Morte In Vacanza*, Death (Fredric March) assumes mortal form and visits the earth to see what humans are all about. He visits Italy and there falls in love with a woman (Evelyn Venable). During his stay, no living things die. Death, in the throes of his newfound passion, realizes he must return to his eternal task. The girl agrees to go with him. The natural order is restored, death is a little less cold, and a unique, rather sentimental love story has been told.

For some inexplicable reason, ABC-TV felt that

Edmund Gwenn and Sydney Greenstreet talk while
Paul Henreid listens on in *Between Two Worlds*.

Kathleen Howard pleads with Death (Fredric March)
not to take her daughter in *Death Takes a Holiday*.

Death Takes a Holiday needed a second telling. They signed Monte Markham as Death, Yvette Mimieux as his love, and in 1971 presented a clinical, contemporization of the moody and romantic original.

On Borrowed Time (1939) took a similar theme and turned it about: Mr. Brink (Sir Cedric Hardwicke) is tricked into climbing a magic tree by an old man (Lionel Barrymore) and is thus held from his appointed rounds. The only way he can leave is to be invited down. The result of Brink's incarceration is that no one dies. Starvation and suffering run rampant; finally, the pain hits home. The old man's grandson (Bobs Watson) is mortally wounded in an accident. To free the boy from an eternity in limbo, Brink's jailor must free his prisoner. Death takes the old man, for whom he had originally come, and his grandson to a bright and cheery afterlife. The film ends happily after all.

It was over a decade before the next film of sombre death was released, illustrating the public's preference for the more light-hearted angel fare. Not surprisingly, it was Ingmar Bergman who reintroduced the character of Death to audiences.

Very few classic fantasy films are also considered classics of mainstream moviemaking, but Bergman's 1956 production *The Seventh Seal* succeeded in carving just such a niche for itself. In the fourteenth century, Swedish knight Antonius Block (Max von Sydow) and his squire Jons (Gunnar Bjornstrand) return from a decade in the Holy Land only to find their country being ravaged by buboinc plague. On the road, Block meets a black-cloaked, pasty-faced death who has come to claim him. The knight does not believe his time has fairly come and challenges the interloper to a game of chess with his life as the stakes.

The game lasts over a broken period, during which time Block and Jons meet other people who sense that they will soon die. Among them are Plog, a smith, and his wife Lisa; a priest-turned-thief; a mute girl who takes up with Jons; a witch, who ends up being burned at the stake; a painter; and an actor, Jof, his wife Mia, and their baby son Mikael. By the end of the film, Block has lost his game of chess, but has succeeded in distracting Death that others may survive. The knight returns to his castle where he, his wife, and their party are claimed by the Grim Reaper. The final shot of the film, the most famous, has Death, his scythe upraised, leading his victims across an open meadow to their fate.

Effective publicity still for *On Borrowed Time*. Pictured are, from left to right, Bobs Watson as Pud, Eily Malyon as the hated Aunt Demetria, Lionel Barrymore, and Sir Cedric Hardwicke as Mr. Brink.

The Seventh Seal is based on Bergman's own play *Wood Painting* and is, for all intents and purposes, just that: a medieval tapestry come to life. There is symbolism throughout, and allegory on the paradox of meaning and futility in life. We see everything through the eyes of our nihilstic knight who, after these many years of disappointment in far-off lands, is able to work a small but satisfactory manipulation of fate. In this respect, despite the brooding and plague-ridden narrative, there does come a beacon of promise at the end. Jof, Mia, and Mikael, the innocents, survive.

Technically, the black-and-white film is remarkable. If *The Seventh Seal* were nothing more than a loosely packaged tale without depth or metaphor, it still would be stunning to watch and study. It, more than almost any fantasy film within memory, succeeds in removing the viewer from his own secure environment and thrusts him into the midst of controlled chaos.

As if filmmakers were afraid to raise the gauntlet and try to equal Bergman's achievement, the next film about death was some six years coming. *Carnival of Souls* (1962) was an extremely low-budget black-and-white film that works with its lack of gloss to create a stark, haunting vision of

Death claims a victim in *The Seventh Seal.*

death. A young woman (Candice Hilligoss) survives a car accident and is faced with a world that does not acknowledge her presence. People she meets are like mannequins—stiff and unmoving. This suddenly cruel world drives her ever more frantic. She is finally reduced to running from one person to another begging that they see or hear her. The girl's prayers are answered. She is recognized by a crowd of corpselike wraiths who embrace her. The party dances, and it is then she learns that she is dead, drowned when her car went off the bridge.

Throughout *Carnival of Souls*, our only vantage point is that of the girl, and we come to believe that it is the world has gone mad and not she. Only in the last moments of the film is our viewpoint objective. We see living, breathing people towing the heroine's car from the bay and she is dead behind the wheel. What has gone before, her subjective views, become immediately more frightening because for seventy-nine minutes we *believed* them. In essence, we have experienced one filmmaker's view of death: a world of isolation, fear, and that which we cherish most—life—turned cold and unresponsive.

In contrast to the drab world of both *The Seventh Seal* and *Carnival of Souls*, Roger Corman's *Masque of the Red Death* (964) took a full-color look at plague-ridden lands whose lord, Prince Prospero (Vincent Price) is as diseased of mind as are his subjects of body. The film is an earnest attempt to translate the classic work—combined with another story by Edgar Allan Poe, *Hop Frog*—to cinematic terms, merging the author's striking symbolism with film's vivid realization of period, mood, and color.

As twelfth-century Italy crumbles, Prospero lives in his closed world of elegance, sadism, devil worship, and some affection, especially for Francesca (Jane Asher), a lovely village girl he has kidnapped to live in his castle. But, as it must, the facade of security topples. During a lavish costume ball, Red Death, in his traditional cloak and sporting Prospero's face, has come to take the prince. This accomplished, he joins Yellow Death, Blue Death, and the others as they continue their journey. If justice has not triumphed, then fate has at least proven itself more powerful than man.

Masque of the Red Death is an eye-filling, well-acted, and literate fable, which came closer than any other film to embellishing what Bergman did in his *Seventh Seal*.

Unlike ghosts and angels, one aspect of the afterlife that has never found a strong niche in film is reincarnation. *Let's Live Again* (1947) was an early, silly stab at the subject with an atomic scientist's (John Emery) brother reincarnated as a dog. Lacking a cast and budget, the film made no impression on the ticket-buying public. Ten years later, Hollywood tried a different tack. They used reincarnation to turn people into monsters and filmgoers loved it. Two films from the fifties dealt with hypnotic reincarnations of ancient beasts. The first was *The She Creature* (1956) in which a sideshow hypnotist, Dr. Carlo Lombardi (Chester Morris), summons a prehistoric sea monster from aide Andrea's (Maria English) ancestral past. The monster, a scale-encrusted amphibian, menaces a seaside community. The second film of this type was remarkably similar: *I Was A Teenage Werewolf* (1957) with Michael Landon (*Bonanza*) as the victim of a deranged psychiatrist (Whit Bissell). The good doctor sends Landon's mind back to the Stone Age and the boy becomes a snarling brute. The film, which costs $150,000, became one of the top-grossing films of 1957, in the company of such

Paul Blaisdell as the monster in *The She Creature*.

Michael Landon as the monster in *I Was a Teenage Werewolf*.

efforts as *The King and I* and *Bridge on the River Kwai*.

Since it was the monsters that had sold these two pictures, other films about reincarnation slipped by relatively unnoticed. There was Roger Corman's *The Undead* (1956) in which a psychotherapist learns that his prostitute patient is the reincarnation of a medieval witch. Traveling psychically back in time, our hero fails to prevent her ancestor's death and ends up tinkering his modern-day self out of existence. Elsewhere, Jock Mahoney was certain *I've Lived Before* (1956), as a World War I fighter pilot; *The Search For Bridey Murphy* (1956) ended when twentieth-century American housewife Teresa Wright is proven, under hynosis, to be the reincarnation of the nineteenth-century Irishwoman; and Liliane Montevecchi was the modern corporealization of an ancient Mayan god in *The Living Idol* (1957).

Christopher Lee faced *Terror in the Crypt* (1963), a Spanish-Italian co-production in which the friend (Ursula Davis) of Lee's daughter (Audry Amber) is possessed by the murdering spirit of a dead witch. One year later, Vincent Price suffered a similar problem in Roger Corman's *Tomb of Ligeia*. The setting is England in 1821, and Price portrays a widower, the spirit of whose deceased wife Ligeia haunts his new bride. Pressing onward, restless spirits visited the unsuspecting William Campbell, the descendent of a vampire who is possessed by the creature in *Blood Bath* (1966), a film of the same inexpensive caliber as *Creature of Destruction* (1967), a remake of *The She Creature*. A more creditable picture was *The Crimson Cult* (1968)

starring Boris Karloff, Christopher Lee, and Barbara Steele. When a young man disappears, his brother Robert (Mark Eden) goes to the country inn at which he was staying. He arrives as the proprietor J.D. Morley (Lee) is hosting the three-hundredth anniversary of the burning of Lavinia (Miss Steele), the Black Witch of Greymarsh. Through Morley's niece Eve (Virginia Wetherell), Robert learns of his brother's death as part of Lavinia's curse to destroy the descendents of her accusers. Morley, her agent, is about to kill Eve and Robert when Professor Marshe (Boris Karloff) and his servant Basil (Michael Warren) find the sacrificial altar. Morley sets the place on fire, the innocents escape, and before he perishes, the innkeeper reveals himself to be the reincarnation of Lavinia.

The Crimson Cult belongs to its three stars, who skillfully flesh-out the lean story based on H. P. Lovecraft's *Dreams in the Witch House*. Unimpressed by this tasteful and restrained effort starring their alumnus Lee, Hammer films of England went the gore route with their own tale of reincarnation, *Hands of the Ripper* (1971). Based on the short story by Edward Spencer Shew, Jack's restless spirit possesses his daughter, forcing her into all manner of bloody mayhem. Then in the midst of all this standard but exciting horror product bloomed a flower that quickly withered and died. Barbra Streisand, who can sing like an angel, cannot work miracles. She pulled the genre from its masters and failed to make a killing in the tacky screen version of the Lerner and Lowe musical *On A Clear Day You Can See Forever* (1972). Psychiatrist Marc Chapot (Yves Montand) falls in love with one of Daisy Gamble's (Barbra) previous selves, an eighteenth-

Barbara Steele as Lavinia Morley in *The Crimson Cult*.

33

Lord Percy Moorepark (Lauri Main) is the husband of Melinda (Barbra Streisand) in *On A Clear Day You Can See Forever*.

century aristocrat named Melinda Tentrees, who has been hypnotically summoned from Daisy's past. The complication, of course, is that the doctor and his patient begin dating, but it's not the twentieth-century incarnation he wants. Daisy is deeply hurt by this; so much so that a song ensues: *What Did I Have That I Don't Have*? In the end, a confident Daisy leaves Marc and learns, courtesy of the title song, that "the glow of your being outshines every star."

Perhaps, because reincarnation features a more subtle kind of psychology than most other fantasy—not unlike Miss Giddens' disintegration in *The Innocents*—the public quickly becomes confused by it. There is no tangible menace or presence to hold on to. This would account for reincarnation

having stayed a thing of the past until the last effort of this type to date, the poorly received *Reincarnation of Peter Proud* (1975). Though the picture rode on the star of *Exorcist*-spawned interest in the supernatural, the public stayed away. The story details how a man's (Michael Sarrazin) previous identity begins to dominate his current self to the point of complete possession.

One thing is clear. Reincarnation walks a thin line between the unknown world of death and the darker domain that lies ahead, the kingdom of black magic where death is only the beginning! Thus, we move from the sphere of the human-spawn to the realm of the devil-spawn with our first stop being Satan's servant the witch.

Michael Sarrazin stoops beside the tombstone of his previous incarnation in *The Reincarnation of Peter Proud*.

3
WITCHCRAFT AND VOODOO

Witchcraft has been with us since prehistory. Because a woman's fertility was tied to the mysterious moon, and she had knowledge of the gathering and fixing of strange herbs, her natural place was to serve as a liaison between man and the gods of nature. In time, she mastered many of nature's secrets, and turned to metaphysics for greater insights into healing, planting, etc. This progression from "white" magic to "black" magic was, therefore, a natural progression of the curious mind.

It took filmmakers nearly four decades to discover the witch in film. Although there were scattered short subjects such as George Melies *The Witch* (1906)[3] and documentaries like the 1921 Swedish film *Witchcraft Through the Ages*, it wasn't until *I Married A Witch* (1942) that the subject came of age. Unfortunately, the beginning was a pandering one.

Based on the novel *The Passionate Witch* by Thorne Smith and Norman Matson, *I Married A Witch* features Veronica Lake as Jennifer, the title sorceress, burned at the stake with her father Daniel (Cecil Kellaway) in seventeenth-century Salem by Wallace (Fredric March). Freed from imprisonment in a tree by a bolt of lightning, the pair returns to haunt Wallace's twentieth-century descendents. Eventually, March and Miss Lake marry, and she gives birth to a baby witch. It's all very innocent fun, though not as interesting as *Weird Woman*. Based on Fritz Leiber's novel *Conjure Wife*, the film stars Lon Chaney Jr. as university professor Norman Reed. Reed's jealous exgirlfriend, Ilona Carr (Evelyn Ankers), uses witchery to try and win

Norman from his new bride Paula (Anne Gwynne). The professor uncovers Ilona's plot and sets a trap for the witch, which leads to her accidental hanging. The film was remade in 1961 as *Burn, Witch, Burn* in which Professor Norman Taylor (Peter Wyngarde) and his witch-wife Tansy (Janet Blair) are hounded by Flora Carr (Margaret Johnson), the ambitious wife of a college instructor. She wants Norman's post for her spouse. In the end, Flora is destroyed when she is crushed by a large stone gargoyle she had brought to life to do her bidding.

The Woman Who Came Back did so in 1945, and her story dealt with witchcraft in twentieth-century New England. Nancy Kelly was the reincarnation of a witch burned at the stake some three-hundred years before. Twin versions of *Macbeth*, one helmed by Orson Welles (1948) and the other produced by Hugh Hefner and directed by Roman Polanski in 1971 feature the famous trio of witches: "By the pricking of my thumbs, something wicked this way comes!" Though their screen time is limited to alerting the war hero Macbeth that he will one day be king, their prophecy drives the troubled thane to kill his liege and assume the throne. In the Welles version, we meet the crones as they fashion a clay icon of Macbeth; Polanski has them on a beach burying a severed hand. Based on the play by William Shakespeare, the films also feature the haunting of Macbeth by his friend Banquo, whom the new king has had killed to prevent the realization of another prophesy, that Banquo's sons shall be kings. In the Polanski version, his bloody reappearance to Macbeth during a great feast is ghastly and

Peter Wyngarde is the victim of a voodoo effigy in
Burn, Witch, Burn.

unnerving. The Welles treatment is considerably more subdued.

Rex Harrison turned down the lead in the next witch film, a screen adaptation of John Van Druten's play *Bell, Book, and Candle* (1958). James Stewart got the part, portraying a New York City publisher who, just before his marriage, is enraptured by the charms of witch-artist Kim Novak. This mildly diverting film costarred an admittedly uncomfortable Jack Lemmon as a warlock. It also made clear the fact that no one knew quite how to handle effectively the witch in film. Italian cinematographer-turned-director Mario Bava showed them how. Bava's *Black Sunday* (1960) is based on Nikolai Gogol's story *The Vij*. It was the first film to deal skillfully with the classic visions of witchcraft, dwelling on the one day in every century when the Devil and his agents are permitted to walk

freely amongst men; hence, the film's title. The focus of Bava's atmospheric tale is on one witch, played by Barbara Steele, who, during an eighteenth-century inquisition in the province of Moldavia, has the spiked and golden mask of Satan pounded to her face. She is mercifully thereafter burned at the stake, joined, in death, by other victims of this witch and vampire hunt.

On the evil twentieth-century day, Miss Steele returns to haunt the descendents of her executioners. A vampiric aide (Ivo Garrani) rises from his grave to join her, his mission being to procure blood that his mistress might become strong enough to walk the earth forever. Fortunately, a young doctor (John Richardson) stumbles upon her plan and the revitalized sorceress is once more burned at the stake.

Lavish sets and sensitive black-and-white pho-

James Stewart visits the occult art store of Kim Novak in *Bell, Book, and Candle.*

tography highlight a motion picture filled with striking visions of horror: Garrani's clawing from his muddy grave; Miss Steele's initial murder, attended by hooded priests, lifeless trees, the flickering shadows of cleansing flames, and a swirling, ominous mist; the slow-motion journey of a coach through a dank, foggy wood; and so forth. It's all very classic and classy work, a film that pulls the viewer into another time and world, a place governed by a decidedly different set of laws from those with which we are familiar. Sorrowfully, Bava's subsequent efforts, *Black Sabbath* (1963), *Blood and Black Lace* (1964), and *Planet of the Vampires* (1965) did not live up to the promise of this minor masterpiece.

Along similarly haunting lines was the release, that same year, of a tightly packaged black-and white mood piece entitled *Horror Hotel,* with 250 year-old warlock Christopher Lee posing as a Professor of Demonology. It's all a front, however, as he is also the proprietor an an inn in Whitewood, Massachusetts, the guests of which become sacrifices for his devil cult. One of Lee's students (Venetia Stevenson) is sent by her instructor to the hotel from which vantage point she intends to do research for her paper *Black Magic in America.* When the girl disappears, her brother (Dennis Lotis) comes to Whitewood to investigate. He uncovers Lee's cult and, although he is too late to save his sister, rescues another would-be victim (Betta St. John). Angered with the failure of his disciples, Satan burns them all to ash during a mass. The final scene in the cemetery, with the shadow of a huge stone cross setting the cult members ablaze, is brilliantly executed.

Leaving behind these intelligent Italian and British witch efforts, we turn to H. P. Lovecraft's *The Case of Charles Dexter Ward,* which became a mediocre Roger Corman film *The Haunted Palace* (1963). The title belongs to a poem by Edgar Allan Poe, from which the film draws chunks of narrative to tell the story of warlock Curwen (Vincent Price) who is burned at the stake in 1765. He swears vengeance and puts a curse on all the villagers. Moving a century forward, his descendent Ward (also Price) arrives in town to find many of the residents thereof horribly mutated by his ancestor's curse. Arriving at Curwen's mansion, Ward gazes upon his great great grandfather's portrait and, through it, is possessed. He wreaks terrible havoc upon the New England villagers until, in the end, the house is set afire, the painting burns, and Curwen is exorcised. Or is he? The redeemed Ward, in the final shot, looks more like Curwen than himself, and even his wife (Debra Paget) resembles Curwen's mistress. The film co-starred Lon Chaney Jr. as Ward's vicious butler Simon Orme.

Barbara Steele goes up in flames for a second time at the end of *Black Sunday.*

Haunted Palace is typical of the Corman-Price school of horror, in that it is handsomely mounted in full, rich colors that do not compensate for the drab nature of the narrative. Much better was cinema's next venture into the occult, *Witchcraft* (1964). In this low-budget but meticulously made film, Lon Chaney Jr. portrays warlock Morgan Whitlock, head of an age-old family of witches. For three-hundred years, the Whitlocks have been fighting the neighboring Laniers, one of whose ancestors condemned a Whitlock to be burned at the stake for practicing black magic. But the real trouble begins when an old cemetery is dug up as part of a construction project, and the original Whitlock witch, Vanessa (Yvette Rees) returns to destroy the Laniers. The plot is further complicated by the fact that Amy Whitlock (Marie Ney) is in love with the doomed Bill Lanier (Jack Hedley). In the end, Amy must make the supreme sacrifice by remaining inside her burning home to be certain that the entire Whitlock coven is destroyed forever.

This largely overlooked work was eerily photographed and evokes a healthy respect for the supernatural powers of the Whitlocks. Particularly striking were the gloomy appearances of the lovely Vanessa as she went about her punitive murders. One sad aspect of *Witchcraft* is that it marked the end of the black-and-white occult film. The public wanted color—particularly red—and they got it, in unrelenting doses. This will become more evident in our upcoming look at vampires and werewolves.

Chaney returned the next year in *House of Black Death* as a horned warlock battling rival sorceror John Carradine. It was a low, low-budget film that

Yvette Rees about to cast a spell in *Witchcraft*.

did nothing to embellish the career of either actor.

From the dread we turn to the light-hearted. *Witch Without a Broom* was a Spanish-American co-production in which an American college professor (Jeffrey Hunter) teaching in Madrid finds himself drawn to a lovely blonde girl (Maria Perschy) in one of his classes. The lady is a witch, and she falls in love with Hunter, bringing him home with her to sixteenth-century Toledo. Outraged, the instructor demands that he be returned to the present. Our incompetent heroine gives it a whirl but has her problems: the pair journeys through time and space, landing in the Stone Age, in Ancient Rome, and finally on Mars in the twenty-second century. At long last, Hunter does make it home and finds himself in a hospital bed. Convinced it was all a dream, he looks up to find that his nurse is a familiar-looking blonde.

Witch Without a Broom is a pleasant little film, certainly better, for what it is, than the television series of somewhat similar design, *I Dream of Jeannie*. In a more brutal vein was *The Devil's Own* (1967) with witch Kay Walsh sacrificing virgins in an attempt to gain eternal life for the members of her coven. This surprisingly sturdy film received abyssmal distribution, which denied horror fans the chance to see recreations of some truly blood-curdling rituals celebrating the black arts. Poor circulation in terms of flowing crimson was not a problem suffered by one of the most sadistic witch hunts in film history, *The Conqueror Worm* (1968). Vincent Price portrays Matthew Hopkins, the famous Witchfinder General who roamed Great Britain's countryside during that nation's great Civil War. Based on the novel by Ronald Bassett, the film's only real break with historical fact is that Hopkins is shown to be gratuitously hacked to death. In fact, he died in his sleep. Not that the film was intended to be a history lesson. It is simply a showcase for brutality and gore. There are grisly witch-burnings galore, liberal floods of blood, and a classically malevolent Price who makes his living on the burnt flesh of young maidens. The title, incidentally, is from a poem by Poe, but there is no relation between the two. The tag was American International Pictures' attempt to ride on the star of their successful Poe adaptations *Masque of the Red Death, Pit and the Pendulum*, and others into which we will look later in the book.

Not to be outdone by these various forays into witchery, Hammer films came up with *The Devil's*

Simon, King of the Witches prepares to make a blood sacrifice.

Bride (1968), based on Dennis Wheatley's novel *The Devil Rides Out*. Christopher Lee portrays the Duke of Richleau, a twentieth-century warlock who comes to the aid of a friend who is being pursued by a coven of witches. After battling the Black Warlock Mocata (Charles Gray), the angel of death, and a monster spider, Lee is victorious. This well-made and rather traditional effort was followed by an incidental work entitled *Night of the Witches* (1970), in which a charlatan preacher (Keith Larsen) gets involved with a coven in contemporary California.

A more interesting film was *Simon, King of the Witches* (1971). Simon (Andrew Prine) is a warlock who dwells in a storm drain. When his home is washed away by rain, the sorceror views it as the doing of fickle gods and swears vengeance. He intends to become their equal. To do this, he first tries the sexual sacrifice of the virgin Linca (Brenda Scott) followed by the blood sacrifice of the homosexual Stanley (Richmond Shepard). Failing at this, he puts a curse on the city and is hunted by a city official for his efforts. When Simon kidnaps the

man and murders him, two of the warlock's aides panic and kill Simon. As a once-only parody, *Simon, King of the Witches* is a bizarre curio but fun nonetheless.

The most recent witch film is the low-budget *Touch of Melissa* (1972). A young man (Michael Berry), wandering along a New England road, meets Melissa (Emby Mellay) a beautiful 125 year-old witch. They fall in love. A jealous younger sister creates problems for the pair and in the end, during sex, Melissa shrivels and returns to her true age.

From witchcraft we move to voodoo and black magic where the change is more one of geography than metier. Films of witchcraft, as we have seen, most often originate in the seventeenth or eighteenth century and are set usually in England or New England. Voodoo and the dark arts are associated generally with the West Indies.

Within this genre, one of the most prevalent themes is the reanimation of the dead: the creation of zombies. Despite these creatures' lack of personality, they have had a remarkable history in film. This is all the more curious when one considers that no zombie film or novel has ever had the cultural impact of the more popular *Frankenstein* or *Dracula*. Still, filmgoers have displayed an enduring interest in the perambulating dead, which has resulted in dozens of fantasy films starring glassy-eyed and laconic corpses snatched from the hand of God by the claws of Satan.

White Zombie (1932) was the earliest of the zombie films and starred Bela Lugosi two years after his box-office triumph as *Dracula*. The film introduces Madeline Short (Madge Bellamy) who has come to Haiti for her marriage to Neil Parker (John Harron), a bank employee at Port-au-Prince. On the boat trip over, Madeline meets plantation owner Charles Beaumont (Robert Frazer) who invites her to be married in his mansion. She accepts, unaware that the man wants her for himself. In Haiti, Beaumont calls on Murder Legendre (Lugosi), the island's voodoo master. Legendre agrees to help him. He places a poisoned rose in the bride's bouquet and, at her wedding, she falls, apparently dead. After her funeral, Madeline is revived. The zombie king then double-crosses Beaumont by poisoning him as well. Both are now his slaves.

When Neil finds Madeline's grave untenanted, he calls on Dr. Bruner (Joseph Cawthorn), a local missionary. Together, they track down Legendre. When Bruner clubs the sorcerer, Beaumont snaps

Bela Lugosi (third from right) stands above the cataleptic body of Madge Bellamy in *White Zombie*.

from his stupor, charges his erstwhile master, and both men fall from a cliff to their death. Madeline is free of the spell and rejoins her lover.

White Zombie is an excellent film, and one of the few starring roles in which Lugosi did not rely on exaggerated theatrics. His Legandre is a poised, restrained, and menacing figure whole malevolence is disguised with a veneer of wicked confidence. The picture is plain and stark, which works to its advantage. It underlines the cold, colorless world in which the zombies live. These zombies do all of Legandre's dirty work, from kidnapping to murder. The unflinching human shells became the stereotype for all screen zombies to come, particularly in terms of their hollow temperament. This attitude was best emphasized in the famous scene wherein the zombies are working at Beaumont's mill, grinding sugar cane to powder. When one of the creatures tumbles soundlessly into the pit, he is ignored by his fellows, nor does he seek to cry out as they toss their crop upon him, grinding the corpse and the cane both into dust.

The producers of *White Zombie*, Victor and Edward Halperin, satisfied with the enormous return on their investment, reentered the fold with a new, low-budget feature *Revolt of the Zombies* (1936). This time around, the Haitian locales were dropped in favor of a more unique Cambodian setting. The walking corpses of Indochinese were used by French soldiers to battle in their stead during World War I. This new Halperin film, with its antiwar flavor, was poorly received by the

public. While this stopped the brothers, it didn't deter filmmakers from venturing further into the realm of the zombie.

Noble Johnson, the native chieftan in *King Kong*, portrayed the zombie in *Ghost Breakers* (1940), a Bob Hope film we discussed in chapter 1. However, his bald, lumbering monster was played strictly for laughs. *King of the Zombies* (1941) was, then, the next serious zombie effort featuring silent-film star Henry Victor as Dr. Dangre, a magus who creates zombies via voodoo for axis agents. This film was followed by the equally topical *Revenge of the Zombies* (1943). John Carradine toplined as Dr. von Altmann, a Nazi scientist busy recruiting a zombie army for Hitler's war effort. His base of operations was a Louisiana swamp into the boggy marshlands of which, at the film's conclusion, he was dragged by his zombified wife Lila (Veda Ann Borg) leading the doctor's mindless corpse corps.

After years of dearth came what is largely considered to be the finest zombie effort of all-time: Producer Val Lewton's doggedly authentic *I Walked With a Zombie* (1943). The film derives its name from a series of newspaper articles written by Inez Wallace under the *I Walked With a Zombie* masthead, and was Lewton's admitted attempt to transmute *Jane Eyre* to the West Indies. Deeper than self-indulgence, it is a striking film because the acolytes of its on-screen mysticism are not wild-eyed, monosyllabic extras; they come across as real people. As such, they give the film an added dimension of realism.

Lewton's director for what would become his favorite film was Jacques Tourneur, with whom he had worked before on *The Cat People*. The scenario has a young nurse Betsy (Frances Dee) hired by a West Indies sugar planter, Paul Holland (Tom Conway) to care for his somnambulistic wife. The locals view Catherine (Christine Gordon) as a zombie, although logical explanations for her catatonia are offered, anemia being one such rationale. Discouraged with Catherine's state, Betsy takes her to the local Mama-Loa, the witchdoctor, and is shocked to learn that she is none other than Mrs. Rand (Edith Barret), Paul's mother. The shaman explains that she plays along with the natives' superstitious fears in order to give them valid medical treatment. It was also she who, through scientific or voodoo means (we are not certain which), put Catherine in this bizarre state. Meanwhile, the bloodless, speechless girl is shot in the heart with an arrow by the planter's half-brother Wesley (James Ellison) who is himself destroyed by a giant zombie named Carre Four (Darby Jones). The nurse, who has always loved her employer, is now free to marry him.

The voodoo rites pictured in *I Walked With a Zombie* were supervised by actual practitioners of the black arts. Every effort was made to translate the primitive tribal flavor of voodooism to film.

A year later, Bela Lugosi found himself married to a zombie in *Voodoo Man.* Lugosi's quest is to find a girl with the same mental plane as his wife onto whom he might transfer her curse. With the aide of voodoo priest George Zucco, he succeeds only in turning the other women into mindless automations. By the final reel, Lugosi is destroyed, of course, and the ladies freed from their trance. Lugosi was gone only a few months, however: hard upon he was riding herd on the infamous *Zombies on Broadway* (1945). When PR men Wally Brown and Alan Carney journey to the West Indies in search of zombies for a nightclub act, they encounter Lugosi and his collection of misshapen undead. The film series that had begun so fitfully a decade before had now slid to the stygian pits of mediocrity. It should come as no surprise that this inept little film put the lid on the zombie film for over a decade.

In 1957, guarding an undersea diamond mine, were ten of the *Zombies of Mora-Tau.* When the treasure is destroyed, the monsters vanish with it. Thus went the inauspicious return for the walking dead. Better by far was the next zombie programmer, *Voodoo Island* (1957). Boris Karloff portrayed Dr. Phillip Knight, an investigator of the supernatural who visits the Hawaiian island of Kauai to learn why a party that had been searching-out sites for a new hotel has vanished. In due course, his aides Mitchell (Glen Dixon) and Schyler (Elisha Cooke) are turned into zombies, and interior decorator Claire Winter (Jean Engstrom) is eaten by a monster plant. Knight and the remaining explorers are confronted by the island chief (Frederick Ledebut) and are permitted to leave, but only if they promise never to return. A taut little film, *Voodoo Island* provided Karloff with a welcome change of pace as the hunter rather than the hunted. *The Disembodied* was also released that year, a psychological thriller with voodoo-induced personality transference.

Moving from the tropics to the moors, we next encounter *The Four Skulls of Jonathan Drake*

(1959). In this opus, the male members of an accursed family all die of decapitation at the age of sixty. Their heads are then shrunken and preserved by Paul Wexler, a two-hundred-year-old white man whose head was sewn onto the body of a black witchdoctor some nine-score years before. Eventually, the dire proceedings come to an end when scientist Edward Franz intercedes. Zombie Wexler, his age catching up with him, disintegrates. A largely overlooked film, *Four Skulls of Jonathan Drake* has many moments of grating terror, all of them supplied by Wexler. His lips sewn shut, the actor has an ominous glower with which he creates a character of brooding presence. Less frightening, but with a greater emphasis on characterization, was *Macumba Love* (1960). The film is about an author (Walter Reed) who is researching a voodoo cult in South America. *Macumba Love* was actually filmed on location in Brazil, which added tremendously to its authenticity. Clyde Kelley was filmland's next zombie, *The Dead One* (1961), a voodoo creature who is destroyed by sunlight.

One of the more unusual entries in this zombie renaissance was the Italian-period piece *War of the Zombies* (1963). John Drew Barrymore stars as a

Paul Wexler invades private property in *The Four Skulls of Jonathan Drake.*

sorcerer in Caesar's Rome who reanimates the bodies of slain warriors. His plan is to conquer the world. Said ambition is cut short with the destruction of his mystic idol. Next came *Curse of the Voodoo* (1964), which delved into the transference of pain from a man tortured in Africa to the protagonist living in London. This British picture was followed into release by another Italian film, *Terror Creatures From The Grave* (1965). The title beings are born when an occultist, researching a medieval plague, is murdered. Before dying, he summons forth the plague's ancient victims to slaughter his murderer. After they do his bidding, the zombies move mindlessly about, killing everyone in sight until they are destroyed by rain.

As if on cue, Hammer films, famous for their exciting reworkings of old horror standards (*Curse of Frankenstein, Horror of Dracula, The Mummy*) jumped on the zombie bandwagon in 1965. *Plague of the Zombies* is set in nineteenth-century Cornwall where the owner of a tin mine (John Carson) uses the undead to dig at his lode. This taut little thriller sports excellent makeup and production values, especially in the dream sequence when the monsters crawl slowly from their age-old graves. A less poetic vision of voodoo was *The Oblong Box* (1969). In his brief role as a country doctor, Christopher Lee is killed by a man who had been slave-trading in Africa and was disfigured by a witchdoctor's curse. Back in England, he is secreted away and grows restless. After committing several murders he dies, but not before biting brother Vincent Price and infecting him with his malady. Not a bad film, *The Oblong Box* was another Poe "adaptation," although like *Conqueror Worm* it had little to do with the author.

Mexico's answer to Hammer films, Azteca, gave us a short-lived series about a practitioner of voodoo in *Dr. Satan* (1966) and *The Return of Dr. Satan* (1967), with Joaquin Cordero in the title role. By the time their *Snake People* was released (1968), even Boris Karloff's Damballah, high priest of a voodoo cult in the tropics, was insufficient to breathe life into an atrophying mode. It remained for George Romero to give zombies new life with his bizarre *Night of the Living Dead* (1968).

Johnny (Russ Streiner) and Barbara (Judy O'Dea) are visiting the grave of their father when they are accosted by a pasty-looking derelict. The silent man knocks Johnny unconscious, but Barbara escapes in their car. Night falls and she enters a

Vincent Price as the eroding victim of the curse of the *Oblong Box*.

farmhouse. There, amidst gnawed corpses, she meets Ben (Duane Jones). He, too, is being sought by a mounting number of walking cadavers. According to the black man, the creatures are all over the place and feeding on the flesh of the living. The pair boards up the besieged house with broken chairs and furniture. Soon, they are joined by Harry (producer Karl Hardman), his wife Helen (Marilyn Eastman), their daughter Karen (Kyra Schon), and lovers Tom (Keith Wayne) and Judy (Judy Ridley). Karen is weak from a ghoul-bite.

Marshalling their courage, Ben, Tom, and Judy try to drive off and get help, but their efforts are futile. Only Ben makes it back to the house alive. The five terrified survivors listen to television commentators who explain that all over the country newly deceased are returning to life. Speculation is ripe that a plague brought to earth from a Venus Explorer Satellite is responsible for the zombies. A scientist explains that shooting the creatures in the head will destroy their motor nerves and stop them dead. He also warns that those who have been bitten by the living dead will become like them.

Meanwhile, the creatures attack and enter the

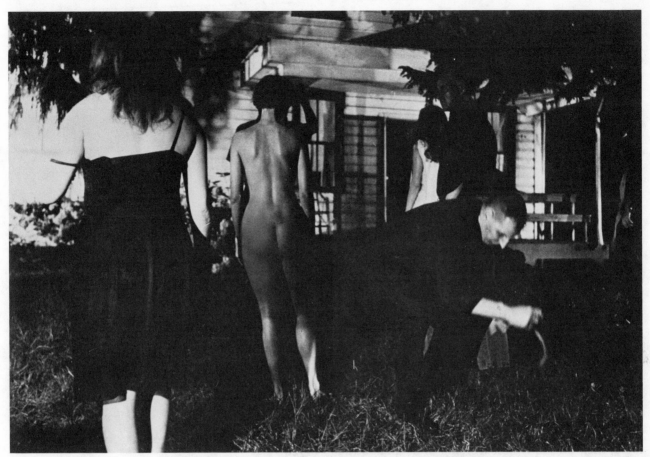

The besieged household in *Night of the Living Dead*.

house. Harry dies, the mutated Karen kills her mother with a garden hoe, the monsterized Johnny drags off his sister, and Ben is left alone, barricaded in the basement. Morning arrives, along with the sheriff and his men who are busy shooting zombies. Things look a little less gloomy. Ben pokes his head through a window and calls; the deputies shoot him dead. The picture, like the night of terror, is over.

There are those who claim that *Night of the Living Dead* is a classic horror film. Others find the movie revolting in its explicit details of cannibalism and murder. Both arguments are valid, but given the drive-in theatre market at which the independent movie was aimed, the gore was a requisite drawing card. In its favor, the film is an unbearable suspense treat with fine performances and a taut script. Produced for under $150,000, *Night of the Living Dead* went from being a cult curiosity to becoming a

national institution. It has since grossed millions of dollars in general and arthouse release, spawned a popular paperback novelization, and is a favorite of television's late late-night movie crowd. It is interesting to consider that Romero's next film, *The Crazies* (1972), about an accidental dumping of war chemicals in a town's water supply, received none of the first film's critical or financial success. Backed, now, by a healthier budget, Romero's more polished product also lost its sponteniety.

Strangely, no major filmmaker tried to emulate Romero's product and it wasn't until *Sugar Hill* (1974) that zombies returned. This time, the vehicle was a brutal "blacksploitation" film. A not-very-clever attempt to snatch patrons from the lines of *The Exorcist* and *The Godfather*, Sugar Hill, the title heroine, uses zombies to wreak vengeance on gangsters. If nothing else, the film is clearly a sign of the times.

4
THE DEVIL

Voodoo has no ties to the European culture in which most of our supernatural films have their roots. As we have seen, this caused films of the species to become stale in the retelling: they had one primary locale, stereotyped players, power-mad or vengeful occultists, lifeless zombies, and so forth. However, redundancy is not a problem suffered by our next topic, the more universal worship of Satan and the devil's own strangely paternal interest in mankind. It is to this bottomless reservoir of human possession, visits to the underworld, and deals with Lucifer that we now turn our attention.

The first screen vision of Satan came in the *Student of Prague*. Two German versions (1913 and 1926) of Poe's *William Wilson* tell the story of Baldwin (Paul Wegener in 1913; Conrad Veidt in 1926), a student who desires the hand of a rich young woman. He trades his mirror image to the devil in return for wealth. The evil image begins to haunt him, however, and eventually Baldwin is forced to shoot it. Destroying the evil in himself, the young man commits suicide. A routine tale by today's standards—it is the kind of story that often turned up on television's *Twilight Zone*—*Student of Prague* set the stage for more extravagant deals with the devil to come.

Quite appropriately *The Divine Comedy* gave us the screen's premier vision of the steamy pit itself as *Dante's Inferno* (1924). Hades appeared on-screen only briefly, however, as part of the dream of a millionaire who has just read the poem. In a 1935 remake, the vision is even briefer: we see hell as a sideshow barker Spencer Tracy sees it, a place of

racking punishment for those who have been damned. Both movies capture the writhing heat and carnality of hell, but neither film manages to frame it with a story that is generically fearful. Thus, as he was first in so many other cinematic developments, it was D. W. Griffith who gave us our first feature-length epic of deviltry, *The Sorrows of Satan* (1926).

Unlike the novel by Marie Corelli, the film opens with the epic battle from *Paradise Lost* between Satan's minions and the Heavenly Host. After the fall of the rebellious angels, Griffith brings us to the present with Satan come to earth disguised as Prince Riminez (Adolphe Menjou) to lure a young writer

The rebellious angels attack the Heavenly Host in *Sorrows of Satan*.

(Ricardo Cortez) from his fiancee (Carol Dempster) by way of an alluring seductress (Lya de Putti). Only in the end does Riminez lower his polished exterior to reveal the bat-winged, spike-tailed, and goat-horned Satan of legend. Although the writer sees the devil directly, he is only a shadow to the audience. In the end, the devil gives our impoverished protagonist wealth beyond imagining, but he returns to his beloved.

The next screen Satan came to us courtesy of A. Merritt's classic pulp novel *Seven Footprints to Satan*, first published in 1928 and made into a movie a year later. It was one of the last silent fantasy films and, indeed, after its release a soundtrack was added. Although, unlike the book, the film's deviltry is exposed as a hoax perpetrated on our world-adventuring hero James Kirkham (Creighton Hale) by his Uncle (Sheldon Lewis) who is after a diamond, owned by Kirkham's girl Eve (Thelma Todd), the illusion to that point is effective. Since that time, the grand old novel has been announced for refilming at least once every year, but thus far nothing has come of it.

The devil himself was given a rest for a decade while, between *White Zombie* and *Revolt of the Zombies*, the Halperin brothers tried their hand at *Supernatural* (1933). In this polished and engrossing fantasy, the demonic spirit of an executed murderess (Vivienne Osborne) takes over the body of a young, innocent, and quite lovely Carol Lombard, forcing her to perform evil deeds. Beyond the film's historicity as an early version of spiritual possession, it is interesting to note that Lombard's boyfriend was played by up-and-coming Western star Randolph Scott. H. B. Warner, DeMille's original *King of Kings* portrayed a doctor-cum-medium in the film.

Oddly enough, seven years later—the length of the devil's deal in our next film—Stephen Vincent Benet's *The Devil and Daniel Webster* was brought to the screen as *All That Money Can Buy*. The screenplay, co-authored by Benet, has downtrodden young New Hampshire farmer Jabez Stone (James Craig) sell his soul to an impish Mr. Scratch (Walter Huston) for seven years of prosperity. At the end of this period, the devil comes to collect his due, but our married hero refuses to go. Daniel Webster (Edward Arnold) successfully defends his client in a trial conducted before a jury of the ghosts of American traitors. As we have seen, it was not the first time the devil would be denied his charge. Bearing no malice for his defeat, however, Satan

(Laird Craiger) remains an affable fellow and a just spirit in *Heaven Can Wait* (1943). He receives the newly deceased Henry van Cleve (Don Ameche) in a luxurious office where he hears the man's life story. Although Ameche views himself as the nineteenth-century's answer to Don Juan and a heel, Satan feels otherwise. In the end, the devil sends Henry to heaven.

For variety's sake, possession was back in 1945 as a mildly diverting grade-B film called *The Phantom Speaks*, in which the spirit of an executed murderer takes over the body of a scientist and forces him to avenge his death. The film was just over an hour long, which was enough time for it to get in and out without adding to or detracting tremendously from the category.

Back in Hades, Satan grew a little colder because of his various upsets and looked for revenge on mankind in a classy and intelligent devil film called *Angel On My Shoulder*. Satan (Claude Rains who, some five years before, had played the angel in *Here Comes Mr. Jordan*) sends a murdered hoodlum (Paul Muni) back to earth as a respected judge with instructions to hand down rather dubious decisions from his devil-spawned bench. As ever, love—for the title heroine Anne Baxter—and conscience win out. Muni abandons his assignment and outwits the devil to remain on earth as a reformed human being. Undaunted, Satan (Ray Milland) sends forth a temptress (Audrey Totter) to corrupt a crusading district attorney (Thomas Mitchell) in *Alias Nick*

Walter Huston offers James Craig great wealth in *All That Money Can Buy*. All Craig need do is sign over his soul.

45

Beal (1949). Failing at that, the Lord of the Underworld (Stanley Hollaway) locates an earthman who looks like him (also Hollaway) and, in *Meet Mr. Lucifer* (1953), orders his lackey to introduce three clean-living families to television. Through the evil box, he hopes to corrupt them. Thwarted even in this attempt, the time for subtlety was plainly at an end. Thus, with the help of Jacques Tourneur, the devil's next screen appearance scared viewers out of a year's growth and remains, to this day, one of the great fantasy films of all-time: *Curse of the Demon* (1958).

Based on the M. R. James short story *Casting of the Runes,* the film opens with the death of Professor John Harrington (Maurice Denahm). Pulling into his driveway one night, he is torn to pieces by a giant, fiery demon. The next day, John Holden (Dana Andrews) arrives in England for a convention of scientists studying the psychic. He is shocked to learn of the professor's death and decides to carry on his expose of an alleged devil cult. Later that day, while searching for an old volume of occult lore, Holden is met at the library by Dr. Karswell (Niall MacGinnis), the head of the cult. Unnoticed by the investigator, Karswell slips him a parchment covered with runic symbols. This paper, we later learn, is the holder's passage to hell.

That night, while dining at his hotel with Professor Harrington's daughter Joanna (Peggy Cummins), Holden finds that as of a few days hence, every page has been torn from his desk calendar. Following this, the mystic scrap passed to him by Karswell flies toward the fireplace, as if by its own will, only to be stopped by a grating. Had it burned, Holden's fate, as illustrated by the calendar, would have been irrevocable. As it stands, he learns he must pass the paper to someone else or the demon, when it arrives, will do to Holden what it did to Harrington. Tailing Karswell on a night train out of town, Holden is able to slip him the parchment. It flies from the warlock's hand and, as he chases it along the tracks, the monster materializes, on schedule. It picks up the horrified sorcerer and tears him asunder. No longer disbelievers, Holden and Joanna walk off into the dreary night.

Curse of the Demon builds from a film of omen and suggested menace to one of absolute terror. While the opening of the picture tends to give away too much too soon, such as the existence of the demon, it also sets the stage for the horrors to come. For one thing, we gain an immediate respect for Karswell since it is shown that he's *not* a charlatan. For another, a lightning-filled cloud pursues Harrington down the road before the creature appears. When this same cloud reappears midway through the picture, we know what it portends. Indeed, the occasion for this is the most frightening part of the film. Holden, unable to find adequate resource material at the library, breaks into Karswell's country estate one evening to examine his library. After grappling with a housecat turned inexplicably into a leopard, Holden leaves and is pursued through the dark and misty forest by the demon cloud. Since it is not yet Holden's time to die, the beast does not appear. However, in the scientist's frenzied flight from the spectral fog, Tourneur has raised his audience to a fever pitch in preparation for the climactic appearance of the beast.

Even before Holden had become too deeply embroiled in cult affairs to back out, Tourneur treated us to one of the films many quietly unnerving scenes, one wherein Karswell, dressed as a clown, uses his magic skills to entertain local children at his home. Holden comes to visit and makes a crack about there being no such thing as magic. In response to this glib assertion, Karswell summons forth a storm that grows from a mere rustling of trees to a violent display of the elements. Although surprised, Holden is far from convinced.

The title monster from *Curse of the Demon*.

Later, at his hotel, the scientist is again faced with the bizarre: he hears a strange melody in the air. It has no traceable origin that he can discover and, when he repeats the tune to an Indian friend who has come to London for the convention, the older man gasps. It is a song universally associated with the devil.

In interviews, the late Tourneur was oft-quoted as having said that the demon, itself, was forced on him by the studio as box-office insurance. While this is probably true, the monster in no way detracts from the picture's quality. Designed after four-hundred-year-old woodcuts made by devil worshippers, the beast is ferocious and so well constructed that it is nothing worse than frosting on Tourneur's devil's food cake.

The performance of Dana Andrews is properly cynical, but it is Niall MacGinnis who steals the show. Although anxious for power, MacGinnis' Karswell is a sympathetic character who has the inenviable task of defending himself from the ravages of his self-righteous critics. Too, that he takes time to entertain children softens the sting of the terrible justice he metes out to adults. Andrews, on the other hand, is an obnoxious and meddlesome bastard who, like Professor Harrington, *drove* Karswell to murder in self-defense; in essence, they *made* him the villain. This offered the players an unusual shift in the traditional hero-villain relationship that, in its resolution, shakes Andrews' vaunted confidence to the core and destroys Karswell entirely.

A masterful film, the black-and-white picture played nationally on the lower half of a double bill with Hammer's colorful but standard *Revenge of Frankenstein*. More curious than the mysteries of the devil are the minds of distributors.

Back From the Dead (1958) was a return to the more standard ghost and evil-spirit fare of the thirties and forties. Based on the novel *The Other One* by Catherine Turney, *Back From the Dead* featured Peggy Castle as a girl possessed by the spirit of husband Arthur Franz's first wife. *The Devil's Partner* (1958), on the other hand, was an hour-long reworking of the Dorian Gray theme wherein, through the invocation of Satan, Edwin Nelson becomes a younger version of himself. A more novel twist—or decapitation, as it were—was the living severed head of a sixteenth-century devil worshipper. Based on David Duncan's *Water Witch, The Thing That Couldn't Die* (1958) was buried in a

The Thing That Couldn't Die meets with two of its hypnotized servants.

chest by Sir Francis Drake. When freed, some four centuries later, the title character takes over the mind of a girl who is forced to unearth the evil creature's body. When reassembled, but before he can wreak further havoc, the satanist is destroyed by a magic amulet.

Along with this disembodied cranium, 1958 gave us Lola, the exciting temptress of *Damn Yankees*. Based on the successful Broadway play, *Damn Yankees* stars Ray Walston—who later became *My Favorite Martian*—as the devil, Gwen Verdon as his vivacious aide, and Tab Hunter as an aged fan of the Washington Senators baseball team whom the devil makes young to defeat the New York Yankees. Walston's Satan is played for laughs, Miss Verdon for grinds, and although the tunes and production are lively, the movie lacks the sparkle of the stage. Still in all, this film, along with our next picture, serve to illustrate a basic truth about art. No matter what the quality of the enterprise, the various forms of art can skillfully accommodate diverse extremes in theme and style.

A case in point: if *Damn Yankees* represents the contemporary American musical theatre's view of Satan, as a gambling, spirited rogue, then Ingmar Bergman's *The Devil's Eye* (1960) is its antithesis, the classic Satan. The Satan who is less interested in amassing souls than he is in eroding morality. Unfortunately, while Bergman's picture supports our postulate as a work of art, it unfolds with all the sloth and rhetoric of a medieval miracle play. As such, it serves to entertain only the most devout of Bergman devotees. In it, Bibi Andersson (Mia from

Gwen Verdon informs Tab Hunter that, "Whatever Lola Wants, Lola Gets!" in *Damn Yankees*.

The Devil shows Don Juan a picture of the girl he wants deflowered in *The Devil's Eye*.

The Seventh Seal) portrays an afianced young woman whose virginity has given the devil a sty in his eye. Annoyed, Satan sends Don Juan (Jarl Kulle) from his domain to seduce the girl. Naturally, the emissary falls in love with her and does not steal away her chastity. He has, however, kissed the girl who, on her wedding night, lies to her husband claiming she has never been kissed. This small infidelity is sufficient to cure Satan's sty and all ends happily.

Between the extremes of comedy and allegory is the conceptually unique but ultimately routine effort *The Skull* (1965) from Britain's Amicus films. Based on a story by Robert Bloch *(Psycho)*, *The Skull* is all that remains of the sadistic (sic) Marquis de Sade, and occult collector Peter Cushing owns it. Unfortunately, the remnant is not quite vacant. The restless soul of the Frenchman still resides therein, takes possession of the Englishman, drives him to kill friend Christopher Lee and others, and finally forces him to take his own life. The film would have been a sublime psychological thriller save for one eviscerating effect: the skull can float, and does so lazily from room to room at will. Luckily, Cushing has an amazing ability to offset the bizarre with his own balanced skills. He carries the film through many of its stickier moments.

Still in Britain, Stanley Donan, not content with having directed just one devil film, *Damn Yankees*, brought together England's marvelous comedians Peter Cook and Dudley Moore (of the plays *Beyond the Fringe* and *Good Evening*) in *Bedazzled* (1967). Cook plays the Devil Mephisto, under the pseudonym of George Spiggott, and Moore the

The Devil (Peter Cook) stops Dudley Moore from hanging himself by offering him great riches in *Bedazzled*.

Wimpy Bar employee who, on the verge of suicide, sells Spiggot his soul. In return, he gets seven wishes. From this point forward, lunacy reigns supreme. Our hero has very few of his dreams fulfilled and quickly learns that the deal was hardly a wise one. Even if the duo's insane humor is not your cup of tea, there's a very picturesque Raquel Welch on hand as the devil's righthand woman, Lillian Lust, caretaker of the seven deadly sins. If you find *that* dull, then perhaps the fantasy staple *Dr. Faustus* (1967) is more your cup of hemlock. This eighteenth and most impressive version of the play by Christopher Marlowe was produced and directed by Richard Burton, who also stars as the man who sells his soul to Mephistopholes for eternal youth. As one might expect from the actor who has portrayed tragic heroes ranging from Hamlet to Marc Antony, the emphasis is not on hell but on Faustus' loss of God. Burton's wife Elizabeth has a cameo as Helen of Troy and again as the spirit who drags Faustus through the floor and into hell. Andre Teuber's Mephistopheles is superb, a bitter, beaten creature who, like Faustus, is apart from God and inner peace. Despite—or because of—the film's very stagelike, straightforward production and lofty musings, the public stayed home. Or perhaps they were saving their ticket money for *Rosemary's Baby* (1968).

Rosemary's Baby, like *The Seventh Seal*, is one of those rare fantasy films that made a sizeable impression on the general moviegoing public. Based on the

Peter Cushing lies dead, the final victim of *The Skull*.

Mephistopholes strikes a deal with *Dr. Faustus*.

Mia Farrow and Ruth Gordon in *Rosemary's Baby*.

best seller by Ira Levin *(The Stepford Wives),* the film was produced by one-time horror quickie filmmaker William Castle and was directed by Roman Polanski *(Macbeth, Chinatown)*

Newly moved to New York City, Rosemary (Mia Farrow) is the innocent victim of a cult of Manhattan-based devil worshippers. Unbeknownst to Rosemary, her down-and-out actor husband Guy (John Cassavetes) has sold her to Beelzebub in return for a juicy part in a play. Satan wants a child; our heroine is to be the unsuspecting mother. Rosemary is raped by the devil and recalls the experience only as a ghastly nightmare. In the months that follow, a neighbor, Mrs. Castavets (Ruth Gordon) gives Rosemary cakes and milk shakes filled with strange herbs. The woman has also suggested a Dr. Saperstein to the girl, a medic who gives her strange medicines to take to assure a healthy baby. After a while, Rosemary starts to wonder about these bizarre goings-on. She asks an old friend, Hutch (Maurice Evans), to help her get to the bottom of things. Shortly thereafter, Hutch dies. Before she learns the truth, Rosemary's baby is born and the girl is told that it has died. Then, one night, she hears a strange wailing from the apartment next door. Breaking in, she finds Guy, Mr. and Mrs. Castavets, the doctor, others, and her child. The cloven-hoofed little demon horrifies her, at first, but after a while, overcome by maternal affection, she accepts the child amidst the cries of "God is dead."

One of the frightfully vivid aspects of *Rosemary's Baby* is that Guy and Rosemary's apartment could have been *our* apartment; their fears and wants not unlike our own. Indeed, Guy's collapse in the face of temptation is nothing less than human. The catalyst is that Guy has a way out. On another level, in the form of seemingly unrelated throwaways, the picture builds subtle hints that all is not well. Even before we've settled into our seats, the Castavets' lodger, a young lady, jumps from the apartment window and dies in a bloody heap on the street. Shortly thereafter, the actor who was to have played the part that Guy had wanted goes blind. Rosemary has those weird, unholy dreams. Hutch dies. Since neither Rosemary or the viewer is in on Guy's deal, these incidents gnaw at us, play on our fear that something terrible is going to happen. Which it does.

Enough has been written elsewhere about the high quality of the directing and acting, especially that of the Oscar-winning Ruth Gordon. Still, it should be pointed out that *Rosemary's Baby* is perhaps the only film of the recent spate of horror-fantasies that achieves its shock without resorting to cheap gimmicks such as bloodshed, green bile, ghastly tortures, or grotesque makeups. It is simply a well-made nightmare that richly deserved its great popular success.

Surprisingly, no one followed in the footsteps of Mia's devil child, and in 1969 Satanic rites returned in *The Dunwich Horror*. This Roger Corman production was of a more traditional slant than *Rosemary's Baby*, based on the work of H. P. Lovecraft. Although the film suffers without the bravura presence of Vincent Price, it did find strong players in Sam Jaffe, as the high priest of a New England devil cult, Sandra Dee, Dean Stockwell, and others. A more grotesque brew was a loose adaptation of Poe's *Facts in the Case of M. Valdemar*, Japan's *The Vampire Doll* (1970). A young girl is put into a deep trance just before death. At the moment of expiration, her soul becomes damned because her body lives on as a flesh-eating monster. Meanwhile, Gordon Hessler, the director on *The Oblong Box*, also turned to Poe for a plot in the well-made *Cry of the Banshee* (1970). Vincent Price stars as the medieval Lord Edward Whitman who, while out riding, kills the children of a devil worshipper, the title banshee Oona (Elizabeth Bernger). In retaliation, she places a curse on the Whitman family. Within days a wicked madness has infiltrated the Whitmans. Edward has become more sadistic than ever.

While this is going on, one of the Whitman servants, Roderick (Robert Hutton) has been turned into a Sidhee, a devil spirit. Unfortunately, Roderick does not know of the curse. He kills one of the Whitman children and butchers the Lord's wife. Then, one night, Whitman stumbles upon his daughter Maureen (Hilary Dwyer) making love to Patrick. Angered, the nobleman orders the servant chained in a dungeon. There, Oona calls on him and he breaks free. Roderick goes to kill Maureen, but Edward intercedes. As the men struggle, the girl shoots her former lover. Roderick is buried and, several days later, Edward, his son Harry (Patrick Mower), and Maureen climb into a coach and leave the accursed town forever. In a truly frightening conclusion, Edward turns to address his children. They fall over dead. Glancing up at the driver, the Lord screams: it is Roderick.

The monstrous Sidhee from *Cry of the Banshee*.

Fine production values, strong performances, and tight direction elevate an ordinary property to one of the screen's finest Poe "adaptations." Even the gratuitous sex and gore does not detract from the film's building horror as the world of the smug Lord Whitman slowly crumbles. Although Price's character is reminiscent of Prospero in *Masque of the Red Death*, he fills it with his own brand of pungent evil, which in its familiarity eliminates the need for extraneous exposition.

Having enjoyed some popular success with *The Crimson Cult*, Tigon films stayed both in and out of the red with *The Blood on Satan's Claw* (1970), which despite its galvanic title is a taut little chiller. In eighteenth-century England, a farmer uncovers a bone implanted with an eye and turns it over to local authorities. It soon evolves that the bone and eye were the buried remains of an ancient demon who returns to spiritual life and allies himself with a lovely young lady, Angel Blake (Linda Hayden).

With recruits, she hacks a young man to death, has a virgin raped and sacrificed, and finally tries to seduce the local clergyman Rev. Fallowfield (Anthony Ainley). She fails at this, and eventually the coven is defeated by a local purifier known as The Judge (Patrick Wymark).

The film enjoyed decent play, but only at second-rate houses; a pity, since it was an honest effort to blend devil worship, period atmosphere, and eroticism in a mature fantasy film. Less satisfying was a devilish reworking of *Dr. Jekyll and Mr. Hyde* as the Philippine-made *Beast of the Yellow Night* (1970). Vic Diaz played the devil to whom Eddie Garcia sold his soul. In return, he possess a succession of men, drawing the evil from each. When enough wickedness has been absorbed, our protagonist becomes a monster.

In the wake of these sundry and unusual excursions into the occult, filmmakers experimented with relevence and artiness, both of which failed to

Barbara Parkins and an accursed Labrador Retriever in a publicity still for *The Mephisto Waltz.*

their service of Lucifer. They go after children, dutifully destroying their parents with toys-gone-mad and other tools of the supernatural. Despite token resistance by the small town's sheriff (L. Q. Jones, who also wrote the novelization based on the film), and two visitors, Ben (Charles Bateman) and Nicky (Anna Capri), the coven wins out. This continues a twist made popular by *Rosemary's Baby* in which, at the climax, the devil comes out on top.

As has been evidenced by the recent successes of both *The Godfather* and *Jaws,* source material is a great factor in describing both the budget and play a film will receive. Thus, the big bestsellers of 1972—*The Other* and *The Exorcist*—were made into big-money movies in 1973, one good and the other awful. Directed by Robert Mulligan *(To Kill A Mockingbird* and *Summer of '42) The Other* is a fine period adaptation of the novel by actor-turned-author Tom Tryon. A small Connecticut town of the 1930s is the setting for this story of twin brothers, Niles (Chris Udvarnoky) and Holland Perry (Martin Udvarnoky), only one of whom is alive, but both of whom walk the earth. Harboring a belief in the existence of his dead brother, Niles acts

satisfy a basic demand of any motion picture: it must also entertain. For this reason, 1971 saw two major financial and critical disappointments. *The Possession of Joel Delany* is the story of a young Puerto Rican murderer who is, himself, killed. His spirit enters the body of Joel (Perry King). As a result, the title character goes around slaughtering New Yorkers until his life, too, is ended. Not ready to surrender, the restless spirit takes over Joel's sister Norah (Shirley Maclaine). The film is long on character study—rich protagonist possessed by the spirit of a ghetto dweller—with which it does an adequate job, at the expense of plot. Likewise, director Paul Wendkos' *Mephisto Waltz* is an earnest but hugely belabored affair wherein Duncan (Curt Jurgens), an aged pianist, has the devil transfer his spirit into the body of Myles (Alan Alda), a more youthful musician. Cuts made by the producers left Wendkos with a beautifully photographed but disjointed film.

The failure of this strange duo did not discourage other filmmakers from delving into the occult. One stand-out effort was *Brotherhood of Satan* (1971), in which a dozen elderly devil worshippers decide it's time to procure new bodies in which to continue

An atmospheric publicity still showing the bizarre twins in *The Other.*

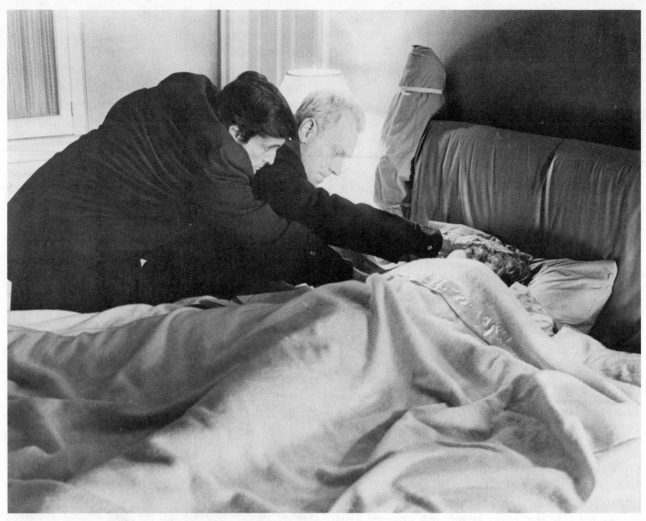

Jason Miller and Max von Sydow attend the possessed Linda Blair in *The Exorcist*.

out both lives, with one brother being a thing of evil who kills off members of his family one by one. A magnificently crafted film, *The Other* plays well as both a psychological or supernatural drama in the tradition of *The Haunting*. It's a pity that this well-crafted film did not receive the public accolades thrust on that shard of excrement known as *The Exorcist*.[4]

The whole world went to see *The Exorcist,* and only God knows why. Perhaps the devil, and his twin brother the Hollywood publicist, made us do it. There were very few genuine shocks in the film, and even old hands like makeup man Dick Smith did not perform up to snuff.

The story, for posterity, tells of young Regan MacNeil (Linda Blair) who is possessed by the devil. Although just why Regan has been so-honored is never explored, we must assume that, ala Bergman's *The Devil's Eye,* her purity was a sty in his eye. In any event, after urinating on the floor before her actress-mother (Ellen Burstyn) and her dinner party—a crude and silly omen of the evils to come—Regan goes upstairs where, a few scenes later, her tribulations start to build. Her bed begins hopping up and down, after which, when it is stable, she floats above it; her tongue turns green and her face becomes horribly scratched and corroded; finally, she speaks with the voices of those deceased. In the end, where science and medicine have failed, religion succeeds: two priests exorcise the spirit, although it costs them both their lives. Max von Sydow dies of the strain and, in an admittedly excellent scene, Jason Miller takes the evil spirit within himself. Immediately thereafter, according to one's interpretation, he either tosses himself or is tossed by the devil from a second-story window.

This leaves us with an intriguing postscript: although he's been exorcised, the devil has claimed two "bishops" for a "pawn." By any reckoning, as in the other films of this era, the devil has been triumphant.

All the subtleties used by Hitchock, Tourneur, and others to evoke emotion were flagrantly discarded by director William Friedkin in favor of gross sensationalism. Clinical gore and tastelessness are as freely exploited as contemporary mores allowed; in a way, we deserve *The Exorcist*. About the only positive achievement Friedkin *(French Connection)* managed was to create a very casual feel about Regan's home life prior to her possession. No doubt this was intended to show us, and properly so, that anyone can be possessed. However, Friedkin failed to embellish this hypothesis by playing on the theme's most frightening aspect: the inequitable juxtaposition of the ultimate innocence, a young girl, and the ultimate evil, the devil. This is something Robert Wise did much better with his confrontation between Aimee and the Headless Horseman in *Curse of the Cat People*.

In terms of acting, Jason Miller distinguishes himself as Demian Carras, the lonely, determined priest. Max von Sydow is wasted in a cameo role that is as unrounded and unconvincing as the film's technical effects. Linda Blair is too sweet to be credible, and Ellen Burstyn, 1974's *Best Actress* Oscar-winner for *Alice Doesn't Live Here Anymore*, works much too hard at being natural. In all, a pretentious, overblown, and overrated effort.

Like the forthcoming *Exorcist, Part II* in which the grownup Regan is repossessed, a black version of *The Exorcist* was an inevitability. Thus was born *Abby* (1974), a schlocky piece of cinema that puts a black woman in the place of Regan. It was followed by *Behind the Door* (1975), a remake of *The Exorcist* in which the devil is after a child that lies aborning in Juliet Mills' womb. To get at the baby, Satan possesses its mother. The film uses the same gimmicks as its predecessor including floating junkets, rasping voices, buckets of pea-colored vomit, and eroded facial features. Better than all of the above was the most recent devil film, *The Devil's Rain* (1975). Ernest Borgnine stars as the head of a cult of eyeless zombies who exact vengeance on people whose forbears had oppressed them. Thus, having run full-circle to what might accurately be called *Black Sunday: 1975*, we end our look at devil worship and Satan's various personifications. But our journey has taken us farther from the rational world to a point where we can now enter the somewhat more challenging and fanciful sphere of the monster.

5
THE VAMPIRE

A vampire is considered the most damned of creatures. He walks the earth between dusk and dawn to drink the blood of others. He is vulnerable only to garlic, a religious icon, sunlight, or a wooden stake driven through his heart. Beyond these defenses, like Satan, the vampire is a godless eternal.

The key word is godless.

The drinking of human blood has been a not-uncommon practice since prehistory. From the Stone Age through the unholy Roman Empire, warriors sought to abet their strength by consuming the crimson essence of fallen foes. Even today, the Christian euphemism of drinking the blood of Christ has great ritualistic significance. The point, then, is that the act itself is less damnable than the insacred trimmings that surround it.

Legends of vampirism are not tied to one region or historical period. Chinese vampires, for instance, were green and glowed in the dark; Russian vampires sucked blood directly from the hearts of their victims. The ways in which one becomes a member of this cannibalistic clique likewise vary: in Scotland, for instance, if a cat jumped over a corpse the dead man became a vampire. In Poland, those born between the new and full moon were especially sensitive to the curse.

It wasn't until Bram Stoker's novel *Dracula*, however, that the vampire legend gained a "class" stature. Its author had read Sheridan La Fanu's great vampire tale *Carmilla*, published in 1872, and joined the macabre prose of that earlier work with legends of the fifteenth-century Transylvanian Count Voivode Dracul, whose surname meant *dragon*. Voivode was a vengeful lord whose favorite pastime was the impaling of criminals, whores, or foreigners on large wooden stakes. Over one-hundred-thousand people were so-destroyed making it poetic justice that Stoker's vampire carry Dracul's bloody standard into literary history. Published in 1897, the novel *Dracula* was a great success and spawned an equally popular stage play by John Balderston and Hamilton Deane. Indeed, one of the theatrical *Draculas* was Bela Lugosi, who later gained immortality in the motion picture version. More on Lugosi later.

One of the first and finest film versions of *Dracula* was *Nosferatu* (1922), made by the German director F. W. Murnau *(Sunrise, The Last Laugh)*. Set in 1838, the film opens with Hutter (Gustav von Vangenheim), a businessman, visiting the castle of Count Orlock (Max Schreck) to sell him land in England. During their transactions, the Count is entranced by a picture of Hutter's wife Ellen (Greta Schroeder) and, leaving a terrified realtor behind, sails to Bremen to make her his own. En route, Orlock kills everyone onboard and when he arrives, a plague erupts in Bremen caused by rats that have followed the vampire. Hutter, who has left Transylvania, tells Ellen that Orlock is the cause of this sickness and she resolves to destroy him. That night, Ellen sacrifices her own life to keep the vampire by her bedside until dawn.

It was a well-publicized fact that the last name of

Nosferatu menaces the crew of a ship transporting him to greener pastures.

An early portrait of Bela Lugosi.

the Orlock actor, Schreck, means *terror* in German. It's an accurate label. Pale, thin, and with arched eyebrows and pointed ears, Schreck is the perfect *Nosferatu*. Beyond his appearance, however, the film built around him is a quality production, filled with murky sets and all the great gimmicks that would soon become familiar to horror-film fans: the driverless coach that carries Hutter to the castle; Orlock's lunatic aide (Alexander Granach); the doors that open and close by themselves; etc. Seeing these for the first time, in 1922, audiences must have found the effects unnerving.

Bela Lugosi's *Dracula* (1930) was next, a generally overrated film that fails to capture the menace of Murnau's presentation. Despite his ultimate association with the role,[5] it is Lugosi's performance that remains largely unsatisfying.

Menace is an intangible quantity, a presence that can make or break a horror film antagonist. Vincent Price can suggest menace with a gesture; Karloff with his voice. Lugosi's forte was his devilish hands and stare. Unfortunately, the role of *Dracula* is much more than blazing eyes and supple fingers. It is sexuality, or more properly a sense of physical lust that the very melodramatic Lugosi just didn't possess.

Drawing more from the play than the novel, director Tod Browning *(Freaks, London After Midnight)* had intended the role for Lon Chaney Sr. Unfortunately, the great silent star died that year and Broadway's *Dracula* stepped into the film. The plot is not remarkably dissimilar from *Nosferatu*

with Renfield (Dwight Frye) sitting in for Hutter, and Mina Seward (Helen Chandler) the object of Dracula's attention. The one addition was Dr. Van Helsing (Edward van Sloane) whose goal it is to prove that vampires really do exist. It is he, creeping

Bela Lugosi and Helen Chandler in *Dracula*.

57

Bela Lugosi in the stage version of *Dracula*, which toured the country during the forties.

through age-old catacombs, drives the fatal stake through Dracula's heart: *off-screen!*

Although the cob-webbed sets and gothic mood are legendary, and quite rightly so, the film is too much a stage play to qualify as effective cinema. It was photographed in a very static, pedestrian manner with much of the novel's allure—such as Dracula's turning into a wolf and the deaths on the ship—spoken of but never seen. Equally staid was Lugosi. His fans are legion, yet beyond his strange, unsettling voice and the piercing stare, the Hunga-

Bela Lugosi and Arthur Lucan in *My Son, the Vampire*.

rian actor creates an impression of one less undead than one uninspired. His Dracula is a cardboard villain for whom we feel neither pity or hatred. He is simply a part of the unearthly goings-on. Only Dwight Frye, who becomes Dracula's maniacal aide, is at all electric.

Despite these drawbacks, which even in 1930 must have been glaring, *Dracula* became Universal Pictures' top-grossing film of the year. It was certainly more widely embraced than Danish director Carl Dryer's more personal effort, the esoteric *Vampyr* (1931). An independently financed effort, *Vampyr* was released in the United States as *Castle of Doom*, a severely edited, voice-over narration abomination that went largely undistributed. Only recently has the picture resurfaced in its original form. Based loosely on *Carmilla, Vampyr* is the saga of David Gray who, through a series of weird events, is lured from a quiet country inn to the dark embrace of a vampire family. In the end, he destroys the matriarch of the clan to free an unaffected daughter. The remaining bloodsuckers are pursued and killed by the ghosts of their victims.

The striking realism of *Vampyr*—it was shot entirely on location—is balanced by the eerie *look* of the picture. The film was photographed through a strip of gauze, which gave it a mystic, haunting quality. The dialogue, as one critic so aptly observed, is only "half-heard" and the consumate effect is that of watching a dream turn slowly into a nightmare. However, *Vampyr* moves from the normal to the paranormal so gently that the viewer never experiences a lapse in credibility, despite the film's strange narrative. This, of course, does not always work to *Vampyr*'s advantage. Part of the fantasy film allure, in general, is that the settings are natural, while the people or monsters are figments of illogic. *Vampyr,* with its vague and arcane imagery, sacrifices that quality of fun in its quest for effect.

That the picture was made during the heyday of the American horror cycle was coincidence. It was simply a project that Dryer wished to undertake. Ultimately, accustomed to the shocks generated by Chaney and Karloff, America paid scant attention to *Vampyr.*

By the time Universal had finished counting the profits they made on *Dracula*, the studio was ready with their second vampire film, *Dracula's Daughter* (1936). Based on Bram Stoker's short story *Dracula's Guest*, Gloria Holden stars as Countess Marya

Universal Pictures produced a Spanish-language version of *Dracula* (1930) using the same sets as the Lugosi film. Pictured are Dracula (Carlos Villarias Villar) and Dr. Van Helsing (Barry Norton).

Irving Pichel and Gloria Holden in *Dracula's Daughter*.

Zaleska, Dracula's daughter, and Edward van Sloane repeats as Van Helsing. In a unique plot development, Van Helsing goes on trial for the murder of Dracula, whom the police don't really believe was a vampire. He is defended by former pupil psychiatrist Jeff Garth (Otto Kruger) as, in a nearby glen, Dracula's body is cremated. The Countess and her aide Sandor (Irving Pichel, who went on to direct *Destination Moon* in 1950) are among the observers. Zaleska vows to escape her father's curse of vampirism and duly seeks Garth's help. During the course of their work, she falls in love with the doctor and asks him to spend eternity with her. He refuses and Sandor abducts his fiancee (Marguerite Churchill) to Zaleska's Transylvanian castle. Garth follows and the Countess orders him to marry her or his sweetheart will die. Jealous, Sandor fires a wooden arrow through his mistress' heart. Arriving on the scene, Van Helsing and the police commissioner shoot Sandor to death.

Dracula's Daughter gives us a dimensional heroine in Zareska, who is vulnerable in spirit yet a monster, cursed by her birthright. Highlighted by fine performances, the film is far less-stilted and anemic than its predecessor.

PRC's *Dead Men Walk* was released six years later, vampires with incredible strength in the persons of Elwyn (George Zucco) and his hunchbacked slave (Dwight Frye). Zucco also portrayed his twin brother Dr. Clayton in the film. It was a nice vehicle for the critically underrated Zucco, and bare though it was in terms of literacy, *Dead Men Walk* was a giant step above Columbia's

Lon Chaney Jr. about to introduce himself to Robert Paige in *Son of Dracula*.

Return of the Vampire (1943) in which Lugosi once again donned his infamous black cloak. For *Return of the Vampire*, the one-time Dracula was Count Tessla, whom we encounter in 1918 as he terrorizes a sanitarium. Destroyed, the fiend remains dormant, a stake in his heart, until the German bombing of London jars him to wakefulness. With his werewolf aide Andreas (Matt Willis), the vampire murders freely until he sets his eyes and fangs on a girl with whom Andreas has fallen in love. Enraged, the werewolf pounds a stake into Tessla's heart. Having thus destroyed his own source of strength, the accursed servant dies.

It was only a matter of time before the inevitable *Son of Dracula* (1943) appeared, courtesy of Universal, with Lon Chaney Jr. assuming the title role. Chaney, while not a performer of great range, was a fine monster star. He had inherited both the Mummy and Frankenstein Monster roles from Karloff, created his own monster in *The Wolfman* (1940), and was the logical choice for the new Dracula. Although lacking Lugosi's continental polish, and a bit too broad for the role, he gave his Dracula a harsh authority that worked out rather well.

The Hungarian Count Alucard (Chaney) arrives in Louisiana at the home of Katherine Caldwell (Louise Allbritton), a girl he had met while on vacation. Katherine is lured to a swamp where Alucard's coffin bobs to the top of a lagoon. Water vapor seeping from the closed pine box assumes the shape of the Count, who takes the hypnotized girl to a Justice of the Peace where they are wed. When Katherine's fiance Frank Stanley (Robert Paige) finds out about the nuptials, he hastens to Katherine's house where he shoots Alucard. The bullets pass through his body and kill the vampire's new wife. Believing he has committed murder, Frank surrenders himself to the police. Later, revived by Alucard, Katherine visits Frank's cell. The prisoner realizes who Alucard is—perhaps by spelling his name backwards—and escapes. He finds the Count's coffin in a drainage tunnel, burns it, and the unholy monster turns to dust at sunrise. Katherine is likewise destroyed.

A change in locale and some atmospheric sets save *Son of Dracula* from being just a standard vehicle for the first of many blasphemies that would be drawn from the original characters. Having realized tremendous success with their other monster movies, the Frankenstein and Wolfman films,

Boris Karloff agrees to keep the stake from John Carradine's heart only if the vampire agrees to serve him. From *House of Frankenstein*.

the Universal monster series continued, but with the trio of monsters united. *House of Frankenstein* (1944) was the first of three teamups and is a veritable who's who of monsterdom. Boris Karloff portrayed Dr. Gustav Niemann, a mad scientiest who had been sent to prison for having vivisected animals. He manages to escape the penitentary and, with the aide of his hunchbacked assistant Daniel (J. Carroll Naish), kills the proprieter of a traveling horror show, Dr. Bruno Lampini (George Zucco). Niemann takes his place, withdraws a stake from the display skeleton of Count Dracula (John Carradine), and the vampire is reborn. Niemann uses Dracula to exact vengeance on those who sentenced him to prison. Unfortunately, the vampire is late in returning to his coffin one night, and is reduced to ash by the rising sun. Niemann, journeying to Dr.

Frankenstein's castle, finds the Wolfman (Chaney) and Frankenstein Monster (Glenn Strange)[6] frozen in ice. Unthawed, the Wolfman returns to his evil ways and is shot by a silver bullet; the Frankenstein Monster revives and carries Niemann into a pit of quicksand. All was quiet, then, until the next year and the *House of Dracula*. This time, both Dracula (Carradine) and the Wolfman (Chaney) return inexplicably to the country of Vasaria. There, hoping to be cured of their afflictions, they seek out Dr. Franz Edelmann (Onslow Stevens) who is more concerned with reviving the Frankenstein Monster (Strange) than helping his unusual patients. In the end Dracula dies, the Wolfman is cured, and the doctor goes mad. Finally, in *Abbott and Costello Meet Frankenstein* (1948), the monsters met for the last time. Dracula (Lugosi) plans to put Costello's brain in the body of the Frankenstein Monster (Strange). The Wolfman (Chaney), however, comes to Lou's rescue by leaping from a cliff with Dracula's batform in his grip. Surprisingly, the film is quite good with excellent production values. Chaney's transformation to the Wolfman is masterfully done in full view of the audience, but it is Lugosi's on-screen and excellently animated change from man to bat that is the standout segment. A fitting denouement to the careers of Universal's great monsters.

Vampire's Ghost (1945) was the four-hundred-year-old vampire leader of West Africa's underworld, but his story was inconsequential: its running time was less than an hour. Gone, too, were the traditional trappings: John Abbott's vampire could walk about freely during the daylight hours and was destroyed by mere fire! Clearly, the vampire no longer represented healthy box-office returns. Even Bela Lugosi as a vampire was not enough to sell tickets. As *My Son, the Vampire* (1952), the poor and unhealthy Lugosi—he died four years later—was a would-be vampire in an unstartling addition to the British *Old Mother Riley* (with Arthur Lucan in the continuing title role) series.

Herman Cohen mixed youngsters and bloodsuckers in *Blood of Dracula* (1957), a vampiric reworking of his *I Was a Teenage Werewolf* theme with Sandra Harrison hypnotized into believing she is a vampire. *Return of Dracula* (1957) was next, a run-of-the-mill melodrama in which Dracula (Francis Lederer) trades in his cloak for a suit and tie and deserts Transylvania for the more plentiful pickings of Carleton, a city in Southern California. There, he menaces young lovers Tim (Gage Clarke) and Rachel (Norma Eberhardt) before falling into a pit and landing on a proprietously sharpened spike. It was time to inject some new blood in the legend. Fortunately, Britain's Hammer studios accepted the challenge, returned to Stoker's original tale, and created what is widely considered to be the finest horror film ever made, *Horror of Dracula* (1959). It also began a horror boom that has run, unabated, for sixteen years.

Horror of Dracula had a cast of actors, not just performers, who breathed energy and excitement into the shopworn tale. A rerun of *Nosferatu*, the film starred Christopher Lee *(Three Musketeers, Man With a Golden Gun)* as the Count and Peter Cushing *(The Skull)* as Van Helsing. Cushing and Lee became *the* horror team of the late fifties, sixties, and early seventies, wielding the same box-office clout as had Karloff and Lugosi in their heyday. Lee's Dracula is, furthermore, a foreboding presence—Lee is 6'4"—and his deep, sonorous voice gave the character an aura of great power beneath the superficial cordiality. This strength is vividly displayed early in the film when Jonathan Harker (John Van Eyssen), in Transylvania to sell Dracula British property, is bitten by a lady "guest" of Dracula's castle. From out of nowhere, the Count comes hissing and leaping over furniture to swat the girl ruthlessly aside and carry her through a bookcase. Lee also fulfills the requisite sexuality of Dracula. Anticipating the vampire's nocturnal visitations, his victims lie in bed with breathless expectation. When the bloodsucker arrives, he stands framed in the doorway and, draped in his black cape, walks slowly to the hostess' side. His kisses are passionate, planted on breast, shoulders, and arms. Finally, caressing their necks, he feasts. Yet, despite Lee's evil, carnal creature, there is pathos in his personality. It is the tragedy of the hunted, and issues from the cool, logical Van Helsing. The doctor's one fervent desire is to slaughter all vampires, and his passion makes the already damned Dracula's lot an even less enviable one. Indeed, this balance makes for a brilliant climax wherein Van Helsing tracks Dracula to his castle. When the physician arrives, the vampire is busy burying his latest victim to serve as future sustenance. The sun is rising and, with a great sense of panic, Dracula drops the body into a hastily excavated grave and darts urgently for the shadowed safety of his

Jonathan Harker is shown his room by Dracula in *Horror of Dracula*.

domain. Inside the castle, the vampire batters his nemesis mercilessly until, caught in the rays of the rising sun, Dracula is held there by a crucifix Van Helsing forms with twin candelabras. In a magnificent special-effects scene, the vampire slowly rots and turns to dust, thus ending his reign of terror.

The *Horror of Dracula* sets are all lavish and photographed with a great feel for movement. The direction, by Terence Fisher, is superb. There is no fluff or padding in the film and Fisher's shocks are genuine; the suspense issues from plot and characterization rather than pertinacious bloodshed. The film is *the* masterpiece of the genre, and with its companion film *Curse of Frankenstein*—starring Cushing and Lee as doctor and monster, respectively—gave the horror film a jolting rebirth from which it has not yet recovered.

After *Horror of Dracula*, Lee was borrowed by Italian filmmakers for *Uncle was a Vampire* (1959) in which he portrayed the bloodsucker responsible for turning a nobleman (Renato Rascel) into the title fiend. That was the same year *Curse of the Undead* came riding out of the sunset. The film starred Michael Pate as a vampire-gunslinger who is finally done-in by a bullet on which a preacher has etched a cross.

When Lee returned to Hammer, he was gauzed up and starred with Cushing in *The Mummy* (See chapter 7). Meanwhile, the studio went full ahead on what would become the longest and most profitable vampire series in film history. *Brides of Dracula* (1960) followed *Horror of Dracula* by just over a year, with David Peel replacing Lee in the central role. *Brides of Dracula* is the story of a young girl (Yvonne Monlaur) who is stranded by an accident and forced to stay at the castle of an old Baroness (Martita Hunt). In due course, she finds the woman's son Baron Meinster (Peel) chained to a wall in his room. Unlocking his silver shackles, the girl has no way of knowing she has just set loose a vampire. Free now, the creature procures his "brides" from among the young ladies at a convent school. He even attacks his mother, who becomes a bloodsucker and turns to Dr. Van Helsing (Cushing) for help. With the fearless vampire killer on the case, the young Baron flees. While attempting to escape, he is caught in the shadow of a cross formed by the arms of a windmill and is destroyed.

Boasting a superior cast and mounted with the same care as its predecessor, *Brides of Dracula* was a great success for Hammer. Curiously, it would be

David Peel makes an exit in *Brides of Dracula*.

five years before their next picture, during which time filmgoers were treated to some unusual independent vampire fare. *World of the Vampires* (1960) was a Mexican film in which Mauricio Garces used organ music to both control and destroy vampires. A nicely conceived picture, *World of the Vampires* was marred by poor dubbing for American release and a low budget. Better was *Blood and Roses* (1960), another adaptation of *Carmilla*, although drawing more from the original story than had *Vampyr*. The French-Italian co-production was directed by Roger Vadim *(Barbarella)* and was an attempt to create a delicate mood piece in which Annette Vadim is possessed by a vampire ancestor and is driven to drink blood. Her victims are rival beauties such as Elsa Martinelli. Despite vivid sets and costumes, *Blood and Roses* is a slow, droll film that delivers neither the chills or fantasy one might expect. For contrast, a more rewarding effort was *Vampire and the Ballerina* (1962). While on a European tour, Francesca (Tina Gloriani) and Louisa (Helene Remy), two members of a ballet troupe, desert their companions to go sight-seeing in a nearby forest. By nightfall they are lost, and Francesca's worried boyfriend Luca (Walter Bran-

Elsa Martinelli goes for a walk in *Blood and Roses*.

di) goes looking for the girls. He finds them just as a thunderstorm breaks; the group runs to an old castle for cover. There they are met by a lovely Countess (Maria Luisa Rolanda) who, later that night, seduces and bites Louisa. When the trio returns to town, the bloodsucker follows and continues to drain the dancer. Luca, realizing that Louisa first grew weak at the castle, returns to investigate. Francesca comes along and they meet the Countess, who admits that she and her servant (Iscaro Ravaioli) are vampires. Francesca and Luca run into the forest, but the monsters pursue. Without realizing it, the demons stray far from their castle and are unable to return before dawn. Touched by the first rays of morning, the vampires perish.

Vampire and the Ballerina is a simple gothic fantasy without pretense and unwarranted gloss. In a curious way, it is not unlike a fairy tale with its young innocents lost in a forest of evil, the wicked vampires lurking nearby, and the purifying rays of sunlight hiding just beyond the horizon.

Before urging Christopher Lee back into his cape, Hammer produced a catch-penny but intriguing effort called *Kiss of the Vampire* (1963). Noel Willman played the leader of an early twentieth-century vampire cult that terrorizes a Hungarian township. In a clever finale, the devil is invoked to destroy his own with a swarm of lethal bats. Another film with a gimmick was *Billy the Kid vs. Dracula* (1965), although it was not in a class with even the lowliest Hammer production. Despite John Carradine's able performance as Dracula, the picture is geared to the lowest element of the schlock-theatre crowd. The Count poses as a wealthy Easterner, uncle to rancher Betty Bentley (Melinda Plowman). Soon the killings start, and reformed outlaw-turned-Bar-B foreman Billy (Chuck Courtney) gets suspicious. Eventually, Dracula abducts his own "niece" and the one-time gunman follows the Count to a mine. There, he slays the vampire with a stake pounded home via gun butt. This tongue-in-cheek effort played a double bill with the equally tepid *Jessee James Meets Frankenstein's Daughter*.

Back in Britain, *Devils of Darkness* (1965) dealt with a cult of immortals whose leader is Count Sinistre, a vampire. However, the more substantive entry from England that year was Christopher Lee's long-awaited return as Stoker's vampire in *Dracula, Prince of Darkness*. Two couples vacationing in Carpathia visit Castle Dracula out of curiosity. They are made welcome by Klove (Thorley Walters) who, later that night, kills Allan (George Woodbridge) and hangs his body above Dracula's coffin.

Christopher Lee strikes a dynamic pose in *Dracula, Prince of Darkness*.

His ashes made corporeal by Allan's dripping blood, the count attacks Allan's wife Helen (Barbara Shelly). The other couple, Charles (Francis Mathews) and Diana (Suzan Farmer) escape to a monastery where they seek the aide of Father Shandor (Andrew Kier). Eventually, Helen is destroyed and Dracula, caught on the frozen moat of his castle, has the ice shot from beneath his feet and drowns.

With the same high-caliber performances and production values as *Horror of Dracula*, *Dracula, Prince of Darkness* was a success. Although produced for less than $300,000, the money was well spent on refurbishing and redecorating old sets, and gathering up a strong, largely "no-name" cast. There were, unfortunately, two refinements made in Lee's persona: his lack of dialogue—the vampire was given not a single word to speak—and a red-lined cape. The silence made him less sinister since it forced some rather strained gestures, and the cape was jarring due to its blazing color. The logic of these changes is, at best, elusive.

Leaving Lee behind, for the nonce, we find *Blood of Dracula's Castle* (1967), a very minor effort starring Alex D'Arcy as a Dracula who, with his Countess (Paula Raymond) find themselves competing with a werewolf for victims. *Taste of Blood* followed that same year, offering viewers a subjective look at vampirism. The modern-day descendent of Dracula drinks a cup of wine laced with blood and is afflicted with his ancestor's curse. The unfortunate victim of fate is thus forced to kill the relatives of those who had staked his namesake. Feeling the genre had been bled dry, Roman Polanski decided it

The original ad-art for a Hammer double bill. Note theatre giveaways on top.

was time for a satire. Thus was born *The Fearless Vampire Killers or Pardon Me, But Your Teeth Are In My Neck* (1967). A blatant satire of *Nosferatu* and *Vampyr*, the film stars Ferdy Mayne as the patriarch of a vampire family, and details the efforts made by Professor Abronsius (Jack McGowran) and his assistant Alfred (Polanski) to destroy them. This results in a happy ending for the monsters, a twist that, as we have seen, was just becoming the vogue and which Polanski himself favored in *Rosemary's Baby*. The humor in *Fearless Vampire Killers* is geared to the knowing horror audience with such bits as a Jewish vampire tittering gaily at the ineffectiveness of a crucifix. When all is said and done, however, it is Polanski's homage to the genre; that the integrity of the classics survives this clever parody is a tribute to their stature.

Back at Hammer, Christopher Lee returned for his third vampiric outing in *Dracula Has Risen From the Grave* (1968). By this time, however, some of the seams were beginning to show on Hammer's Transylvanian backlot. The script wasn't as tightly written, nor the film as carefully paced and directed as previous efforts. The performances were excessive, either overly urgent or underplayed. Of course, the picture did have the overpowering presence of Lee, and he managed to carry the film through many turgid spells. A year after he had fallen into the moat, Dracula's wicked presence still held the surrounding villages in an almost hypnotic spell of terror. A visiting monsignor (Rupert Davies) feels this icy chill and forces the local priest (Ewan Hooper), a drunkard, to help him exorcise Castle Dracula. Climbing the mountain with a near life-size crucifix, the local priest stumbles and cuts himself. His blood drips to the moat and seeps through to Dracula. The vampire is reborn and finds the cross attached to his castle door. Enraged, Dracula finds and hypnotizes the weak priest and kills the monsignor. Before dying, however, the religious man tells his son-in-law Paul (Barry Andrews) to carry on and destroy Dracula. The vampire, meanwhile, entrances Paul's wife Maria (Veronica Carlson) and heads for the castle. The priest, who has struggled from Dracula's spell, joins forces with Paul and they arrive just as Maria throws the cross to the still-frozen moat. Paul and the bloodsucker battle. After furious combat, Dracula trips and falls from the battlements to find himself impaled on the holy symbol. The priest quickly mouths a proper Latin prayer and, for the third time, the nasty Count has been destroyed.

Despite its numerous shortcomings, *Dracula Has Risen From the Grave* does give us the single most effective sequence of the Hammer series. After the monsignor's death, Paul finds Dracula asleep in his coffin and pounds a stake into his heart. The attack wakens Dracula and Paul withdraws. The tormented priest, who has been awaiting his master's coming, begs Paul to invoke God's help or the stake will be ineffective. An atheist, Paul is unable to mouth the necessary prayer. Screaming and snarling, blood shooting from his chest, Dracula climbs from the coffin. With great effort he stands, gropes awkwardly at the pike, and pulls it from his chest. The suspense is great and the characterizations play well off one another: the stupid hero, weak clergyman, and dominant, angry vampire.

The next few years saw Hammer literally flood the market with vampires. By this time, however, the emphasis in their pictures had switched from horror to sex and gore. *Taste The Blood of Dracula* (1970) was the mildest of these, with Lee returned to life by three men who become bored with their existence and dabble in Satanism. Dracula takes the occultists' children under his spell, and fosters much mayhem before being trapped in a church and disintegrating on the altar. Sadly, Dracula was nothing more than a two-dimensional killer in a one-dimensional thriller. It was followed into release by Lee's fifth film in the series, *Scars of Dracula* (1970), a work of considerably greater merit. Revived by drops of blood from the fangs of a bat, Dracula once more takes up residence in his castle. When Simon (Dennis Waterman) and his girlfriend Sara (Jenny Hanley) come looking for the young man's missing brother, they arrive at the castle and are invited, by Dracula, to spend the night. Klove (Michael Gwynn), however, likes the couple and warns them to leave. They flee to the local church and the Count murders his aide for this bit of treason. Simon leaves Sara with the priest and returns to the castle where he finds his brother's corpse. Dracula appears and chases Simon to the rooftop. There, about to skewer his prey with a metal rod, the vampire is struck by lightning and is electrocuted. Although slightly contrived, the film at least had creditable acting and some atmospheric sets. Clearly, though, much of the character's range had already been exploited. However, since Lee's Dracula was still big box office, the sequels would continue. At this time, Hammer also readied a new selection of unrelated vampire films to capitalize on the sex and blood market.

Countess Dracula, Vampire Lovers, and Lust for a Vampire were all released in 1970. Countess Dracula had nothing whatsoever to do with vampires. It was the story of Elizabeth Barthory, the notorious noblewoman of history who maintained her beauty by bathing in the blood of young girls. While the "Dracula" title was simply a box-office ploy, the film's format and gothic overtones made it a blood relation to the other films. Vampire Lovers was yet another picture based on Carmilla. Young Mircalla Karnstein (né Carmilla) (Ingrid Pitt) has come from the grave to avenge the slaughter of her vampire family. After seducing and killing the daughters of General Van Spielsdorf (Peter Cushing) and other responsible parties, she is herself destroyed through decapitation. But not for long. In a sequel, Lust for a Vampire (with Yutte Stensgaard replacing Miss Pitt), Mircalla's skeleton is washed with blood and she is reborn. The vampiress menaces a girl's school and one of its professors, Richard LeStrange (Michael Johnson) falls under her spell. Unfortunately, while the bisexual heroine goes about killing young ladies, she falls in love with LeStrange. Finally, both are trapped in a burning mansion. A charred rafter breaks loose and pierces the vampiress' breast; Richard is saved from the inferno by a friend.

Marred by excessive sadism and an ultimately distracting preoccupation with bloody and naked flesh, these latter Hammer films remain a sad reflection of our changing tastes in entertainment: fangs, flesh, and flagellation is a more bankable combination than talent and integrity. This dismal state of affairs can be placed in a different perspective. While Hammer's very erotic product was thriving, an intelligent and faithful Spanish adaptation of Stoker's novel entitled Count Dracula (1970) was made, with a mustachioed Christopher Lee in the fore. It received little European or American distribution, and has not even appeared on television. In light of this, it is interesting to speculate how different the work of Tod Browning or James Whale (Bride of Frankenstein) might have been given today's lascivious freedom.

Two films that had considerable impact in 1970's vampire deluge, and indeed spawned a sequel apiece, offer a possible answer to that question. Both pictures were rather anachronistic, old-fashioned fantasies, true in theme to the work of the masters.

The cult-honored, low-budget Count Yorga: Vampire (1970) and its followup film Return of Count Yorga (1971) feature Robert Quarry's vampire in the contemporary world, but with all the classic contrivances. The first film opens with a seance of young people, over which Yorga presides. After the gathering, he is given a ride to his gloom-shrouded estate outside Los Angeles. There, the van driven by Paul (Michael Murphy) and Erica (Judith Lang) becomes stuck in mud and the duo is forced to stay the night. Paul is killed by Yorga's servant Brudah (Edward Walsh) and Erica is transformed into a vampire. Yorga goes prowling again and Donna, another girl from the seance, is his target. Meanwhile, her boyfriend Michael (Producer Michael Macready, son of actor George) and a Dr. Van Helsing-like Dr. Hayes (Roger Perry) deduce who and what Yorga really is. In a surprise ending, Michael destroys the Count with a stake in the heart, after which the vampirized Donna attacks and inflicts her lover. On that happy note, the film ends. Since it made a great deal of money, there was the not unexpected Return of Count Yorga. No rationale was offered for the vampire's return; Yorga was simply there and living on the outskirts of San Francisco. At a masquerade ball in an orphanage, Yorga selects social worker Cynthia Nelson (Mariette Hartley) as his new mate. That night he sends out his female vampire entourage, collected in the last film, and they kidnap Cynthia. After much to-do, her fiance Dr. David Baldwin (Roger Perry) is able to convince the police to investigate. They visit Yorga's house, rekill Brudah, and are themselves destroyed by the accursed women of Yorga. Only David gets through and, while he battles the vampire, Cynthia hacks at Yorga with a battle axe. He is killed for a second time. Unfortunately, in a twist lifted from the first film, David has been afflicted with Yorga's bite and attacks Cynthia as the curtain falls.

The unique aspect of these unspectacular, very plain productions is Yorga himself. He seems very much thrilled with being a vampire, and relishes taunting others with his powers. Indeed, at one point in the first film he boasts to Dr. Hayes about how, in all his years, he has accrued "the wisdom of the ages." This is certainly not the tortured vampire of Stoker, Lugosi, or lee. Too, the lack of budget—the pictures cost $200,000 apiece—caused the film crew to seek out real locations and forced the actors to dispense with theatrics. These would have been out of place in the very stark settings. Thus, without an overabundance of prurience or human lapidation, the Yorga films proved that there was still a market for a comparatively old-fashioned thriller.

Equally traditional but more expensively crafted, were a pair of films based on the television soap opera *Dark Shadows* (chapter 17). Here it is the gothic atmosphere and slow, controlled build to a climax that are most important. Set in twentieth-century Collinwood, an estate in New England, *House of Dark Shadows* (1970) opens with handyman Willie (John Karlen) entering the family crypt in search of the lost Collins treasure. In a hidden vault, he finds a chained coffin, which he opens. Shortly thereafter, the Collins family of Roger (Louis Edmonds), his son David (David Henesy), his sister Elizabeth (Joan Bennett), and her daughter Carolyn (Nancy Barrett) is visited by one Barnabas Collins (Jonathan Frid), who claims to be a cousin from England. Since he much resembles the painted portrait of the eighteenth-century Barnabas, they take him at his word. Soon the deaths begin, including that of Carolyn. Dr. Julia Hoffman (Grayson Hall) and Professor Elliot Stokes (Thayer David) are convinced the killings are the work of a vampire. Their theory is borne out by Carolyn, who returns from the dead, attacks her fiance Tod (Donald Briscoe), and is spiked to death for her efforts. Unfortunately, Julia falls in love with Barnabas, the head vampire, and tries to cure him through medicine. He agrees to the treatment, but spurns her affections. Crushed, Julia sabotages the formula and, when Barnabas drinks it, he is made to look his real age of 175 years. Enraged, the vampire kills Julia and renews his youthful appearance by drinking the blood of governess Maggie (Kathryn Leigh Scott). As he carries her off, Maggie's fiance Jeff (Roger Davis) arrives. The young man spears Barnabas through the heart, a remedy sufficient to *keep* Barnabas dead, despite the arrival of a sequel.

Television series regular, artist Quentin Collins (David Selby) who has inherited the estate, was the center of attraction in *Night of Dark Shadows* (1971). Though not a vampire film, it is of the same archaic school. Briefly, Quentin sets up studio in a strange tower room and is troubled by visions: of a nineteenth-century funeral, of struggles between deceased Collinwood residents, etc. When it becomes clear that the room is haunted by Angelique Collins, Quentin realizes that he is the reincarnation of her lover Charles. In the end, both spirits are exorcized, *Dark Shadows* went off the air, and producer Dan Curtis turned his attention to the production of such television films as *Night Stalker* and Jack Palance's *Dracula*.

Theatrically, *Lake of Dracula* (1971) was the next vampire movie, a Japanese production from Godzilla's home studio of Toho. Beside the Lake of Dracula, Mori Kishida, a descendent of the original Dracula, dies and is transformed into an albino vampire with golden eyes. This oriental interpretation of an old European theme is interesting, but something is lost in the translation between cultures.

Dracula, A.D. 1972 (1971) was the next Christopher Lee-Hammer opus, with bored rock star Johnny Alucard (Christopher Neame) holding a black mass at the church in which Dracula had died a century before, as seen in *Taste the Blood of Dracula*. Resurrected by the Satanic celebration, the vampire has victims brought to the church, where he sets up shop. The fiend is finally stopped when doused with a jug of holy water by a descendent of the original Dr. Van Helsing (Cushing).

Another vampire sequel, this one the third in Hammer's *Carmilla* series, was also released in 1971 as *Twins of Evil*. Two identical twin sisters, Mary and Frieda Gellhorn (Mary and Madelaine Collinson), one introspective and the other outgoing, come to live with their uncle, Gustav Weil (Peter Cushing), a notorious Witchfinder General. The teenage orphans enroll in school, while, nearby, the rakish Baron Karnstein (Damien Thomas) has accidentally revived his ancestor Mircalla (Katya Wyeth) who turns Frieda into a vampire. In the end, Weil decapitates Frieda, the innocent Mary is rescued from a fiery stake by Anton (Harvey Hall), a local choirmaster, Weil is hacked to death by Karnstein, and Karnstein himself is speared through the heart by Anton. Confusing, yes, but well-acted and with some depth and variety in character. *Twins of Evil* seemed to indicate that things were looking up for the Hammer produce. Certainly their next film, *Vampire Circus* (1971) bore this out. Emil (Anthony Corlan), the Circus of Nights owner-vampire, is traveling about early nineteenth-century Serbia exacting retribution for the killing of his cousin Count Mitterhouse (Robert Tayman). With the blood of one of his victims, Emil brings Mitterhouse back to vampiric life. Eventually, the villagers revolt and set fire to the sideshow caravan, thus burning the loathesome relatives to death.

The locale of the circus offered exciting creative opportunities for director Robert Young, who keeps his story moving at a rapid and interesting clip. Particularly impressive was Emil's changing from panther to man, in which form he commits

Madelaine Collinson has been transformed into a vampire, and partakes in her first meal. Mentor Damien Thomas looks on approvingly in *Twins of Evil*.

murders, and the use of a house of mirrors in the flaming finale. This latter is a less-showy display than the mirror conclusion of Orson Welles' *Lady From Shanghai* (1948).

There were, as ever, a number of independent vampire films that year, among them *Bloodsuckers* and *Dracula vs. Frankenstein*. *Bloodsuckers* starred television's *The Avengers'* Patrick Macnee as a physician whose sexual frustrations drive him to practice vampirism. The British effort boasted Peter Cushing in a supporting role, but the film was more psychological than fanciful. *Dracula vs. Frankenstein*, on the other hand, was a poor American quickie in which Dracula (Zandor Vorkov) locates Dr. Frankenstein (J. Carroll Naish) and asks him to

William Marshall as the title vampire in *Scream, Blacula, Scream.*

create a serum that will enable him to move about freely in daylight. Using a house of horrors for cover, and a zombie called Groton (Lon Chaney Jr.) for assistance, Frankenstein agrees. As added incentive, Dracula unearths the Monster's corpse and gives it to the scientist. In the end, of course, Dracula must fight the monster and literally rips him to shreds before perishing with the first rays of dawn. *Dracula vs. Frankenstein* is all very commercial schlock, which is fine, except that in its haste it wastes the considerable skills of Naish and Chaney.

Establishment Hollywood, in the meantime, was at the zenith of its "blacksploitation" cycle and saw the dollar sign screaming from the wall. After coming up with a black Godfather they created a black Dracula called, naturally enough, *Blacula* (1972). The one great accomplishment of this condescending motion picture was to bring the superb Shakespearean actor William Marshall to a mass audience. Marshall portrays Mamuwalde, an African chieftan damned by the original Count Dracula (Charles Macauly) for having tried to abolish slave trade. Centuries pass, and a pair of interior decorators arrive at Dracula's castle to add the Count's furniture to their collection. Among the artifacts they snare is Mamuwalde's coffin. Once in Los Angeles, the vampire claims the pair. At their funeral, Blacula is intrigued by Tina (Vonetta McGee), one of the boys' friends who is there with her sister Michelle (Denise Nicholas) and Michelle's fiance Gordon (Thalmus Rasulala), a police pathologist. Tina has the misfortune of resembling Mamuwalde's long-dead Luva, and the next night Blacula follows the trio to a restaurant. It's love at first sight between Tina and the Vampire. Gordon, however, is worried. He believes that Blacula is responsible for the recent spate of deaths and *un*deaths, which include the resurrection of the interior decorators. Gordon and the police eventually trap Blacula at a warehouse where Tina is accidentally shot. To save her, Blacula turns the girl into a vampire. Horrified, Gordon stakes her to death and Blacula, filled with remorse, walks freely into the morning light.

Scream, Blacula, Scream (1973), a sequel, moved the vampire to Louisiana where, through a voodoo ceremony, he is returned to "life." Indeed, the film shows how, through voodoo, Mamuwalde tries to rid himself of his curse. Instead, he is destroyed when his black magic effigy is stabbed in the heart. Not an overwhelming commercial success, Blacula's second outing was also his last. Christopher

Lee's beleaguered Dracula was not as fortunate. Starring in the *Satanic Rites of Dracula* (1973), Lee did so under protest due to the puerile nature of the screenplay. The film had the vampire trying to conquer the twentieth-century world via biological warfare. Most fortuitously, Cushing's Van Helsing traps the Count in a Hawthorn bush from which, for vampires, there is no escape. It would appear, if Lee's disappointment with the quality of these films is not dispelled, this demise will be permanent.

If Lee were displeased with Dracula in modern times, one of his countrymen was not. David Niven played the count in *Vampira* (1973), a film that had Dracula and his daughter (Teresa Graves) commute from Transylvania to London on very legitimate fiscal business. During the course of the film, the vampire saves a girl from muggers, is interviewed by *Playboy* Magazine, and makes himself a very respectable man-about-town. If it were not a glib observation, the author would note that a tongue-in-cheek film like *Vampira* is sufficient to make the real Count turn in his grave. Speaking of which activity, Duane Jones, who was buried at the end of *Night of the Living Dead*, crept from his sarcophagus to star in *Ganja and Hess* (1973), the story of a professor who is stabbed with a mite-infested knife and becomes a vampire. He infects Marlene Clark with his disease and both go on a killing spree. Eventually, weary of his lethal existence, Jones stands before a crucifix and is destroyed. Miss Clark, not as brave, remains among the unliving. Luckily, she was some five centuries too late to have crossed paths with *Captain Kronos: Vampire Hunter* (1974). In this surprisingly sturdy Hammer film, Horst Janson starred as a professional vampire slayer who, with the aide of Professor Hierony-mous Ghost (John Carter), cut a swath through medieval Europe in search of the undead. This particular adventure pit him against the House of Durward, vampires who were wont to suck youth, not blood, from their victims. And as of this writing, Hammer has just released a film entitled *Legend of the Seven Golden Vampires* (1975), billed as *The First Kung-fu Horror Spectacular*.

From *Nosferatu* to kung-fu, it's been a long and often frustrating journey for Dracula. Perhaps, though, the last word on this matter of vampirism has been had by Andy Warhol. Due to the success of his 3-D *Frankenstein* (1973), Warhol sponsored a new *Dracula* (1975). Although the author has not yet seen the movie, he was on a New York based talk show with director Paul Morissey. Based on the filmmaker's comments, one thing seems a relatively safe bet: when Dracula sucks, it will not be blood he's after. If this is so, and if film as an entity is truly a mirror of the culture from which it springs, then we, and the Count, are in for some troubled times ahead.

6
THE WEREWOLF

Not unlike the vampire legends, stories of the human in wolf form are ancient and worldwide. These tales originated primarily in agricultural localities where wolves were wont to prey on farm animals and, in rare instances, on their keepers. In such lands any murderer, beggar, or alleged witch was fit game for the werewolf hunters. Too, in medieval Europe, the clergy was all-powerful, and kept the masses in line by fostering superstition. The only salvation was through worship, which kept the church solvent. Too, enemies of the church were done away with by being tagged as devil worshippers who, as part of their ceremonies, became wolflike creatures and feasted on human flesh.

Oddly, the werewolf never achieved the widespread film following of the vampire, as evidenced by the fact that there have been some fifty vampire films produced internationally as opposed to a mere twenty pictures about the werewolf. Perhaps the complex makeup process is in large part responsible for this situation. The shaggy monster takes four or five hours to prepare which, for an actor struggling under hot floodlights while trapped beneath layers of crepe hair, greasepaint, and nose putty, is hardly cause to celebrate. In a more commercial vein, there has never been a classic novel about the werewolf. True, Rudyard Kipling, Guy de Maupassant, Guy Endore, Ambrose Bierce, and others had written short stories dealing with wolfmen. But these tales hadn't the impact of *Dracula* or *Frankenstein*. Thus, while Stoker's character came to the silent screen, and Mary Shelley's manmade monster was brought to filmic life by Edison in 1910, the werewolf did not

reach the cinema until 1935, four years after Lugosi's *Dracula*. The film was *Werewolf of London*, also from Universal Pictures, and it starred Henry Hull as Dr. Glendon, a London botanist who journeys to Tibet in search of the Mariphasa Lumina Lupina, a rare flower that blossoms only under lunar light. Finding the plant high in the Himalayas, Glendon is attacked and bitten by a hairy humanoid beast that, as quickly as it had appeared, vanishes into the night.

Back in London, Glendon is visited by a strange Asian scientist named Yogami (Warner Oland) who had also been searching for the Mariphasa. In a puzzling, roundabout conversation, Yogami tells Glendon that this plant is the only known antidote for lycanthropy: the curse of werewolfism. Glendon scoffs and asks Yogami to leave. That night, Glendon's nerves become frayed. He is short with his wife Lisa (Valerie Hobson); even the cat is uneasy and will not go near him. Glendon runs from the house to the laboratory. En route, his hands become claws, his face grows shaggy, and in his mouth there sprouts a full set of fangs. Arriving at the lab, the newborn werewolf is horrified to find the one-blossomed Mariphasa missing. Running into the night, he attacks a lone woman and, after he has feasted, takes a room at a seedy downtown hotel. There, Glendon spends the night to be away from Lisa. As Yogami had warned him, the werewolf always kills the one it loves most.

The next night, Glendon again suffers the transformation and, at the zoo, releases the howling wolves from their cages before slaughtering another

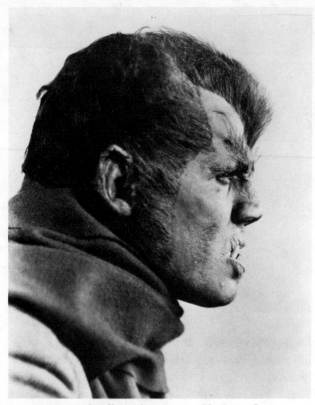

Henry Hull as the *Werewolf of London*.

thus limiting the intricacy of Jack Pierce's design—*Werewolf of London* is a classic film. In contrast to his subdued visage, Hull imbues Glendon with an infectious and mounting terror. This is climaxed by the first man-to-monster sequence, a remarkable segment in which, as Hull hurries from his home to the adjoining lab, he passes behind a series of pillars. As he emerges from behind each pole, we see that his visage has grown more grotesque. The columns were a contrivance, of course, to allow Hull to disappear from view, the camera to stop rolling, the makeup to be applied, and then filming resumed with the progressively altered Glendon emerging from the other side. It's a wildly effective scene that is superior to the technically excellent but rather dreary full-view transformation that became a standard of the Chaney werewolf films. Another plus is the movie's variety of interesting subplots, something missing from most horror-fantasy films. There is Glendon's neglect of Lisa, which leads to her taking a lover; Yogami's sly and ominous enterprises; the investigation of Scotland Yard's doubting inspector; the cacklings of the local botany club that well contrast the insolent sobriety of Glendon; and a marvelous bit of comic relief supplied by Ethel Griffies and Zeffie Tilbury as nervous, drunken residents of the hotel at which Glendon stays for his first full night as the werewolf.

Thematically, it is interesting to note the variance of emphasis on the fantastic element in this, Universal's finest werewolf picture, and their second, *The Wolfman* (1941). In *Werewolf of London*, Hull is destroyed by an everyday .38 caliber bullet. Too, he is a scientist that invites comparison with *Dr. Jekyll and Mr. Hyde*. By the time *The Wolfman* went into production, the studio had created an entire and now-legendary mythos about the werewolf, trying to evoke a more gothic feel for the monster. This changed attitude was most likely the result of a lukewarm reception at the box office for the Hull film.

The Wolfman, as we noted earlier, gave Lon Chaney his first "original" monster. It also gave Jack Pierce, who had created Karloff's Frankenstein Monster and Mummy makeups, one of his greatest challenges. He had to personify, in a glance, the same virile, grunting attitude that Chaney planned for his monster. Both men succeeded brilliantly in their respective tasks and were given top support from a grand supporting cast and smashing production values.

woman. Returning to the lab, Glendon works feverishly through the next day to force a new bloom from the stubborn Mariphasa. He succeeds, but while his attention is elsewhere, Yogami enters, steals the flower, and rubs it into his skin. Enraged, Glendon now realizes that Yogami is the creature that attacked him in the mountains. The two struggle, during which altercation Glendon becomes the monster. Killing the Asian, he hurries into the night. Glendon goes to a nearby estate that he owns and orders the caretaker to lock him in the tower. Just then, below his lofty window, Glendon sees Lisa and her lover Paul Ames (Lester Mathews) arrive. The werewolf jumps the several stories to the ground and attacks the couple. They run and the werewolf follows Lisa inside. Before he can pounce, however, Glendon is shot to death by the Chief of Scotland Yard (Lawrence Grant) whom Yogami had alerted earlier to keep an eye on the scientist. The monster crumples to the floor where he reverts back to his human form. "In a few moments," he gasps, sprawled at his wife's feet, "I shall know if this all had to be." So saying, Glendon dies.

Despite its relatively tame monster makeup— rumor has it that Hull disliked a lengthy application,

Bela Lugosi, as Bela the fortune-teller, sees *misfortune* in the palm of Fay Helm. From *The Wolfman*.

Lon Chaney Jr. as *The Wolfman*.

The Wolfman is filled with the supernatural touches that made *Dracula* so colorful. As a result, it had more atmosphere than the clinical *Werewolf of London*. While the wild-eyed hysteria of Chaney's Lawrence Talbot cannot match the precise disintegration of Hull's pompous and elite Glendon, he is more ruggedly bestial, which gives the film some of its finest moments.

Young Talbot returns from school to his home in Wales. While shopping in town, he meets Gwen (Evelyn Ankers), a girl who runs an antique store. He's attracted to her, and buys something to break the ice, a cane capped with a heavy silver wolf's head. There's a star engraved on the walking stick; Gwen explains that it's a pentagram. Legend has it that a werewolf will see this mark on the palm of his next victim. Larry shows little interest in the story and asks Gwen if she'll go with him, later that night, to a nearby gypsy camp. She agrees, but brings along a friend Jennie Williams (Fay Helm) as a chaperone. At the caravan, they are greeted by a fortune teller (Bela Lugosi), and Jennie is ushered into his tent. Larry seizes the opportunity to be alone with Gwen and they go for a walk. Meanwhile, as the seer gazes into Jennie's palm he is horrified to see the pentagram. He chases her away, but it is too late. The gypsy becomes a werewolf and attacks the girl. Larry and Gwen hear his howl followed by Jennie's scream. Leaving his date, Talbot runs to their chaperone's aid. A large wolf has her pinned, his teeth gorging her throat. Clubbing the beast to death with his silver-topped cane, Larry is bitten and passes out. Gwen and an old gypsy woman Maleva (Maria Ouspenskaya) arrive at the grisly scene simultaneously. They load Talbot into a cart and drive him home. Alerted, the local chief of constables Montford (Ralph Bellamy) hurries to the scene of the crime. There, he finds the corpse of young Jennie, the dead fortune teller, and Talbot's cane.

The next morning, Larry is confronted with the evidence. Since his allegedly severe wounds have mysteriously healed, no one believes his story. To end pointless speculation, Sir John Talbot (Claude Rains), Larry's father, concludes that a wolf killed Jennie, ran away, and the gypsy was injured in the confusion. This resolution satisfies everyone but young Talbot who, several days later, runs into Maleva in the forest. She tells him about her son's curse and how it's been passed on to him. That night, alone in his room, the disbelieving Talbot is racked with a strange, pounding sensation, as if his body were being forced apart from within. His mind slips from his control: Larry has become the Wolfman. Padding into the night, he kills the first person he encounters, a gravedigger working nearby, and returns home. The next day is a tortured one as Larry awakens and finds the footprints of a wolf by his window. He anxiously awaits the second change. That night, after becoming the monster, he rushes into the forest where he meets Maleva. She mouths a special prayer and Talbot is cured of his bloodlust, but for this night only. At sunrise, he hurries to see Gwen, but panics when the pentagram appears on her palm. Hastening home, Larry asks his father to strap him to a chair and lock him in his room. Reluctantly, Sir John agrees and that night, with all the townspeople searching for a wolf, Larry is transformed and breaks free. Running through the woods he finds Gwen, who was out looking for him. She faints and as Larry goes to tear out her throat, Sir John happens along. He beats the beast with the silver-topped cane and the monster falls dead. Before the older man's disbelieving eye, the werewolf becomes his son. When the villagers arrive, they assume that Larry saved Gwen from the wolf and died in the process. Sir John keeps the truth to himself.

As in *Werewolf of London,* there are many marvelous touches that spice the road to the eventual transformation. After he has been bitten, Larry visits a shooting gallery where he is unable to fire on the likeness of a wolf. Later, a usually friendly dog belonging to the Talbots' gamekeeper growls when Larry approaches. Unfortunately, the build from Larry's return home to his becoming the monster is far too long and made to seem even more so by the weight of his trivial relationship with Gwen. Henry Hull's decaying marriage in the earlier film was far and away the more interesting of the two.

Inspired by the success of Universal's pileous fiend, Twentieth Century Fox brought forth its own pseudo-werewolf in *The Undying Monster* (1942). John Howard starred as the heir to a curse that has been passed through one family since the crusades: the eldest male of each generation is transformed into a werewolf. However, the monster element in this picture is quite secondary to the picture's prime function, which was to serve as a murder mystery. Not a powerhouse in the horror field, Fox wanted to be certain they could also market their film simply as a suspense picture. Thus,

John Howard as *The Undying Monster*.

Simone Simon and psychiatrist in *The Cat People*.

the creature is seen only briefly and in long-shots or cut-away closeups, which hide its not very horrific features. However, even *The Undying Monster* was less camera shy than our next manimal, Simone Simon as one of Val Lewton's *Cat People* (1942). Irena (Miss Simon)—whom we met in the sequel *Curse of the Cat People*—is a New York fashion designer who learns that she is descended from a race of women who, in medieval times, became huge cats when sexually or emotionally aroused. Because of this fear, Irena is unable to consummate her marriage to Oliver Reed (Kent Smith), a naval draftsman. Oliver turns to a psychiatrist (Tom Conway) for Irena and to a mistress, Alice (Jane

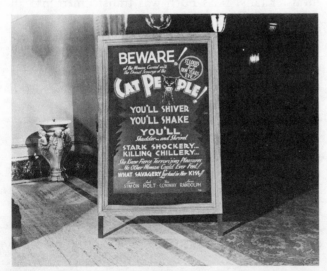

An in-theatre announcement for the coming of Val Lewton's *The Cat People*.

Randolph) for himself. Jealous, Irena becomes a large creature that stalks Alice at night. Fortunately, in each encounter, the young girl eludes the beast. Meanwhile, Oliver's psychiatrist friend tries to allay Irena's fears of metamorphosis by seducing her in her apartment. While so involved, he is mangled by an unseen creature, whom he manages to wound before dying. Shortly thereafter, Irena stumbles from her building, obviously hurt, and walks to the Central Park Zoo. There, amidst the great cats, she dies.

Although laden with what were even then standard elements of the were-animal film, such as Irena's walking into a pet shop and driving the animals berserk, director Jacques Tourneur infused his picture with shadowed, suggested images that leave an ultimate resolution up to the audience. Was or was not Irena a were-leopard? There is nothing in the film to offer a conclusive answer. This suggestive approach thrilled critics immensely, and raises an interesting point about the fantasy film as a whole. Movie historians are inclined to down the straightforward presentation of monsters such as *The Wolfman*, while lauding Tourneur and Lewton's more psychological approach. Granted, the tension of the cat pursuing Alice, first in the park and later in the darkened swimming pool of her hotel, is nerve-wracking cinema. One must keep in mind, however, that Irena's mental and personal anguish, the question of her sanity, is really what the picture's *about*. It's not a *monster* movie. Thus, an absurd comparison between it and *The Wolfman* is unjustified. Yet critics insist that the Chaney or Hull

75

films would have benefited greatly by adopting the unseen-menace technique of *The Cat People*, which is to miss the point entirely of the fantasy film. The genre affords a suspension of disbelief that is not to be found in "real" life. Stories like *The Cat People*, while fantastic, can be torn from most any psychiatrist's notebook. While this does not dilute its value as a fantasy film, by the same token it does not invalidate the Hull or Chaney representations, or make them any less sophisticated. While they demand a greater tolerance for the impossible— which is a certain type of sophistication in itself— the reward is a look at a reality different from our own. People who want their monsters fully rationalized are looking to be comforted, not stimulated. The only "comfort" we find in fantasy is that its very existence proves we have not lost our ability to dream in the face of technological advances.

Returning to werewolfery, we return, as well, to Val Lewton. Overwhelmed by the public acceptance of *The Cat People*, he unleashed a less prestigious effort the following year, a thriller called *The Leopard Man*. Although executed with the ingenuity of *The Cat People*, the film is less horror than sickness: we are led to believe that a leopard escaped from a traveling circus has been responsible for a clutch of grisly murders. It is, in fact, the film's hero (Dennis O'Keefe) who is the psychopathic killer.

Back at Universal, things were a little less sensational. The highly touted teamup of *Frankenstein Meets the Wolfman* (1943) was a silly, uninteresting effort with Chaney's second appearance as the Wolfman and Bela Lugosi's once-only rendering of the Frankenstein Monster. His final resting place disturbed by grave robbers, Larry Talbot is exposed to the rays of the full moon and once again becomes a monster. Locating Maleva (Maria Ouspenskaya), the pair journeys to Vasaria in search of the one man Talbot hopes can cure him, the legendary Dr. Frankenstein. Unfortunately, the Baron and his monster perished in a fire, as seen in the *Ghost of Frankenstein* (1942) for which, ironically, Chaney played the monster. Locating Frankenstein's daughter (Ilona Massey), Talbot begs the girl to lend him her father's notebook. She refuses. Only when the monster returns to life and menaces Vasaria does she agree to give the book to Talbot's friend Dr. Mannering (Patrick Knowles), and only then on the condition that he destroy the monster before curing the Wolfman. Naturally, Mannering becomes ob-

sessed with the creature and tries to bring him to full potency. The monster breaks free, does battle with the Wolfman, and both are swept away when angry villagers explode a dam above Mannering's mountain workshop.

The climactic battle is genuinely uninspired, with an obvious double (Eddie Parker) stepping in for Lugosi. It is painful to see Lugosi play the monster in this slap-dash production. It was a part he had turned down when Universal was casting the first *Frankenstein*. Lugosi didn't want to play a character in which his distinguished voice would not be used, or his features hidden beneath a quantity of foam rubber and latex. The role went to Boris Karloff. *Frankenstein Meets the Wolfman* was thus the first of an endless string of professional indignities Lugosi would suffer. The fact that his Monster is nothing more than a chemical contribution—there's little "acting" to it—makes his decline all the more tragic.

Frankenstein Meets the Wolfman was followed into release by the films we mentioned in our vampire study, *House of Frankenstein*, *House of Dracula*, and *Abbott and Costello Meet Frankenstein*. It should be pointed out, in context, that by the time this last film rolled around, the Wolfman was no longer just a pathetic victim of fate, but a good guy. As we mentioned, he sacrifices his life that Costello might survive.

Over at Columbia Pictures, *Cry of the Werewolf* (1944) was Nina Foch's wail or terror when she learned that her mother's affliction of turning into a wolf is hereditary. A disappointing picture for monster fans, Miss Foch was transformed into an *actual wolf* which is, in fact, the werewolf of legend. That didn't save it from appearing drab by comparison to the Universal monster. Another quickie, although this one sporting a bonafide monster, was *Catman of Paris* (1946). Robert Wilke played the fanged feline who is unwittingly covering for the picture's real killer, Douglas Dumbrille. Despite Wilkes' convincing portrayal as the monster, we'd seen it all before. It was time for poetry to replace the gruesome Hollywood pros.

One of the most popular fables of all-time is *Beauty and the Beast*, based on the tale by Madame Leprince of Beaumont. The story's theme, the attraction of the monster to the beautiful heroine, was the basis for many other films, such as *King Kong* (1933) (see chapter 10), but it remained for poet-filmmaker Jean Cocteau to do a literal version

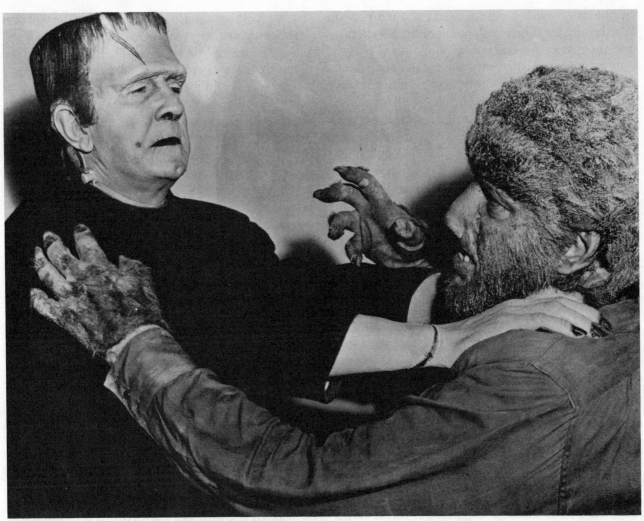

Bela Lugosi and Lon Chaney Jr. as, respectively,
Frankenstein Meets the Wolfman.

Catman of Paris.

Jean Marais peers into an enchanted mirror in Cocteau's *Beauty and the Beast*.

77

of the fairy tale. Cocteau spent six months on location in the Loire Valley shooting his picture, and the results are staggering.

It's the seventeenth century. A merchant (Marcel André), the head of a proud and wealthy family, faces complete financial ruin. One day he goes to meet a ship at port and finds that his creditors have taken everything. Bankrupt, he journeys slowly homeward through a strange, dark wood. Night falls and he becomes hopelessly lost. Finding an old, torch-lit manor, he enters and is at once wrapped in a thick mist. When it clears the merchant finds himself in a dining hall with food and refreshment spread before him. He eats and, later, walks in the garden of this seemingly deserted estate. Recalling a promise he had made to bring home a rose for his youngest daughter, Beauty (Josette Day), the visitor plucks a flower. Suddenly, a man (Jean Marais) appears. He introduces himself as the Beast, and the name is clearly appropriate. He is a large man with the head of a lion. He is also the lord of this mansion, and the roses are his prize possession. The theft, he decrees, must be punished with the merchant's death, or the death of one of his daughters. The old man asks for three days. After that time, the merchant promises to meet the sacrifice with his own life. The Beast agrees to the stay of execution and gives him a white horse by the name of Magnificent who, when given the command, will carry him back through the tortuous forest to the Beasts's lair.

The saddened father returns home and the two elder sisters, Felicity (Nane German) and Adelaide (Mila Parely), berate him for his stupidity. Only beauty is sympathetic to her father's plight, and offers to go in his stead. He will hear none of it, so that night she sneaks into the stable and orders Magnificent to take her to the Beast. Arriving at the palace, the girl enters and walks about, finding all manner of oddity therein. Suddenly, the Beast appears and Beauty, startled by his appearance, faints. The maned-man, struck by her loveliness, carries her to a bed and when she awakens asks if he might watch her dine. Beauty conceals her shock and, that night, as it is to be for many nights thereafter, the monster visits her at dinner. They become great friends, the Beast even confiding that he has vast wealth hidden in a great pavilion nearby. Then, one day, glancing in an enchanted mirror, Beauty sees that her father is dying. She longs to visit him, and the Beast agrees to let her go, but only for

one week. If she doesn't return by then, he will die. The Beast gives her a magic glove and, slipping it on, Beauty is transported home. There, she finds her formerly regal sisters dressed now as paupers, while she, herself, is robed like a queen. Beauty also finds her old beau, Avenant (also Marais) envious of the love she harbors for the Beast. In truth, the boy is jealous but compounds this with greed when he hears of the monster's treasure. He convinces Beauty's sisters to ask that she remain another week, under some pretence, while he seeks out the Beast. However, the monster's castle is too well-hidden to be easily detected, and Avenant's efforts prove futile. Meanwhile, we see the Beast as he walks silently, sadly through Beauty's room. Overcome with grief, he sends Magnificent to fetch her. When the horse arrives at the stable, Avenant, who knows the password to send the animal homeward, climbs on its back and rides to the Beast's castle. At the same time, in her enchanted mirror, Beauty sees the dying Beast. The looking-glass shatters. Hurriedly, she pulls on the glove and joins the accursed lord. When she arrives, he is laying prone by the side of a pond. Beauty begs him to live, but he hasn't the will. At that precise moment, Avenant is killed by the arrow of a statue guarding the Beast's treasure pavilion. As he falls dead, his face becomes that of the Beast; the monster, in turn, becomes a man. Rising to his feet, he explains that Beauty's love has both saved and changed him. After a long embrace, the pair is spirited magically skyward, to vanish in the clouds.

Beauty and the Beast is filled with many sublime visions of fantasy, a veritable market place of ethereal wonders. These accoutrements, the enchanted mirror, Magnificent, the magic glove, and so forth, are all very romantic touches. However, they serve the film rather than dominate it. The magic of *Beauty and the Beast* lies not in these superficial trimmings but in the deeper realities the film probes. The very human values of hate, love, fear, and devotion. Unfortunately, to analyze Cocteau's perspective on each would take us an entire volume. Indeed, the director's diary on the making of the film is available in book form (see bibliography) and offers valuable insights into the mind of a uniquely gifted filmmaker.

There are fantasy elements other than those we have mentioned, and they are all rendered with sensitivity and a feel for the genre. In the Beast's dining hall, for example, the food is served by disembodied hands; the walls are lined with sculpted faces inset with human eyes that follow the actors about the room. Arms bearing torches and candelabras protrude from the wall to direct Beauty about the mansion on her first visit; voices come from out of nowhere to address the girl. It's a grand and mystic world in which the story unfolds, perhaps a land in which we would all enjoy a few days respite. A land where, for Cocteau, honesty is the basic virtue and love its ultimate result.

Crucial to the effectiveness of the film was the presentation of the Beast. His presence, in a word, is awesome. His first appearance, to the merchant in the garden, brings with it a chill that causes the leaves in surrounding trees to wither and fall. His visage, too, is masterfully executed, the makeup applied ala Jack Pierce, hair-by-hair, by Cocteau himself.

It is coincidence, of course, that after *Beauty and the Beast* time stopped for the werewolf. Only the release of *Abbott and Costello Meet Frankenstein* remained, with its fifth rehashing of the Chaney creation. It would be fully a decade before someone took another stab at lycanthropy. The drought-breaker was called, appropriately enough, *The Werewolf* (1956), and it worked out rather well, budget and storyline considered. By the midfifties, science and the atom bomb had impinged upon the genre. Thus, our monster became not a lunar werewolf, but an irradiated one. Steven Rich was the victim of research to find a cure for radiation poisoning. In the process, his system became un-blanced and he turned into a werewolf. After the obligatory rash of murders, the monster was destroyed. Leopards, too, made a comeback that year with *The Cat Girl*. Barbara Shelley starred as the victim of yet another family curse, this one enabling her to transfer her mind into the body of a leopard. It was a veritable rerun of *The Cat People*, without Lewton or Tourneur's flair for drama. The mistaken monsters theme resurfaced for the first time since *Catman of Paris* as Gloria Talbott, *The Daughter of Dr. Jekyll* (1957), was made to believe that she had inherited her father's "ability" to become a monster. Actually, she was being duped to protect the guilty Arthur Shields, her late father's associate, to whom the doctor had transmitted his werewolfery. Obviously, the screenwriters were not up on their classics or they'd have realized that the good doctor's affliction was psychological rather than physical.

With the sixties came a lemon and a jewel. The lemon was *Werewolf in a Girl's Dormitory* (1961) and the gem was Hammer's only film of this type, *Curse of the Werewolf* (1962). *Werewolf in a Girl's Dormitory* was an Italian import with Curt Lowens as the lycanthropic superintendent of a girl's school. No one connects the principal with a series of gruesome campus murders until a dog snarls at him. At this, the picture's hero (Carl Schell) gets wise to Lowens and eventually does him in. Abyssmal dubbing and cuts made by the American distributor ruin whatever good there might have been in the original production. What survives is nothing with any more depth than the screen's most mindlessly ferocious werewolf mangling pretty young coeds. Fortunately, Hammer's product was of far greater merit. Not only was it one of the studio's great pictures, ranking alongside *Horror of Dracula*, but it was the first film of its kind to place emphasis on the anti-Christian aspects of the werewolf, something that we saw was inherent to the earliest European werewolf legends.

The Marquis of Castle Sinestro (Anthony Daw-

Oliver Reed in a gruesome closeup from *Curse of the Werewolf*.

79

son) is a sadistic nobleman of seventeenth-century Spain. Into the castle, during his wedding feast, comes a poor beggar (Richard Wordsworth) and the Marquis makes him beg for his food. When the guests have had their fun with the pauper, he is thrown into the dungeon near where the nobleman's hunting dogs are kept.

Years pass. The Marquis is old now, and crippled with syphilis. When a lovely young servant girl (Yvonne Romain) spurns his advances, he has her thrown into the same dungeon as the beggar. By this time, the poor man has all but become a canine. He rapes the girl and dies of the exertion. She manages to escape, kills the Marquis, and runs into the surrounding woods. There, she falls into a lake and would have drowned had not Don Alfredo Carido (Clifford Evans) happened along. He saves the girl and takes her into his home. There, on Christmas Eve, her baby is born. The mother dies, and Leon is adopted by Alfredo.

Again, the years slip quickly by. Leon (Justin Walter) is six and there are bloody attacks made on sheep belonging to surrounding farmers. One man manages to shoot the wolf that has been preying on his flocks. Hard upon, Leon arrives home bleeding from gunshot wounds. A local priest is called in and recognizes the symptoms. He explains to Carido that his son is a werewolf. The anguished father hopes that by showing the boy love he can be cured.

As Leon reaches manhood (Oliver Reed), he falls in love with Christina (Catherine Feller), the daughter of a nearby vineyard owner. The wolf-curse has been all but forgotten. Then, while at a dance hall with a friend (Michael Ripper), Leon feels strangely unsettled. The full moon has appeared and, rushing outside, he becomes a werewolf. Leon kills both his friend and a performer at the dance hall, after which he butchers a shepherd.

The next day, Leon begs his father for help. Don Alfredo asks him to go to a monastery where, during the full moon, he will be kept in chains. The young man refuses to live like an animal and runs to see Christina. He is with her when the full moon rises again and, not wishing to harm the girl, hurries away. He does not get far, however, as the authorities have been on his tail and quickly apprehend him. Thrown in jail, Leon feels the transformation coming on. He tears the door from its hinges and murders the jailor. Rushing to the rooftop, he encounters Don Alfredo who carries a gun. In it is a silver bullet fashioned from a crucifix. Leon pleads

with his father to kill him, and the old man reluctantly obliges. While a mob of villagers cheers from below, Leon falls dead and the curse is ended.

Although this is not made entirely clear in the picture, Leon's werewolfery was not passed to him by the rabid beggar. Legend has it that any child born on the Eve of Christ's birth will be taken by the devil. Although Leon's conception by rape was an unpropitious beginning, the inopportune birthdate sealed his fate. In the movie, his possession is made explicit in two brief scenes, which are among the most terrifying ever filmed. Leon's birth is the first. Don Alfredo is sitting alone in the livingroom while, upstairs, his womenfolk help the servant girl through labor. Suddenly, a wolf's howl is heard from above, shading gradually into the wail of a newborn baby. Don Alfredo is shocked, but he pushes the incident to the back of his mind. There it remains, forgotten until Leon's baptism. As the priest immerses the baby, the water in the holy font begins to boil. This, as we mentioned earlier, is a return to the religious roots of the werewolf, and is used to excellent advantage by the moviemakers.

Apart from its thematic brilliance, another marvelous aspect of *Curse of the Werewolf* is the makeup by Roy Ashton. The beggar, after his years of incarceration, is a crusty and bestial creature with a scraggly, dirt-caked matte of hair and a face worn ragged by the decade of dank, sunless isolation. His grizzled appearance is a marked contrast to the werewolf, however, which is Ashton's showpiece. It's the first lycanthrope to sport pointed ears *atop* his head, along with a full chest and back of gleaming, silvery fur. The cinema's previous lupines all sported shirts buttoned more or less to the neck.

The production itself is immaculate, an accurate recreation of the dirty, pestilent era in which Leon lived. Upon this already depressing stage, Hammer built its horror. However, the studio chose not to powder their film with crawling mist and decayed monuments. Rather, they structured their mood through the person of Oliver Reed, and the reactions to his plight of people around him. Reed, who has since gone on to gain international stardom in such films as *The Three Musketeers* and *Royal Flash* gave us our finest screen werewolf. His physique and virile good looks lent presence not only to the monster, but to Leon as well. Reed's desolation consisted of more than Chaney's studied and forlorn looks skyward.

Curiously, *Curse of the Werewolf* was Hammer's

Mark Damon as the monster in the *Beauty and the Beast* remake.

only werewolf film. Perhaps fans were annoyed that they had to wait until the picture's end, when Reed was in jail, to see the werewolf. Or it might have been that the public just wasn't as interested in lycanthropy as it was in vampirism or the Frankenstein Monster. Aesthetically, of course, *Curse of the Werewolf* was a huge success, the artistic antithesis of *Beauty and the Beast*. Hammer's product was shot in color and is coarsely authentic. Cocteau's black-and-white film is a more delicate tapestry that hardly ever lets the real world intercede. Yet both are classics and stand as prime examples of the range and power of the fantasy film.

Beauty and the Beast returned in 1963 with Mark Damon and Joyce Taylor in the leading roles. The film was an attractive one, played strictly as a supernatural adventure on a very juvenile level. Wearing one of the last monster makeups ever created by Jack Pierce, Damon became the beast only at sunset. Considering its low budget, the film

succeeds as a colorful entertainment. Not as polished were the *Werewolves on Wheels* (1971), members of a motorcycle gang who were punished with werewolfism by a coven of satanists. Less traditional was the Rowan and Martin romp entitled *The Maltese Bippy* (1969). In it, Dick Martin only dreamt he was a werewolf. Even Kerwin Mathews (*Seventh Voyage of Sinbad*) donned fangs and fur for *The Boy Who Cried Werewolf* (1973). Unfortunately for both the film and the supernatural genre, all the fur the public cared to see was living on the *Planet of the Apes*. The heirs/hairs apparent to the hirsuit crown of the werewolf, it is curious how these were-monkeys have so dominated the media for nearly a decade. It is an enigma into which we will look later in the book. For now, however, we must leave the werewolf and his kin for the moldering world of the mummy, one of filmdom's most bizarre and, as will soon become clear, "Kharismatic" creations.

7
THE MUMMY

It is interesting to consider that Universal Pictures never teamed the Mummy with their other screen monsters. The gauze-encrusted Kharis/Im-ho-tep appeared in six Universal Pictures to the Wolfman's five and Frankenstein's eight, yet he remained a loner. Certainly, a plot contrivance could have brought the millenia-old monster to Europe from his Middle Eastern stomping grounds. And, just as assuredly, a film entitled *Frankenstein Meets The Mummy* would have had no less box-office appeal than *Frankenstein Meets The Wolfman*. What, then, would account for the Egyptian's isolation?

The answer lies in the nature of the beast. For one thing, until Christoper Lee essayed the role in Hammer's *Mummy* (1959), the character was utterly lacking in vitality. He would simply plod through his movies and fulfill the curse of death promised those who had defiled his tomb. What's more, in several screen appearances he had a game leg, which he dragged behind him, and one arm taped to his chest. In single combat, the Wolfman, the Frankenstein Monster, or even Dracula could have kicked the tar from the lumbering Mummy. Thus, due to the simple incongruity of the pairing, the Mummy remained an entity unto himself, unapproached by friend or combatant. Another curiosity that distinguishes the Mummy from his cinematic kin is that, while we had *The Bride of Frankenstein, Dracula's Daughter*, were-women in *The Cat People* and *Cry of the Werewolf*, and even an *Invisible Woman* (1941), there was never a female mummy. In pictures where the Mummy was *protecting* a princess' tomb, she would never be seen on

screen; in movies where he was *seeking* his stolen princess, it was always her reincarnation or look-alike that he found. There was never a dyed-in-the-gauze lady mummy. No explanation for this will be offered; it is simply food for thought.

One final consideration about the Mummy is that, of all the classic screen monsters, he's the only one who really exists. Although the mummies of Tutankhamon, et al, are by no means ambulatory, they do possess a certain aura—the mystery of antiquity is as good a phrase as any—that carries into their celluloid brethren. While the concept of a man becoming a bat or a wolf is comparatively far-fetched, who's to say that somewhere, well preserved within those still-warm, still-moist wrappings, is not the seed of life?

Like the Wolfman-werewolf character before it, the Mummy offered Universal's creative heads not a single classic novel or story on which to base their tale. Thus, as they had done for the Hull and Chaney films, the studio made up their legends. And they gave the role of Im-ho-tep to the man they hoped would succeed Lon Chaney Sr. as their top horror star: the man who had just set the world on its ear with his brilliant performance as the Frankenstein Monster, Boris Karloff. The choice was ideal. Karloff imbued his Mummy with an elusive quality that is superficially sanguine, yet is filled with a deep and abiding evil.

The Mummy (1932) opens in 1921. Three men, Sir Joseph Whemple (Arthur Byron), his assistant Ralph Norton (Bramwell Fletcher), and Egyptologist Dr. Muller (Edward van Sloan), uncover an

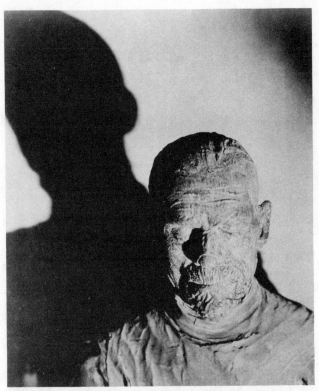

Boris Karloff in a rare publicity still for *The Mummy*.

ancient tomb in a Middle Eastern desert. Inside they find a casket and a box. Hieroglyphics reveal that here are the remains of High Priest Im-ho-tep, a man buried alive for having tried to raise his beloved, the pharaoh's daughter, from the dead. Turning next to the small container, Muller translates a curse etched on the lid: *Eternal punishment for anyone who opens this casket.* Whemple and the doctor leave Norton with the find. Believing that they have uncovered the Scroll of Thoth, the spell by which the God Osiris was raised from the dead by his sister Isis, the young man opens the box. It is indeed the scroll, and he reads the inscription aloud.

Unbeknownst to Norton, the Mummy's hand moves. The eyelids open, shedding flecks of dust and crumbling gauze. The Mummy comes to life and walks slowly to the young archeologist's side. Later, when his associates return, they find Norton hysterical, his mind, and the mummy, gone.

One day, ten years later, a pasty-looking old man walks into the camp of Frank Whemple (David Manners), whose father has gone on to become a curator of the Cairo Museum. The newcomer introduces himself as Ardath Bey and leads Frank's party to the hitherto uncovered burial place of Princess Anck-es-en-amon. Ardath is, of course,

the Mummy, although he has doffed his cloth cacoon. After the discovery, the strange Bey disappears until he is found by the elder Whemple one night, staring at the Princess' remains. After the archeologist leaves, the Mummy kneels and offers a strange prayer before the body of his beloved.

In another part of town, young Helen Grosvenor (Zita Johann) leaves a party at her home and hurries to the museum. It's closed, and she faints on the steps. Frank Whemple finds the girl and rushes her home. Dr. Muller, the Egyptologist, and her psychiatrist arrive as she begins to mutter phrases in an Egyptian dialect that has been dead for over two thousand years. The next morning, Frank, who is attracted to the lovely girl, asks why she has been under Muller's care. Helen explains that of late she has found herself strangely drawn to the museum. The doctor is trying to find out why. Later that day, Muller puts forth an incredible theory: that the Mummy of Im-ho-tep was not, as they had believed, stolen, but that it and Ardath Bey are one and the same. Just then, from another room, the men hear Ardath talking to Helen. She is in a strange trance. Frank hurries the girl away while Muller confronts Im-ho-tep with his thesis. The Mummy admits to the truth, then demands that Muller return the Scroll of Thoth. The doctor refuses and Bey departs. Muller then asks Sir John to burn the parchment, for it has given life to the Mummy and has made Helen a prisoner of his mighty will. The elder Whemple leaves to do as friend has asked. Meanwhile, by the sacred pool in his residence, the Mummy wills the death of Sir John and orders the scientist's servant (Noble Johnson) to bring him the parchment. Then he calls out to Helen. She heeds his summons and they go to the museum. There he explains that she is the reincarnation of his princess. While he could reanimate the body of Anck-es-en-amon, she would be but a heartless shell. Thus, he must sacrifice Helen to Anubis and merge his soul with hers for eternity. Terrified, Helen prays to a large idol of Isis for help. As Im-ho-tep prepares to stab the girl, the goddess raises her Scepter of Life and fires a searing bolt at the Mummy. He falls to the floor, a smouldering mound of dust, just as Frank and Muller arrive and reclaim Helen, body and soul.

A very slow, very nonshocking fantasy, *The Mummy* manages to scare us through Karloff's brittle, confident presence. His Im-ho-tep is a desperate character who fully intends to regain his princess. This determination is evident in Karloff's incomparable delivery, his posture, and especially his glance. Through his eyes, the Mummy subjugates and destroys. Karloff's own eyes reflect this unfathomable power and cause the master to upstage his very theatrical co-stars.

After *The Mummy*, Karloff did a few pictures for other studios, after which Universal cast him in two more Frankenstein films, *The Raven* (1935), and other horror classics. By the time the next mummy film went into production, Karloff was busy with other projects. Thus, ex-Western star Tom Tyler inherited the title role in *The Mummy's Hand* (1940) because of his striking resemblance to Karloff. Unlike Im-ho-tep, however, Kharis remained in wrappings throughout. To emphasize the monster's great age, Tyler also originated the shuffling gait and mute mentality that would remain the Mummy persona in all films that followed. He was also the first mummy to sample another standard, the now-famous Tana Leaves. The Universal ritual, torn liberally from their *Wolfman* screenplay, dictated that three leaves be served once during the cycle of every full moon to keep Kharis alive; nine would give him mobility. The ritual was carried out by High Priests through the ages.

The Mummy's Hand featured Dick Foran as Steve Banning, head of an archeological expedition that uncovers the tomb of Egyptian Princess Ananka. Inside, instead of Ananka, they find the Mummy of Kharis, a man who was buried alive after stealing the sacred Tana Leaves to raise his beloved from the dead. Meanwhile, Andoheb (George Zucco), the current High Priest of the Sun God, plans to punish those who have desecrated Ananka's resting place. Thus, he feeds nine of the life-giving Tana Leaves to the Mummy instead of the usual three. The Mummy rises from a slab to strangle Professor Petrie (Eduardo Ciannelli). The doctor screams, but by the time help arrives, Andoheb and the Mummy have fled.

That night, Marta (Peggy Moran), daughter of the expedition's backer, translates the markings on a vase Steve had discovered in a Cairo market place. They delineate Ananka's precise burial place, through a hidden tunnel in the tomb. The crew decides to search out the new passageway on the morrow. Kharis and Andoheb have other ideas. The Mummy kidnaps Marta and brings her to the temple. There, the High Priest intends to make her Priestess. Unfortunately, Andoheb is shot dead by

Tom Tyler in a publicity still for *The Mummy's Hand*.

Babe (Wallace Ford) who, with Steve, is searching the tomb for Marta. Steve finds her tied to an altar and tries to free her when Kharis attacks. Grabbing a brazier of live coals, the archeologist dumps them on the Mummy and he goes up in flames.

Plainly, the fanciful and exotic additons to the legend left Kharis little more than a ravaging brute. He lacked Im-ho-tep's penetrating eyes, caustic tongue, and thus the qualification to be an archvillain. Accordingly, the studio gave him an evil master in Zucco on whom the audience could vent its hisses and boos. He became the villain while the Mummy was simply a monster. And a very profitable one! *The Mummy's Hand* proved a runaway smash so Universal swathed Lon Chaney Jr. in one hundred and fifty yards of fabric and set him loose in *The Mummy's Tomb* (1942). Picking up where the last film left off, we find Stephen Banning (Dick Foran) twenty years older, and at his home in Massachusetts. With him are his sister Jane (Janet Shaw), his son John (John Hubbard), and John's fiancee Isobel Evans (Elyse Knox). Stephan tells them the story of his encounter with the Mummy. This is really a recap for the audience, who sees it all in flashbacks from *The Mummy's Hand*. As the story ends, and the listeners scoff, the elderly Banning voices regret that his late wife Marta is no longer alive, or she would verify the tale.

Simultaneously, in Egypt, Andoheb (George Zucco) is telling the same story to Mehemet Bey (Turhan Bey) who is to be the new High Priest. Andoheb explains that Babe's bullets only wounded him and that Kharis was merely singed by the fire, not destroyed. With his dying breath, the aged High

Priest makes Mehemet swear to murder the Banning family.

Mehemet brings Kharis to the United States where the High Priest becomes caretaker of a cemetery. On the night of their arrival, he feeds Kharis nine Tana Leaves and the monster treads slowly forth. At the Banning residence, he finds and slays Stephen. The next day, after searching through his father's papers for clues to the killer's identity, a frustrated John calls on Isobel. They are spied upon by Mehemet, who is entranced by the girl. Later, John picks up Babe (Wallace Ford) at the train station. He has come to town for his old friend's funeral. Again, Kharis sets forth, kills Jane, and later that night strangles Babe. When John finds a strip of moldering gauze in the bushes of his home, he realizes what they're up against: his father's old nemesis Kharis. Meanwhile, Mehemet sends Kharis to kidnap Isobel, ostensibly to stop her from marrying John and continuing the Banning line. In truth, he wants her for himself. Back at the Banning house, when Isobel's abduction is discovered, John and the sheriff question the gathered townspeople and learn that an Egyptian has recently assumed the post of caretaker of the cemetery. Putting two and two together, John hastens to the graveyard and confronts Mehemet, who has a gun. Before he can shoot the young man, however, the sheriff fires and Bey falls dead. Inside the makeshift temple, Kharis picks up Isobel and walks off. John tracks him to his home where the Mummy beats him back. Kharis climbs the stairs to the second-floor balcony. Outside, the frightened townspeople take torch to the terrace and the Mummy goes back inside. With the house blazing out of control, Banning and Isobel escape via an arbor. The Mummy dies in the blaze.

The next year he was resurrected, appropriately enough, as *The Mummy's Ghost*. By this time, though, the narrative thread was growing stale. High Priest Youssef Bey (John Carradine) comes to America to reclaim Kharis and the remains of Ananka, these latter having been sent to Massachusetts' Scripps Museum between *The Mummy's Hand* and *The Mummy's Tomb*. Meanwhile, at a local college, we meet students Tom Herbert (Robert Lowery) and Amina Mansori (Ramsay Ames). The girl, we will soon learn, is the reincarnation of Princess Ananka, and is eventually taken over by her spirit. Elsewhere, the school's Egyptologist, Professor Norman (Frank Reicher), is busy translating hieroglyphics and learns the secret

of the Tana Leaves. He burns nine of them and their vapor rises into the night air. These are sensed by Kharis, who had escaped the burning Banning house and has been roaming about a nearby forest. The Mummy enters the room and kills Norman. After several more murders, Kharis is summoned by Youssef, who has established headquarters in a shack by a swamp. Bey's first move is to try and regain Ananka. He visits the museum and hides there until after closing, at which time he admits Kharis. The Mummy embraces his age-old bride and she crumbles beneath his touch. Clearly, her spirit has fled and Youssef wants it. This means kidnapping Amina, which Kharis does. He brings her to the High Priest who falls in love with her. Jealous, Kharis kills the priest. Tom, in the interim, has tracked the Mummy and follows Kharis as he carries Amina into the swamp. As they walk, the girl literally becomes Ananka and ages accordingly. The Mummy and his crumbling beloved sink into quicksand as the shocked Tom looks on. He should have been more patient, for Chaney and a new Ananka (Virginia Christine) returned that year in *The Mummy's Curse*. A reclamation project in the bayou unearths the ancient pair. With the aide of a

Lon Chaney Jr. as the Mummy in *The Mummy's Curse*.

A sample of the antics expected when *Abbott and Costello Meet the Mummy*.

In this publicity still for *Curse of the Faceless Man*, Elaine Edwards is carried off by the title villain.

new High Priest (Peter Coe), who sets up shop in an abandoned monastery, both Kharis and his princess are revived. Ananka immediately turns beautiful, but the Mummy stays his decrepit self. In any case, the keeper of the monastery (Martin Kosleck) wants Ananka for his own and, still jealous, the Samson-like Mummy brings the temple crashing down. Buried beneath tons of debris, the Mummy went unseen for a solid decade.

Actually, when *Abbott and Costello Meet the Mummy* (1955), it was not Kharis but *Klaris* they encountered, and the actor was no longer Lon Chaney but Eddie Parker. Parker, you will recall, doubled for Lugosi as the Frankenstein Monster in *Frankenstein Meets the Wolfman*. The comedians played a pair of bungling treasure hunters who became involved with thiefs likewise engaged in robbing the tomb. Both groups bear the wrath of the Mummy, but it was the audience that suffered most. This was the last film of the *Abbott and Costello Meet . . .* series and, with its strained, familiar humor, and the aging duo looking painfully bored, it's not difficult to see why.

The Pharaoh's Curse (1956) was not in the form of a mummy, per se, but belonged to the same school: an age-old being (Alvaro Builliot) protected the sanctity of an ancient tomb by killing members of an archeological expedition. A similar fate was endured by scientists who came face to crust with *The Curse of the Faceless Man* (1958). In an interesting fabrication, Bob Bryant was a resident of Pompeii who was buried when Vesuvius erupted A.D. 79. He returned to life in modern times to kidnap Elaine Edwards, under the mistaken notion that he was saving his girlfriend of some nineteen centuries before.

Clearly, not unlike the werewolf pictures, the Mummy and related creatures repeated a very specific cycle. Even the Frankenstein Monster, although not a part of this study, went through a similar evolution. Universal maintained a rigid formula throughout the midforties, after which the formula was spoofed, and finally some bizarre notions were hauled in from left field to revitalize the mode. And with the Mummy, as ever, it was Hammer films that ultimately offered something fresh to the legend. Before we look at the British productions, however, it should be pointed out that the Mummy was also the basis for a very popular series of films made in Mexico. Spain and Mexico have long been involved in the production of horror and monster films, although few of these efforts ever

The Aztec Mummy as seen in one of his latter films, *The Robot vs. The Aztec Mummy.*

see widespread release in this country, either theatrically or on television. In Mexico, however, one character in particular, the Aztec Mummy, has enjoyed a popularity akin to that of the Universal monsters in the forties. These films are not as bad as literal translations of their titles seem to indicate: *The Aztec Mummy* (1958), *Robot vs. The Aztec Mummy* (1959), *Curse of The Aztec Mummy* (1959), and *Wrestling Women vs. the Aztec Mummy* (1964).

Hammer's *Mummy*, unlike their versions of *Dracula* and *Frankenstein*, was not based on the original movie of the Universal series. Rather, it is a combination of *The Mummy's Hand* and *The Mummy's Tomb*, transported from the present to the year 1895. The film opens with Stephen Banning's (Felix Aylmer) discovery of the tomb of Ananka. Like Bramwell Fletcher's Ralph Norton before him, the old man is driven mad when he sees the guardian Mummy Kharis (Christopher Lee) walk about the room. Thus, it remains for his son John (Peter Cushing) to exhume the Princess and bring her to England. The High Priest Mehemet (George Pastell), in turn, brings Kharis to England to destroy those who disturbed Ananka's resting place. As in the Universal picture, everyone is slaughtered with the exception of John Banning. The young archeologist escapes a vicious attack by the monster when his wife Isobel (Yvonne Furneaux) happens along. She looks and sounds exactly like Ananka and Kharis obeys her commands to leave. He returns, however, to kidnap Isobel, after which the High Priest orders Kharis to kill her. Instead, the Mummy murders Mehemet and heads for the moors. There, riddled with bullets, he sinks slowly into the swamp.

Despite the hackneyed plot, *The Mummy* is a marvel to behold. Peter Cushing, as ever, gives John Banning far greater personality than the John Hubbard enactment. He's a curious, brave, and compassionate human being and thus plays well against the cold, fanatic Mehemet, who comes to live as his next-door neighbor. The discussion of Egyptian theology between the men, when Banning welcomes the newcomer to England, is rapier sharp and a high point of the picture. Too, Cushing gives Banning a very sympathetic limp, the result of a broken leg suffered while on the Ananka dig. Lee, on the other hand, his face slathered with the muck of eternity, can do little with his part other than grunt and destroy. Of course, he is very good at the latter, Lee's height making him a formidable mummy. When, for instance, he enters Banning's home by battering down the door, surviving twin shotgun blasts, and ignoring a spear thrust through his body, the audience knows that this is a Mummy with which to reckon.

As with most every Hammer production, the sets, costumes, and especially the attention to period detail, are superb. A nice gothic atmosphere is achieved with the wonderful marshland locales, thus giving the film an added dimension in terms of mood. On the other side of the coin, there is an impressive flashback sequence to Kharis' attempt at raising his beloved Ananka from the dead. Wisely, the script places this segment away from Egypt

proper so as to avoid the necessity of crowd scenes and expensive sets. There is, however, a lavish funeral sequence, and a nicely appointed set that serves as Ananka's tomb. It is in this set that the film's only unfortunate artistic slip occurs, and that is the cutting out of Kharis' tongue for having misused his powers as High Priest. It is with tasteless relish the film dwells on the actual disfigurement performed by two nubian slaves. Beyond this minor quibble, the picture is top-drawer entertainment, and easily the best Mummy film since Karloff.

Hammer's second stab at the children of Thoth came in 1964 with *Curse of the Mummy's Tomb*. Dickie Owens portrayed the Mummy Ra-Antef who, in classic manner, went traipsing through fog-covered streets in search of the infidels who disturbed his sleep. Owens was followed to the screen by stuntman Eddie Powell who, in *The Mummy's Shroud* (1966), stopped the party of Sir Basil Walden (Andre Morell) from troubling the peace of Pharaoh Kah-to-bey. For the record, and to commend the technicians responsible—Bowie Films—the one truly excellent scene in this otherwise run-of-the-mill exercise is the finale: a mystic incantation robs the Mummy Prem of life and he slowly decays, eventually toppling in on himself. It's the only such scene ever created to equal the brilliant climactic disintegration of Christopher Lee in *Horror of Dracula*.

After several years leave from the deserts of Egypt, Hammer came up with a break in the old theme. In *Blood of the Mummy's Tomb* (1972), the tomb of Queen Tera is entered by Professor Julian Fuchs (Andrew Kier), who ships her perfectly preserved, unmummified corpse back to England. It's a nasty find he's made: the queen, as we know from an unnerving prologue, held all Egypt in fear of her supernatural powers. Indeed, when she died, the priests took especial care to sever the hand on which she wears her mystic ring.

On the twenty-first birthday of Julian's daughter Margaret (Valerie Leon), he gives her a ring taken from Tera's finger. Slowly, the spirit of the queen possesses the girl and drives her to murder. Joined by Corbeck (James Villiers), one of her father's most vociferous opponents, she kills members of the expedition to recover artifacts taken from her mausoleum: statuettes of a cobra, a cat, and a jackel, to be used as part of an occult ritual. In the end, as Corbeck tries to reanimate the real Tera with the

Peter Cushing tries to spear Christopher Lee in **The Mummy**. Notice shotgun hole in the monster's right side.

Scroll of Life, Fuchs breaks in and destroys the body. This unleashes incredible spiritual forces that tear down the building and bury the professor, his daughter, and Corbeck. Only the girl survives, and as she lies in a hospital bed wrapped from head to toe in symbollic bandages, we are left to wonder if it is Margaret or Tera.

In many ways, *Blood from the Mummy's Tomb* is a return to the wicked nature of the Karloff characterization. Tera's evil hold on people, her ruthless way of dispatching enemies, and the inexplicable nature of the queen's incredible power add up to a grand tale of evil fantasy. It is even more fitting that the film is based on *The Jewel of Seven Stars,* a short story by Dracula's creator Bram Stoker. This blood relation gives kinship to the often diverse roads of fantasy at which we have looked thus far. Many of these themes reappear in our next chapter, a review of the monster melting pot, humanoid creations that are neither vampire, werewolf, or mummy.

8
THE MONSTER

*Holstenwall Fair,
including sideshows
of all kinds,
and marvels never before
seen!*

So proclaims a handbill passed to the hero in *Cabinet of Dr. Caligari* (1919). It's also a remarkably apt description of this chapter. Unlike the common backgrounds shared by the legends of the vampire, werewolf, and zombie, there is no single thread to bind the films herein. They all feature fantastic beings that range from borderline reality—the somnambulist in *Caligari*—to impossible fantasy like *The Golem*. Some belong to ancient folklore, such as *The Abominable Snowman of the Himalayas*, while others, like the *Creature from the Black Lagoon*, are more modern abstractions.

Of them all, *Cabinet of Dr. Caligari* has the distinction of being among the early classic fantasies that has never been equaled. Filmed in Berlin's Decla Studios, the picture was directed by the largely undistinguished Robert Weine after Fritz Lang (*Der Niebelungen*, *Metropolis*) had turned it down. It was written by a pair of young men, Carl Mayer and Hans Janowitz, who were distressed with the Great War recently passed and wanted to down the horrors of autocracy. *Cabinet of Dr. Caligari* was designed by three studio art directors who conceived the sets in very expressionistic style. This meant that the natural shapes of props and backgrounds were distorted for effect, thus satisfy-

ing producer Erich Pommer's desire to create a film that was visually filled with horror, sensationalism, and current artistic vogue. This accomplished, the filmmakers faced another problem. The studio had almost exhausted its month's ration of electricity, making lighting a problem. Pommer, therefore, had his artists *paint* the lights and shadows on their backdrops and sets, thus eliminating the need for hard lighting. The resultant film was strange both in design and story.

Jane (Lil Dagover), a beautiful girl, passes like a ghost before two men sitting in a garden. Francis (Friedrich Feher), the younger man, introduces her as his fiancee and proceeds to tell his friend Dr. Olson (Rudolf Lettinger) an incredible story.

To the Holstenwall Fair comes hypnotist Dr. Caligari (Werner Krauss) who wishes to put his somnambulist Cesare (Conrad Veidt) on display. Caligari asks the town clerk for permission to maintain a booth at the fair, and the clerk, after belittling Caligari, grants him a license. That night, the clerk is murdered. The next day, Francis and Jane visit Caligari's tent while touring the grounds. Inside, Caligari explains that Cesare has been asleep all his life and is roused only occasionally to fortell the future. Waking the creature, Caligari fields questions from the audience. One man, Alan (Hans Heinz von Twardowski) asks for how long he shall live: "Until dawn" is the somnambulist's answer. Later that day, to fulfill his prophecy, Cesare murders Alan. Francis comes to believe that the hypnotist is responsible for these killings, so

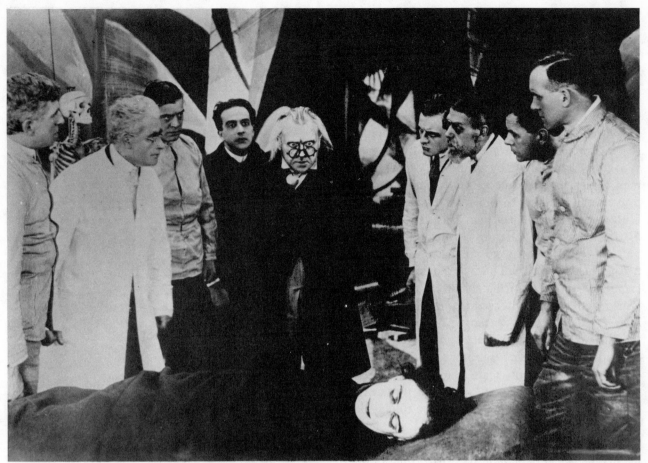

The bespectacled Dr. Caligari goes into shock at the sight of his deceased monster (Conrad Veidt) in *Cabinet of Dr. Caligari.*

Caligari sends Cesare forth to kill Jane. The monster goes to stab the sleeping girl but, taken with her beauty, decides to kidnap her instead. The townspeople set off in pursuit, over bridges, roads, and rooftops, until the zombie dies of exhaustion. Francis, meanwhile, has learned that Caligari is the head of a nearby insane asylum and is, himself, somewhat deranged. When the hypnotist learns of Cesare's death, he goes berserk and has to be put in a straitjacket.

Francis finishes his story at which point Caligari steps into the garden. He is the head of *this* asylum, and explains to Dr. Olson that he is trying to cure Francis of his delusions. We see that Cesare and Jane are also inmates of the institution, and the film concludes with a shot of Caligari's face that leaves us to wonder just where sanity lies.

The story of Francis, the framing narration set in the asylum, was an afterthought to the original tale.

Suggested by Weine, this prologue and epilogue enraged the authors. Their theme had been perverted, coming as it did from an acknowledged madman, into a pro-authoritarian commentary.[7] Nonetheless, putting aside the moral issues stirred by *Cabinet of Dr. Caligari*, it's a grand motion picture. It gives us one of the screen's great villains in the hypnotist, and a truly demonic creation in the somnambulist. Veidt (*Man Who Laughs, Hands of Orlac*), garbed in black leotards, his dark-shadowed eyes blazing from a pasty white face, gives every appearance of a man on whose soul some terrible evil is feeding. His subjugation by the wicked Caligari, his single flash of sympathy—the sparing of Jane's life—and his subsequent death make Cesare one of the silent era's great tragic characters.

This element of audience empathy for a monster is crucial: the character must *touch* the viewer and/or awe him in order to be successful. Therein lies the difference between the somnambulist's ilk and our next screen monster, *The Golem*. Cesare was the slave of Caligari, a victim. The Golem, an avenger of stone, was also a slave, but far from a victim. Strangely, the sequel to *The Golem* came first, in 1914. Entitled *The Golem: The Monster of Fate*, this German film directed by Paul Wegener—who also played the monster—has Rabbi Loew's incredible stone giant found beneath the floor of an age-old synagogue and bought by an antique dealer. The old man brings the monster to life through a cabalistic prayer and puts it to work as his housekeeper. Unfortunately, the clay man falls in love with his master's daughter. Chasing her through the house, he tumbles from a tower and shatters on the street below. This first film faded quickly outside of Germany since, immediately after its release, the world went to war. The second picture, *The Golem: How He Came to Be,* was made six years later. It is the story of what happened *before* the events described in the earlier picture.

Popular complaint against Hebrew sorcery—alchemy and astrology—has reached its peak: the Jews of fifteenth-century Prague are told to leave the city. For protection, old Rabbi Loew (Albert Steinrueck) readies for life the ancient Golem he has in his cellar. He summons forth the spirit of Astaroth to reveal the mystic word that will animate the great stone man. The disembodied head of the demon appears, and with it comes a blazing ring of fire and forceful winds. They surround the Rabbi as Astaroth mouths the forbidden word *Aemaer*. Loew scratches this incantation on a scrap of paper and slips it into the Star of David on the Golem's chest. Slowly, the monster opens his eyes and starts walking about the room. When the Rabbi twists the amulet again, the monster stops, as though rooted to the spot. In the days that follow, Loew has the monster chopping wood and even shopping for groceries, a basket around his arm. The holy man leaves the administration of the monster to his associate Famulus (Ernst Deutsch).

One day, the Rabbi brings the Golem to see the emperor. During their audience, the ceiling cracks and the monster, its arms upraised, keeps it from falling. In return, the potentate pardons the Jews. Returning home, the monster resists when Loew tries to turn it off. Acting quickly, the Rabbi grabs the life-giving Star of David and the stone man goes still. Loew is worried, for this is the first time the Golem has shown a will of its own and the desire to

Albert Steinruck (right), as Rabbi Loew, and his assistant move *The Golem* to the clergyman's basement.

live. Puzzling over what to do next, Loew happens across his daughter Miriam (Lyda Salmanova) in the arms of Florian (Hanns Sturm), the king's aide. Angered, the Rabbi revitalizes the Golem. The monster smashes his way into Miriam's room and Florian attacks it with a dagger. The knife breaks and the official runs to the astrology tower, the Golem in pursuit. The beast captures the official and hurls him to the street below. Then it grabs Miriam and carries her downstairs where he is met by Famulus. The apprentice tries to shut the Golem down, but the monster pulls a burning ember from the forge and sets the house on fire. Famulus runs to fetch the Rabbi, who is at services. By the time Loew arrives, the giant has fled and the house has collapsed, hiding Florian's corpse. Miriam was pulled from the inferno by the clay man and left lying on a boulder. Looking to join some children at play, the monster smashes the ghetto gates. Cuddled in the monster's arms, one of the youngsters accidentally touches his talisman. The Golem becomes still. Loew and his friends arrive and carry the monster home; he has served his purpose and must now be retired.

Photographed by Karl Freund—who went on to direct Karloff's *The Mummy*—this second Golem picture is both visually and technically superb. It accurately re-creates the ancient ghetto, painting a filthy, claustrophobic picture of Prague. Wegener, as the stone man, is also well conceived, properly awkward and lumbering as befits the role. Indeed, the only scene in which Wegener's credibility fails is when the monster goes shopping for food, a woven basket slung about his arm. Although this sequence is supposed to show the Golem as docile and obedient, thus setting the stage for his subsequent rebellion, it is incongruous and unintentionally comedic. Beyond this discrepancy, however, the picture is a powerful period piece and a grand portrait of religious mysticism. Although it would be three times remade, in 1933 and 1966 by French filmmakers and again in Britain called *It!* (1966)—in which the monster survives a direct hit from an atom bomb—the 1920 film remains the finest and most popular version.

There were few silent fantasy tales after *The Golem*, the deformed but decidedly nonsupernatural characters of Lon Chaney Sr. fairly dominating the genre. The sound period brought with it the series films, and it wasn't until the midforties that new and bizarre monsters made their way to the screen.

Gorillas have always been popular players, featured as stars in their own right—such as *King Kong* in 1933 (see Chapter 10)—or as cameo killers in a Tarzan or Jungle Jim picture. An offshoot of these shaggy brutes are the Yeti, the abominable snowman, and the missing link. Although these movies were generally set in the mountains of Tibet, there were exceptions. One film that broke from legend was *White Pongo* (1945), which was also the most routine effort of this type. A creature of high intelligence, the albino African gorilla was thought to be the missing link between man and the monkeys. Alas, no one ever finds out what he really was since Pongo kidnaps the heroine (Maris Wrixon) and is killed for his efforts. Understandably, other Yeti were reluctant to show their faces for a full

A publicity still for *White Pongo*.

decade. In the meantime, Hollywood brought forth an avalanche of hybrid creatures ranging from humanoid to impossible.

The Flying Serpent (1945) was Quetzacoatl, the great Mexican bird God. George Zucco, after resigning as the Mummy's High Priest, starred as professor Andre Forbes, discoverer of the lost treasure of Montezuma. He keeps it hidden in a cave guarded by the feathered carnivore. Complications

The Flying Serpent takes to the air. Notice the wires leading from his back, just above the tail, and from the horns on his head.

arise when friends and associates begin to bother the scholar. He leaves one of Quetzacoatl's feathers hidden somewhere on the antagonist's person, and his demon flies out to kill them. In the end, of course, Zucco is destroyed by his own monster.

Leaving the air for the sea, we find *Miranda* (1948), which gave us Glynis Johns as a mermaid, a nonhostile phenomenon who rescues physician Griffith Jones from drowning. To show his appreciation, the Englishman fulfills Miranda's greatest wish, which is to visit London. She moves in with Jones and his wife Googie Withers, after which the mermaid becomes openly promiscuous. This causes problems for all involved, especially the uninformed theatre-goer who had been anticipating fantasy along the lines of Hans Christian Anderson. At least the sequel, *Mad About Men* (1954), made no attempt to hide its metier behind an amorphous title. On the other hand, *Mr. Peabody and the Mermaid* (1948) was a more innocent production. Based on the novel *Peabody's Mermaid* by Gus and Constance Jones, it featured William Powell as a businessman from Boston who, while on a winter vacation in the Caribbean, captures a mermaid (Ann Blyth). As the title suggests, it's an innocuous little comedy-fantasy that, like its companion efforts, fails to dip into the vast sea of mystical lore about the ocean's strangest creature.

Although failing to start a trend with the mermaid, studios were hard at work employing amphibious creatures to a more horrific and interesting end. *The Maze* (1953), filmed in 3-D, is the story of an old British castle whose viscount is a giant, two-hundred-year-old frog. Although the monstrous lord keeps visitor Richard Carlson hopping throughout the picture, it is the striking sets and photography that are the movie's real star. Director William Cameron Manzies, who had helmed *Things to Come* (1936) and was art director on *Gone With the Wind* (1939) and *Thief of Bagdad* (1940), had a flair for visual storytelling and innovation that was second to none. Menzies' contribution to the genre will be more fully discussed later. Meanwhile, sticking with the dipnoan family, the following year saw Universal add another name to its list of classic monsters, *The Creature From the Black Lagoon*. The Creature, a cross between man and fish, is explained to be a member of an aquatic branch of evolution that developed along lines similar to our own. Because of curiosity fermenting in the mind of his biological cousin, the amphibian man is thrice

The Creature from the Black Lagoon.

forced to pit his extraordinary might and mind against twentieth-century man. In the first of the Creature movies, Dr. Maia (Richard Denning) finds the fossilized hand of an incredible monster in the banks of the Amazon River. Returning to Morajo Bay, he gathers up frogman David Reed (Richard Carlson), his secretary and girlfriend Kay Williams (Julie Adams), and Dr. Mark Williams (Whit Bissell), and they mount a well-appointed expedition to locate additional remains. They find, instead, the petrification's living counterpart. From a clandestine vantage point, the Gill Man (Ben Chapman) keeps an eye on the crew and takes a liking to Miss Williams. Eventually, the monster's lagoon is drugged and the unconscious Creature is shackled onboard the ship. Before long he breaks free, rips away Dr. Williams' face, and kidnaps Kay. Maia and Reed go after the monster with spearguns. They find Julie alive in the Creature's suboceanic cavern and, when discovered by the amphibian, shoot him to death. In the last shot, he sinks slowly into the murky depths of the lagoon. Not wishing to let dormant creatures lay, Universal resurrected this new box-office giant in *The Revenge of the Creature* (1955).

An expedition returns to the Black Lagoon where, it develops, the Creature (Ricou Browning) was only stunned by the bullets. This time, a better-equipped Dr. Maia and company succeed in bringing the beast back to civilization. Imprisoned in a high-walled pool at the Ocean Harbor Aquarium, the monster finds he is still enamored of Kay (Lori Nelson). Battering his way to freedom, the Creature traces Miss Williams and her boyfriend (John Agar) to a nightclub, reduces the place to rubble, and abducts the girl. Pursued, the monster is riddled with bullets, drops his delicate parcel, and stumbles into the ocean. By the time the third film rolled along, a new approach was needed. In *The Creature Walks Among Us* (1956), the monster (Don Megowan) undergoes plastic surgery after being captured by Jeff Morrow and Rex Reason. Since his gills have been removed, the reprocessed Creature can no longer breathe underwater. Understandably piqued, the monster bursts from an electrified prison and wreaks havoc in the seaside town. After murdering Morrow and coveting his wife (Leigh Snowdon), the monster finds he is choking. Something has gone wrong with the operation. Suffocating and riddled with bullets, the monster stumbles to the ocean and vanishes.

The Creature trilogy is one of the few instances in which sequels maintained the same high quality of the original. The core of this greatness is twofold: the element of pathos, established by director Jack Arnold in the first two films, and the stunning design of the monster.

Arnold has always managed to render his protagonists with empathy. Usually, in the case of *The Incredible Shrinking Man* (1956) or the stranded Xenomorph in *It Came From Outer Space* (1953), the hero is somehow different from the rest of us, and is therefore being hunted by irresponsible men or haunted by unjust fate. This, quite properly, forces our sympathies to the victim, which in this case is the Creature. His lot is the same as that of King Kong or the Frankenstein Monster whose violence is justified by the actions of their antagonists. Indeed, if the Creature is, in fact, only one member of an intelligent race that developed parallel to our own, the sin is greater than the oppression of a supersimian or a man built from dead tissue. It is a crime against nature. In this perspective, *The Creature From the Black Lagoon* serves as a precursor to *Planet of the Apes* where man is strapped to an operating table while his erstwhile laboratory animals, the monkeys, wield the surgeon's scalpel.

Ricou Browning doffs his headgear between takes on *Revenge of the Creature*. Notice snaps just below Ricou's neck. Photograph courtesy of Ricou Browning.

Curiously, the invigorating fight put up by the Creature in Arnold's twin efforts is replaced by brooding depression in last film, directed by John Sherwood. The butchered Gill-man, dressed in clothes and locked in a cage, has been reduced from a noble to a pathetic figure. Perhaps, in a larger sense, it is another of the fifties' many comments through fantasy and science fiction films on man's haphazard approach to science and nature. Of course, this higher postulate is not what packed the houses for Creature films. The first picture was shot in 3-D, which added to its appeal; Julie Adams' fetching garb—or lack of it—made the going easier for fathers who brought their kids to the Black Lagoon. The real draw, however, was the design and execution of the Creature itself. The face is that of a fish, with slightly more sinister eyes; the body is antediluvian, though not the lumbering form of a dinosaur. In terms of personality, he is the perfect hero, the uncorrupted being who does not hesitate to defend his home against the encroaching scientists. Both as a monster and a character, then, the Gill-man pleased those who came looking for a good story, plenty of action, and one of film history's finest monsters.

The suit itself was of airtight molded sponge rubber built at a cost of over $15,000. For the many underwater sequences, air was fed to the Creature by way of a long rubber hose. Lengthy takes were required of Messrs. Chapman, Browning, and Megowan, and this required not only great stamina, but the ability to perform intricate subsea stunts as well. Browning performed these latter for all three films. One segment in particular, from the first picture, stands out as the best in the series. Julie Adams goes swimming in the lagoon while the camera watches from some twenty yards below the surface. Into the frame, between the girl and the camera, swims the Creature, who paces Miss Adams, supplely miming her motions without exposing his presence. It's a unique and poetic segment that removes the viewer from the festering lagoon surface to the quiet world underwater. Like everything about the Creature films, it was executed with style and grace.

Although the Creature imitations were pre-ordained—along with Creature model kits, poseable action dolls, board games, paint-by-number kits, wallets, Halloween costumes, and comic books—they would not appear for several years. In the meantime, filmmakers picked up where *White Pongo* had left off. Sparked by Sir Edmund Hillary's conquest of Everest in 1953, the studios set off in pursuit of the Abominable Snowman.

The first legitimate Yeti picture was *Snow Creature* (1954), a not-very-subtle "remake" of *King Kong*. On an expedition to the Himalayas, the wife (Leslie Denison) of botanist Paul Langton is carried off by an Abominable Snowman. Later, the creature is himself shanghied and transported to Los Angeles where he escapes, goes on a city-wide rampage, and is destroyed. *Man Beast* (1955), on the other hand, didn't stray from the snow-covered peaks of Everest. This made for some nice studio re-creations of the Himalayas on which hero Rock Madison encountered the shaggy white monster. Unfortunately, while the picture had plenty of action, it lacked the depth of *The Abominable Snowman of the Himalayas* (1957). In this Forrest Tucker-Peter Cushing vehicle, the creatures were portrayed as beings that craved only anonymity. Accordingly, whenever the snowmen appeared, they were shown from the nose up and then in but brief takes. Although effective, well written, and smoothly played, the picture tended to bog down in talk and didactics. Thus, the best of the Yeti films remains

The surgically altered Creature finds he can no longer breathe underwater in *The Creature Walks Among Us*.

Half-Human (1955), a Japanese effort padded for American release with scenes shot in Hollywood. In the "new" version, the body of a young snowman is brought to scientist John Carradine. Through this contrivance, the exposition is delivered in conversation and the picture shifts to a Northern Japanese mountain range. There, under the able direction of Toho's top fantasy director, Inoshira Honda *(Godzilla)*, a group of young people on a skiing excursion encounter a family of gorillalike snowmen. Eventually, the child is shot down and the parent destroyed in a lava pit, thus ending the race. As one might imagine, the public's appetite for the snowman was quickly sated by these efforts, which, like the mermaid films, failed to exploit the lore and legend of the monsters to their fullest.

Shifting our attention from the frigid top of the earth to the hot and clammy tropics, we find the son of an African chieftan become the monster star of *From Hell it Came* (1957). Knifed and dumped into a pit of quicksand, the creature, a monstrous treeman, sallies forth to avenge his death. In a similar resurrection, this one a continent away, *The Giant From the Unknown* (1957) returned from the grave to menace Central America. Buddy Baer was the monster, an eight-foot-tall Spanish Conquistadore brought back to life by the perennial favorite,

The Monster watches as the girl who killed his former, nonabmoninable self drowns in quicksand. As seen in *From Hell It Came*. Notice assassin's dagger, which is still in the creature's heart.

The Monster From Piedras Blancas studies a gruesome souvenir from one of his many seaside raids.

the stray bolt of lightning. Still in Mexico, a cousin of the *Creature From the Black Lagoon* made his sole screen appearance in *The Monster of Piedras Blancas* (1958). The beast came from the sea to menace an oceanside lighthouse. Unlike the Creature films, however, this picture was simply a monster-gone-mad story with no attempt at characterization or subtlety. Of the same school was *Eegah!* (1960), a giant prehistoric man who was discovered in a cave and fell in love with a modern-day-lady (Marilyn Manning).

Not a shop to rest on their laurels, Universal Pictures tried to create another running character in *The Mole People* (1955), but failed by relegating their monsters to all but a few brief appearances. When Dr. Bentley (John Agar) and his crew of archeologists entered a newly formed fissure, they found a race of albinos whose civilization sank beneath the surface world in 3,000 B.C. The mutated Mole People are kept as slaves by these ancients who, it develops, were at one time the Sumarians. The newcomers stop taskmasters from whipping their beastly charges and, as a result, when the Sumerians try to kill their upper-world visitors, the monsters come to their aid. A final earthquake destroys the city; only Bentley and Dr. Bellamin (Hugh Beaumont) survive.

In addition to Universal, Roger Corman, Dean of the Poe films, made his mark on the man-monster genre. His contributions were mostly in terms of science fiction: *Day the World Ended* (1956), with its atom-spawned mutants, and *Night of the Blood Beast* (1958), an astronaut turned into a crusty tendrilled being by an outer space creature, are examples. Corman also produced and directed less technological films in this very prolific grade-Z period. Among them were *Monster From the Ocean Floor* (1954), about a cyclopean cell beneath the sea; *Beast From the Haunted Cave* (1959), about a humanoid arachnid who wraps his victims in cocoons, in this case a bunch of skiing gangsters who commit the perfect crime only run into the Beast; and *Creature From the Haunted Sea* (1961), this one awash with teens and monsters. Not a widely seen film, it did serve as a model for Del Tenney's more successful *Horror of Party Beach* (1963) in which radioactive waste dumped into the ocean mutates plankton and algae into incredible monsters. *Beach Girls and the Monster* (1964), in turn, borrowed the same theme and put adventure star John Hall in the seaweed monster suit. There was no limit to the

A fully mutated John Agar near death in *The Hand of Death*.

kinds of plagiarism in which Hollywood would indulge for their monster movies. They all made money. Even without the teenage elements, ghoulish goings-on drew a crowd in the early sixties. A holdover from the technology scare of the fifties took a pot-shot at the military, giving John Agar *The Hand of Death* (1961), a lethal Midas' touch that eventually turned him into a loathesome monster; there was even an attempt to literally scrape the bottom of the barrel with *The Slime People* (1963), gloppy beings from center earth who tried to take over the world.

Of course, amidst this more sensational and crudely produced product was some genuine polish. Animals, for example, were many times used as aggressors and killers in films like *The Birds* (1963), *The Hellstrom Chronicle* (1970), *Frogs* (1973), and *Bug!* (1975). Each film featured nature in revolt, all the little Davids of the animal kingdom stinging, pecking, and biting at man, the wanton Goliath.

The Birds, of course, was Alfred Hitchcock's stab at the fantastic with gulls, crows, and pigeons turning on the residents of Bodega Bay in Northern California. Beyond the thematic slap at man's overrated opinion of himself—the aviates are never bested; things simply and inexplicably return to normal—*The Birds* illustrates an even greater irony about the folly of man. And it has nothing to do with the plot of the film. Hitchcock's superb special effects were created by Ub Iwerks, the man who designed Mickey Mouse for Walt Disney. Pit against *Cleopatra* in the 1963 Oscar race, Iwerks' magnificent technical work lost the award to a crew that was unable to make even Elizabeth Taylor's asp seem exciting. Judgments based on uninformed popular opinion rather than on real merit is every bit as dangerous as an island of crazed birds! *The Hellstrom Chronicle* fared better, winning the Oscar as Best Documentary of the Year. The film was a literate account composed of filmed scientific studies showing how bugs will eventually inherit the earth. *Frogs*, however, was convinced that the insects would need help. Thus, in addition to rebellious spiders and scorpions, amphibians and reptiles on an island off the Southern Coast of the United States joined the revolt and sent mankind fleeing for his collective life. In Los Angeles, the struggle was somewhat more incredible. *Bug!* saw foot-long incendiary cockroaches crawl from the earth's core. Based on the popular novel *The Hephaestus Plague*, *Bug!* was released at the same time as *Jaws*, and was lost in the shuffle.

With the end of the fantasy and science fiction boom of the fifties, man-monsters and their ilk were fewer in number than before. Hammer gave us *The Reptile* (1966), a fine film about a voodoo curse. Harry Spalding (Noel William) and his wife Valerie (Jennifer Daniel) journey to Claymoor Heath in England to learn the cause of Harry's brother

Jacqueline Pearce attacks Jennifer Daniel in *The Reptile*.

Peter's death. When they arrive at the late man's home, they meet Dr. Franklyn (Ray Barrett) who is looking for his missing daughter Anna (Jacqueline Pearce). Later, the girl shows up at the Spaldings and invites them for dinner. When they arrive, the couple is shocked to find that Anna's father has locked her in her room. After dinner, Harry leaves to dig up Peter's corpse. He finds a gruesome wound on the man's neck. Late that night, he sneaks into the Franklyn house to question Anna. He finds, instead, a scaly, fanged monster that bites him and flees. Valerie nurses the wound and visits the Franklyn house herself. There, she realizes that Anna has been transformed into a snake woman. The doctor is arguing with a Malaysian servant over his daughter's sleeping body. He kills the housekeeper and during the scuffle overturns a lantern. The house catches fire just as Harry arrives. The burned physician explains that he had once stumbled upon Borneo's *Ourang Sanco*, the Snake People. For meddling in their affairs, he was punished by having his daughter turn regularly into a monster whose bite is fatal. Just then, Anna awakens and gnaws her father to death. With the house an inferno, only the Spaldings escape.

The successful combination of gothic horror, voodoo, and interesting characterization made *The Reptile* a unique little film, tastefully done and executed with flair. Unfortunately, the motion pictures immediately following in the man-monster field were returns to the standard fare of yesteryear. As ever, some were good and some were not. In *Mad Doctor of Blood Island* (1969) science created a chlorophyll man; the sequel, *Blood Beast* (1970) offered more of the same. *Trog* (1970) was Joe Cornelius as a prehistoric man living in a secluded cave in England. Dr. Brockton (Joan Crawford) found the Trogledyte and introduced him to civilization, but the apeman was hardly appreciative. He murdered left and right in response to our mad world, finally committing suicide with a stalactite from his lair. Less sociable was *Bigfoot* (1971), the American Northwest's answer to the Abominable Snowman; *Legend of Boggy Creek* (1972) followed similar lines, purportedly the true story of a gorilla-like beast that preys on people who wander near his swamp. There was even a Lagoon Creature hybrid in *Octoman* (1971), an octopus with legs who menaced the party of star Kerwin Mathews, wrestled an alligator, and so forth. The film was commendable for the surprisingly effective costume by Rick Baker, whose design makes the monster's many appendages all seem lively. And finally, returning to the occult beginnings of *Cabinet of Dr. Caligari*, there came twin creatures from England, the second of which provides us with a strange sense of deja vu: *Horror Express* (1972) and *Creeping Flesh* (1972). Significantly and fittingly, both films starred Peter Cushing and Christopher Lee. *Horror Express* is, in reality, the trans-Siberian railroad, circa 1905. In its hold is a crate containing a prehistoric fossil discovered in Hangchow, China, by Alexander Saxton (Lee). Drawing life essence from the passengers, the remains regain their corporeal form, that of an intelligent simian who had been shipwrecked on earth. With great effort of will, the alien passes his consciousness into the minds of passengers, questing knowledge and the one passenger who might know how to fabricate steel. With this formula, the alien would be able to build a spaceship and return to his own world. Unfortunately, his probings obliterate the victims' brains. Thus, Saxton and his rival Dr. Wells (Cushing) have no choice but to destroy the fiend. They derail the train and it tumbles off a mountain peak exploding in the valley below. Among the destroyed: Telly Savalas in a co-starring role as a Cossak. In *Creeping Flesh*, Dr. Emmanuel Helder (Cushing) learns that evil incarnate once walked the earth in the form of an awesome alien monster. Helder finds its skeleton while on an expedition and tries to use the bone matter as a vaccine against evil, which he believes to be a bacterial disease. Unfortunately, the skelton comes in contact with water, the (creeping) flesh is regenerated, and the monster comes to life. After the creature disappears into the countryside, the film takes a Caligariesque twist—again proving that history, in life or in art, is cyclical. The narrator, Helder, is shown to be an inmate in the sanitarium of his half-brother James Hildern (Lee). Thus, the doctor's battle for peace through the conquest of evil is shown to be ultimately futile. Both films are, however, examples of quality improvements on, and not just reworkings of, the old standards.

To this point, our study has been limited to fantasy that presents man with an intelligent humanoid or spiritual nemesis, vengeful fauna, or the incarnate evil of the human soul. During the next few chapters, our tolerance for the fantastic will shift to a higher level. No longer will the menace be localized or intimate. When our upcoming monsters *pounce*, a city crumbles!

9
THE DINOSAUR

The fantasy films in this chapter and the next feature creatures that are, if not more unusual than any we've yet encountered, certainly the *largest* monsters in this book. Over the years, the gargantuan beast and the dinosaur have enjoyed great popularity. He is one of the most difficult characters to capture on film, not only because of the technical challenge a credible representation poses, but because it is difficult to evoke audience identification with, or sympathy for, a five-hundred-ton behemoth. Nonetheless, we will analyze their appeal by examining, first, what happens when man invades the dinosaur's lost island, seething plateau, or hidden valley. In the next chapter, we will transpose that same monster to man's world and watch some very diverse and interesting results.

The creator of Sherlock Holmes, Sir Arthur Conan Doyle, gave us our most famous book of dinosaur fiction, *The Lost World*. Published in 1912, the novel received its most famous screen treatment from the team of Willis O'Brien and Marcel Delgado in 1925. The simple plot is largely in accordance with Conan Doyle, although the dinosaur element was enhanced to suit better the visual medium of film. To the base of a dank, isolated plateau in South America comes the expedition of Professor Challenger (Wallace Beery). After encountering a few traditional jungle beasts by the banks of the Amazon River, the scientist takes his party up the plateau. They cross a large fallen tree to negotiate a deep ravine and are at once in another world. They find flying reptiles and fierce prehis-

toric carnivores: the group even uncovers an apelike and very antagonistic caveman (Bull Montana). Eventually, the lost world is shaken by a cataclysmic volcano. While the dinosaurs tumble into fissures and trample each other in a mad effort to avoid immolation, the explorers escape via a rope ladder. Challenger, however, has not yet had his fill of monsters. In his zeal, he captures a pair of dinosaurs and carries them back to London. There, both beasts break free when their cage shatters upon unloading from the ship. The winged pteranodon roosts in Parliament. The long-necked brontosaur rampages through the city, smashing buildings and crushing people underfoot, before falling through a bridge into the sea and swimming home.

The Lost World was a silent, ten-reel epic that enjoyed a great popular success. The public was much taken with the novelty of seeing live dinosaurs on screen. The process through which the animals were brought to life is stop-motion photography, still the most effective way of creating giant monsters for the screen. Each creation was a foot-high model built of clay and rubber molded atop jointed, poseable wooden skeletons. The animals were set in position, exposed to one frame of film, moved a fraction of an inch, exposed to a second frame of film, and so forth. When the completed strip of celluloid was run through a projector, the illusion was one of movement. This is much the same principle as cartoon animation with 3-D characters substituting for the flat, two-dimensional drawings. A staple of the fantasy film, stop-motion

Two of Willis O'Brien's monsters have at one another
in the original *Lost World*.

photography was also the process that, through the years, gave such television characters as Gumby, Speedy Alka-Seltzer, and the Pillsbury Poppin' Fresh Doughboy their unique appeal. Beyond the animation, however, was the problem of photographically enlarging the monsters. Since *The Lost World* was made in an era before the invention of the optical printer—a device that combines several strips of film into a single image—the movie enlarged its models via miniature sets or double exposure: running the same roll of film through the camera twice, photographing first the actors and then the monsters. This second process was used extensively in the London sequences. The small, scaled sets were used predominantly for the plateau segments with plaster cliffs, sculpted trees with tin leaves, and sandy stretches all glued carefully in

place. Should a boulder, "leaf," or grain of sand have jiggled between frames, the on-screen result would have been a seemingly alive, animated terrain!

The special effectsmen behind *The Lost World*—and indeed, this was a special effectsman's movie—were Willis O'Brien, the animator, and Marcel Delgado, the model-maker. O'Brien was thirty-years-old when he undertook the movie. Ten years before, he had brought a sixty-second roll of film to a producer in Los Angeles, a reel showing an animated clay dinosaur and a caveman playing together. Impressed with the young man's work, the producer gave him enough money to create a longer, more polished version of this effort. The resultant film, *The Dinosaur and the Missing Link* (1914) was sent to the Edison Company in New York and proved a great financial success. This inspired O'Brien to leave his job as a stonecutter and, backed by Edison, he made an entire series of stop-motion shorts, capped by *The Ghost of Slumber Mountain* (1919), which returned over $100,000 on its $3,000 investment. His reputation as a "magician" secure, O'Brien yanked Delgado from the Otis Art Institute and put the skilled sculptor to work constructing rubber dinosaurs that wouldn't eventually melt under the heat of the floodlights. Together, they built and animated over fifty monsters for *The Lost World*.

It's become a glib phrase to justify any silent film that has become dated due to technical inferiority, but "for it's time," *The Lost World* was an awesome achievement. While not every creation in the film is fluid and lifelike, the fight between a styracosaur and the predatory tyrannosaur is equal to anything Hollywood has turned out since. The animation is perfectly smooth and the struggle lively and well directed. Other high points are the fight between two allosaurs; the first appearance of a dinosaur, a feeding pteranodon; and the chaotic stampede of the many dozen monsters fleeing the volcano. Although refinements in technique and materials have improved the quality of the optical and process work, *The Lost World* has a charm and innocence—some would call it naivete—that would become lost in many of the more sophisticated productions that follow.

Eight years after *The Lost World*, O'Brien and Delgado tackled the awesome challenge of animating *King Kong*. Despite its legendary dinosaur footage, *Kong* is the meat of our next chapter, where the great ape can be put in perspective with his gargantuan progeny. Thus, after cameo appearances in *Kong* and *Son of Kong* (1933), dinosaurs were extinct in Hollywood until 1940 and *One Million B.C.*

Producer Hal Roach and director D. W. Griffith were determined that their picture be a romantic semidocumentary account of the life of cave people. Unfortunately, they were not prepared to weather the time or expense involved in stop-motion photography. They elected, instead, to draft their screen dinosaurs from among the ranks of live lizards adorned with plastic fins and men wearing monster suits. Curiously, although the results were ludicrous, the film has achieved a "classic" status among film buffs. This is due, perhaps, to a nostalgia they hold for stars Victor Mature and the late Carole Landis. In any case, the picture painted a sound-stage portrait of man in his infancy with Mature as Tumak, of the warlike Rock Tribe, and Miss Landis as Loana, one of the peaceful Shell People. When Tumak has an argument with his father, Akhoba (Lon Chaney Jr.), who is also the tribal chieftan, he is banished from their midst. Wandering into the lakeside camp of the Shell People, he kills an allosaur that threatens to devour a young girl and is accepted into the tribe. There, he falls in love with young Loana and the two of them face many adventures together. They are among the few who survive a climactic earthquake and volcano.

Despite an admittedly spectacular finale, *One Million B.C.* was nothing more than a bland pastiche of uninspired characters and situations. *The Lost World*, for example, was a showcase for monsters. Everything was constructed to give O'Brien's work center-stage. In *One Million B.C.*, which purported to be the story of prehistoric survival, the dinosaurs were simply window dressing to a weak and anachronistic soap opera. There was naught to hold an audience's interest. Compounding this problem was the film's lack of spoken dialogue. The producer wanted his cavemen to grunt. Griffith was adamant that they speak fluent English. Roach got his way, Griffith resigned before the picture was completed, and the film became an almost intolerable bore.

For the duration of World War II, Hollywood shied away from dinosaurs. Even the spawn of King Kong would not surface until after the hostilities had ended. The financial crush was tight for other than proven formulae, and prehistoric subjects were still relatively novel. Despite a formidable showing at the box office by *One Million B.C.*, it may have been a freak, something about which the public was simply curious, as they had been about *The Lost World*. It's success didn't guarantee widespread acceptance of the mode. Then there was another consideration. Unlike today, where a single theatrical showing of a motion picture is followed by its sale to television, the gross from reissues was a necessity. A novelty film like *One Million B.C.* might not have the drawing power of a straight action, romance, or horror film. Thus, Hollywood stayed with the more bankable features until after the war. When the strife ended, and fiscal matters stabilized, Hollywood was not long in reacquainting itself with the dinosaur. Unfortunately, it was a compromise return. Believing that audiences might have outgrown the excitement of a giant monster,

A rare publicity still of Carole Landis and Victor Mature in *One Million B.C.*

studios ground out low-budget fare with the emphasis less on logic and special effects, then on action and adventure in which the dinosaur played a small part. Accordingly, *Unknown Island* (1948) was a virile adventure film with scientist Phillip Reed using fiancee Virginia Grey's money to finance a photographic expedition to an alleged land of dinosaurs. Their sea captain Barton Maclane learns that when World War II pilot Richard Denning had bailed from his stricken plane over the site, he had seen several of his buddies devoured by the beasts. Since then, the flier's been a drunkard. However, he does know his way around the island and is persuaded to return with the explorers.

After a sea voyage filled with mutiny and the dour glances of Maclane, who has designs on Miss Grey, the party reaches the dread land. By film's end,

Maclane has been eaten by a dimetrodon, Reed has proven himself a coward by not standing up to the captain—only the dinosaur saved Miss Grey from his slimy clutches—and the always dependable Denning has taken both the show and Miss Grey for his own. *Unknown Island* was a spirited, well-played adventure film that worked hard to build a foreboding atmosphere about the time-forgotten island. Unfortunately, it was all for naught, as the picture is a perfect example of how shoddy special effects can ruin an otherwise solid effort. A trio of stiff, lifeless tyrannosaurs attacking a fallen native bearer is laughable. Even worse was the sad attempt to re-create the giant ape-tyrannosaur battle from *King Kong.* Two costumed extras slugged it out at the edge of a cliff and, after a dull exchange, went tumbling into the ocean below. Yet, in light of these insurmountable deficits, *Unknown Island* is a masterpiece when compared with *Prehistoric Women* (1950). The only "dinosaur" in evidence was a fictitious flying creature whose occasional raids served barely to liven this witless tale of how cavewomen won their mates. Another tedious effort was *Two Lost Worlds* (1950), in which James Arness journeyed from Dodge City to nineteenth-century Australia trying to rescue Laura Elliott from pirates. This he did, only to shipwreck his crew on an island inhabited by stock-shots from *One Million B.C.* Luckily, the following year saw a slight upswing in the field's integrity as Cesar Romero took a hearty crew to *The Lost Continent* in search of a misfired missile. There, they encountered some nicely realized stop-motion monsters in a land where uranium deposits had preserved the prehistoric environment. After a series of deadly battles with the inhospitable fauna, the men fled as a violent earthquake sent the dinosaurs and their home into the sea. By this time, however, Willis O'Brien had returned with help for the genre that he had sired.

In 1955, O'Brien and his former apprentice, Ray Harryhausen, animated a magnificent twenty-minute segment in Irwin Allen's documentary *Animal World*. Allen's film detailed the evolution of life on earth from creation to the present. Despite publicity-stills promising women menaced by lusting dinosaurs, the prehistoric segment was played strictly for fact. Using well-researched miniature sets and meticulously crafted monster models, the animators created the most realistic visions of the dinosaur ever filmed. Particularly striking were the hatching of a baby brontosaur from its egg; the battles between the monsters; and an awesome earthquake reminiscent of O'Brien's *The Lost World* finale. Also effective were the full, rich colors and unusual camera angles. The only real flaw in the film was an occasional closeup of lifesize mechanical heads intercut with the stop-motion footage. Since the "robots" were limited in range and mobility, their plodding movements slowed the action down. The nonsaurian aspects of the documentary were well done, however, and though they lacked the

A ceretasaur and stegosaur battle in *Animal World*.

A tyrannosaur chases Jock Mahoney and Shawn Smith in *Land Unknown*.

A sequence showing the appearance of the Fire Monster at the climax of Irwin Allen's *Lost World*. Note cord that loops around the monster's waist, used to raise it from the pool of "lava."

stylistic flair of Disney's *True Life Adventures*, the film was quite good.

The failure of *Animal World* to elicit a strong box-office response inspired filmmakers to return to the medicrity of yore. Jock Mahoney and crew stumbled upon *Land Unknown* (1957) when their aircraft crashed in the midst of an Antarctic oasis. There they found men wearing lacquered dinosaur suits and a pulley-operated pteranodon. Dinosaurs were also featured prominently in the excellent 1959 film *Journey to the Center of the Earth*. Although the beasts were, again, lizards, they were less

offensive than most. For one thing, the monsters at the earth's core were supposed to be dimetrodons, beasts that closely resembled their modern-day screen counterparts. Thus, the substitution of the rubber-fined creatures was not irreverent. Too, the monsters were shot at high speeds which, when projected, gave the illusion of slow motion and, thus, mass. The non-saurian aspects of this film will be discussed more fully in Chapter Four.

There is a terrible paradox in the 1960 remake of *The Lost World*. Although Willis O'Brien was commissioned to handle the special effects, producer Irwin Allen decided to play it safe. Allen put his money on name actors Claude Rains, Jill St. John, Michael Rennie, and Fernando Lamas and thus precluded the use of expensive stop-motion work. Lizards were recruited, and it must have been painful indeed for the sixty-four-year-old craftsman to coax along camera-shy gila monsters in lieu of his beloved stop-motion models. In any case, due to an effective ad campaign, with saturation exposure on television during prime children's viewing hours, *The Lost World* was quite successful. And, in all fairness to Mr. Allen, it *is* a fine film, filled with grand character players, excellent sets, and lush color photography. As in *Journey to the Center of the Earth*, high-speed photography and shots taken from extreme low angles gave the lizard-dinosaurs an effective giantism and bulk. Of course, purists wince when Rains' Professor Challenger points at a squat iguana and declares, "That, my friends, is a brontosaur!"; but this is tolerable negligence on the part of Allen. At least he *had tired* with *Animal World*. Less empirical is the judgment most often aimed at the plot: specifically, regarding the film's conclusion. Challenger finds a baby dinosaur and vows to bring it back to London. This cheats the viewer by stopping just at the point where the 1925 picture was building to its climax. However, since the expense of remaking the original verbatim would have been prohibitive, Allen chose to focus on the island itself and save the destruction of London for a sequel. Unfortunately, his involvement with other projects from his *tv* series *Lost in Space* and *Voyage to the Bottom of the Sea* to the motion pictures *Poseidon Adventure* and *Towering Inferno* nipped these plans in the bud.

Leaving Sir Arthur Conan Doyle's seed work, we find his predecessor, Jules Verne, whose *Around the World in Eighty Days* (1956), *Twenty Thousand Leagues Under the Sea* (1954), and *Journey to the Center of the Earth* had proved financial bonanzas for their producers. The great fantasy novelist did not fare as well in *Valley of the Dragons* (1961), the screen adaptation of his novel *Off on a Comet*. The talented Cesare Danova, who had just lost the role of *Ben-Hur* to Charlton Heston, played one of two duelists swept to the surface of another world as it passed close to earth. There, they found the sixth reusing of dinosaur footage from *One Million B.C.* along with a race of Neanderthals thrown in for good measure. Five years later, the same stock footage returned in *Island of the Dinosaurs*, a Mexican film that saw but sporadic play in this country.

As they eventually did with all the established branches of horror and fantasy films, Hammer dipped into the past with a primeval foursome: *Prehistoric Women* (1966), *One Million Years B.C.* (1967), *When Dinosaurs Ruled the Earth* (1970), and *Creatures the World Forgot* (1970). *Prehistoric Women*, which was not a remake of the earlier film by that name, was the weakest effort in the group. An African explorer (Michael Latimer) is struck by a bolt of lightning, which sends him back to the Stone Age. There, he falls in love with a girl (Martine Beswick) who helps him escape the clutches of evil tribeswomen. When Latimer is again smitten by a static bolt and is returned to the present, he meets a girl who looks exactly like Miss Beswick. Inoffensive fantasy and nothing more, *Prehistoric Women* was overshadowed by the unanticipated success of Hammer's next production, a remake of *One Million B.C.*, called *One Million Years B.C.* The storyline followed the Griffith film exactly, but there the similarity ended. Hammer let animator Ray Harryhausen fill the screen with incredible stop-motion monsters that were designed to sate the appetite of even the most avaricious dinosaur fans. For viewers less interested in beasts than breasts, there was Raquel Welch who did an excellent job with the Carole Landis role. John Richardson was Hammer's Tumak.

Filmed on location in the rugged terrain of the Canary Islands instead of on a canvas-backed sound-stage, the film achieved a gritty authenticity with its pounding sun, volanic outcroppings of rock, and uninhabited countryside. Richardson's banishment and trek across a seething desert to the ocean of the Shell People is thus brought vividly to life, embellished by Mario Nascimbene's magnificent musical score. By the time he arrives at the seashore, Richardson is so blistered, sweat-soaked, and beaten that he takes one look at Miss Welch and passes out.

The dinosaurs, in a word, are superb. Harryhausen gave us an archelon, Tumak battling an allosaur, a brutish brontosaur, a lively fight between a ceretasaur and a styracosaur, and a magnificent aerial battle between a rhamphoryncus and pteranodon, with Miss Welch caught in the great talons of the latter.[8] Miss Welch, it should be noted, turned in a splendid performance. As in the original, there was not a word of dialogue spoken, and

The brontosaur from *One Million Years B.C.* Although some footage of this scene was shot, it was later eliminated from the film.

Triceratops (left) vs. ceretasaur in *One Million Years B.C.* Note John Richardson and Raquel Welch by ceretasaur's tail.

everything had to be communicated with grunts, facial expressions, or manual gestures. John Richardson and she worked hard and sincerely to make credible the characters of Tumak, the intemperate exile, and Loana, the peaceful mediator between the newcomer and her passive race. Unfortunately, while everyone else looked prehistoric, Miss Welch was too radiant in her animal-hide bikini to pass as a cavewoman.[9]

Since logic has never deterred the filmgoing public, it flocked to see *One Million Years B.C.* Accordingly, Hammer quickly drew together the same diverse elements and rushed ahead with a "sequel." Since Harryhausen was involved with *Valley of Gwangi* (See chapter 10) Hammer turned, for their stop-motion monsters, to one of George Pal's alumni, Jim Danforth. Danforth had worked on the animation in Pal's *Wonderful World of the Brothers Grimm* (1962) and *Seven Faces of Dr. Lao* (1964) among others, and all of which are discussed later in this book. Similarly, Miss Welch had moved on to bigger and better things, so Hammer signed twenty-one-year-old Victoria Vetri as Sanna, heroine of *When Dinosaurs Ruled the Earth*.

Because of great tremors and volcanoes, lovely Sanna is to be sacrificed to the Sun God. Before the ritual can be completed, however, a storm intercedes and Sanna escapes into the sea. After floating some distance, she is found by Tara (Robin Hawdon) of the Sand Tribe. When he brings her back to camp, the caveman's mate becomes jealous and blames Sanna for a crime she didn't commit. The newcomer is forced to flee for her life into the wilderness, where she befriends a dinosaur and her baby. Then, one day, a member of Tara's tribe locates Sanna and she is captured. As the girl is about to be burned at the stake, a gaseous ball spins into earth orbit, where it cools and becomes our moon. It wreaks havoc among the tides, and in the ensuing floods, all the evil cavemen are destroyed.

Miss Vetri does quite well with the very physical role of Sanna. Unlike *One Million Years B.C.* which is Tumak's story, this is the heroine's film. *She* was the one who suffered exile, while the docile Tara played Loana's counterpart, the arbitor between Sanna and his envious mate. As for the special effects, Danforth came up with some clever twists on an old theme. Instead of the standard brontosaur, he gave us a flippered plesiosaur, which ran amok in the camp of Sanna's evil tribesmen; giant crabs that were stirred to life by a storm and pin-

Tara vs. rhamphoryncus in *When Dinosaurs Ruled the Earth.*

cered a dozen or so cavemen to death; a pterodactyl that chased Tara up a cliff; a triceratopslike chasmosaur; and the mother and baby dinosaurs that were a fictitious hybrid of the stegosaur and tyrannosaur. Danforth's animation on all of these was incredibly lifelike, and Sanna's romp with the man-sized baby monster ranks among the golden moments in stop-motion photography. Unfortunately, his beasts didn't have the detail or sparkle found in the Harryhausen monsters. On the other hand, Danforth devised some incredibly complex shots that broke new ground in terms of combining miniature models with live backgrounds. In all, a remarkable achievement.

By the time *Creatures the World Forgot* came into being, Hammer had decided, and rightly so, to do away with the dinosaurs. Not only had Danforth gone over schedule and budget on this second film—bringing it in for more than it had cost Harryhausen to do *One Million Years B.C.*—but the studio felt they could sell the film without dinosaurs and thus save a considerable piece of change. They were right. The film featured an unclad Julie Ege in the role vacated by Misses Welch and Vetri, and spun a simple story of caveman in conflict. It made a handsome profit, although it has been the last film of the series to date. Meanwhile, other filmmakers were tyring their hand at prehistoric subjects, many of which worked out admirably.

Czechoslovakia produced a rather engaging fantasy called *Journey to the Beginning of Time* (1968), the story of four boys who, while boating down a river, were carried backward in time. They passed from the Ice Age to Creation watching the life-and-death struggles of mammals and dinosaurs, finally arriving at the ocean where life had originally begun. The monsters were stop-motion creations, nicely animated, but not up to American work in this field. Still, the film is spirited fun, and an interesting educational experience for the young. Another foreign effort, this one from Italy, was *When Women Had Tails* (1970) in which seven prehistoric male babies were set adrift in a basket and floated to an isolated island. When they matured, the cavemen tried to return to the mainland, but were windswept, instead, to another island. A claudate Senta Berger was the only inhabitant thereof, and interpersonal strife ensued. This film was followed into release by *When Women Lost Their Tales* (1970), which carried the story to yet a second sequel, loosely based on the play *Lisistrata* and with the unlikely title of *When Women Played Ding Dong* (1971). The epic told of an arms race that developed between rival cave factions. The title, in all seriousness, referred to what the women did when their menfolk finally put down their weapons.

A return to more familiar territory was *The Mighty Gorga* (1970) in which treasure hunters in Africa found a lost plateau of dinosaurs, along with the title creature, a huge ape. Although the film was low-budget fare produced for a quick return, it had a pair of fine leads—Scott Brady and Anthony Eisely—and is commendable for being every bit as good as the recent million-dollar dinosaur disaster *The Land that Time Forgot* (1975). This, of course, does not speak well for the latter film. Despite countless pleas from fans of author Edgar Rice Burroughs—Tarzan's creator—and the urgings of film buffs in general, the author's estate did not insist that Britain's Amicus productions engage Harryhausen or Danforth to do the special effects work. As a result, fine sets and a good performance by star Doug McClure as Bowen Tyler, the submarine-wrecked hero of Burroughs' trilogy, were flagrantly wasted. Huge *papier mache,* wire-operated "dinosaurs" were used, causing the expensive production to look cheap. Even lizards would have been an improvement. The reason for the mechanical models, of course, was that they enabled the special-effects photography to be completed in under eight weeks; this, as opposed to the animation shooting schedule of nearly a year for *One Million Years B.C.* Unfortunately, haste in any technical endeavor is synonymous with bad. In a word, this is the most appropriate description of *The Land That Time Forgot* that one can make.

Thus, on an unhappily sour note, we come to the end of our stay with *The Lost World* and its breed. Turning back the clock, we will pick up the parallel trail of those films in which a prehistoric monster is pulled from his native dwelling place and rapes a defenseless mankind. It is the more colorful of the two genres, and one more laden with Freudian import than adventure!

10
THE GIANT MONSTER

The year is 1925, and Willis O'Brien is busy developing new properties for his stop-motion camera. Despite the success of *The Lost World,* he is unable to find financing for films about Atlantis or Frankenstein. This latter project he conceived over eight years before Universal made the Karloff film. Only one project, for which he shot some test footage and drew hundreds of sketches, was optioned. The germ of a film was *Creation* and the studio was RKO. Shortly thereafter, the company changed hands and producer Merian C. Cooper inherited the properties of his predecessors. *Creation* intrigued him, not because of *The Lost World* theme, but because he saw that O'Brien's vast technical skill could be applied to his own pet project, the story of a gorilla. He called on the special effectsman and had him make a test reel of a stop-motion ape battling one of the dinosaurs pictured in *Creation,* a tyrannosaur. The footage was shown to RKO stockholders and they gave the go-ahead for *King Kong* (1933). The film was a year in production and cost well over a half-million dollars. Once again, O'Brien had Delgado build the monster models and the miniature props. O'Brien himself handled the animation. And the picture, released at the height of the Depression, broke attendance records at New York's Radio City Music Hall and L.A.'s Chinese Theatre. Indeed, so great was the demand for tickets that in Manhattan *King Kong* played the Music Hall and the rival Roxy both.

Drawing narrative sustenance from the brontosaur finale of *The Lost World, King Kong* became the prototype for what is referred to by industry observers as the "monster-on-the-loose" genre. Before *Kong,* only *The Loch Ness Monster* (1932) had had a smattering of this theme, with the beast appearing to a diver near the film's conclusion.

King Kong is largely a reworking of the *Beauty and the Beast* plotline. Movie producer Carl Denham (Robert Armstrong) adds to his all-male film crew the lovely Anne Darrow (Fay Wray) whom he found destitute on the streets of Manhattan. Following the map given him by a sea captain, Denham sets sail for Skull Island. His chosen task is to shoot a documentary on the natives' mythical god Kong. Arriving at the primitive jungle, the men go ashore and try to sneak some footage of an aboriginal ceremony. They are discovered, however, and the chief (Noble Johnson) wants the blonde Miss Darrow as Kong's bride. He offers to trade six of his women for the girl. The movie mogul refuses and the crew returns to the ship. That night, the natives sneak onboard and kidnap Anne. The sailors hurry to the island and run ashore just as the screaming girl is carried away by an enormous ape. Half the group sets off in pursuit and, after battling a stegosaur and a brontosaur, catches up with the gorilla. Unfortunately, the meeting takes place with Kong on a cliff and the men stranded precariously on a large log spanning a great chasm. The ape shakes the bridge and the men fall to their deaths. First Mate Jack Driscoll (Bruce Cabot), who had climbed to a ledge in the face of a cliff, is the only man to survive. Kong

Preproduction sketches for *King Kong*.

tries to nab him, but is pulled from the offensive by Anne's screams. The ape had placed the girl in a tree and arrives as a tyrannosaur is trying to devour her. Kong breaks the creature's jaw and heads, with Anne in paw, for his mountaintop lair. Jack stays close on Kong's heels. When the monster ape becomes entangled with an aggressive pteranodon, Jack sneaks to Anne's side and they descend a long vine to the river. The ape, who has crumpled the bird and tossed it from a cliff, sets out after his bride. Jack and Anne hurry to the native village and Kong arrives shortly thereafter. He tears the flimsy huts to straw and is stopped only when Denham hurls potent gas bombs at the gorilla. At the filmmaker's insistence—"We'll be millionaires, boys!"—his wary men build a raft and Kong is floated to New York. There, he is chained and exhibited in a Broadway theatre. When newsmen arrive on opening night to photograph Kong, Jack, and Anne, the ape becomes riled. He thinks the flashbulbs are intended to hurt his bride. Kong breaks his bonds and Driscoll hurries the girl away. Pounding his way through New York in search of his mate, the great ape finds her in an hotel room. Taking her in his mighty paw, the gorilla scales Manhattan's equivalent to his own lofty home, the Empire State Building. After a furious battle with airplanes, the great Kong, bleeding and weakened, gently puts Anne on the ledge of the tower, releases his grip, and plummets to his death.

Previously unpublished sequence showing brontosaur
attack on the Carl Denham raft in *King Kong*.

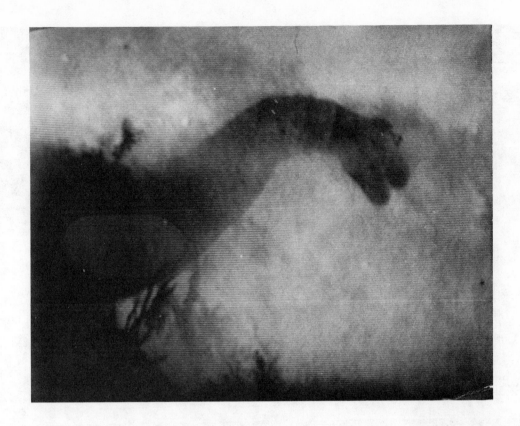

Every rave adjective and the synonyms thereof have been applied and reapplied to *King Kong* and its monumental special effects. Little reaffirmation of these is necessary, and we shall make only a few observations. Forty-three years after its premiere, the film has lost none of its fascination or ability to hypnotize even the most demanding and sophisticated of movie audiences. *Of course* the dialogue appears, today, charmingly blithe; the acting melodramatic. The same may be said of *Hamlet* or *Macbeth*. Much of the picture's allure lies in this whimsical approach to reality. Half a century from now, *The Godfather* or *Jaws*, with their wealth of gore and currently fashionable characterizations will no doubt seem every bit as corny; if, indeed, these films are even remembered with the fondness of *King Kong*. Beyond the acting and story, however, the glow of Kong himself is undiminished. The glorious personality that Willis O'Brien painstakingly gave his metal-boned, rubber-skinned, rabbit-haired model is nothing less than a reflection of our own basic frustrations and challenges. Never mind the metaphor that hindsight has ascribed the great ape, making Kong the oppressed Black man in the White society, man being squelched by his mechanized world, or even the Christ icon seen in the ape's crucifixion pose during his New York stage debut. King Kong is simply a universal victim like the majority of all fantasy characters. Whether or not this allegorical slant was part of the filmmakers' intent, it is one of Kong's greatest legacies. Through it, he will survive as long as the medium of motion pictures itself, this incredible Everyman.

After the first wave of *King Kong's* profits slammed against the shores of RKO, the studio rushed ahead with a sequel, *Son of Kong*. Carl Denham (Armstrong) is hiding from his creditors. Newly indicted by a Grand Jury, the ex-filmmaker flees with his Kong co-captor, Capt. Englehorn (Frank Reicher) to work a shipping route in the Orient. There, they run into Capt. Nils Helstrom (John Marston), the man who gave Denham the map of Kong's island. Helstrom, too, is broke and asks Denham if, during his expedition, he had found the treasure of the island. The mogul admits that he hadn't. The three men hurriedly organize an expedition to Skull Island. En route, a girl, Hilda (Helen Mack), is discovered hiding onboard. Denham had befriended her in port and she was determined to stick by his side.

King Kong on display in New York.

Helen Mack and Robert Armstrong find the *Son of Kong* stuck in quicksand.

During the voyage, the crew decides to forgo a visit to the monster-infested atoll and sets Denham, Helstrom, Englehorn, Hilda, and the cook Charlie (Victor Wong) adrift in a rowboat. Arriving at Skull Island, the party splits up. While searching for a place to establish camp, Denham and Hilda discover "little" Kong, a twelve-foot tall white gorilla. He's stuck in quicksand. Denham pushes a tree into the pit and the friendly ape climbs out. Later, the monkey repays the favor by murdering a huge cave bear and a studio-invented dragon that menace our heroes. By the end of the film, Denham has found the treasure, and the island is rocked by an earthquake. Denham and the giant ape are trapped in a cave; Helstrom is devoured by a sea serpent; Hilda, Englehorn, and Charlie rush to the rowboat. The Son of Kong frees himself and Denham from their craggy prison, but much to their chagrin they find that the island is sinking. While Englehorn and Hilda row quickly to the small nub of rock that remains, young Kong holds Denham above the storm-whipped waters. Only after the adventurer has been placed safely in the boat does the gorilla release his grip and vanish beneath the waves. Denham, the Skull Island diamonds in hand, is once more wealthy and, as we will see, "returns" to the screen in fifteen years, once more involved with a giant ape.

It's unfortunate that *Son of Kong* must live in the shadow of its dynamic predecessor. The young gorilla is played for laughs, his mien that of a cherub

Robert Armstrong bandages *Son of Kong's* finger with a piece of Helen Mack's slip. In this sequence, the arm was actually constructed to scale. It was mechanically operated off screen and could open and close.

rather than a king. Little Kong's gestures—such as looking at the audience and shrugging when he doesn't understand something Denham has done, or barging in on Hilda and Denham in a moment of intimacy and covering his mouth to suppress a snicker—are contrived to make him our pal instead of the towering figure his father was. Therein lies the rub. When King Kong died, we were saddened at the injustice of his demise, the tragic fall of a monarch. We're made to feel sorry for Kong's son simply because he is so cute. His death would be equivalent to watching a puppy drown, and the emotion it inspires is more naggingly superficial than the defeat of Kong. This tacky approach is unfortunate, for the film does showcase, again, marvelous mannerisms and personality drawn from a molded figurine, some clever dialogue, and fine acting. Especially well done is the final cataclysm. Alas, *Son of Kong* simply hasn't the heart of the original. Indeed, it is rumored that O'Brien, dissatisfied with the light approach of the film, did little of the animation himself.

Son of Kong did only moderately well at the box office; audiences responding negatively to the teddy-bear approach of the filmmakers. There were no further sequels, and O'Brien became involved with other projects, such as *Last Days of Pompeii* (1935), *War Eagles*, and *Valley of Mist*. *War Eagles*, the story of natives who attack New York City astride giant birds only to be beaten back by dirigibles was dropped in 1939 after six months of

Son of Kong battles a monster to save his human friends. The idol behind Miss Mack and Armstrong was where they found the treasure of Skull Island.

Original ad-art for *Mighty Joe Young.*

preproduction work. Merian Cooper had been in the army and, upon his return, decided that airships, an integral part of the story, had become obsolete. *Valley of Mist*, built around the discovery of dinosaurs in the American West, was similarly canceled when Paramount and Jesse Lasky Sr. decided it would take too long and cost too much to produce. The film *was* eventually made as *Beast of Hollow Mountain* (1956), using O'Brien's plot but not his animation. This film, in turn, was remade by Harryhausen as *Valley of Gwangi* (1969). More on both pictures later in the chapter.

Valley of Mist was to have spotlighted scenes of cowboys roping dinosaurs. Since footage had already been shot to test the feasibility of the theme, the idea was retained for O'Brien's next project, *Mighty Joe Young* (1949). The result was a somewhat contrived story of a gorilla raised by Jill Young (Terry Moore), mistress of an African plantation. To the veldt comes Max O'Hara (Robert Armstrong), a theatrical entrepreneur who is capturing animals to display in his new Hollywood nightclub *The Golden Safari*. When Joe attacks Max's camp, he is lassoed by the cowboys Max brought along for his bizarre roundup. Snapping the ropes after a ferocious battle, the ape scales a cliff, plucks Max from his horse, and is about to kill him when Jill arrives. She commands Joe to put the man down. Turning to Max's top cowboy Gregg Johnson (Ben Johnson), she explains that they are encroaching on her land. When the showman hears this, it is evident he could care less. He wants Joe and Jill for his nightclub and convinces them to

Primo Carnera battles *Mighty Joe Young* during the nightclub act.

come to Hollywood. After seventeen weeks of standing-room-only performances, Jill realizes she had made a mistake. The ten-foot-tall Joe is terribly unhappy being locked in a jail cell beneath the club. Jill resolves to return to Africa with Joe and Gregg, with whom she has fallen in love. Unfortunately, some drunks get to Joe just after a show and feed him liquor. Inebriated, the gorilla breaks from his cell and destroys the club. The police decide that Joe is a menace and order that he be shot.

Max feels guilty about the verdict and bribes the captain of a steamer to carry Joe back to Africa. Meanwhile, Jill and Gregg sneak the ape from his jail cell into a van. The police pick up their trail and follow. En route to the dock, the refugees pass a burning orphange. At Jill's urging, Joe scales a tree beside the building to save a child trapped on the top floor. Unfortunately, the structure collapses, felling Joe and the tree. The baby is unharmed, but the ape is hurt. Because of his heroism, however, the police spare Joe and he is allowed to return to Africa with Jill and Gregg.

Ray Harryhausen did most of the animation in *Mighty Joe Young*, Willis O'Brien's time being consumed with the designing of intricate technical setups. Marcel Delgado was again on-hand to build the models. For the team's efforts on this film, Willis O'Brien, the father of Kong, won a well-deserved Oscar for Best Special Effects.

Like *Son of Kong*, Joe is the star of his film. His acting range is a marvel, spanning the conditions of fear, indecision, terror, drunkenness, joy, and depression. Again, however, the filmmakers chose to create some very trite situations for a character whose nobility and stature deserved greater respect. The most glaring of these occur one after the other. Chased by the police, the ape pokes his head from the back of the truck and spits at them, wiping his mouth contentedly. Satisfied with this, Joe sits down and starts drumming his knees as though bored and looking for something to do. Like everything else associated with Joe, the technical work is virtuoso; only the sense of it is somehow lacking.

As for the ape's human counterparts, Armstrong's Denham-rehashed is embarrassingly out of date, while Terry Moore's Jill is so pristinely sweet as to make the character depthless. Only Ben Johnson's drawling, easy-going cowboy is at all effective, along with Regis Toomey as Max's exasperated press agent.

A sequence showing the death throes of *The Beast from Twenty Thousand Fathoms*.

Eventually, the Cooper-O'Brien return to Kong's territory crept to a profit. It was not, however, the runaway success that RKO had hoped would justify its considerable cost. Thus, while O'Brien became locked in several ultimately unrealized projects, his student Harryhausen moved to more successfully market his skills. In so doing, he latched onto a career that has given the screen an unbroken flow of first-class fantasies. The first of these was *Beast From Twenty Thousand Fathoms* (1953). A fictitious rhedosaur, the Beast was unleashed from eons of glacial imprisonment by atom bomb tests in the Arctic. The monster destroyed ships and villages along the North Atlantic on its

way to ancestral burial grounds in New York's Hudson River. After flattening Manhattan, the creature came ashore at Coney Island's amusement park where its viscera were reduced to ash by a radioactive isotope fired through a bazooka wound in the monster's neck. Based on the short story by Harryhausen's lifelong friend Ray Bradbury, *Beast From Twenty Thousand Fathoms* started the fear-of-science films that so inundated the fifties. Atom bombs especially brought the world symbolic destruction by resurrecting all manner of prehistoric beast. After rousing the rhedosaur, for example, nuclear tests killed the fish of the ocean, which forced Harryhausen's second creation to surface

120

for food in *It Came From Beneath the Sea* (1955). The enormous octopus descended upon San Francisco where it rent to scrap metal the newly completed Golden Gate Bridge, and caused similar devestation throughout the metropolis before having an electric torpedo drilled into its brain.

Although nature's vengeance against man did not stop with the death of the cephalopod, Harryhausen himself explored new territories. His next fantasy project was *Animal World*, buffered on either side by the science-fiction films *Earth vs. the Flying Saucers* (1955) and *Twenty Million Miles to Earth* (1957). In this latter film—featuring Harryhausen's finest animation to date—an egg from Venus hatched on Earth unleashing a reptilian creature. The *Ymir* grew several yards in height daily, due to the strangeness of earth's atmosphere. When it was large enough to run rampant in Rome, it annihilated the Italian landmarks, killed an elephant, and met its own death in a fall from atop the Colosseum. After the considerable success of this film, Ray and producer Charles H. Schneer took some time off to develop a means of combining stop-motion monsters with live actors in color. The year-long experiments concluded with the patenting of *Dynamation*. Their premiere effort in this process was *Seventh Voyage of Sinbad* (1958), which is discussed in chapter 11.

The five-tentacled octopus—at $10,000 a tentacle, it was all the producers could afford—as seen in *It Came From Beneath the Sea*.

A rare frame blowup showing the Ymir about to further devastate the ruins of Rome in *Twenty Million Miles to Earth.*

Meanwhile, on the other side of the world, a phenomenon was aborning. Japan, the logical seat of antagonism toward the atom bomb, recreated Hiroshima and Nagasaki in *Godzilla* (1954). The "Bomb" was a two-hundred-and-fifty-foot-tall, four-hundred-ton dragon; the plot was not remarkably different than *Beast From Twenty Thousand Fathoms.* A fictitious dinosaur was raised from ages of hibernation by the Bikini atom tests. With mindless intent and a seering incendiary ray, the monster destroyed ships, menaced isolated islands, and finally lumbered from Tokyo Bay to demolish the great Japanese city. His destructive swath was so

absolute as to make the Harryhausen beasts seem like angels of mercy.

Why the Japanese set loose such incredible fury on their homeland is curious. Perhaps, with *Godzilla* coming so soon after the war, theirs was the only stomping ground the destruction of which would not seem the enactment of some vicarious vendetta. However, whatever the reason, there is a strange and frightening catharsis to Godzilla's twin descents on Tokyo. The creature's onslaught was so thorough, so irreovcable that by picture's end the viewer had been saturated with crumbling buildings and blazing city blocks. Whether intentionally or

Godzilla is his first screen appearance.

film became one of that year's great successes in Japan and America.[11] A sequel was rushed into production and other monsters were hurried from the drawing board to the screen.

The first Godzilla followup was *Godzilla's Counterattack* (1955). Of course, it was imposible for even the magic of the movies to revive a monster that had been vaporized. Therefore, to avoid confusion, the picture was retitled *Gigantis, The Fire Monster*. The plot had two Japanese pilots discover Gigantis and a prehistoric quadruped named Angorus battling to the death on a remote island. Eventually, the monsters struggled their way into Japan doing an even more thorough job of destruction than Godzilla. Unfortunately, unlike *Godzilla*, the special effects in *Gigantis* were quite shoddy. The monsters were filmed at normal camera speed, and were shot straight on, rather than from a low angle. Thus, there was no illusion of enormity. The effect was that of an Halloween party gone awry with the two monsters looking very rubbery and very silly. In the end, Angorus was defeated and, back on his island, Gigantis was buried beneath tons of ice, courtesy of a Japanese aerial bombardment.

Toho's next creation, and one that would rival Godzilla in popularity, was *Rodan* (1956), twin pteranodons hatched from age-old eggs by fresh air brought to their subterranean cavern through the world's deepest mine shaft. The enormous birds, one male and the other female, flew forth at supersonic speeds to destroy the air force and a sizeable chunk of Japan. With a wingspread of over five hundred feet, the dinosaurs created winds that carried tanks, bridges, and people through the air, while with beak and talon they tore at buildings. After the Orient was properly humbled, it regrouped its armies and sent a barrage of missiles against the Rodans' mountainside cavern. The projectiles caused it to erupt, drowning the birds in a sea of lava. Shot in color, with the monster scenes filmed at high speeds, *Rodan* was a return to the high quality of *Godzilla*.

It would be several years before the next Japanese monster films, and the interim saw a surge in American elaborations on the theme. An enormous mollusk, released from its suboceanic lair by underwater demolition in Nevada's Salton Sea, attacked a naval research base in *The Monster That Challenged the World* (1956). Unfortunately, his thrown gauntlet was accepted by Lt. Commander

no, Toho International and their late, great special effectsman Eiji Tsuburaya forged a brass-filled symphony of disaster that leaves us gasping for the whisper of woodwinds. It is somewhat sobering to think that we are so voyeuristic as to need the purging of *Godzilla*.

Quite naturally, Tsuburaya and his staff were careful to execute their special effects with precision. Godzilla was a man in a monster suit[10] who traipsed through a soundstage full of miniature sets. Ordinarily, as we have noted, this means of monster-making is inferior to stop-motion. However, the Toho technicians gave their monster costume remarkable flexibility and, since Godzilla was never intended to be other than a mindless tool of destruction, his lack of emotional range was perfectly in tune with the theme. Again, the creature was shot at high speed to give the impression of mass and bulk.

Cornered in Tokyo Bay by a marine and a scientist, Godzilla was asphyxiated by the latter's rather contrived oxygen destroyer, a device designed to eliminate breatheable air from water. The

Angorus vs. Godzilla in *Gigantis, the Fire Monster.*

John Twillinger (Tim Holt), who scalded the monster to death with clouds of steam.

To the south of this crustaceous menace was the long-overdue screen appearance of Willis O'Brien's *Valley of Mist*. Padded with cattle stampedes and gunplay, *The Beast From Hollow Mountain* emerged an unusual Western-Monster film. Strange deaths and missing livestock caused cowboy Guy Madison to investigate a valley that had long been taboo for the local citizenry. Therein he and Carlos Rivas, his rival for the hand of heroine Patricia Medina, found a tyrannosaur. After Rivas was pulled from a cave and mangled by the beast, it attacked Miss Medina, who had taken refuge in a nearby shack. The creature tore down the house, but, using himself as bait, Madison roped a tree limb, swung over a quicksand pit, and lured the monster to his death. In contrast to the twelve-foot-tall mechanical creature used in *The Monster*

That Challenged the World, The Beast From Hollow Mountain was a well-animated stop-motion model that had been built by Marcel Delgado for the *Valley of Mist* project. As well, the tyrannosaur film is noteable for being the first stop-motion monster production shot in color. While the effect was crude, with the raw color film stock ruining many process shots due to its inflexible grain, it was a special effects landmark of sorts.

In another part of the world, atom tests, ala *Beast From Twenty Thousand Fathoms*, melted an ice berg and set free the giant, prehistoric *Deadly Mantis* (1957). Following in the footsteps of such science-fiction bug films as the ant-filled *Them!* (1953), *The Tarantula* (1955), and the radioactivated grasshopper giants in Bert I. Gordon's *Beginning of the End* (1957), the *Deadly Mantis* preyed on landmarks like the Washington Monument before being gassed to death in New York's Holland

An example of the excellent Japanese miniatures used in *Rodan*. Notice how the low angle of the camera gives the monster a sense of giantism.

Rodan is caught in the manmade volcano and is scalded to death.

An example of the schlock publicity stills that proliferated the fifties. From *The Monster That Challenged the World*.

march through London, scorched half the populace to death with his very presence. The monster was finally beaten when a radium-tipped torpedo was fired into his mouth, thus speeding up the natural disintegration process spawned by the atom bomb. For this latter film, O'Brien and Peterson were joined by the team that had animated *Beast From Hollow Mountain*, Jack Rabin and Louis DeWitt.

Both *The Black Scorpion* and *The Giant Behemoth* were technically interesting, although the stories were far from extraordinary. The finest moment between the two came in *The Black Scorpion* when the insects attacked a passenger train. Rather sadly, it forces one to recall King Kong's similar attack on a Manhattan elevated train. As for *The Giant Behemoth*, although care was taken to mold the skin of the stop-motion model directly from a lizard, there is no animation for the first half of the film. Until the monster comes ashore, all we see is a poor, plaster head and neck of the monster that is poked through miniature reconstructions of the Thames and is used to sink a toy ferry boat. In anyone's lexicon, it is unfortunate that these films stand as the final monster animations of the great Willis O'Brien.

Back in Japan, a primitive lizard-god rose from

Tunnel. Another insect monster followed hard-upon, Bert I. Gordon's *The Spider* (1958). The huge tarantula menaced a Midwestern town for which effort he was electrocuted in his subterranean lair.

After completing *Animal World* with Ray Harryhausen, and prior to being saddled with the remake of *The Lost World*, Willis O'Brien helmed *The Black Scorpion* (1956) and *The Giant Behemoth* (1958). *The Black Scorpion* was animated with the help of Pete Peterson and told the tale of an eruption that caused giant insects to crawl from the center of the earth. Carlos Rivas was back to battle the monsters, along with Richard Denning who had only recently returned from the *Unknown Island*. After striking terror into the hearts of Mexican peasants, the title creature descended upon Mexico City where it was burned to death in a sports arena. *The Giant Behemoth*, on the other hand, was another *Beast From Twenty Thousand Fathoms* off-shoot, a prehistoric monster wakened from sleep by atom tests. These blasts also seemed to have irradiated the Behemoth who, on his destructive

An interesting study of the stop-motion allosaur known as *The Beast of Hollow Mountain*.

126

The Beast of Hollow Mountain attacks the shed in which
Patricia Medina is hiding.

his bottomless lake to halt Japanese desalinization of his home in *Varan the Unbelievable* (1958). A careless film, Varan is the only monster that did not return in any of Toho's many sequels. Even worse than the Oriental effort, however, were a pair of American films that, to their credit, made money but contributed nothing to the genre. *The Giant Gila Monster* menaced teenagers in a small New Mexican town, while the *Attack of the Giant Leeches* (1959), a Roger Corman film, carried the action to the swamps of Florida. More interesting was *Caltiki, the Immortal Monster* (1959), a pulsating blob that rose from the pool of an ancient tomb to kill trespassing explorers. Dividing into an army of monsters, Caltiki was vanquished in the end by army flame-throwers. This Italian effort, photographed by Mario Bava, was several notches above its American counterpart, *The Blob* (1959), a gelatinous mass from outer space.

Watching this endless parade of sensationally packaged dross—what youngster could resist a film that showed an incredible monster devouring people and cities both?—the King Brothers of England had the idea to do a high-quality monster-on-the-loose film. They commissioned Eugene Lourie, director of *Beast From Twenty Thousand Fathoms*, to helm their picture and backed the project with well over a half-million dollars. The result was *Gorgo* (1962), a sixty-foot-tall monster stirred from the ocean's depths by an undersea volcano. Captured by two down-and-out seamen, the creature is carried to London where, despite protestations from paleontologists, it is put on display at Dworkin's Circus. Gorgo remains a popular display until its two-hundred-foot-tall mother comes calling. She batters her way up the Thames, destroying London Bridge, Big Ben, Westminster Abbey, and Piccadilly Circus. After freeing her

The plastic, unmoving head of *The Giant Behemoth* attacks a ferry . . .

. . . in marked contrast to the beautifully crafted stop-motion monster that marches through London later in the film.

child, the monsters amble back into the sea.

Gorgo featured $75,000 worth of excellent miniature sets, along with a flawed but satisfying monster. Filmed in a process known as *Automotion*, the creature was alternately a man in a costume, a small mechanical model, and, most startling of all, a full-size replica, which was used when the captured beast was paraded through the streets of London. The giant model, lashed to the back of a flat-truck, came complete with snarls, snapping jaws, and rolling, blinking eyes. The miniature machine, limited to growls, a shuffling gait, and awkward vertical swipes with its arms, was much less convincing. Fortunately, compensation was made by

Lourie who brought us the finest performances this genre has ever seen. Abetted by rich color photography, *Gorgo* was perhaps the slickest of the monster-on-the-loose sagas. Unfortunately, it did not do as well at the box office as the producers had hoped, and there were no sequels.

Shifting from foggy England to the steaming tropics, in *Dinosaurus* (1962) the construction crew of Bart Thompson (Ward Ramsey) discovered a tyrannosaur, brontosaur, and caveman beneath the sea, locked in suspended animation. Revived by lightning, the dinosaurs begin to fight as the caveman prowls the island in search of unprotected ladies. After a time, the tyrannosaur slaughters the

STRIPPING HUMAN FLESH FROM BONE
...CREEPING, MULTIPLYING, DEVOURING
...HUNGRY FOR THE BLOOD
OF A WORLD!

An example of Hollywood hard-sell. The poster for *Caltiki, the Immortal Monster* promises a volcano, crumbling statues, an incredible monster, and decimated cities. There is even the hint of a Frankenstein Monster in the lower lefthand corner. In fact . . .

. . . Caltiki was a rather boring blob who did little destruction. The "Frankenstein Monster" was, in actuality, the eaten remains of the fellow on the floor.

Gorgo levels a London landmark.

Ward Ramsey and his derrick push the tyrannosaur
from a cliff in *Dinosaurus*.

brontosaur and is knocked from a cliff by Thompson's derrick; the Neanderthal is buried in a mine disaster. Produced by Jack H. Harris, the man who gave us *The Blob, Dinosaurus* is untaxing entertainment that highlights average stop-motion models built by Marcel Delgado and animation by contemporaries of Jim Danforth: Wah Chang and Tim Barr.[12] By this time, of course, the cost of quality stop-motion work had soared, prohibiting American filmmakers from dabbling in the special-effects process. For this reason, Harryhausen had shifted his operations from Hollywood to England. Likewise, other motion-picture people were setting up shop abroad. One of these men was Sidney Pink who moved a unit to Denmark where, for a nominal sum, he was able to film *Reptilicus* (1962). Reptilicus is a prehistoric (sic) beast whose tail is unearthed by an oil drill. Taken to a lab, the segment regenerates into a new monster that terrorizes Copenhagen and murders thousands of Danes by spewing forth a viscous white poison. Reptilicus is finally blown to pieces, but the audience is left to wonder, as small fragments of monster flesh begin to quiver, if we have, in fact, seen the end of Reptilicus. Although this was an open invitation for a second film, *Reptilicus* did not make the killing that Pink had anticipated, and no further films appeared. If nothing else, this proved that in 1962 neither an elaborate and thoughtful monster film like *Gorgo*, or a puppet on often-visible wires like *Reptilicus*, could force itself easily into the black. The reason for this, of course, was that Japan had cornered the market. Not only was Japanese labor less expensive than anywhere else, but Japanese technicians had perfected the art of constructing realistic miniatures. They destroyed these with gusto and in great number. On a different level entirely, their beasts were soon transformed from villains to heroes, and youngsters loved it!

Mothra (1961) was the first export of the decade and it made a mint. Although the film was still caught in the original mold of the monster as an avenging angel, kids ran to see the colorful, brilliantly executed tale. Mothra, a huge caterpillar, journeys from its South Pacific island to rescue a pair of six-inch-tall priestesses (Emi and Yumi Ito), who had been kidnapped by Toho's answer to Carl Denham. When the monster centipede reaches Japan, it spins a cocoon on the ruins of the Tokyo Tower and emerges an enormous moth. With a wingspan that causes hurricane winds throughout

Mothra lands to pick up her two High Priestesses.

the city, Mothra batters the populace into submission and the twins are returned. Appeased, the creature flies to its island in peace.

Since *Mothra* hasn't *Godzilla's* fear of the atom-age spun throughout its fabric, the film comes across as a light parable. The destruction wreaked by Mothra is all very impersonal; the human element lies in the exotic natives who honor and worship the monster and their culture, and in the capitalist entrepreneurs who sneer at these traditions. In essence, then, *Mothra* is a victory for fantasy over the cold touch of the dollar bill. While it is not our intent to overintellectualize what is first and foremost a monster film, the picture does portray imagination and magic in a reverent light.

Before the newly recruited members of the monster-movie public could catch their collective breath, the battle of the century was upon them: *King Kong vs. Godzilla* (1962). The famous ape, captured on Skull Island (sic), is transported to Japan. Simultaneously, Godzilla breaks free from the iceberg in which he had been imprisoned at the end of *Gigantis, the Fire Monster.* After destroying their respective cities, Kong is reunited with "Fay Wray" (Mei Hama), and the monsters meet on Mt. Fuji. Despite the havoc wrought by each creature, nationalism takes hold of us and we root for the homegrown monster. Godzilla kicks boulders at Kong, scorches his chest with fiery breath, and laughs with glee at the simian's predicament. Then, as is only fair, the amphibian takes a severe beating from the infuriated ape. Finally, both beasts topple from the mountain slopes into the sea. In the

131

King Kong vs. Godzilla, with Kong getting the worst of
the bargain.

Frankenstein Conquers the World, but first he must deal
with Baragon.

European and American versions, Kong swims home victorious. For the patriotic Japanese audiences, Godzilla wins the struggle. It's all academic, however, since both monsters survived to return in sequels.

A disappointment for both Kong fans—O'Brien's animated monster had been replaced by a man in a stiff monkey suit—and Godzilla fans—the behemoth had been transformed from an engine of destruction to a comedian—the film was on target in terms of what the public wanted to see. Consequently, it was a huge success. The film also gave Godzilla the foundation of his new folk-hero image and, much to the dismay of Toshiro Mifune, established the monster as that nation's top box-office star.

Without taking time to look their gift monsters in the mouth, Toho pit Godzilla against Mothra in *Godzilla vs. The Thing* (1964). Hurricane winds wash Mothra's enormous egg to the Japanese shore. Placed in an incubator, the egg is attacked by Godzilla. Meanwhile, the giant moth has located her missing spawn and beats Godzilla back. The titans struggle and, by battle's end, Mothra has grabbed her nemesis by the tail and dumps him into the sea. The egg hatches, and Mothra returns home with her caterpillar offspring.

After *Godzilla vs. The Thing*, Toho prepared for the eventuality that Godzilla's rat pack might eventually overstay their welcome. The studio therefore explored other areas of the monster genre by concocting *Frankenstein Conquers the World* (1964), in which a child, deformed by the Hiroshima blast, grows to monstrous proportions. After being studied in a hospital—where the late Nick Adams is a physician—the monster goes out into the world to do battle with a giant devilfish and Baragon, an electrically charged dinosaur from inside the earth. Thoughtlessly made, and an ill-conceived melding of the Universal Karloff monster with the Japanese mythos, *Frankenstein Conquers the World* ended up a disappointing, one-shot film. Another once-only monster was *Dagora, The Space Monster* (1964), a tentacled bloblike creature who came to earth in search of food. Since his nutritional craving was for diamonds, earth dispatched the creature with admirable alacrity.

Returning to more familiar territory, Toho introduced yet another creature, *Ghidrah, The Three Headed Monster* (1965). Supported, this time, by Godzilla, Rodan, and the son of Mothra, the film

Ghidrah, the Three Headed Monster battles Godzilla, Rodan, and the caterpillar Mothra (lower right hand corner).

was a great success and made Ghidrah one of the Toho staples. In the studio's most impeccable, most elaborate production, a huge meteor comes screaming through the earth's atmosphere to crash in the Japanese countryside. It soon develops that the cosmic visitor is actually an egg, which hatches and sends forth a huge fireball. Slowly, the flaming issue takes shape and becomes Ghidrah. The winged beast scours the land destroying forests and cities with its fiery breath and mighty limbs. Meanwhile, Rodan has burst from the lava pit in which he had been buried a decade before, the caterpillar Mothra

A rare frame blowup of the monsters from *War of the Gargantuas*. The film played this country on a double bill with *Monster Zero*.

has been sent from her island by the twin priestesses, and Godzilla reappears, all to do battle with Ghidrah on Mt. Fuji. The outer-space visitor is bested, but the monsters are not permitted a respite. Godzilla and Rodan returned to fight *Monster Zero* (1965), who is none other than Ghidrah. This time the two "good" monsters are loaned to an alien world whose surface is being ravaged by the great dragon. Earth's reward for its cooperation is invasion by the aliens, said attack being nipped in the bud by our armies and monsters. *Godzilla vs. The Sea Monster* (1966) was next, with the king of the monsters awakened from slumber in an island volcano to do battle with Ebirah, an enormous lobster. The job proves to be a difficult one, however, and a winged Mothra is called in to assist.

Meanwhile, American star Russ Tamblyn went to Japan for Toho's *War of The Gargantuas* (1967), a film originally slated to star Toho's abyssmal Frankenstein Monster. To disassociate this film from its predecessor, the plot was reworked to tell the story of a peaceful brown-furred giant from whose cells is cloned an evil green twin. The monsters have a bitter dispute over how to deal with humankind. This difference of opinion culminates in a struggle that levels Japan and ends only when a volcanic eruption destroys both monsters. The film did not achieve any greater success than its non-Godzillian predecessor. Clearly, the lesson had been learned that a new monster must be buffered by the presence of a Toho mainstay in order to survive. Thus, the studio's next character was the inevitable *Son of Godzilla* (1968), a precocious and pug-faced creation able to exhale only smoke rings as opposed to his father's mighty radioactive breath. In his film debut, the Son of Godzilla is shown being raised on

King Kong Escapes and battles Gorosaurus, while the mechanical Kong levels the Tokyo Tower.

134

the island last seen in *Godzilla vs. The Sea Monster*. During the course of the film, the father-and-son team battles a trio of giant mantises and a monster spider known as Spiga. Despite their victories, however, Godzilla is dissatisfied with his son's performance. Following the example of human parents, the once soulless creature spanks and chastises his child. So much for Dr. Spock.

Giving the Godzilla family a brief vacation, Toho turned to King Kong for their next film, the juvenile, noncomedic *King Kong Escapes* (1967). The great ape is reunited with his love, Mie Hama, and journeys to Japan for battle with a robot-Kong built by the Red Chinese. Although every plot development is geared to hurry along a confrontation between Kong and his mechanical counterpart, there is time set aside to re-create at least one scene from the 1933 original. When a submarine docks at the gorilla's island, the party—including American actor Rhodes Reason—is attacked by a tyrannosaur, referred to in press releases as Gorosaurus. Kong appears to subdue the beast, although Gorosaurus returns to fight Ghidrah in *Destroy All Monsters* (1968). The men in costumes were hardly as effective as O'Brien's stop-motion models. Their movements were rubbery, and their faces were without expression. For some reason, however, Toho chose to shelve the standard comic histrionics for a more serious confrontation. The results were ludicrous. The spirit that had made the original *Godzilla* so effective had long ago vanished. In its place were fading budgets and gaudy color. Since there was no longer the heart to take their monsters seriously, the only possible approach was with tongue-in-cheek. Any divergence from this path, as in the Kong-Gorosaurus battle, was destined to fail.

As if to support this observation, the next Godzilla film required a scorecard to follow the action. Rodan, the caterpillar Mothra, Spiga, Manda—a giant snake—Angorus, Baragon, Gorosaurus, Godzilla, and his son Minya teamed to battle Ghidrah in the epic *Destroy All Monsters*. As the film opens, we see that the monsters—with the exception of Ghidrah—are all living peacefully on Monster Island. Upsetting this harmony are the alien Kilaaks, rocklike beings who assume human form and take control of the monsters' minds. Turned against mankind, the creatures ravage the world until Japan is able to destroy the Kilaak base on earth's moon. The monsters then turn on the Kilaaks' trump card, Ghidrah, and, destroying him,

return to Monster Island. Following this saga, Toho itself took a breather by issuing an album film of Godzilla's fiercest battles. Entitled *Godzilla's Revenge* (1969), it was superficially the story of a boy who is constantly being bullied about and, for escape, dreams of visiting Monster Island. There, he meets Minya who recounts his father's greatest exploits. When Minya himself is called upon to do battle with a beast many times his size, the boy finds this inspirational. He returns to reality and confronts his own problems head-on. An effective fantasy parable, *Godzilla's Revenge* made a valid point comprehensible to children, while still managing to entertain. Perhaps, in their monsters, Toho has also found a viable alternative to the pretentious *Sesame Street!*

While isolated efforts such as *Gappa, The Triphibian Monster* (1967) came from other Japanese studios, Canadian producer Marvin Newland took an heretical stab at both Toho and Walt Disney. The half-minute long *Bambi Meets Godzilla* (1969) begins with the deer grazing contentedly and ends when a massive reptilian foot descends from above to crush the animal. Currently the most popular art-house short-subject extant, *Bambi Meets Godzilla* was included in Filmways' *Genesis II* (1969) release, a feature-length compilation of great short films.

More orthodox fare, but still a departure from Toho's norm, was the one-shot *Yog, Monster From Space* (1970). A life force from the asteroid belt, Yog inhabits the bodies of such creatures as a crab, a turtle, and an octopus causing them to grow huge. The being is destroyed by ultrahigh frequency sound, but not before he has raped and plundered our planet in typical Toho style. An even more unusual monster than Yog, however, was Hedorah, the second half of the ticket in *Godzilla vs. The Smog Monster* (1971). Hedorah is formed by industrial wastes accumulated in the bay of Suruga City. Growing to a height of two-hundred feet, the Smog Monster flies through the air feeding on atmospheric pollution and the refuse of factories. Enter Godzilla, who battles and subdues the globular mass. Following this bout, the reptile was summoned for his next annual exercise, this time with Ghidrah and an ivory-clawed, web-backed biped in *Godzilla vs. Gigan* (1972). Most recently, Toho's dinosaur has seen action in *Godzilla vs. Megalon* (1974) and *Godzilla vs. Mechagodzilla* (1975), which pits him against Angorus and a mechanical

Two of the forms taken by *Yog*: a monster turtle and a huge lobster.

next seen in *Return of the Giant Monsters* (1967). In this film, Gamera battles Gaos, a flying monster from whose mouth issues a scathing laser beam. The fourth Gamera picture, *Destroy All Planets* (1968) has Viras, a giant alien-controlled starfish, visit the earth to tangle with our heroic turtle. Venturing into space, Gamera next encountered Guiron in *Attack of the Monsters* (1969). Guiron, an absurd knife-shaped monster, is the slave of brain-eating girls whose planet is in earth orbit on the other side of the sun. Hard upon, Jiger, guardian of an ancient stone god, follows the kidnapped stature to Expo '70 where the spear-exhaling monster battles Gamera in *Gamera vs. Monster X* (1970). At one point in the film, the wily Jiger lances Gamera's legs, neck, and arms making it impossible for the turtle to withdraw them and rocket away. Eventually, however, Gamera works the spears free and emerges triumphant. Finally, in the last film to date, *Gamera vs. Zigra* (1971), a monster fish from earth's prehistory.

Because of Japanese saturation in this monster-on-the-loose market, few American filmmakers bothered with it after 1962. Studios like American International were content to simply buy the rights to these foreign films and release them directly to

replica of himself. Will there be no rest for this phenomenal monster? As long as the public continues to be disappointed in its human heroes it will turn to Godzilla for selfless and mighty action.

Despite the overwhelming box-office strength of Godzilla, Japan's Daiei Films brought forth a series monster of their own. Gamera is a giant prehistoric turtle who, like Godzilla, is a friend to mankind. Withdrawing arms, feet, and head into his shell, Gamera is able to spit fire through these openings and soar through space via jet propulsion. In the first film, *Gamera The Invincible* (1966), the titanic tortoise is freed from a glacier by atom-bomb tests. Since he has not yet been domesticated by Daiei, Gamera decimates all of Tokyo before being decoyed into the nosecone of a giant rocket and shot to Mars. Returning to earth later that year—a meteor has knocked the rocket off course and back to earth—Gamera defends our planet against Barugon in *War of the Monsters*. Barugon—not to be confused with Toho's Baragon—fires a ray from his back that immobilizes potential enemies. Despite this power, he was defeated by Gamera who was

An unusual still of Godzilla as he prepares to battle Hedorah in *Godzilla vs. The Smog Monster*.

136

Ray Harryhausen's original sketch showing the roping of Gwangi . . .

. . . and how that same scene looked on the screen. From *Valley of Gwangi*.

A lifesize, immobile model of Gwangi is transported to civilization in *Valley of Gwangi*.

. . . and the cage door comes crashing down on Laurence Naismith. From *Valley of Gwangi*.

United States television. Certainly there was no competing with Toho or Daiei for a share of the crucial overseas ticket. However, at the height of the Japanese hold on the market, Ray Harryhausen and producer Charles H. Schneer decided to join monsters with the big foreign box office of cowboys in *Valley of Gwangi* (1969). This film was more or less a literal adaptation of Willis O'Brien's defunct *Valley of Mist*, which had also gone under the name of *Gwangi*.

Gwangi, a tyrannosaur, is snatched from his Forbidden Valley in Mexico by circus owner Champ (Richard Carlson). Unfortunately, a blind Indian seer Tia (Freda Jackson) had promised death to anyone who tampered with native taboos. She has her midget aide unlock Gwangi's cage. When the curtains rise on opening night, the monster

breaks free. After killing an elephant and storming through town, the dinosaur is trapped by Tuck (James Franciscus) in a nearby cathedral. Snapping at the American, Gwangi tips over a lighted brazier and is killed in the ensuing blaze.

Valley of Gwangi did poorly at the box office. Although it is probably the least remarkable of Harryhausen's films, *Gwangi* deserved more than the ignominious "dumping" that studios are wont to give unobtrusive little adventure films. A more telling complication, of course, was that at the time, with the exception of kiddie matinees, theatres were booking what the public wanted to see: sex and violence. As Harryhausen appropriately observed, "A naked dinosaur just was not outrageous enough."

11
MYTHOLOGY

So far, we have covered a wide spectrum of oddities ranging from apes to zombies, and from ghosts to Godzilla. One common thread between them all, however, is that each of them performs on the stage of our rational world. The laws of nature govern everything but the very fact that these fantastic creatures exist.

In this chapter, we shall look at movies in which not only are the *antagonists* unique, but all of nature itself has seemingly gone mad. Magic and sorcery abounds; superhuman heroes battle extraordinary foes: and the only boundaries we shall find are the limits set by the filmmakers' imaginations.

One of the early film mythologies was the legend of Siegfried as recounted by Fritz Lang in his epic *Der Nibelungen* (1924). Less loyal to Wagner than to the Norse sagas on which his opera was based, the film is broken into two narrative segments. These are *Siegfried* and *Krimhild's Revenge*. In part one, Siegfried (Paul Richter), with magic powers granted him by the dwarflike Nibelungs—creatures of mist and keepers of a great treasure—takes sword in hand and slays the great dragon Fafner. Bathing in its blood, Siegfried becomes invulnerable and returns to collect the trolls' wealth. Word of his great deed spreads, and Siegfried is invited to the castle of Burgandy's King Gunther (Bernard Goetzke). There, the warrior falls in love with Gunther's sister Krimhild (Margaret Schon). He wins her hand by gaining Queen Brunhilde of Issland (Hanna Ralph) for Gunther. Angered with her defeat, the Virgin Queen orders Gunther's vassal Hagen (Theodor Loos) to kill Siegfried. Learning that a fallen leaf had

prevented the hero's total immersion in Fafner's blood, Hagen drills an arrow home during a hunt, killing Siegfried.

In *Krimhild's Revenge*, Siegfried's wife has married Attila the Hun (Hans Adalbert von Schlettow), and invites the court of her treacherous brother to their camp. She has the guests massacred, murdering Hagen with her own hands. Attila, enraged that so great a warrior should meet an ignominious death, orders Krimhild killed. Thus, very much in the manner of William Shakespeare, a tale that began with great spirit and majesty has ended in a mass murder and emotional depression.

While *Der Nibelungen* abounds with the grotesque charm of its fairy-tale monsters, it is not Fafner or the gnomes that give the film its strongest fantasy element. Rather, it is Lang's potent imagery that lifts *Der Nibelungen* from the world of reality. The misty netherworld of *Siegfried* and the grim coldness of *Krimhild's Revenge* are as integral to Lang's fantastic content as were his visions of the futuristic city to *Metropolis* (1925). Too, there is a timelessness about the work that is not evident in other silent fantasies such as *The Lost World*. This immortality is not unique to *Der Nibelungen*; it is present in most films of mythology. While filmmakers are liable to alter or reinterpret our fears, changing Dracula from the gothic to the sexual, or the innocent *King Kong* to the moral-laden *Godzilla*, mythology stays constant. With its roots firmly planted in our childhood fantasies, it is a genre that, were it to grow up, would die.

Moving from Iceland to the Arabian Nights, we

Douglas Fairbanks watches an amazing display in *Thief of Bagdad*.

find a dramatic shift in mood. Where Paul Richter's Siegfried was grim and determined, Douglas Fairbank's *Thief of Bagdad* (1924) is cocky and free-wheeling. This difference was to be expected.

The Arabian Nights are more opulent and exotic than the folklore of any other culture. This is due, in great part, to the fact that these tales were told for adults, not children. Not surprisingly, this increased their eroticism, since listeners were looking to be entertained rather than informed of some great national hero or preached a lofty moral. Unfortunately, Hollywood has yet to fully exploit the delicate sensuality and Middle Eastern flavor of these wondrous tales.

Thief of Bagdad tells the story of a dashing young rogue whose sole motivation in life is his love for the daughter (Julianne Johnston) of a caliph. To win her in matrimony, he must obtain a magic chest by fighting a dragon, a monster spider, a giant bat, a living tree, and other incredible foes. Returning to Bagdad on a magic carpet, he arrives in time to prevent the city's conquest by invading Mongol hordes. Despite the fanciful narrative trappings, however, *Thief of Bagdad* was first and foremost a vehicle for Fairbanks. The silent star gave his fans

what they wanted to see, which was Fairbanks somersaulting around the lavish Arabian sets, slipping through windows and into rooms, and even getting to ride the back of a winged horse. A more athletic picture could not have been conceived for the star! Too, this film was one of the early tinted pictures, with entire scenes dyed a color that best exemplified the mood of the segment. This added tremendously to the mood with its hazy red-market scenes, deep blue nocturnal jaunts, and so forth.

Over a decade slipped by, and only an occasional tale from Bagdad reached the screen, such as *Ali Baba Goes to Town* (1937) with Eddie Cantor on a flying carpet. Producer Alexander Korda *(Things to Come, Elephant Boy)*, depressed by this, and the lack of imagination in world cinema, determined to create the movies' most spectacular fantasy. Dining one night with Fairbanks, Korda asked to buy the rights to *Thief of Bagdad*. Fairbanks agreed, and the producer replaced his droll, devil-may-care character with an intense, sixteen-year-old South Indian named Sabu. Further, Korda made a careful distinction between the sexual and adventurous elements in his film. Only Sabu, as Abu, was permitted to go on mystical journeys; his leading man, King Ahmad (John Justin) remained in the background to long for the love of a beautiful princess (June Duprez).

The story begins with Ahmad deciding to mingle with his people in order to grow closer to their needs. Upon his return, the king, dressed in rags, is apprehended by his traitorous Grand Vizier, the sorceror Jaffar (Conrad Veidt). Ahmad is declared a madman and is sent to the dungeons. That night, the light-fingered thief Abu is also captured and thrown into Ahmad's cell. Abu lifts the jailor's keys and the pair escapes to the kingdom of Basra. There, Ahmad falls in love with the sultan's beautiful daughter (Miss Duprez). Stealing into her garden, Ahmad admits his love for the girl and she reciprocates. Unfortunately, Jaffar arrives the next day with presents for the sultan (Miles Malleson). Among his gifts is a mechanical flying horse for which the monarch willingly exchanges his daughter. Not wishing to marry Jaffar, the princess flees.

Meanwhile, Ahmad and Abu are found waiting in the royal garden. Brought before Jaffar, the rightful king accuses him of treachery and is struck blind with a sweep of the sorceror's hand. Abu is transformed into a dog, and both insurgents are sent into the street. Months pass. The princess is found by slave traders and is returned to Jaffar. The girl, however, is in a trance from which only Ahmad's embrace will release her. Finding the blind sovereign, who has become a beggar, the sorceror leads him to the princess. Embracing her lover, she recovers from her trance and is promised, by Jaffar, that when she accepts him as her lover, Ahmad and Abu will be cured. She complies and accompanies the sorceror to his waiting ship. The curse lifted, the thief and his king board a small boat and set out in pursuit of Jaffar's galleon. Watching their approach, the wizard summons a storm that batters and sinks the tiny craft.

Abu awakens on a beach where he finds a bottle. Uncorking it, he is greeted by an enormous djinn (Rex Ingram) who proposes to crush the lad underfoot. Abu, thinking quickly, claims that he doesn't really believe the giant came from the bottle. Annoyed at the boy's insolence, the djinn returns to his container simply to prove it can be done. Abu slams the stopper in the bottle and bargains with the genie. In exchange for his freedom, the spirit is forced to promise the boy three wishes. Abu's first request is for food. His second wish is to find Ahmad. This can only be accomplished by stealing the All-Seeing Eye, a job after Abu's heart. The crimson jewel is set in the eye of the Goddess of Light, a statue in the Temple of Dawn atop the world's tallest mountain. Flying to the great peak, Abu scurries up inside the great figure, fights an enormous spider, steals the gem, and sees that

Rex Ingram places Sabu inside the Temple of Dawn. From *Thief of Bagdad*.

Ahmad is in a rocky landscape. He orders the djinn to take him there. Together, Abu and his king gaze into the idol's eye and see that the princess is at Jaffar's palace. Bemoaning his fate, Ahmad wishes that he were in Bagdad. Abu idly seconds the wish. Ahmad disappears and materializes at Jaffar's court. He is taken prisoner and the sorceror declares that both he and his stubborn lover will die at dawn. Meanwhile, the genie is free and leaves the thief alone in the middle of a wilderness.

Angrily, Abu smashes the All-Seeing Eye and finds himself in a settlement—modeled, incidentally, after Korda's own heart—ruled by old men. These ancient sages left the unimaginative world many lifetimes before to establish a land where anything is possible when seen through the eyes of a child. The king of this land presents Abu with a flying carpet and a silver crossbow. Hastening to Bagdad, Abu arrives in time to prevent Ahmad's execution. As Jaffar tries to escape astride his flying horse, Abu kills him with a silver shaft fired through his skull. Days later, with Ahmad restored as king and his princess by his side, Abu rides the magic carpet through a rainbow in search of other adventures.

There have been few films as grand and filled with joy of innocence as *Thief of Bagdad*. Paradoxically, the film is so burdened by the splendor of its production and preoccupation with flashy special effects, that it becomes tedious to watch. Indeed, the lavish mounting of the film would have overwhelmed the audience were it not for the marvelous presence of Veidt, Sabu, and Ingram. In his sincerity

Sabu hitches a ride on Rex Ingram's ear in *Thief of Bagdad*.

and amazement, Sabu helps make the unreal credible; his proud, boastful Abu's interaction with Ingram's boistrous, challenging Genie is the picture's greatest strength. In his few scenes, Conrad Veidt is, as ever, magnificent. His satanic gestures and bodily control are as finely honed here as they were in *Cabinet of Dr. Caligari*. By remaining human and fallible, this phenomenal trio serves as the wing that keeps Korda's glorious dream from falling to earth.

Thief of Bagdad was the first color film to make extensive use of the very specialized kinds of movie effects the story required. Although richly deserving the Oscar it won in 1940 over *One Million B.C.*, the very complex trickery does not hold up today as well as *King Kong* or *Things to Come*. Jarring breaks in credibility such as an immovable sculpted dummy used to simulate the flying djinn are painfully in evidence. The process work[13] on both the flying horse and magic carpet scenes leave much to be desired. Indeed, the film is at its technical best when the effects are accomplished primarily through editing and careful use of props, such as the storm-at-sea sequence. Lifesize reconstructions of the genie's hand and foot are moderately successful.

Thief of Bagdad did, however, establish a standard of production excellence that filmmakers had to find antagonizing. Few Hollywood producers could afford the time or budget that the British-made film enjoyed, and it was a good many years before anyone tried to emulate Korda's spectacular film. Unfortunately, the picture did inspire several popularized and generally tepid interpretations of the Arabian Nights theme, all of which served to downgrade public opinion of the genre.

Sabu was to be typecast for the remainder of his brief life—he died in 1963 of a heart attack—doomed to play a succession of loin-clothed roles that were all but pale shadows of the pungent Abu. The first of these characterizations was in *The Arabian Nights* (1942) in which John Hall sought to win the hand of Maria Montez and overthrow his evil brother Leif Erikson. The film also starred John Qualen and Shemp Howard—one of the Three Stooges—as the clowning Aladdin and Sinbad, respectively. Hall and Miss Montez went from this largely forgotten film to *Ali Baba and the Forty Thieves* (1943), perhaps the finest version of the generally nonfantastic Arabian Night.

Rex Ingram was also plagued by his image and repeated the role of a genie in *A Thousand and One*

Phil Silvers and Cornel Wilde, as Abdullah and Aladdin, neatly kibitz their way out of a prison in *A Thousand and One nights*.

Nights (1945). His talents were wasted as Cornel Wilde and Ingram's co-djinn Evelyn Keyes worked wonders to save a throne, while Wilde's sidekick Phil Silvers, replete with black-rimmed glasses, looked on.

With the support of Anthony Quinn and Maureen O'Hara, Douglas Fairbanks Jr. tried to follow in his father's footsteps as *Sinbad The Sailor* (1947), but the color film lacked both fantasy and a respect for the genre. The same can be said of *Aladdin and His Lamp* (1951), an hour-long retelling of the famous Arabian Nights story.

Odd bits of casting sparked a handful of otherwise routine films: Brooklyn-born Tony Curtis was

John Agar and Patricia Medina onboard *The Magic Carpet*.

The Cyclops chases Sokurah onto the beach and is met by Sinbad and his men in *Seventh Voyage of Sinbad*.

143

the *Son of Ali Baba* (1951), Lucille Ball starred as the heroine of *The Magic Carpet* (1952), and Dale Robertson landed the title role in Howard Hughes' 3-D epic *Son of Sinbad* (1955). Sabu, himself, was again forced into the Arabian Nights with *Sabu and the Magic Ring* (1957); rubbing the enchanted jewel, genie William Marshall appeared!

As is evident by the selections listed above, the difficulty in making a successful fantasy film is that it must be taken seriously. That filmmakers failed to do this is plain in the downward spiral of their produce and its integrity. As long as stock footage and standing sets, costumes, and props were available for the new films, they continued. Eventually, because it had a respect for the amazing, science fiction caught the public's imagination. Theatergoers were calling for trips to the moon, not to Bagdad. However, for many years Ray Harryhausen had been developing a theme for an Arabian Nights story, and he felt that the Cold War world of 1958, ripe with tension, was ready for a film that would provide, in his own words, "some escapism and excursions into the world of the child's imagination."

Recall, if you will, that when we last saw Harryhausen in the fifties, he was experimenting with *Dynamation*. The first showcase for this exciting new process was Ray's Arabian Nights masterpiece the *Seventh Voyage of Sinbad*. To prevent a war between the kingdoms of Chandra and Bagdad, Sinbad (Kerwin Mathews) is to marry Princess Parisa (Kathryn Grant). Since the two are very much in love, this marriage of state doesn't bother them at all. Carrying Parisa to Bagdad for the wedding, Sinbad's ship stops at the Island of Colossa to take on food and water. Once ashore, the small party hears screams. These cries belong to the magician Sokurah (Torin Thatcher) who is fleeing from an enormous cyclops. The sailors spear and distract the fifty-foot-tall monster, while Sokurah summons forth Barani (Richard Eyer), the genie of a magic lamp. The djinn builds an invisible barrier between the men and the cyclops, allowing them to cast off. When Sokurah joins them, the protective shield vanishes. Heaving a huge boulder seaward, the cyclops capsizes their rowboat. The men reach Sinbad's ship, but Sokurah has dropped his lamp. The cyclops retrieves it and departs.

In Bagdad, on the eve of the wedding, Sokurah shrinks Parisa to the size of a doll. Called to the court by Sinbad, Sokurah explains that she can only

be restored with a potion made from the eggshell of Colossa's great bird, the Roc. Sinbad recruits a crew from the prisons of Bagdad and, after commissioning a giant crossbow for protection, sets sail. After quelling a mutiny, Sinbad arrives at the island. Dividing the men into two groups, Sinbad's band is waylaid by the cyclops. The warriors are placed in a cage for future consumption. As the monster proceeds to roast one of the men, Sokurah, who has left his group behind, arrives at the cage, laughs at Sinbad's predicament, and enters the cyclops' cave in search of his lamp. His rifling through the monster's treasure chests alerts the cyclops who investigates. Sinbad, meanwhile, reaches into his clothing and withdraws a tiny box. From within the jeweled case steps the six-inch-tall Parisa. The prince places her on top of the cage and she undoes the latch. The men go free, Sinbad blinds the cyclops with a torch, and then tricks the sightless monster into stepping from a cliff. The lamp, lost by Sokurah in the fray, is retrieved by Sinbad. Hurrying his men along, the Prince of bagdad leads them to the breeding grounds of the Roc. They kill a two-headed, twenty-foot-tall baby bird for food and take a piece of its shell. As they dine, the men are attacked by the murdered chick's parent. Sinbad leaves Parisa's small case on a rock while he does battle with the enormous bird. Slipping away, Sokurah kidnaps the princess while the two-headed giant grabs her fiance within its great talons and flies off.

Some time later, Sinbad awakens in a giant nest and, returning to the site of the battle, finds Parisa missing. He still retains the magic lamp, however, and summons the genie. Barani shows him the way to Sokurah's castle, carved deep in the heart of a mountain, where Sinbad creeps past the dragon used to protect the cave from cyclopes. Finding Sokurah's laboratory, Sinbad orders the sorceror to restore his betrothed. This Sokurah does, only to bar the lovers' escape with a living skelton warrior. Sinbad duels and defeats the creature, flees with Parisa, and is met by a second cyclops at the mouth of the cave. The Arabian Knight cuts loose the dragon and the creatures go at one another. The dragon kills his foe and pursues his master's enemies. By this time, however, Sinbad and Parisa have reached the beach. Sinbad fires the giant crossbow and the huge shaft pierces the dragon's heart. The beast falls to the ground, crushing Sokurah, and the lovers sail home.

The two-headed Roc pecks away at one of Sinbad's men
in *Seventh Voyage of Sinbad.*

Although *Seventh Voyage of Sinbad* hasn't the scope or spectacle of Korda's *Thief of Bagdad*, it is the author's personal favorite in this mythological genre. The film's fantasy elements are used creatively and do not overburden the film. Unlike the Temple of Dawn or flying horse sequences in *Thief of Bagdad*—which were marvelous—there are no extravagant displays of special effects that exist solely for their own sake, thus breaking the flow of the plot. Too, in *Seventh Voyage of Sinbad*, the genie, the monsters, and Sokurah's magical exhibitions are all treated very matter-of-factly, as if this sort of thing is an everyday occurrence. In this way, the film successfully builds its own strangely ordered universe. In *Thief of Bagdad*, we are shown *our* world in which magic is a transgressor. This is an impure form of fantasy.

On another level entirely, the effectiveness of *Dynamation* cannot be communicated on paper. The photographs that accompany this piece only *hint* at the realism Harryhausen achieves with his special-effects process. As for the monsters themselves, they are superlative. The satyrlike cyclops and classically rendered dragon are among Harryhausen's finest creations. Abetting the marvelous monsters are fine performances by Mathews, as a robust but admittedly too-Anglican Sinbad, and Shakespearean actor Torin Thatcher. The late Bernard Herrmann contributed a brilliant musical score.

Seventh Voyage of Sinbad made a huge and unexpected profit for Columbia Pictures, which spurred other filmmakers into action. A third version of *Thief of Bagdad* went before the cameras,

The amazing skeleton duel from *Seventh Voyage of Sinbad*.

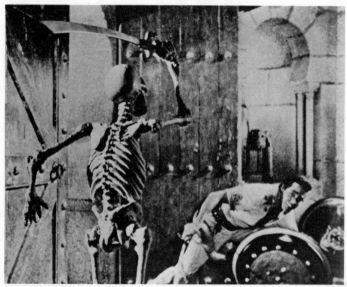

146

Steve Reeves finds Pegasus and its guardian in the third
screen version of *Thief of Bagdad.*

this one more faithful to the Fairbanks original than
to the Korda film. Made in Italy by American
director Arthur Lubin (Claude Rains' *Phantom of
the Opera*), the film starred muscular Steve Reeves
as the brigand who falls in love with a princess
(Georgia Moll). When an evil suitor drugs her with a
love potion, the girl falls into a deep sleep; this,
because she already loves Reeves. Half the kingdom
is promised to he who finds a curative blue rose that
grows on the other side of the world. Many start
the journey, but the road is not an easy one. There
are seven "doors" that lead to the blossom, and each
one conceals an incredible adversary. With the aid of
a court magician (Edy Vessel), the thief also sets out
and is the only one to pass safely through every
impass. He returns with the rose, creates an army of
magic soldiers to save Bagdad from the invading
forces of the jealous suitor, and marries Miss Moll.

Despite the typically poor dubbing and a disin-
terested cast of supporting players, the lavish and
energetic film has a fine performance by the beard-
less Reeves, along with impressive sets and special
effects. Particularly interesting in the technical
department are the cloak of invisibility, the living
trees, and the winged horse. In all, the unjustly
overlooked *Thief of Bagdad* holds its own even in
the company of its more distinguished predecessors.

Dick Shawn, who went on to play Hitler in *The
Producers* (1964), was filmland's next genie as the
Wizard of Bagdad (1960). Returned to mortal
standing for failing to guarantee that a marriage take
place, the dejected djinn regains his powers when
the wedding does, in fact, occur. Subsequently, the
bumbling spirit helps Barry Coe regain his throne.
Following in Shawn's stead, director Vittoria de Sica
played the famous lamp-dweller in the *Wonders of
Aladdin* (1961). He starred opposite Donald
O'Conner's Aladdin for American director Henry

147

. . . only to learn that the court magician has hidden his master's heart!

Levin's (*Journey to the Center of the Earth*) Italian production. The story adheres closely to the Arabian Nights mainstay, with poor Aladdin finding the lamp, getting three wishes, and marrying princess Noelle Adam.

Television's *Zorro*, Guy Williams, became the next Arabian Nights recruit in the colorful *Captain Sinbad* (1963). Directed by Byron Haskin (*War of the Worlds, Time Machine*) and produced by the King Brothers (*Gorgo*), the film pits our hero against a dragon, an invisible giant, and an evil, undying caliph whose sorceror has hidden the monarch's heart in a tower. The prince endures it all, of course, to rescue a beautiful princess (Heidi Bruhl). As ever, liberties were taken with recorded legend; what remained was an exciting swashbuckler having nothing more in common with the Arabian Nights than its four decades of predecessors.

The Middle Eastern fantasies went silent for a decade as Hollywood wrestled with a serious and combustible world situation and, hence, underwent a pseudo-intellectual renaissance. When this had shaded into pretention and passed, Ray Harryhausen returned with a few leagues more for Sinbad in *The Golden Voyage of Sinbad* (1973). Much to the surprise of Columbia Pictures, this modestly budgeted action film became one of that year's top grossing films. It ended a long string of box-office disappointments for the Schneer-Harryhausen team.

While returning to its evil master Koura, a strange homonculus—a foot-tall batlike human—passes over Sinbad's ship. A sailor shoots at the creature, causing it to drop a golden amulet. Sinbad (John Phillip Law) puts the charm about his neck; the carved gold piece gives the adventurer strange visions of great turmoil and a girl with a single eye tatooed upon her palm. That night, a storm blows the ship to the kingdom of Marabia. Going ashore, Sinbad is attacked by a mysterious black rider and his cutthroat assistant. Stealing the latter's horse, Sinbad heads for the city. There, he meets Marabia's Grand Vizier (Douglas Wilmer), who wears a golden mask. This, he explains, is due to Koura's magic. When the sultan died heirless, he left the Vizier with two artifacts. One is a large disc with strange markings. The other is a golden amulet. These are kept in an undergound chamber, which Koura once sent a flaming fireball to destroy. Caught in the holocaust, the Vizier lost his face, but saved the bequests.

Toying with the relics, Sinbad notches his own latticed charm with that of the Minister. He notices that the shadow they cast on the disc forms two-thirds of a nautical chart. Just then, the men see the homonculus spying on them from a corner of the room. They pursue the creature and it turns to ash. The Vizier realizes that Koura, by gazing through the monster's eyes, now knows as much as they do about this strange map. Sinbad provisions his ship for immediate voyage: there is more to this affair than meets the eye!

On the eve of their departure, the sailor meets Margianna (Caroline Monroe), the girl of his vision. Taking the slave girl onboard, he finds that she knows nothing about the meaning of the mark on her palm. Meanwhile, Koura (Tom Baker) has hired a ship and, the next morning, follows Sinbad and the Vizier. Seeking to lose the sorceror, the Prince of Bagdad leads him into the Sea of Mist for which only he has a navigation chart. Realizing that he stands a

The great goddess Kali comes to life to battle Sinbad in *The Golden Voyage of Sinbad.*

Centaur and griffin battle in *The Golden Voyage of Sinbad.*

good chance of becoming hopelessly lost, Koura brings to life the masthead of Sinbad's vessel. The giant figurine snatches the map and, tumbling overboard, brings it to Koura. Fortunately, Sinbad has memorized the course.

Arriving at the continent of Lemuria, Sinbad and his crew consult an oracle to learn the whereabouts of the third golden piece. While they are so involved, Koura seals the entrance to the temple and hastens to follow the seer's directions. Climbing through an opening in the ceiling, Sinbad frees his party and they arrive, just behind Koura, at the temple of the six-armed goddess Kali. The magician brings the statue to life and it promptly attacks Sinbad and his men. The warriors drive Kali to the top of a stone staircase from which height the idol falls and shatters. In her shell is the third amulet. Unfortunately, Koura gets it first as green-skinned Lemurians, in awe of his powers, make their presence known. They seize Sinbad's party and, because of Margianna's ocular marking, turn her over to their one-eyed god. The girl is lowered into a pit while above, a desperate Sinbad orders the Vizier to remove his mask. The ruler's scarred face horrifies the Lemurians. They scatter, leaving the sailors free to rescue Margianna from a giant centaur. As they descend to the pit, a golden griffin—half-bird, half-lion—arrives and attacks the creature. With Koura's help, the centaur wins and is subsequently stabbed to death by Sinbad. The prince next battles Koura, who has made himself invisible. Stepping into a fountain, the sorceror's outline appears and Sinbad slays him. The waters turn red with blood, then change to a golden hue:

the third amulet has led them to the crown of Marabia's sultan. Their prize is the rightful rule of that country. The ornament is placed on the Vizier's head and his features are restored, a blessing of his rightful inheritance.

With fine leading players, and a clever plot, *Golden Voyage of Sinbad* stands as one of Harryhausen's most satisfying vehicles. Particularly gratifying is the high level of art to which the animator has raised his craft over the years. Two scenes in particular indicate Ray's control of the medium, and the eerie drama for which he strives in all his films.

Alone on the deck of Sinbad's ship, the wine-guzzling Haroun (John Garfield Jr.) is sitting beside the masthead, talking to her in his stupor. Slowly, the wooden figure turns and looks at the sailor. Haroun jumps to the deck as his companion tears herself from the prow. It's a brilliantly mystical, flawlessly executed scene that can only have transpired in the world of mythology! Another segment, perhaps more illustrative of the animator's consumate skills, is Kali's descent from her pedestal. The goddess descends from her altar and, reaching the base of the staircase, does an exotic dance. Her six arms writhe gracefully in time, while the statue's head and legs maintain a separate rhythm. When she is through with her display, Koura tosses the goddess a sword; magically, the single weapon becomes six. It's a breathtaking scene that changes, in the span of mere seconds, from the light breath of fantasy to the darker touch of a nightmare. Indeed, the only disappointment in the *Golden Voyage of Sinbad* is the centaur-griffin battle. The two clumsy quadrupeds are not as visually or strategically matched as the nimble cyclops and the lumbering dragon from *Seventh Voyage of Sinbad*. As an historic note, *Golden Voyage of Sinbad* marked a happy return to the Arabian Nights genre of Miklos Rozsa, whose music for Korda's *Thief of Bagdad* and his subsequent scores for *Ben Hur* and *El Cid* won him international acclaim.

After *Golden Voyage of Sinbad* became one of the top-grossing fantasy films of all-time, Columbia reissued *Seventh Voyage of Sinbad,* which itself enjoyed great success this second time around. And, as this book goes to press, the author has received a letter from Ray Harryhausen indicating that, "We have only recently returned to London from a good four-month schedule abroad. Spain, Malta, and Jordan have all added considerably to *Sinbad and*

150

the Eye of the Tiger. I now have a rather long siege for the completion of animation." Originally entitled *Sinbad at the End of the World,* this new picture stars Patrick Wayne—John's son—as the indomitable sailor, and Jane Seymour as his lady-in-waiting.

It would appear that after a long and arduous history, stop-motion magic has finally found its home in a world where imagination has meaning.

As our journey through mythology progresses, we'll encounter the folklore of Russia, Japan, England, and Ireland. Right now, however, we turn to the legends of Ancient Greece, a prolific cache of fables that has attracted more filmmakers than most any other genre in all of film fantasy.

Hercules, his brethren Atlas, Maciste, Ulysses, Ursus, and the replanted Biblical characters of Samson and Goliath account for much of this volume. They became the mainstays of films set between the eighth and first centuries B.C. As accurately as can be determined, what with several different release titles for many of these films, there were nearly forty sword-and-sandal epics released between 1960 and 1963 alone. Remarkably, Hercules himself had not starred in any film, sound or silent, until Steve Reeves tore out a tree by its roots to stop the runaway chariot in *Hercules (1957).* Prior to this, only a strongman known as Maciste the Mighty had appeared on screen, with no ties to either gods or fantasy. His screen debut was in the lusty, sweat-and-dust-filled *Cabiria* (1924), with the pulsing biceps of Bartolomeo Pagano on display. The film was filled with action, spectacle, and sexual overtones, but nothing more fantastic than the

The huge cyclops Polyphemus in *Ulysses.*

presence of a preterhuman. An incredible thirty Maciste films followed *Cabiria,* few of these seeing even limited American display.

Cecil B. DeMille gave the world *Samson and Delilah* in 1949, with its teeming brawn, lavish musculature, and collapsible temples. However, its position as a fantasy film is indistinct. Space limitations prohibit a weighty dissertation of the Old or New Testaments as fantasy or history.

Thus, prior to *Hercules,* only *Ulysses* (1954), with Kirk Douglas as Homer's epic hero, merged period spectacle with fantasy in the Ancient Greek's tilts with the cyclops Polyphemus, the sorceress Circe (Silvana Mangano), and the alluring sirens. Unfortunately, the Italian-American production suffered from an unworkable combination of American and Italian players, along with a pedestrian script. The production, however, was lavish, and Douglas played his hero with sobriety. The larger-than-life hero had had its trial runs: it was time for Reeves and his *Hercules* to put Thebes and its surrounding communities on the filmic map.

As is ever the case with screen adaptations of established works, there were changes made in the the name of cinematic flow. Gone were the Aegean

Kirk Douglas as *Ulysses.*

Hercules vows to retrieve the Golden Fleece after it has
been stolen from the Argo.

stables, the multiheaded hydra, and other established elements of the myth. *Hercules* does, however, offer compensation. The film is a colorful, well-crafted phantom that glides close to reality without ever involving it. The breakwater is Reeves, his aloof, dynamic character refusing to treat the fantastic as anything other than routine. In this manner, he straddles both worlds the way his namesake bore the mark of god and man.

Despite the ridicule that critics have fired at Reeves—"all beefcake and no brain" being the most common discourtesy—he is a fine Hercules. His first appearance in the film is particularly effective. Sylva Koschina's chariot is running wild along a rocky coastline. A tree in her path begins to quake. It rises from the ground with Reeves emerging from beneath the roots and holding the tree above his head. He tosses the oak in front of the stampeding horses and rescues Miss Koschina, whom he learns is a princess. Suddenly, the hero swears: he smells

his dinner burning. Hercules runs to a nearby campfire, plucks a boar from the spit, and begins to gorge himself. His guest comments on Hercules' pitiful manners, but "I can't help it. I'm hungry!" he explains. After spending an uncomfortable repast with the girl, the strongman rides with her back to the palace. En route, she explains how, years before, on a windy, evil night, she was roused from sleep to find the palace in an uproar. Her father, the king, had been slain, and the symbol of his nations' prosperity, the Golden Fleece, was gone. Hercules promises to help retrieve it. In due course, the hero slays the Niemen Lion, travels with Jason in pursuit of the Fleece, fights an army of apemen, battles a dragon, and puts the rightful king on his throne. However, to do this latter as spectacularly as possible, Jason's Argonauts attack the palace, unaware that Hercules has been drugged and chained. Pulling his bonds from the dungeon wall, Hercules wraps the links first around the enemy, then about pillars fronting the usurper's hall. Samsonlike, he pulls the building down on his charging opposition.

Although portions of the film exhibit a disturbing economy of production, such as the soundtrack of Godzilla's roar being used for the tyrannosaurlike dragon, the bulk of the film exhibits care and quality. Lavish countryside panoramas and attractive sets effectively re-create the look and feel of Ancient Greece. These serve to roundout the film, making *Hercules* a sincere and exciting motion picture.

When *Hercules* made its box-office strength apparent—the film grossed over $5,000,000 in American release—*Hercules Unchained* (1959) was hurried into theatres nationwide. A production as fit as its predecessor, *Hercules Unchained* reunited Reeves with his screen-wife Miss Koschina. After traveling with her and their son a great distance, Hercules stops to drink from a stream. This, it develops, is the Stream of Forgetfulness, and Hercules runs off with the Queen of Lidia (Sylvia Lopez). The Queen, who has her lovers stuffed and put on display, falls in love with the son of Zeus. Fortunately, friends of Hercules are captured. They

Steve Reeves as the were-lion in *Goliath and the Barbarians.*

remind the demigod who he is and explain that he must hurry to Thebes where a tyrant has taken power. When the small group escapes, the Queen leaps into a vat of bubbling embalming fluid and perishes. Although melodramatic, this is a fitting end for her highness. Meanwhile, Hercules reaches his kingdom and its public arena in time to save his wife from a maneating tiger. He follows this with an attack on the invaders' siege towers, toppling them with a chariot and grapnel. It's all very rousing adventure, with but one fantasy-oriented battle: Hercules' mountaintop fight with the Son of the Earth (Primo Carnera). Whenever the antagonist is thrown to the ground, his terrestrial mother increases his strength. To solve this nagging problem, Hercules tosses his foe into the ocean.

Hercules Unchained emphasizes feats of strength rather than a world filled with fantasy. It made considerably more money than its forerunner and thus set the pace for strongman mythologies to follow. Reeves' next film—his first picture not to be released in America under the auspices of movie mogul Joseph E. Levine—was *Goliath and the Barbarians* (1960). In it, Goliath battles Mongol hordes who swarm into Italy from over the Alps. Although *Goliath and the Barbarians* is nothing more than a straightforward adventure film, Reeves does don a marvelous were-lion disguise, the claws of which he uses in clandestine strikes against the Asians. After this picture, the former Mr. Universe went on to star in less-standard fare such as *Thief of Bagdad, Last Days of Pompeii* (1960), and *Morgan the Pirate* (1960). His roles and their kindred characterizations fell to other players, most of whom were without presence or talent.

The Revenge of Hercules came to America in 1960 as *Goliath and the Dragon*, since American International Pictures had had a great success with the Reeves Goliath film. Star Mark Forest tried hard to fill his predecessor's sandals, but his sincerity and build were not enough to negate his lack of acting ability. For the fantasy-film fan, however, there were a battery of interesting mythological characters such as Cerberus, the three-headed canine guardian of Hades; a centaur; a giant bat; and the title dragon. This last creature, incidentally, was a stop-motion model built by Marcel Delgado and animated by Jim Danforth. For the closeups, a full-scale mockup of the monster's head was used.

Surviving these hellish denizens, Forrest returned to the fold as the *Son of Samson* (1960), falling prey to the magic love charm of an evil sorceress. Breaking her spell, the hero saved the throne of Egypt.[14] After this effort, Forest was replaced by Brad Harris who, in *Goliath Against the Giants* (1960), fought sea monsters and Amazons. This was followed by the Kirk Morris Maciste film *The Witch's Curse* (1960), in which our hero faced hell and all its demons to free a spellbound British settlement. That same year saw *Hercules In Rome* as Alan Steele rescued a kidnapped princess (Wandisa Guida).

In a lighter vein, Jayne Mansfield was but one of the *Loves of Hercules* (1960), some of Mickey Hargitay's foes being a three-headed giant, a cyclops, and magic that turns men into trees. More literate, although barely so, was *The Minotaur* (1960), an Italian-made retelling of the half-man, half-bull story. Olympic runner Bob Mathias portrayed Theseus who, in a version different from recorded mythology, is befriended by a sea goddess and given a magic sword to slay the creature.

Just when it seemed that the entire series would become nothing more than mindless pap, the finest of all screen Tarzans, Gordon Scott, went to Italy and fought the zombie army of vampire Guido

Gordon Scott in *Goliath Against the Vampires*. **The title creatures are in the background.**

Celano in *Goliath Against the Vampires* (1961). This was a Maciste film more marketably titled for American release, as was Scott's *Samson and the Seven Miracles of the World* (1961). In the latter picture, Maciste carries his battle against the Mongols to China where he moves a mountain and causes the climatic earthquake. After this conflict, Scott took on Steve Reeves in the lavish *Duel of the Titans* (1962), playing Romulus, one of the legendary founders of Rome, to Reeves' Remus. Scott, like Reeves, gave the portrayals class. Watching him, one is aware of the actor's desire to do more than showoff his build and batter Italian extras.

Mitchel Gordon took a once-only swing at the genre as *Atlas in the Land of the Cyclops* (1961), after which he passed the sinewy scepter to Reg Park, one of the best in the long line of post-Reeves he-men. In *Hercules and the Captive Women* (1961), he is shipwrecked on a living island that devours all who, like Hercules, are washed upon its shores. There, the Greek hero encounters Proteus, a maleable monster that attacks him as a ball of fire, a python, a lion, an eagle, and finally as a huge amphibious monster. By defeating this creature, Hercules has bested the island itself. It surrenders up a former victim, a lovely girl, whom Hercules takes to her home of Atlantis. There, he becomes embroiled with the power-mad Antinea, Queen of the continent (Fay Spain). Her goal is to place Zeus' corrupt father Uranus on the throne of the Gods; since Zeus sired Hercules, the hero sets out to destroy the Temple of Uranus, the tabernacle of

Rossana Schiaffino in the clutches of *The Minotaur*.

Reg Park battles Proteus in *Hercules and the Captive Women.*

which is made of the god's own petrified blood. Locating the chapel inside a mountain, Hercules finds Uranus' pulsing, inanimate body, defeats its guardian force of superhuman albino warriors, and smashes a hole in the cliff that the sun's rays might enter and destroy the temple. The resultant eruptions sink Atlantis and our hero sails on to his next adventure, *Hercules in the Haunted World* (1961). Directed by Mario Bava *(Black Sunday)*, the film pits Park's Hercules and Theseus (Giorgio Ardisson) against Christopher Lee's Leiko, king of Hades' vampire legions. After retrieving the Golden Apples of the Hespirides, and defeating a loathesome rock monster, the pair enter hell's gates to find the magic stone that will restore life to Hercules' comatose girlfriend Dianara (Leonora Ruffo). Returning to the surface world with the jewel, Hercules is pursued by Leiko's army, which ascends to earth through a cemetery. Although Leiko is crushed by a huge boulder, he crawls from beneath

it to finish drinking the blood of Dianara. Propitiously, the sun rises and the monsters are destroyed.

With excellent production values, sincere performances, and intelligent scripts, *Hercules and the Captive Women* and *Hercules in the Haunted World* remain the first peaks in the Italian sword and sandal spectrum since Steve Reeves left the mode for more fertile grounds.

Alas, things went quickly sour. Hollywood gave us *The Three Stooges Meet Hercules* (1961) in the person of Samson Burke. They also meet a two-headed cyclops—two men squeezed into a large woolen costume—and other genre standards. In a more serious vein, Maciste (Mark Forrest) returned, under the American pseudonym the Son of Hercules, in *The Mole Men Battle the Son of Hercules* (1961). No relation to the Universal Pictures *Mole People*, these creatures are scientifically advanced albinos who live inside the earth and to whom sunlight is fatal. To halt their plans for world

One of Leiko's henchmen keeps Hercules (background) and Theseus under wraps in *Hercules in the Haunted World.*

conquest, Forrest splits the earth above their domain, and the creatures are immolated. That year also saw the introduction of a new hero, *Mighty Ursus* (Ed Fury), whose premier epic was shown in this country under its original title. The film tells how a young boy, raised by lions, grew up to become a superman and rescue his beloved from interlopers. The picture did poorly at the box office, which is why the second Fury-Ursus film was released as the more commercial *Son of Hercules in the Land of Fire* (1963).

Tangling further with the confusion of character duplication, *Ulysses Against the Son of Hercules* (1963) was, in fact, Homer's Ulysses battling the *original* Hercules. When the Sea God Neptune complains to Zeus about the havoc Ulysses (Georges Marchal) has wreaked in his domain, the King of the Gods sends his son (Michael Lane) after the Odyssian hero. Instead of capturing him, however, both demigods become involved in a series of lively adventures, which include a battle with the vicious Bird-men and capture by a tribe of Neanderthals. In the end, the strongmen become fast friends and Zeus forgives Ulysses his trespasses. In an only remotely serious followup, *Hercules, Samson, and Ulysses* (1963) (Kirk Morris, Richard Loyd, and Enzo Curusico, respectively) join forces to battle a rampaging sea monster.

Because these lesser-quality productions were now bypassing theatrical release in America for the more lucrative sale to television, much of the care and polish that had been evident in even the post-Reeves epics vanished. However, the

scenarists came up with some interesting storylines to keep our heroes busy. Time-traveling fight promoters confronted *Hercules in the Vale of Woe* (1963), proposing a match between Hercules (Frank Gordon) and Maciste (Kirk Morris). Gordon Scott returned to the fold as Moloch, the mighty prince, in *Conquest of Mycene* (1963), while Maciste (Kirk Morris) was revived—literally raised from the dead by a magic potion—in *Samson vs. the Giant King* (1963). *Samson in King Solomon's Mines* (1964) saw Reg Park back in action, escaping the aforementioned lode by drowning his foes in a sea of molten gold.

Maciste was allowed to appear under his own name in *Samson and the Mighty Challenge* (1964) simply because Samson himself (Alan Steel) was in the film, along with Hercules and Ursus. The name was changed, however, for subsequent Maciste movies: *Hercules, Prisoner of Evil* (1964), with Reg Park fighting werewolves and witches; *Hercules Against the Barbarians* (1964) in the person of Mark Forest; and *Hercules Against the Moon Men* trying to find enough sacrificial blood to revive their queen and take over the world. Finally, with Mark Forrest repeating the role of Maciste, there came *Hercules of the Desert* (1964), in which our hero battled warriors whose voices caused landslides.

Following these low-grade efforts was one final fling for Hercules himself. Don Vadis donned loincloth and sandals to play *Hercules the Invincible* (1964), fighting a dragon to earn title and was back again in *Hercules vs. the Giant Warriors* (1964). This time, Zeus strips his son of his strength as punishment for defiance, restoring it when Hercules is faced with ten giant bronze soldiers. Winding up the long chain of Italian films, Mark Forrest was *Hercules Against the Sons of the Sun* (1965), fighting Incan sun worshippers, and Rock Stevens starred as *Hercules and the Tyrants of Babylon* (1965), battling an evil sorceress. However, the crowning—or clowning—comment on six years of Italian spectacles was had by *Hercules in New York* (1970), Zeus sent Arnold Strong to the twentieth century that he might star on Broadway. Placed under the watchful eyes of comedian Arnold *Stang*, he suceeds. Thus, the genre begun with sincerity and vigor ends with tongue in cheek. An ignoble irony: the great characters of legend, who had survived countless demons and monsters, finally found their match in the power of Hollywood!

Ray Harryhausen's sketch of Cerberus, with Jason and Medea on the left. A scene planned but not executed in *Jason and the Argonauts*.

Unfortunately, this flood of tripe soured the public's taste for mythology and doomed Ray Harryhausen's high-quality contribution to the field, *Jason and the Argonauts* (1963). The story of Jason's quest for the Golden Fleece had been recounted in *Hercules*, of course, and again in the Italian-made *Giants of Thessaly* (1960), a loose interpretation of the legend with Jason (Roland Carey) and Orpheus (Massimo Girotti) fighting monsters and Circe en route to the gilded ramskin. By the time two more years of muscular antics had rolled across theatre screens, distributors and the public were inclined to lump any classical-sounding film with the generally turgid Italian lineup. Thus, *Jason and the Argonauts* was unfairly dismissed as "just another muscle-popper". It is not. With a lavish budget, an excellent cast, and Harryhausen's special effects, the film is a beautifully crafted work of art.

Another Harryhausen sketch of a scene excluded from *Jason and the Argonauts*.

As in *Hercules* and *Giants of Thessaly*, Jason's task is to provide a symbol around which his people will rally to depose the tyrant Pelias (Douglas Wilmer). He proposes to find the Fleece. Summoned by the Gods to Olympus, Jason (Todd Armstrong) is told that Hera, Queen of the Gods (Honor Blackman), will assist him six times during his quest, the number of times his slain sister had called upon her the night Pelias took power. With this guarantee, Jason assembles a crew of Greece's bravest men, including Hercules (Nigel Green) and the weak but resourceful Hylas (John Crawford). Hylas earns his place on the voyage by skipping a discus farther into the ocean than Hercules is able to throw it. Unknown to Jason, however, Pelias' son Acastus (Gary Raymond) is also onboard to sabotage the mission and seize the Fleece for his father.

The Argonauts' first stop is the Isle of Bronze where Jason tells his men they may take only food and water. Hercules and Hylas, chasing goats, find a large statue in whose pedestal is the jewelry cache of the Gods. They steal an oversized broach pin to use as a javelin, and Talos, the metal guardian of the store, comes to life. He smashes the adventurers' ship and proceeds to kill the sailors for Hercules' indiscretion. Jason calls to Hera for help and she guides him to the giant's heel. There, Jason spots a plug. Working it loose, Jason drains Talos' life essence onto the beach and the monster falls to pieces. Hylas is crushed beneath the monster's fragmented chest, but Hercules won't believe that he's dead. He stays behind to find the boy.

Repairing the ship, Jason's men visit the blind prophet Phineas (Michael Gwynn), whose island is plagued by a pair of batlike harpies. To gain Phineas' favor, the Argonauts trap the creatures in cages. In exchange, they ask the old man how to get to Colchis, the land of the Fleece. Phineas gives them directions as well as a charm to get them safely through the clashing rocks. The men set sail and, arriving at the Sympeglades, watch as a ship from Colchis is crushed and sunk. Jason tosses Phineas' charm to the water and the Sea God Neptune rises to push the cliffs apart. The danger passed, Jason rescues the lovely Medea (Nancy Kovaks) who is floating amidst the wreckage of the vessel from Colchis.

In the land of the Fleece, Acastus betrays the Argonauts' intent to King Aeetes (Jack Gwillim), who has the pirates thrown in jail. Medea, however, cannot deny her love for Jason and sets them free. While the Argonauts flee, Jason, Medea, Argus

. . . and Jason returns the monster's warm welcome.

(Laurence Naismith), and two other men hurry to steal the Fleece. There, Jason defeats a seven-headed Hydra and snatches away the priceless treasure. Aeetes arrives after the struggle and gathers together the Hydra's teeth. He follows Jason and, casting the teeth to the ground, watches them erupt into an army of skeleton warriors. Handing Medea and the Fleece to Argus, Jason and his two companions hold the monsters at bay. When his friends are safely away, and the two brave Argonauts have been slain, Jason leaps from a cliff and swims to the Argo. His mission completed, Jason kisses Medea while, up in Olympus, Zeus promises further adventures for the hero.

These adventures were never to be, of course, since the film was a disappointing failure; a pity when one considers the care, attention, and love that went into its making. To further comment on the quality of Ray Harryhausen's special effects would be superfluous; suffice it to say that *Jason and the Argonauts* features the most meticulous animation and process work of his career. In terms of acting, the film also gave Harryhausen his finest cast. Nigel Green's lusty, brawling, empty-headed Hercules is especially refreshing after the many rehashes of

Reeves' pristinely righteous characterization. The Gods of Olympus are also carefully interpreted, played with enough self-parody to keep them from becoming ludicrous. Niall MacGinnis—Karswell in *Curse of the Demon*—is perhaps most at ease as the laconic, all-powerful Zeus. Only Todd Armstrong's Jason is a disappointment. He is as chipper as a college freshman and too superficial to be credible in this quixotic journey. As ever, Bernard Herrmann provides a striking musical accompaniment to the film, while Wilkie Cooper, the perennial Schneer-Harryhausen cinematographer, captures the story in all of its varied hues and grandeur.

Considering the failure of *Jason and the Argonauts*, American filmmakers were understandably reluctant to finance further Greek myths. Thus, the next such effort came from Italy with opera star Maria Callas portraying Jason's wife in *Medea* (1970). However, there is little fantasy in evidence; the film is primarily a classic tragedy in which Medea beheads her brother, knifes her children to death, and sets her lover's wife afire. This, to find true happiness.

Unlike the prolific films based on fantastic Greek

Jason battles and slays the Hydra in *Jason and the Argonauts*.

legends, the cinema's representation of Norse folklore has been primarily in terms of the Vikings. Like the Italian Maciste films of the thirties, these pictures were brawny adventure films ranging from Kirk Douglas' excellent *The Vikings* (1958) to the adequate Italian opus *Last of the Vikings* (1960). Only *Der Nibelungen* borrowed from Scandanavian *fantasy* folklore, as did Roger Corman's bizarre *Saga of the Viking Women and Their Voyage to the Waters of the Great Sea Serpent* (1970). Again, however, this was less a mythology than a sword-swinging adventure film as the viking men, captured by enemies, are rescued by the viking women who tangle briefly with a papier-mache sea monster.

It is perhaps significant, in view of the distortions that surround cinematic interpretations of most mythologies, that the country best suited to make such pictures was the country on whose legends they were based. This is certainly so with the films that came from Russia and Japan, whose folktales have a unique cultural genesis that is difficult to translate for American tastes. To understand, in perspective, how these stories benefit from a non-Western telling, imagine how absurd an Oriental version of Paul Bunyan would seem to American eyes!

Russia has long enjoyed filming the adventures of its national heroes, such as *Alexander Nevsky* (1938) and *Ivan the Terrible* (1944). During the fifties, when the Russian cinema was trying to recover from

the war, very few Soviet films reached the United States. It was the era of McCarthy's witchhunts, and, as ever, political intrigue seriously affected the arts. When the furor died down somewhat, and a few Soviet motion pictures reached American screens, the product was shown to be quite excellent, particularly the fantasies. The first Russian fable to be imported was done so, fittingly, by Roger Corman. Thus, *Sadko* (1952) became *The Magic Voyage of Sinbad*. Based on the opera by Rimsky-Korsakov, the film details a minstrel's search for the Bird of Happiness, in which quest he is aided by all manner of strange being. However, certain aspects of the film—such as the Kingdom of Neptune segment with its dancing octopus and light-hearted seahorses—were regarded as frivolous by American audiences, which is a fair assessment. The film *is* frivolous, like so many foreign fantasy films where reality is less treasured than the creation of a fairy-tale sensibility. Our inability to accept this slant would be analogous to the Russian audience that declares as *dangerously* frivolous the American preoccupation with overstated screen violence. Another consideration is that *The Magic Voyage of Sinbad* was created for a young audience and, as such, is not representative of the finest that Soviet fantasy has to offer. Rather, the eleventh-century exploits of Ilya Mourametz provided Russian filmmakers with a vehicle for one of the most impressive sword and sorcery epics ever made,

159

Sword and the Dragon (1959). Released in America on a double bill with *Frankenstein 1970*, *Sword and the Dragon* is a rugged mythology uncluttered by gloss or pretense.

The ruthless Kalin (Alexi Shvorin) is ravaging the Ural countryside with his brutal Tugar barbarians and a fire-breathing dragon named Zuma. He attacks the village of Goldonia where the brave Ilya Mourometz (Boris Andreyev) lies paralyzed from wounds suffered in a previous encounter with the invaders. He watches helplessly as his beloved Vilia (Natalie Medvedeva) is spirited away. Meanwhile, the great warrior Invinsor, who has long fought the Tugars, has grown old. In the mountains of Goldonia, he hands his magic sword to passing pilgrims and turns to stone. The travelers head for the village where Ilya gives them food and drink, and apologizes for his lack of mobility. In return for his kindness, the visitors give him the dew from magic foliage, which restores life to his limbs. The strang-

ers also give Ilya the sword of Invinsor. Thus armed, the warrior leaves to serve the court of Prince Vanda.

En route, the Goldonian comes to an enchanted forest, which a raven warns him to avoid. Ignoring the omen, Ilya rides deep into the woods where he finds an incredible dwarf sitting in the branches of a dead tree. The creature introduces himself as the Wind Demon and his breath causes hurricane winds that lash at the twisted terrain. Hurling his sword, Illya severs the limb on which the creature is perched and carries him to Prince Vanda. For capturing the dread monster, Ilya is honored with a ring from the nobleman. Just then, an emissary from Kalin arrives demanding tribute. Enraged, Ilya slays the Mongol and becomes a hero of the court. Several days later, seeking out Tugar campsites, he finds Vilia a prisoner of one such band. Killing her captors, Ilya frees the girl and returns to the court where they are wed. Months pass, and Ilya is once

**Ed Stolar and Ann Larion with a friendly octopus.
From *The Magic Voyage of Sinbad*.**

Ilya Mourometz displays the captured Wind Demon in *Sword and the Dragon*.

again off to fight the enemy. He puts Vilia safely onboard a caravan, which the Prince is sending far from the strife. Before she leaves, the woman gives her husband a magic cloth she has woven.

When the caravan is destroyed by Tugars, Prince Vanda is convinced by traitors in the court that Ilya should have been present to prevent the disaster. The lord places Ilya in a dungeon. Meanwhile, in Kalin's prison, Vilia gives birth to Ilya's son. The two are incarcèrated for many years, during which time Vilia refuses Kalin's amorous advances. Because of this, the Tugar adopts her boy and raises him as a Prince of his own people. Before the lad is taken from her, however, Vilia gives him the ring that Vanda had once given her husband.

Years pass, and Little Falcon (Andrei Abrikosov) has grown to manhood. He is ready to lead the Tugars against Prince Vanda. Emissaries demand that the Russians surrender. The Prince realizes that only Ilya can save them, and resolves to beg his forgiveness. He goes to the dungeon and is surprised to find Ilya healthy and strong. The warrior explains that he has been nourished by food from Vilia's magic cloth. Ilya accepts his liege's pardon and, leading the Russian army, confronts his son on the battlefield. Locked in hand-to-hand combat, Ilya notices the ring. Convincing the boy of his heritage, Ilya sends him back to find his mother. The young man locates her, frees the Russian slaves, and returns to the battle just as Zuma, the flying dragon, is released. The three-headed monster attacks the castle as the father and son warriors slaughter the beast. Meanwhile, the Tugars are routed and their chieftain is stuffed into a sack and carried off to trial.

The Mourometz family is reunited, Invinsor's sword is passed from Ilya to his brave son, and both are saluted by the liberated Russians.

While the fight with the full-scale, completely— and surprisingly—mobile Zuma is the highlight of the picture, it is by no means the film's sole attraction. The Enchanted Forest and Wind Demon are superbly realized as are the passing of Invinsor and the Disney-like scene of Valia weaving her magic cloth. For the latter, she is joined, in song, by animals of the forest. The battle scenes are spectacular and the sets lavish, their design purposely unpolished. This creates the ruggedness of which we spoke, an attempt to capture the mud, dirt, and sweat of this bygone era of monsters and warriors. A film too-long neglected by genre historians, *Sword and the Dragon* stands alongside Korda's *Thief of Bagdad* and *Jason and the Argonauts* as one of the screen's few truly epic fantasy adventures.

Like their Russian counterparts, Japanese screen fables deal with the tough, proud, land-tied commoner. However, while thematically the same, the Eastern approach is decidedly more fragile. From Toho's over three-hour-long *Three Treasures* (1958) to the Majin films of 1966, even in holocaust do the images retain the delicacy of a finely brushed watercolor.

It should come as no surprise that gods and magic figure prominently in Japanese fantasy. Like Americans, who take very seriously their own religious beliefs, the Japanese treat their five-thousand-year-old mystical heritage with respect. Too, they have always been a visually oriented people. Their written characters are less letters than pictures; Japanese decorative work on kites, shades, screens, and clothing is legendary. Keeping all of this in mind, then, it would seem only natural that Japanese fantasy deal with wizardry and feudal strife—a period of supreme belief in the supernatural—with an emphasis on the careful delineation of on-screen images.

Japanese fantasy did not become a mainstay of their industry until after World War II. For one thing, Japanese filmmaking itself was halted after a series of earthquakes in 1926 leveled the fledgling industry. So great was the public demand for movies, however, that tents were erected and movies shown amidst the ruins. These, of course, were pictures imported from abroad, and they proved very popular. In order to regain their audiences, then, the Japanese were forced to create homegrown fare, movies of topical interest. This, naturally, precluded fantasy, which was brought in from other nations. *Godzilla* changed all of that. The industry was recovered from the war and was now anxious to *compete*. Using the giant monsters to batter a niche for Japanese fantasy, the filmmakers then turned their lenses to antiquity.

One of the first legend-spawned efforts was the aforementioned *The Three Treasures* starring Toshiro Mifune. In its epic swath, the film covered the origin and growth of Japan and the Shinto religion as they pertained to gods and monsters. With an hour snipped from its original length, the film did weak business in America. This had both a positive and negative effect on subsequent films. On the one hand, they were not overly spiced with Western trappings for the American market. Not as fortunate was the fact that it would be five years before Toho again tried a fantasy film based on native myths. It was produced largely for the Japanese market with a margin of profit assured by sale to American television. The film was *The Lost World of Sinbad* (1962), with Mifune again in the fore, and it has nothing to do with the Arabian Nights. In Japan the picture was known as *Samurai Pirate,* the adventures of a swashbuckling thief at odds with an evil witch who can become a small-winged harpy or turn men to stone with her gaze. The medusa is destroyed when forced to look upon her own mirror image. Not as elaborate as *The Three Treasures,* this new film did strike a balance between economy and artistry without compromising on its cultural origins.

Toei, one of the newer Japanese studios—twenty-five-years-old as opposed to Toho's forty and Daiei's thirty—was responsible for the next medieval fantasy, *The Magic Serpent* (1966). This film concerns a young magician (Hiroki Matsukata) who helps a princess depose the warlord father who abandoned her and her mother years before. Meanwhile, a rival sorcerer has killed the magician's mentor and sets his minions after our hero. These are defeated when the magician hides his head in a tree, leaving him indestructible and free to vanquish his opponents with magic. In the end, the wicked ruler, in alliance with the evil sorcerer, is deposed by the hero's monster—a giant frog—which is then pitted against the power-mad wizard's sea serpent. If the story sounds slightly convoluted, consider just one of its subplots: our hero falls in love with a peasant girl, saves her from the warlord, and joins her astride a giant eagle to fly into the sunset at picture's end.

Considering the limited expenditure on *The Magic Serpent,* the film succeeds admirably in creating the imagery and awe of magic we mentioned earlier. Most startling of all is the scene in which Matsukata's kimono-draped body fells the masked, sword-wielding attackers, while his head looks on approvingly.

That same year, Gamera's home studio of Daiei released two films based on the character of a huge stone idol. In both *Majin* and *Return of the Giant Majin,* peaceable peasants are subjugated by a ruthless tyrant who is ultimately destroyed by the Majin. What audiences came to see, after the rebellions and battles had been dispensed with, were the last fifteen minutes of the film wherein the Majin came to life. In this respect, the second film is the more impressive of the two. The Majin's priestess Sayri (Shiho Fugiama) has been tied to a crucifix and the idol blown to pieces. After the explosion, its head landed in the sea. Leaders of the village revolt are placed on stakes, about to be burned to death, when the ocean parts where the statue's head had fallen. The giant Majin appears and walks slowly forth, each footstep reverberating throughout the land. He pursues and destroys the invaders, toppling their palaces and crushing them underfoot. Returning to the sea, the monster presses his hand to his face: the grim visage disappears, replaced by smooth, emotionless stone. Watching him, Sayri sheds a tear that runs down her cheek to splash on the ground. As it hits, the Majin evaporates and becomes one with the sea.

These two films, with their excellent period detail, superb special effects, and brilliantly designed stonelike Majin costume, are the finest example of pure Japanese fantasy, a balanced blend of adventure, religion, and the icons of an era-gone-by. Like *Sword and the Dragon,* the Majin films are unacknowledged showpieces of the genre.

Unlike the countries at which we have thus far looked, Germany and Ireland have seen limited screen representation in terms of their folklore. Only Siegfried and Baron Munchausen from the former, and leprechauns from the latter have made an impression on the creative spirit of filmmakers. Munchausen, the famous teller of tall tales, was created by novelist Gottfried Burger and has been the subject of short films made by France (1909), Russia (1929), Germany (1943), Canada (1947), and most prominently the Czechoslovakian film *Baron Munchausen* (1961). A combination of stop-motion, live action, and cartoon animation, this engraving-come-to-life has Munchausen greeting astronauts on the moon, meeting Jules Verne and Cyrano de Bergerac, being mauled by a giant roc, traveling underwater, and so forth. Although the braggart-liar is hardly a reputable character, his inflated narratives have an air of nobility about them that is a fair personification of the nineteenth-century drawing-room adventurer. His sole purpose in addressing others was to outdo their exploits in war, travel, exploration, or hunting. Munchausen is simply this self-satisfied but honorable caricature carried to its ultimate, and thus humorous, extreme.

While Munchausen had his enormous sea serpents, Hercules his dragons, Sinbad his cyclops, and Jason his bronze god, the Irish folktale seems to have taken a different turn entirely. Their literature is filled with the pranks and exploits of the "little people." Surprisingly, though, leprechauns have seen but little film exposure. Only Walt Disney featured them prominently in his magnificent work *Darby O'Gill and the Little People* (1959). This largely overlooked film—it has yet to appear in any of the Disney retrospectives—is a phenomenal work of fantasy and horror, containing several of the most frightening visions ever put on film.

Lord Fitzpatrick, owner of the manor at which old Darby O'Gill (Albert Sharpe) and his lovely daughter Katie (Janet Munro) work as caretakers, is displeased with the elder man's work. Regretfully, he retires the O'Gills at half pay, gives them a

The leprechauns present Darby O'Gill with a fiddle in *Darby O'Gill and the Little People.* (c) Walt Disney Productions.

cottage nearby, and brings in young Michael McBride (Sean Connery) to do the job. Darby introduces Michael to Katie as an assistant and asks for a week to tell her the truth: Katie was born in the gatehouse, where they have always lived, and will be heartbroken. Meanwhile, the widow Sugrue (Estelle Winwood) is trying to fix Katie up with her lazy son Pony (Kieron Moore).

As Michael's first day on the job comes to an end, Darby leaves him to find the horse Cleopatra, whom he lets graze on the mountainside. Night has fallen, and Darby carries a lantern to the windswept and foreboding hill. As the horse peeks into a well, Darby approaches. Suddenly, Cleopatra looks up at her master, her face glowing a ghastly green, her nostrils red and flaring. She rears back and knocks the old man into the well. Darby lands hard but does not lose consciousness. Looking about, he notices a pair of leprechauns who introduce themselves as such and lead him to King Brian Conners (Jimmy O'Dea). Conners is aware of Darby's having lost his job and feels sorry for him. Thus, he has brought O'Gill to the kingdom of the little people to live out his days in happiness, drink, and song. Darby protests, but Brian says that he can never leave. Darby appears to accede and asks for a fiddle that they may make merry; Brian snaps his fingers and an instrument appears. The old man plays a mad, frenetic tune, which fills the leprechauns with uncontrollable verve. They hop on their tiny horses and, with a flash of lightning, pass through a fissure that appears in one wall of their cave. They ride vigorously into the night, unable to help themselves, while Darby escapes. He gathers up Cleopatra—who is free, now, from Brian's enchantment—and returns to the barn. There, Darby readies a jug of poteen. Since Brian will be after him, Darby intends to hold the imp until daylight. Accomplishing this, the leprechaun's magic power will vanish until nightfall. When Brian arrives, the old man tricks him into drinking whiskey until dawn. Brian is helpless, and Darby threatens to sic his cat Ginger on the leprechaun unless he grants him three wishes. Brian agrees—noting that a fourth wish will nullify the others—and Darby's first command is that Brian remain in the barn until he decides what to do with the other two wishes.

That night, pleased with his catch and wanting to boast, Darby puts Brian in a sack to show to Michael. When the young man sees nothing, Darby

An example of the amazing special effects in evidence throughout *Darby O'Gill and the Little People*. (c) Walt Disney Productions.

orders the leprechaun to appear, which he does: as a rabbit. Tricked by Brian, Darby thinks carefully so as not to squander his third wish.

Meanwhile, the widow Sugrue is going through the town's mail, which Pony delivers. She reads a postcard addressed to Michael from Lord Fitzpatrick. It orders that he prepare the manor for the nobleman's arrival. Since the widow had wanted Darby's job for Pony, she coaxes him to drive Michael out of town. Also, with malicious intent, she has the letter delivered directly to Katie. The girl's father still had not gotten around to breaking the news to her and she is crushed. She berates Michael for taking Darby's position. He tries to explain what really happened, and also that he loves her. Katie refuses his proposal of marriage and runs off.

At the pub, with Brian still in his sack, Darby prepares to make a third wish. No one, of course, believes that Darby has the leprechaun and he opens the bag to prove it. Out jumps a rabbit that runs away. Just then, Katie arrives. She yells at her father for not having told her why Michael had really joined them. Hurrying back to the gatehouse, Katie goes to fetch Cleopatra from the hillside. It's dark out; she stumbles, hits her head, and falls unconscious. Meanwhile, Pony has snuck into the manor, clubs Michael, puts a liquor bottle by his side, and leaves him where the arriving lord will see him "drunk." Shortly thereafter, Darby arrives. He rouses Mike and both men go looking for Katie. They find the girl and carry her home, where she

lingers between life and death. A dejected Darby steps outside for some air. There, he is met by a faceless banshee who wails hideously at the approach of Katie's death. Petrified, Darby slams the door shut, but to no avail. There is a clap of thunder and, running outside, Darby sees the Costa Bower—the Death Coach with its headless driver—descend through the rainclouds above. Once it sets out, it cannot return empty. Just then, Brian appears. Darby has called him to honor his third wish: that the Death Coach take him instead of Katie. Brian reluctantly agrees and, in an instant, Katie regains consciousness. Conners joins Darby in the carriage. When Brian says he'll miss Darby, the old man agrees, wishing that the imp could go along. Having made a fourth wish, Darby is returned to the house, his other wishes surrendered. Katie is well and, for once, Death has been cheated. After a brief stop in town, during which Michael beats the daylights out of Pony, the three settle into the gatehouse. Darby is permitted to stay on the job with Michael, Katie marries the lad, and all ends happily.

The small Irish mythologies and local touches such as the Costa Bower, Banshee, ghost horse, and leprechauns all serve to make *Darby O'Gill and the Little People* one of the fantasy films' most flavorful brews. As embellished by the Disney staff, scenes such as the sudden appearance at Darby's door of the irridescent-green ghost, or the rain-soaked approach of the Costa Bower, its horses' hooves beating an empty sky beneath the black rider's whip, take on the dimension of gripping horror. It is not the kind of mood or effect for which the Disney staff is famous; it is, paradoxically, the kind of work in which they are second to none. Too, since Disney is careful to build an air of light-hearted fun and merriment, scenes such as these are all the more terrifying.

As for the special effects, they are of a sort to give film buffs a chill up and down their spines. The technical work is the finest the studio has ever done, surpassing the overrated *Mary Poppins* (1964) and most any other special-effects production that one cares to mention. Indeed, so absolute is the illusion that, in press releases and advertisements, the credits listed King Brian as being played by himself.

When one reflects on the flawless nature of *Darby O'Gill and the Little People*, it is puzzling to consider how the same shop could turn out *The Gnome-Mobile* (1967). This story of the discovery

Walter Brennan argues with his leprechaun double in _The Gnome-Mobile_. (c) Walt Disney Productions.

of leprechauns by Walter Brennan in a California redwood forest is as faulty as the earlier film is brilliant. No rationale for this discrepency will be offered, save, perhaps, for the single thought that this was one of the first films the studio made after the death of Walt Disney.

Next door to the legends of leprechauns, we find, once again, giants and dragons governed by evil magicians, and battled by great heroes. While tales of knights and their travails abound, only a small handful of fllms have bothered to tap the rich well of fantasy that issues from medieval England. Before we look at the best and most fanciful of these, some history is in order.

When Ray Harryhausen first conceived _Seventh Voyage of Sinbad_, he took a presentation consisting of hundreds of drawings and a plot outline to several Hollywood producers. One of the men to whom he offered the package was Edward Small who, like the other filmmakers, turned it down. When the picture was eventually made, and became a big hit, Small naturally regretted not having made the picture. Deciding to repent, the producer planned a similar effort, hired Kerwin Mathews and Torin Thatcher—Sinbad and Sokurah from the Harryhausen film—to star, and collared Jim Danforth

and company to handle the stop-motion work. The result was _Jack the Giant Killer_ (1962), a remarkable pastiche built around the legends of sorcerors and giants who lived in Ancient Cornwall.

The wizard Pendragon, banished for having coveted the throne, returns to Cornwall disguised as Prince Elidorus of Tarquin Isle. He presents the Princess Elaine (Judi Meredith) with a twenty-first birthday present, a yard-tall doll called Cormoran. To the girl's surprise, the charming figurine climbs from its small castle and dances with her. That night, when Elaine has gone to sleep, Pendragon appears at her window. Small lightning bolts shoot from his eyes and strike Cormoran's box: the doll comes to life and, growing giant, kidnaps the princess. Brushing aside knights and guards, the monster batters his way through the castle gate and escapes.

The next morning, a young farmer named Jack (Mathews) spots the monster and, after a battle in his hay loft, kills Cormoran with a scythe. For his bravery, King Mark (Dayton Lummis) rewards Jack with the title Giant Killer and makes him Elaine's official bodyguard. Mark then sends his daughter and Jack by boat to a convent in Normandy, where Elaine will be kept until Pendragon is apprehended. However, a spy in the court, Lady Constance (Anna Lee), gets word of these plans to Pendragon, who sends forth an army of demons. They intercept the vessel, seize Elaine, force her into an airborne coach, and bring her to Pendragon. The wizard puts a spell on the princess making her, like Lady Constance, a willing servant to the devil. She can only be freed from this enchantment with the destruction of her mirror image, a reflection of her now-blackened soul.

Meanwhile, back on the ship, the crew has refused to pursue the monsters. They toss Jack and his loyal cabin boy Peter (Barry Kelley) overboard where they are picked up by a lone Viking fisherman (Roger Mobley). Since their host loves an adventure, the three of them set sail for Pendragon's castle. That night, the lusty, good-natured sailor shows Jack a bottle he fished from the sea: in it is a leprechaun. The little man (Don Beddoe), who speaks in rhymes, promises to help the men if they, in return, guarantee to set him free at adventure's end. The bargain is struck and, after a long voyage, the crew arrives at Pendragon's island. With the imp's bottle tucked behind his belt, Jack goes ashore and is met by giant zombie warriors. His sword useless against the creatures, the Giant Killer calls to

A frame blowup of Cormoran from *Jack the Giant Killer*.

Cormoran, the princess in hand, straddles Jack's wall . . .

. . . and does battle with *Jack the Giant Killer*.

Cormoran heads for Pendragon's waiting ship, where he will deposit the princess. Unfortunately, *Jack the Giant Killer* intercedes and rescues her highness.

In many ways, *Jack the Giant Killer* is a better movie than the one it was trying to imitate. The story has more interesting twists and turns, and the characters are more human than the cardboard cutouts offered in *Seventh Voyage of Sinbad*. Indeed, Don Beddoe's far-from-confident leprechaun and Thatcher's swaggering, sneering Pendragon stand out as some of the genre's more successful characterizations. The element of magic vs. magic running below and parallel to the men vs. monsters thread is also a welcome asset. In terms of technical facility, singularly impressive are the final cataclysm that levels Pendragon's domain, and the monsters' attack on the ship. Unfortunately, the stop-motion models and animation are not nearly as convincing as Harryhausen's *Seventh Voyage of Sinbad* work. The physical proportions of Cormoran and Galligantua are comical—the beasts are both top-heavy—and their features have none of the textured detail or emotional range of Harryhausen's twin cyclopes.

Despite this, the film is a grand flight into fantasy, made with care and a telling respect for the genre. Surprisingly, a well-mounted publicity campaign and the promise of the wonders wrought in Fantascope did not work magic. *Jack the Giant Killer* was an unqualified box-office disaster. Perhaps audiences mistakenly felt that they were in for a storybook retelling of *Jack and the Beanstalk!*

A similar fate of general nonacceptance greeted Bert I. Gordon's *Magic Sword* (1962), also a film of high quality and integrity. Gordon's version of St.

the leprechaun for help. Jack is told to pick up the arm of a nearby skeleton. It becomes a magic whip and, with every snap of its black length, another soldier is destroyed. Entering Pendragon's chamber in the castle, he comes face to face with the wizard. Pendragon turns Elaine over to Jack who is drugged by the spellbound princess. The Giant Killer awakens in irons and is ordered by Pendragon to reveal the secret of his magic. Jack refuses; the sorceror brings forth the Viking and Peter, whom he turns into a dog and a monkey. Pendragon then gives Jack one hour for the information or he will die. Left alone with the monkey and dog, Jack coaxes Peter to undo his bonds. Grabbing Elaine, he forces her in front of a mirror, smashes it, and the foursome flees. Pendragon sends the two-headed giant Galligantua in pursuit, but Jack has his imp summon a sea serpent for protection. The monsters battle and the ogre is destroyed. Enraged, Pendragon waits until his enemies have set sail before calling forth all his dark powers to transform himself into a huge gargoyle. The winged dragon attacks the vessel and Jack climbs upon its back. The two struggle high above the waves until the Giant Killer succeeds in driving his sword through the winged beast's neck. They plummet into the sea and Jack is rescued by his friends. A storm cloud envelops Pendragon's castle, destroying it with multicolored explosions and lightning. The menace is ended.

Escaping from Pendragon, *Jack the Giant Killer*, the princess, and friends combat the sorcerer's strange guardians.

. . . and how the monster looked on screen.

168

The gargoyle battles *Jack the Giant Killer* in a preproduction sketch.

Bert I. Gordon's interesting mechanical dragon as seen in *The Magic Sword*.

George and the Dragon pits George (Cary Lockwood) and a half-dozen knights against the sorceror Lodac (Basil Rathbone) to rescue a maiden in distress. Lodac has captured Helene (Anne Helm), a princess of fourth-century England. Despite the wizard's warning that seven curses await any would-be rescuers, Sir Branton (Liam Sullivan) accepts the king's offer of half his kingdom and Helen's hand in marriage for her safe return. From among the peasantry there is also a volunteer, George, the adopted son of the sorceress Sybil (Estelle Winwood). To aid his crusade, Sybil gives her son invulnerable armor; Bayard, the world's swiftest horse; and Ascalon, the Magic Sword. With the blade, George frees six knights who had been imprisoned in stone by Lodac. Together, they ride to the palace and, joining the reluctant Sir Branton, set out in search of Lodac's castle.

The party's first stop is the Ogre's Forest, where a twenty-five foot-tall monster kills two knights ere George, riding rapidly and in tight circles about the beast, causes it to grow dizzy and tumble to earth. The second curse comes hard upon, a misty glen housing a whirlpool of boiling lava into which one of the knights falls. When they clear the foggy terrain, one of George's peers finds a lovely maiden whom he stops to kiss. As they embrace, the girl's face becomes a mask of grotesquery and her fangs come close to piercing the warrior's neck. Only a quick appearance by George saves the knight. Meanwhile, riding on, Dennis and James have stumbled upon the next curse, a pulsing fireball that incinerates the pair.

Watching her son's progress, Sybil becomes worried lest his protection prove insufficient. Looking to ameliorate George's powers, she accidentally removes them. Defenseless, the brave lad, Sir Branton, and the one remaining knight, Patrick, press onward. After traveling a distance in the desert, George asks Branton why the heat is not affecting him. Taken by surprise, the knight hasn't an answer and flees. George pursues him only to find that his powers have fled: the mighty Bayard is unable to overtake Branton's mount. Following him into a cave, George and Patrick are attacked by fire demons. As George's partner grapples with one of the creatures, he is transformed into a monster. In a final act of fealty, Patrick burns down a wall of the cave so that George can escape.

Reaching Lodac's castle, the warrior finds Helene's cell and sets her free. As they flee, Lodac, his monster aides, and Branton appear to block the way. Lodac gives Helene to the traitorous knight who, in turn, gives Lodac a ring that will make him the most powerful sorceror on earth. This was their agreement, which the wizard has no intention of keeping. "Helene" turns out to be the vampiric hag from the road. With the ring in his possession, Lodac kills Branton and has George imprisoned. He is to watch as the real Helene dies. However, after tying him to a rack, one of Lodac's monsters accidentally overturns a cage of shrunken people. The vengeful creatures carry Ascalon to where George is bound and set him free. The brave warrior hurries to a courtyard as Helene is to be devoured by a huge two-headed dragon. In the nick of time, Sybil manages to restore George's powers and hurries to his side in the form of a small bird. While the hero slays the monster, Sybil flies to Lodac's hand and stealthily snatches away his ring. Transforming herself into a panther, she then kills the wizard and his curses vanish. The six slain knights are restored to life and, with George, his mother, and Helene, journey to the castle for a royal wedding.

The Magic Sword has a captivating charm about it. For one thing, there is a greater diversity of characters than in most other mythologies. There is the evil wizard and the cleancut hero, of course, but there are also the bumbling Sybil, the treacherous Sir Branton, and a bizarre cast of supporting players. These include Sybil's two headed assistant, Lodac's pinhead slaves, and the shrunken people. As is Gordon's bent, the monsters are all men in costumes, with the exception of a mechanical dragon. This latter is effective, but doesn't hold up as well as the werewolflike ogre, the gruesome vampiress, or the excellent makeup created for the two knights that are burned to death by the third curse.

By and large, the performances are splendid. It is a pleasure to watch Rathbone and Miss Winwood steal the show with their hammy panache. Lockwood and his associates are simply figures of granite, which is not to their discredit. This is what literature and history have come to make of their legendary heroes. Thus, as a filmic interpretation of a popular fairy tale, *The Magic Sword* is well packaged and fitfully spun.

After the disappointing scores tallied by these two British-based legends, English folklore went long unseen in film. Only recently has it resurfaced with the indomitable Monty Python comedy troupe starring in *Monty Python and the Holy Grail* (1975). In this insanely funny retelling of the Arthurian legend, the bold servants of God encounter a million-eyed dragon, destroyed by the on-screen death of the animator; the wizard Tim who causes explosions with his finger; a man-eating bunny; and the twenty-foot tall "Knights Who Say *Nyee*." The noblemens' quest is never fulfilled, of course, since the police arrive to arrest the knights for having murdered an innocent bystander. This is certainly a departure from where we began this chapter, with the four-hour long *Der Nibelungen.* It is with great restraint that a film historian avoids the temptation of looking too deeply into this strange diversity, seeking a moral about man's changing attitudes toward his heritage. Better to simply enjoy the films as self-contained units rather than clearcut pieces in a puzzle. To analyze the route that lead filmmakers from Siegfried to Monty Python might drive even the strongest reviewer mad!

12
FANTASTIC SCIENCE

In this chapter, we will discuss sixteen films that are on the borderline between science fiction and fantasy. The events they describe are rooted in technology, although the science is not as much an end in itself—as in *2001: A Space Odyssey* or *Forbidden Planet*—as it is a springboard for fantastic goings-on. Too, much of the technology in these films is largely implausible; we can safely say that the existence of a time machine in 1899 or an atom-powered submarine in 1870 are tools of the fantasist, not the scientist.

Of all the novels by Jules Verne that have been rendered in celluloid, *20,000 Leagues Under the Sea* (1954) is the finest. Verne wrote it, and his other great works, during the middle of the nineteenth century. This was not an era known for its great technological advances, and yet, incredible machines proliferated Verne's work. The author tinkered with this gadgetry for himself, of course, which is the reason he had turned to writing novels in the first place. They proved a far more lucrative and viable outlet for his imagination than the operettas on which he had, until then, been working.

20,000 Leagues Under the Sea was brought to the screen by Walt Disney. At the time, Disney had wanted to produce a live-action film that would retain the polish and artistry of his animated cartoons, without losing their sense of wonder. No less than *Snow White* (1938) or *Pinocchio* (1941) he wanted to create a showpiece. For one thing, Disney was anxious for a class film to release through his new distributing company, Buena Vista. The or-ganization was established to give Disney complete control over the release of his pictures, and to reap him a larger percentage of their profits. For another, he would be shooting in the new, ultrawidescreen CinemaScope process to give audiences the opulent adventure they couldn't get from that new kid on the block, television. After several of Disney's live-action movies—tentative, inexpensive family fare such as *Treasure Island* (1949), *Rob Roy* (1950), and *Robin Hood* (1952)—proved popular, the studio was ready to commit to a $5,000,000 project. Walt turned to Verne for his material.

Professor Aronnax (Paul Lukas) and his assistant Conseil (Peter Lorre), onboard a warship in the South Pacific, are researching reports of a sea monster. Also with the team is harpoonist Ned Land (Kirk Douglas). The explorers find that their serpent is, in reality, Capt. Nemo's (James Mason) submarine the *Nautilus*. The monsterlike craft rams Aronnax's ship. Ned, the professor, and Conseil go overboard and are rescued by the martinet captain.

A rare, preproduction sketch of the Nautilus from *Twenty Thousand Leagues Under the Sea.* (c) **Walt Disney Productions.**

Undersea exploration *Twenty Thousand Leagues Under the Sea.* (c) Walt Disney Productions.

He explains that his is an atom-powered vessel purging the world of warships. However, on one such crusade, off New Guinea, a cannon shell damages the Nautilus and it is forced to submerge. No sooner has the submarine gone under than it is attacked by a monster squid. Nemo surfaces and his men combat the sea giant. Ned's harpoon kills the

James Mason as Captain Nemo in *Twenty Thousand Leagues Under the Sea.* (c) Walt Disney Productions.

beast and, in so doing, saves the Captain's life. Nemo softens now, and tells his guests that he had wanted Aronnax on board to serve as his ambassador to the nations. Nemo plans to give mankind the secret of atomic power, but only if the world will lay down its arms. Unfortunately, warships find Nemo's island sanctuary, and a gun battle accompanies his entrance into the harbor. The Captain is wounded, and orders his ship to submerge for the final time. Land, Arronax, and Conseil escape in a skiff as an atom blast destroys the Nautilus, Nemo's island, and the attacking vessels.

Putting aside the Oscar-winning special effects—Disney seldom falls down on matters technical—only character motivation in *20,000 Leagues Under the Sea* leaves anything to be desired. In many ways, the players are less animated than the giant squid. In contrast to the multileveled confusion of the bomb-ridden fifties, Disney gave his audiences a film that had made all the decisions beforehand; his people are all black and white with few subtleties muddying the water. In its defense, this simplification permitted fuller development of subplots, such as Ned's unrelenting efforts to escape the *Nautilus*, the squid sequence, a battle with cannibals, an underwater funeral, etc.

Much of the picture was shot on location in the clear waters of the Bahamas, and a short subject detailing this work was shown on the weekly *Disneyland* television series. It won Walt television's Emmy Award. The studio scenes, such as the sets and sinking of miniature ships, were also executed with great care. In fact, the battle with the squid was filmed twice: the first version failed to impress the meticulous Disney.

When *20,000 Leagues Under the Sea* became one of Disney's top-grossing films of all-time, other filmmakers realized the goldmine to be had in the works of Verne. His aegis was one of the few that allowed studios to film the kind of technical fantasy that science was fast causing to become obsolete. The first post-Disney Verne movie to appear was the hugely successful *Journey to the Center of the Earth* (1959). The producers wisely called upon Captain Nemo, James Mason, to star in the film. He was a readily identifiable figure of fantasy, and gave this character substantially more pathos than the inflexible Nemo. As in the Disney film, tantamount attention and expenditure were given the sets and special effects. Inner earth is re-created with all the trimmings one would have expected to find in a

Pat Boone in one of the magnificent subterranean sets from *Journey to the Center of the Earth*.

Verne film adventure: crystal caverns, multicolored and scintillating; phosphorescent stalagmites; giant mushrooms and plants. No effort was spared to make this a quality production.

The picture spends a great deal of time getting us not only to the earth's core, but to the actual expedition as well. Trivial relationships are explored and dropped. However, when this exposition is through, we are thoroughly familiar with the personalities of Professor Lidenbrock (Mason), his associate Alec McCowan (Pat Boone), their aides, and the antagonists. This latter group is related to Arne Saknussemm, the long-dead explorer whose unsuccessful attempt to reach the center of the earth paved the way for Lidenbrock's journey. Understandably, the Saknussemms believe that the fame and subsequent wealth that will come from the voyage should be theirs.

Following Arne's trail, the Lidenbrock Expedition faces subterranean floods, an avalanche, great middle-earth winds, dinosaurs, and the murderous Saknussemms. Surviving these, the party reaches the center of the earth. There, they find incredible oceans along with a ruined city they decide is Atlantis. Unfortunately, the expedition's stay is not a long one. A blast set to clear a passageway back to the surface world causes a volcano to erupt. The explorers climb into a huge ceremonial dish and are shot through the mountaintop to outer earth.

It was only a matter of time before someone thought to do a sequel to *20,000 Leagues Under the Sea*; that someone was Ray Harryhausen. Using Verne's *Mysterious Island* as its framework, the 1961 Charles Schneer production details the daring escape from a Confederate prison camp by a party of Union soldiers onboard an observation balloon. A violent storm carries the craft westward, setting the five refugees on a lonely Pacific Island. Two shipwrecked women share in the subsequent enounters with mammoth bees, birds, crabs, mollusks, and a pirate ship, the strangers are aided by a mysterious unknown who ultimately reveals himself as Captain Nemo (Herbert Lom). He also explains that the crippled *Nautilus* lies hidden in a nearby grotto. Indicating the giant animals, Nemo tells the party that he's seeking to put an end to war by increasing the world's food supply. Having found the means to do this, with his giant animals, he must now return to society with his discovery. Unfortunately, a volcano threatens the island with complete destruction. Nemo uses the power from his immobile submarine to refloat the pirate ship. Because he is trapped in the *Nautilus*, everyone but the Captain escapes. Having been twice stung by fate, when Nemo next returned it was as the master of a sprawling suboceanic domain in *Captain Nemo and the Underwater City* (1965), with Robert Ryan as the legendary adventurer.

Because the *Nautilius* is an impotent set piece in *Mysterious Island*, the film fails to generate the electricity of *20,000 Leagues Under the Sea*. The craft's death has taken the bite out of its captain. Although Lom's brooding Nemo offers an alternative to the fiery Mason personification, it makes for very dull goings-on. As ever, Harryhausen's monsters take center-stage and perform with distinction. The giant bees in their honeycomb are especially well animated, standing among Harryhausen's most realistic creations.

Nemo's literary brother, another of Verne's paradoxes, the heroic villain, was Robur. In the novels *Robur the Conqueror* and *Master of the World* he made the antics of the *Nautilus* seem pale. The film version of *Master of the World* (1961) opens with a volcanic eruption in the Appalachian Mountains. Three men and one woman in a balloon seek out the source of the blast and find that it is electrical repair work being done on an incredible airship parked in the mountain's crater. The craft is the *Albatross*, and its commander, Robur (Vincent Price), like Nemo, is trying to abolish warfare. Robur captures the balloonists, one of whom is American governmental agent Strock (Charles Bronson).

Herbert Lom as Captain Nemo in *Mysterious Island*.

Two subsea explorers from the silent *Mysterious Island* (1929).

As the ruthless Robur crosses the Atlantic, sinking warships and delivering ultimatums, Strock works to destroy the ship. When the *Albatross* comes within range of two warring European armies, it is fired upon. Damaged, the ship limps away. While Robur tries desperately to keep the craft aloft, Strock plants dynamite in the engine room. He and the other balloonists escape via rope as TNT explodes the world's first heavier-then-air vehicle, and it sails helplessly into the ocean.

Master of the World and *Robur the Conqueror* lack the flair and invention of Verne's other novels and are not among his more popular works. However, they do make for an interesting film in *Dynamagic*. Although the picture is clearly a redundancy of *20,000 Leagues Under the Sea*—even to the Masonesque performance by Price—*Master of the World* works hard to maintain its own personality. On the surface, it is more brutal than the Disney film, and certainly more juvenile. However, there is also a graceful majesty about it that is lacking in *20,000 Leagues Under the Sea*. The *Albatross* bears Robur aloft like an avenging angel. Nemo must slink about underwater to achieve his goal. The irony, of course, is that both autocrats end up in the drink. Still, their parallel paths are entertaining, although Disney's is the more polished effort.

While American producers were busy with the Verne brain-children, Czechoslovakian filmmaker Karel Zeman decided to resurrect the original. *The*

Robert Ryan as Captain Nemo in *Captain Nemo and the Underwater City*.

The prehistoric phororhacos, Gary Merrill (prone), Beth Rogan, and Joan Greenwood in *Mysterious Island*.

A glass-shot from *The Fabulous World of Jules Verne*.

Fabulous World of Jules Verne (1961) follows very closely the visual style of Zeman's aforementioned *Baron Munchausen* (1961), using animation and live actors to tell the story. In the film, spies kidnap a noted professor who is pursued through the fantasy worlds of Jules Verne by his devoted assistant. Drawing primarily from *Face the Flags* with bits of *20,000 Leagues Under the Sea* and *Robur the Conqueror* thrown in for contrast, *The Fabulous World of Jules Verne* tried, very successfully, to bring to life the engravings of the period and the spirit of their author.

A major fantasy filmmaker who has thus far gone largely unmentioned plays an important role in the remainder of our study. He has long been one of the genre's most avaricious participants. In 1939, when Nazi Germany bared its fangs, and the hot breath of war covered Europe, George Pal left Holland and came to America with his wife and son. He had built a reputation as the best and most commercial stop-motion artist in Europe, where his short films and theatrical advertisements were universally applauded. Starting from scratch in a tiny Los Angeles garage, he established the new George Pal Productions. With a small staff he produced dozens of eight-minute long Puppetoons for Paramount, each stop-motion movie taking a month and a half to make. After seven years, though they had always earned a profit, these Puppetoons became too costly to produce. Thus, in 1949, after toying with several projects, Pal obtained backing from Eagle Lion films to produce a picture called *The Great Rupert*. The story of a trained squirrel, executed in stop-motion, *The Great Rupert* makes his down-and-out owner (Jimmy Durante) wealthy when he finds a hidden cache of money. Though well received, and a popular family entertainment, the film was fully eclipsed by Pal's next production, the Oscar-winning, big box office *Destination Moon* (1950), a semidocumentary tale of the first lunar landing. *When Worlds Collide* (1952), *War of the Worlds* (1953), *Conquest of Space* (1955), *Tom Thumb* (1958), and *The Time Machine* (1960) followed, an unbroken string of box-office hits.

Pal had wanted to film *The Time Machine* for over eight years, ever since he first tackled another work by H. G. Wells, *War of the Worlds*. Unfortunately, it took the weight of his many successes to convince MGM to let him make the picture.

Wells is not as intimately associated with science-fiction gadgetry as Verne; rather, his forte gravitated to theme and moral. His pleasure in writing was to expound on some of man's harder doctrines. Pal, however, is more like Verne, an

Yvette Mimieux in a publicity still for *The Time Machine* that can best be described as "tatty."

uncommon in fantasy films, people came to see the Oscar-winning special effects, Pal's fifth in the category out of seven films. And they are, in fact, a wonder to behold. As the time traveler journeys into the future, cities rise and fall about him, seasons pass in seconds, and mountains erode before his startled eyes. It's a *tour de force* that required techniques ranging from stop-motion to time-lapse photography, to such incredible details as small electric lights in the eyes of the subterranean Morlocks. These monster guises, incidentally, were the work of Bill Tuttle, who would himself win an Oscar for disguising Tony Randall as all of Pal's *Seven Faces of Dr. Lao* (see chapter 5).

Although scenes of sincere human drama are, conversely, not generally a part of the fantasy genre, one scene in *The Time Machine* stands as unique in all film history. The time traveler, in his home before taking off for the future, domonstrates to friends a prototype of his machine. Three of the four guests scoff; the fourth man (Alan Young) tells him to be careful. When Taylor heads into the future, he comes across his friend in 1917, looking as youthful as ever. When the voyager calls him by his father's name, Young explains that he is the son; the father

inveterate tinkerer. He did away with the novelist's philosophical meanderings to give the audience one-hundred minutes of solid entertainment.

Our time traveler (Rod Taylor) leaves London on New Year's Eve, 1899. He stops during World War I, World War II, and finally, in 1966, World War III. Disconsolate with the depths to which man had sunk, the explorer pushes far into the future, stopping in the year 802,701. There, he finds a world of sprawling countryside and a passive fair-haired people called the Eloi. The time traveler falls in love with Weena (Yvette Mimieux), but soon learns that the docile Eloi are dominated by cannibalistic mutants known as Morlocks. When the monsters take Weena as part of a group destined to be dinner, the Englishman forces the Eloi into rebellion. The fight against the Morlocks is filled with fire and frenzy as, ultimately, the creatures' underground machinery is blown sky-high. After the battle, Taylor goes back to 1899, picks up some tools and books, and returns to his beloved Weena.

Fine performances and careful attention to period detail make their presence felt. However, as is not

Yvette Mimieux and a Morlock from *The Time Machine*.

Martha Hyer and Charles H. Schneer on the Cherry Cottage set of *First Men in the Moon*.

both touching and frightening, made all the more so when interrupted by the distant explosion of an atom bomb. It is the kind of confrontation which, again, is unique to our genre.

After *The Time Machine*, Pal produced his first financial failure, *Atlantis, The Lost Continent* (1961). A young fisherman (Anthony Hall) leaves his native waters in Ancient Greece to find the legendary land of super science. After being accosted by King Neptune and Atlantean submarines, he finds a nightmare world where rays are made to disintegrate solid matter, and experiments are performed to turn men into animals. In the end, of course, all the technology of Atlantis cannot save it from nature's wrath and stock footage of the burning of Rome as seen in *Quo Vadis*.

Leaving, for now, the work of George Pal, but staying with H. G. Wells, we return to one of the animators who cut his teeth on the puppetoons, Ray Harryhausen. Wells' *First Men In the Moon* was originally filmed by the great French fantasy producer George Melies as *A Trip to the Moon* (1903). In that silent classic—generally considered to be the first science-fiction film—a line of scantily clad bathing beauties launches Melies and friends to the earth's satellite via space bullet. After striking the Man in the Moon square in the eye, the men disembark and are confronted by antlike humanoids called Selenites. Sixty-two years later, Harryhausen's plot followed a remarkably similar and equally innocent thread. An antigravity substance known as Cavorite sends the coughing, eccentric

died in the war. Upset, but pressing on through time, Taylor meets the aged and haggard Young at the onset of World War III. The old man recognizes the time traveler, but can in no way comprehend how he has retained his youth. Their interplay is

Lionel Jeffries and Martha Hyer relax between takes on *First Men in the Moon*.

Selenites electrocute the lunar centipede in *First Men in the Moon*.

Professor Cavor (Lionel Jeffries), writer Arnold Bedford (Edward Judd), and his fiancee Kate (Martha Hyer) to the moon, circe 1890, in a huge metal sphere. They navigate through space by ingeniously raising or lowering cavorite-coated window shades and, arriving on the moon, claim it for Queen Victoria. Donning diving suits, the men go romping about the lunar surface, encounter one of Harryhausen's monsters—not the moon-calf of the novel, but a giant centipede—and are taken prisoner by the Selenites. A scientist, Cavor is thrilled with the creatures; Bedford, realizing that the monsters will never allow them to leave, is not. Cavor elects to submit passively to the Selenites. Arnold and Kate fight their way to the sphere and blast off.

Years later, a NASA moon landing discovers the ruins of a once-great civilization. Astronauts also find the British flag left behind by Cavor, and track down the one surviving member of the flight. Bedford, now old, decrepit, and living in a nursing home, says simply, "Poor Cavor. He did have such a terrible cold."[15]

For the first time in all the Harryhausen filmography, the scenery and monsters do not upstage the performers. This is due to the fact there was only one giant creature in the picture. Neither script nor plot was contrived to work in additional beasts. Thus, character development and personality conflicts were more pronounced than usual. There was meat on which the actors could chew, although only character actor Lionel Jeffries seized the opportunity and gave a wonderful performance as the scientist torn between discovery, challenge, and obligation. He easily overshadowed the dry Judd and the melodramatic Hyer, who seemed ill-at-ease in the period dress and manner. In any case, *First Men In The Moon* is a colorful, marvelously anachronistic adventure that spits in the eye of technology and shows how, in the world of fantasy, all it takes to reach the moon is a diving bell and a can of Cavorite!

Jane Fonda in one of her bizarre *Barbarella* predicaments.

Less innocent fun, although spiced with equally incredible science, was one of the most criticized films of its time, *Barbarella* (1967). Based on Jean Claude Forest's erotic French comic strip, this Roger Vadim film tells how the space heroine (Jane Fonda), barely clad and facing such ominous alien devices as an orgasm organ, saves the earth from destruction in the year 40,000. Her consort, an angel (John Phillip Law), dies in the process, martyred on the cross. Unfortunately, the era of camp had already seen its most halcyon days. Consequently, this tongue-in-cheek effort, playing on film's new sexual permissiveness and its own imagined inventiveness, failed at the box office. So much for adult fantasies! Of course, childrens' adventures were also having a difficult time of it. Such costly efforts as Ian Fleming's tale of a crazy inventor (Dick Van Dyke) and his flying car *Chitty Chitty Bang Bang* (1968), and Road Dahl's sensitive, very excellent *Charlie and the Chocolate Factory*, which became the musical *Willy Wonka and the Chocolate Factory* (1971), also failed to impress theatergoers. Neither picture did as well as expected. This is, not surprisingly, an injustice. The latter film, especially, had interesting sets, a witty and well-written script, the hit tune *The Candy Man*, and an inspiring theme for the fantasist, the song sung by chocolate candy czar Wonka (Gene Wilder): "There is no world I know to compare with pure imagination . . ." Fortunately, the genre did find a foothold with the public in its horror films, and such enormously popular science-fiction efforts as *2001: A Space Odyssey* and *Planet of the Apes*, both released within a month of each other in 1968.

Planet of the Apes is unique in the realm of fantasy in that it has spawned four sequels, a short-lived television series, and an animated cartoon series. Only *Godzilla* and *King Kong* can make similar boasts. The stories told by the five films have been oft-repeated and merit only brief resume. Three astronauts land on a planet where evolution has seemingly gone mad: humans are the uncivilized savages and apes the articulate masters. One of the spacemen is dissected and stuffed, another is lobotomized, and the third, Taylor (Charlton Heston) escapes into the planet's Forbidden Zone. There, he finds the wreckage of the Statue of Liberty and realizes that this insane world is earth of the future. In *Beneath the Planet of the Apes* (1970), a rescue ship visits the monkey planet. Only one astronaut, Brent (James Franciscus) survives the crash-landing and is taken into custody by the apes. Escaping, Brent is captured by the telepathic mutant humans who live underground in the Forbidden Zone. Their God is an atomic warhead, and their sport is forcing the new arrivals Taylor and Brent to battle. In the end, the apes invade the mutants' domain and Taylor detonates the warhead, blowing up the planet. Before this happens, however, three apes had boarded one of the spaceships and, in *Escape from the Planet of the Apes* (1971) did just that, fleeing to Southern California of 1973. There, they are shot and killed. Only a baby ape survives, and he is raised by a carnival owner. The fourth film, *Conquest of the Planet of the Apes* (1972), introduces this ape. Caesar (Roddy McDowall), at adulthood. In the year 1990, a space plague has killed all the earth's dogs and cats, and apes are kept as pets. Trained to do menial labor, the simians quickly tire of their cruel taskmasters. Led by Caesar, the monkeys revolt and end the rule of man on earth. Finally, in *Battle for the Planet of the Apes* (1973), we see how the ape civilization rose to power, how the mutants went undergound, how human beings were enslaved, and how the world became the *Planet of the Apes*.

The genre has never really known a phenomenon that rose and fell as quickly as did the ape films. Built on a gimmick, they never had the staying power of James Bond or Dracula. Yet, in their brief reign, the apes loosed up more ticket and merchandising money than all the Universal and Toho monster movies combined. This was no doubt due to the appeal of the costly ape makeups and plot twists with which the writers kept coming up. The former consisted of $2,000,000 worth of rubber muzzles, foreheads, and noses applied directly to the actors' faces for realistic movement; the latter was built on both making the apes heroes, and bringing the saga full circle. With satire for the adults, and adventure for the kids, the apes proved that you *can* please all of the people all of the time.

As of this writing, the last of the so-called scientific romances to reach the screen has been the Walt Disney studios' disappointing adaptation of Ian Cameron's novel *Island at the Top of the World* (1974). When their airship explodes, a group of explorers is stranded on a volcanic island in the North Pole. The island, they soon discover, is inhabited by Vikings who are far from enamored of the outer-world trespassers. The film becomes, like Disney's earlier and better *In Search of the Casta-*

A case of life imitating art! These candies are currently among the most popular in America! (c) Concorde Confections, Division of Sunmark, Inc.

The Oompa-Loompas, green-skinned candymakers, come to the aide of a little girl who's been transformed into a human blueberry. From *Willy Wonka and the Chocolate Factory*.

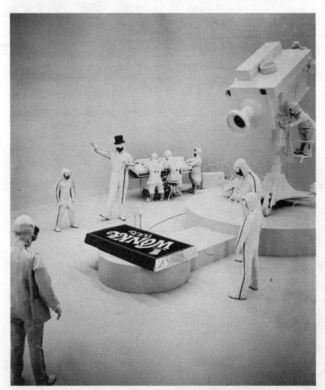

To pack all the taste possible into a single candy bar, the employees of *Willy Wonka and the Chocolate Factory* build their bars huge, then shrink them.

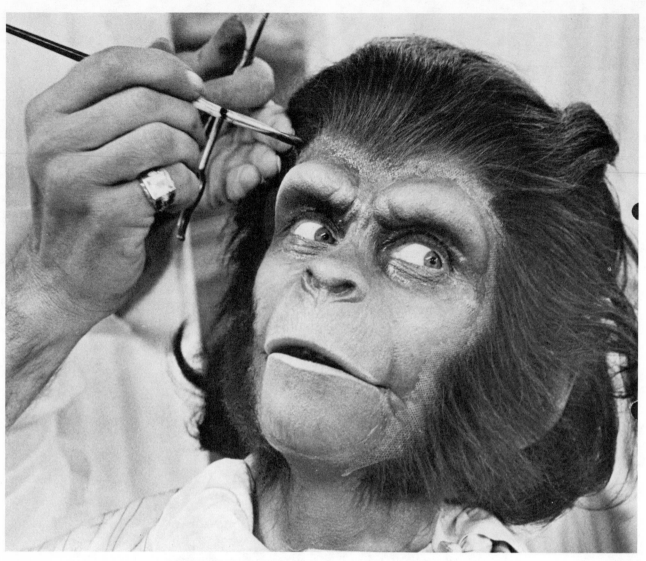

Kim Hunter is made up for her role as Dr. Zira in
Planet of the Apes.

Kim Hunter and Arthur P. Jacobs on the set of *Escape
from the Planet of the Apes.*

Chimpanzee Roddy McDowall clowns with a crew-member between takes on *Planet of the Apes*.

Dr. Hasslein (Eric Braeden) prepares to inject Cornelius (McDowall) and Zira (Kim Hunter) with truth serum, while Lewis (Bradford Dillman) looks on. From *Escape from the Planet of the Apes*.

ways (1962), one series of near-escapes after another. The difference between the films, of course, is the lackluster production of the latter. Nowhere is the reported $8,000,000 budget in evidence. The acting and sets are poor, a pale shadow of *20,000 Leagues Under the Sea*, and the special effects—particularly the glass paintings [16] and miniature sets—are downright awful. Thus, *Island at the Top of the World* raises the inevitable question: if our cinematographic technology keeps improving, why do the majority of our films become increasingly worse?

13
INCREDIBLE LANDS

One of the marvels of fantasy is the amazing variety of strange places to which it constantly carries us. We have already seen a number of bizarre lands in the context of mythology and the supernatural. Now, through the courtesy of William Shakespeare, Jonathan Swift, James Hilton, and others, we will look at the fantasy film worlds of classic literature.

Sir James Barrie's *Peter Pan* has had its most famous screen versions courtesy of Mary Martin and Walt Disney (see chapter 7). However, the Scottish novelist's book and play about the boy who never grew up, and his adventures with Wendy and her brothers in Never-Never Land, was also an interesting silent film. Made in 1924, this alternately theatrical and cinematic film—photographed by James Wong Howe (*Prisoner of Zenda, Hud*)—is notable for its effective flying sequences, elaborate costuming, and sincere, if ultimately disappointing, attempt to put a man in a crocodile suit. It is important to our study as one of the first films to tell a feature-length fantasy story and sustain its credibility. That year also saw the first film treatment of *The Wizard of Oz*, a silent adaptation of the L. Frank Baum classic with a screenplay written by the author's son. In this version, Dorothy (Dorothy Dwan) dreams that she and two farm workers are swept to Oz in a tornado. There, the girl becomes Queen of Oz and the hired hands disguise themselves as a scarecrow and a tin man. After meeting the thin, bespectacled wizard, our heroine comes-to and the vision is ended. A generally forgotten little picture, *The Wizard of Oz* boasts the presence of two men who became giants of the industry: film

editor Sam Zimbalist, the producer of MGM's *Ben-Hur* (1959), and none other than Oliver Hardy, of Laurel and Hardy fame, as the tin Woodsman.

Another tale that has had many incarnations is *Alice in Wonderland*. Silent shorts based on the Lewis Carroll novel appeared in 1903, 1915, 1927, and 1928, but the first feature-length production did not reach the screen until 1933 when Charlotte Henry essayed the role of the impetuous girl. The film had a fine screenplay and superb art direction, both by William Cameron Menzies, a marvelous score by Dimitri Tiomkin (*High Noon, The Thing*), and a supporting cast that included Gary Cooper, W. C. Fields, Cary Grant, and many others. Currently, Disney's 1951 cartoon is enjoying a tremendous renaissance (See chapter 7), despite the failure of a lavish live-action remake in 1972.

In his 1903 operetta, *Babes in Toyland*, Irish-born composer-conductor Victor Herbert told the story of how Alan and Jane, shipwrecked in Mother Goose's Toyland, called forth an army of wooden soldiers to destroy the dictatorial dreams of a wicked toymaker. Twenty-one years later, with a few small changes in the plot, this classic entertainment became Laurel and Hardy's *Babes in Toyland*. The comedians portray laborers in a toy factory who thwart the monstrous bogey-man forces of the evil Barnaby (Henry Kleinbach). They are assisted in this by an army of one-hundred six-foot-tall wooden soldiers who attack to the tune of the memorable *March of the Toys*.

Several decades later, Walt Disney tried his hand

184

The silent *Peter Pan* (1924).

Captain Hook convinces the crocodile to swallow a clock in *Peter Pan* (1924).

Oliver Hardy, Dorothy Dwan, and Larry Semon in *The Wizard of Oz* (1924).

at a literal adaptation of what was, for his studio, very suitable material. The new *Babes in Toyland* (1961) retained the title, but little else of the Herbert original. Ray Bolger starred as the villain, while Tommy Sands and Annette Funicello played the romantic leads. With new songs and a disappointing lack of verve, the picture was one of Disney's least successful efforts and quickly appeared as a special effects-ful two-parter on his *Wonderful World of Color*.

During Hollywood's very opulent thirties, musicals were a popular form of escape from the crushing

The Cat (of The Cat and the Fiddle fame) and Stan Laurel listen to Oliver Hardy describe the mouths of the Bogeymen. From *Babes in Toyland*.

reality of a national depression. Accordingly, studios turned to properties like *Babes in Toyland* that assured enough trade familiarity to breed a financial return. If the material were in the public domain, all the better. Unfortunately, while this theory was viable on paper, it did not always work in practice. Felix Mendelssohn's classic ballet *A Midsummer Night's Dream*, based on the play by Shakespeare, is a prime example of this. It was a spectacular, star-studded financial failure in which four lovers Hermia (Olivia de Havilland), Helena (Jean Muir), Lysander (Dick Powell), and Demetrius (Ross Alexander) meet in the woods of a mythical land and there become embroiled with six dull-witted tradesmen who are rehearsing a play for their king, Theseus (Ian Hunter); Theseus falls in love with Hyppolyta, conquered Queen of the Amazons (Veree Teasdale); and the King and Queen of the Fairies, Oberon (Victor Jory) and Titania (Anita Louise), parry one another in matters political and amorous. Although the 1935 production is a vastly impressive visual achievement, the largely American cast was signed for its box-office strength rather than its training in the stage or in Shakespeare. Confused by the intent and legitimacy of this halfway production, audiences stayed away. However, since this is not the place to argue the sanctity of the Bard, *A Midsummer Night's Dream* features incredible visions of fantasy that tend to leave the viewer breathless. From the magic worked by the impish Puck (Mickey Rooney) to the transforming of tradesman Touchbottom (James Cagney) into a half-man, half-mule, the scenic aspects of Shakespeare's dreamworld are faithful and lush. Sprawling forests, dew-washed and filled with glitter and pearl as fairies flit through the air spinning clothes from spiders' webs, are as imaginative and extravagant as any sets ever created in Hollywood. The pity lies in their having gone to waste in a compromise film that tried, unsuccessfully, to spoon-feed Shakespeare to the moviegoing public.

Perhaps the problem with Shakespeare for the masses is the incompatability of his medieval tongue with our modern ear. Fortunately, other classic fantasies had no such problem. *Lost Horizon*, for example, made a sizeable impact on the moviegoing public in 1936. Based on the best-selling 1933 novel by James Hilton *(Goodbye Mr. Chips)*, the Frank Capra film was also more successful than the recent musical remake. One cannot blame old English for *everything!*

James Cagney and Joe E. Brown "kiss" in a performance of their play. From *A Midsummer Night's Dream*.

In our chapter on Angels, we saw how director Capra's *It's A Good Life* was very much concerned with the ultimate dignity of a single human life. Moreso than his latter effort, the entire fabric of *Lost Horizon* is a reaffirmation of this belief. A planeload of Europeans flees the heart of a Chinese revolution. Much to the foreigners' consternation, when they land to refuel it is on a vast, wind swept plateau from which point their plane is flown to Tibet. Their destination: the valley of Shangri-La, a paradise lost high in the snowcapped mountains of the Himalayas. In this placid setting of white-walled and stately buildings, reflecting pools, and gentle garden paths, the High Lama (Sam Jaffe) offers the newcomers contentment and eternal life, but only if they promise never to leave the great city. Unfortunately, only one man, Hugh Conway (Ronald Colman) is content to stay. He has fallen in love with one of the Tibetans (Jane Wyman). The others elect to leave, and Conway reluctantly joins them. On the mountain peaks, all save our hero perish. Realizing the mistake he has made, Conway decides to return to Shangri-La. The film ends as he scales the white Himalayan slopes in search of lost peace, his fate in the viewers' hands.

Life beyond Shangri-La is a heaving, mindless mass of people lacking in good sense or grace. In this formless, faceless hotbed of the Chinese insurrection, Capra has found his deplorable universal man. Although one may quibble with this simplistic representation of the human animal, *Lost Horizon* is not an irresponsible film. Its purpose is to laud the effort of the single man, and in this respect the movie is both commendable and successful. A parable coated with the gloss of romanticism, the message of *Lost Horizon* would soon be lost, ironically, in the cancerous spread of World War II.

When it was announced, in 1970, that popular composers Burt Bacharach and Hal David would write the score for a musical version of the Hilton original, there were groans to be heard from those to whom Capra's vision remained vital. Bacharach's light, bouncy style did not even seem right, in the telling, for Hilton's weighty theme. The resultant failure of *Lost Horizon* (1973) at the box office was not unexpected. In its behalf, the tunes, out of context, are excellent, and the acting by Peter Finch and Michael York is also quite good. Unfortunately, the tatty retelling, sloppy sets and special effects, and corny supporting players—particularly George Kennedy's gold-lusting engineer Sam Cornelius and Bobby Van's second-rate entertainer Harry Lovett—make the film an embarrassing exercise in pretention. Producer Ross Hunter, who's made such audience-pleasing pictures as *Airport*, should

The tranquility of Frank Capra's Shangri-La in *Lost Horizon*.

The main palace and garden from Ross Hunter's *Lost Horizon*.

have known better than to try and schmaltz up both Capra and Hilton.

In 1937, when MGM decided to film *The Wizard of Oz* anew, they were set to borrow Shirley Temple from Twentieth Century Fox in exchange for the loan of Jean Harlow and Clark Gable. Unfortunately, Miss Harlow died and the deal fell through. Thus, the studio cast Judy Garland as the dream-seeking Dorothy. At the time, the young singer-dancer hadn't a remarkable career behind her. She had had a few bit parts in films, including a handful of short subjects. However, the former Francis Gumm surprised the movie brass and made the film her own. Through it, she became one of the screen's most enduring legends.

When the house of Dorothy's aunt and uncle is flung to Oz by a great tornado, the girl finds that she has done a great deed for the dwarfish inhabitants thereof, the Munchkins. The structure, on landing,

had crushed the evil Wicked Witch of the East to death. Although Dorothy is pleased to have been of service, she wants to go home. A good witch (Billie Burke) tells her to follow the yellow brick road and see the great Wizard, the only man in Oz who can help her. Along the way, Dorothy picks up traveling companions: a scarecrow in search of a brain (Ray Bolger); a tin woodsman who wants a heart (Jack Haley); and a cowardly lion who desperately craves courage (Bert Lahr). Throughout their journey, the foursome is terrorized by another sorceress, the Wicked Witch of the West (Margaret Hamilton), who covets a pair of magical slippers that Dorothy took from the dead witch's feet.

Arriving, finally, in the Emerald City of Oz, the group is brought before the wizard who explains that he will grant their requests only if they bring him the broomstick of the surviving witch. The brave party invades the fiend's castle and is cap-

Margaret Hamilton, Judy Garland, Ray Bolger, and
the yellow brick road in *The Wizard of Oz*.

Margaret Hamilton and two of her monkey-aviates
from *The Wizard of Oz*.

tured. As the sorceress sets the scarecrow on fire, Dorothy grabs a bucket of water to extinguish the blaze. The liquid covers the witch and she melts. The victors return to Oz with the broomstock only to learn that the wizard is a charlatan. However, in their adventure, each of Dorothy's companions had earned the object of his quest. Even the girl's wish is granted when the Munchkins' good witch appears and tells Dorothy that a click of her ruby heels will send her home. Moments later, Dorothy awakens in bed, having been knocked unconscious by the twister. Through it all, however, she did learn that despite her problems, and a longing for that wonderful land over the rainbow, "there's no place like home."

Released in 1939, the film was a great success and properly so. The movie is a childhood fantasy come true, a native American dreamworld of extremes, alternately pleasant and light, frightening and drab, filled with song and terror. The picture spans even the cinematographic rainbow, sporting black and white photography for the scenes in Kansas, and full, rich color when Dorothy arrives in Oz. Of particular note to fantasy fans, especially in the context of our earlier look at witches, is Margaret Hamilton. She provides the screen with one of its most skillfully characterized sorceresses, a classic vision replete with pointed hat, broomstick, and gnarled, twisted carriage. Truly, in song and story, one of the great adventures of imagination.

Returning to earth from Oz, we find quite a different approach to fantasy in Oscar Wilde's 1891 novelette *A Portrait of Dorain Gray*. Filmed, first, in 1945, the story is that of a young man who, in the presence of an enchanted Egyptian cat goddess, makes a wish on his oil portrait: that the painting age while he, himself, remains young. Miraculously, this is what happens. Dorian (Hurd Hatfield) is thus able to live a wicked life without showing his physical age or the weight of his sins. Instead, his portrait grows ever more corrupt. Decades pass and finally, unable to bear the loathesome picture and his own superficial purity, Dorain rends the canvas assunder. To his own person is transferred its myraid evils, and Dorian dies before the painting. With credible box-office sense, the sombre, justice-be-done mood of this excellent film was replaced by an explicit rendering of Dorian's sins in the second telling, *The Secret of Dorian Gray* (1971). However, lacking enough naked flesh to be accurately labeled pornographic, the film failed at the box office, although it did manage to exploit the very moral decay it was condemning. Only Herbert Lom, as Dorian's homosexual lover and an observer to his erosion, survives the picture by playing it with tongue-in-cheek. Everything else about this low-budget abomination is unworthy of serious consideration.

Mark Twain's light-hearted tale of *A Connecticut Yankee In King Arthur's Court* became a Bing Crosby musical in 1948. The contemporary New Englander telepaths himself backward in time. After introducing modern thought to Arthur's England, he is labeled a wizard and is forced to fight for his life. A generally tepid effort, *A Connecticut Yankee in King Arthur's Court* is typical of how fantasy becomes silly when forced into the mainstream by people who have no understanding of or feel for the genre. Another of literature's most misunderstood magicians was *The Pied Piper of Hamelin*. In the 1953 film, based on a poem by Robert Browning—which is itself based on an ancient legend—Van Johnson's piper lures a plague of rats from the medieval German town. When his job is completed, he learns that the townspeople never had any intention of paying him for his efforts. As a result, the piper is forced to whistle away the local children. Made for television, the film was also a great theatrical success. Less appreciated was the 1971 remake, with rock star Donovan in the title role.

In several of this chapter's films there was the very potent moral warning that man must mutate or die. Perhaps the patriarch of this school, and still the most cleverly conceived satire of its type, is Jonathan Swift's *Gulliver's Travels*. Although Swift went mad at the end of his life, the only madness inherent in his novel is the folly of the creatures and peoples that Gulliver meets on his journeys. These include the midget Lilliputians, the giant Brobdingnagians, the residents of the flying island of Laputa, and the literate horse beings known as Houhynhms.

The first complete publication of the Englishman's allegedly factual voyages was in 1735. Two-hundred years later, in 1939, the first screen version of *Gulliver's Travels* premiered, a feature-length cartoon created by Max Fleischer (see chapter 15). Twenty years later, Ray Harryhausen's *Three Worlds of Gulliver* was released. Although Swift's satire of the eighteenth century was edited and made more universal for the film, the screenplay is faithful in theme to the original.

William Bendix as Sir Sagramore (left) helps Bing Crosby into a proper disguise in *A Connecticut Yankee in King Arthur's Court.*

Ray Harryhausen considers last-minute details (left), while Kerwin Mathews and hairdresser prepare to shoot a scene for *The Three Worlds of Gulliver.* In this sequence, Mathews will be helping a Lilliputian prisoner escape from prison.

The movie is a condemnation of man's selfish ignorance, the brunt of which is borne by Dr. Lemuel Gulliver (Kerwin Mathews). His tour of duty as a ship's doctor is cut short when he has an argument with fiancee Elizabeth (June Thorburn) and a storm tosses him overboard. Washed onto

Lilliput, the giant learns that this incredible nation is at war with the neighboring island of Blefescu. The king explains to Gulliver that the enemy insists on breaking eggs at the large end; as everyone knows, the dignified way to break eggs is at the small end. When Gulliver suggests that the countries compromise and split their eggs in the middle, the king dismisses this as barbaric. Thus, the potentate insists that Gulliver conquer Blefescu or he'll not be permitted to build a ship for return to England. Not wishing to hurt anyone, Gulliver does nothing more than haul Blefescu's warships out to sea, thus ending the strife. After becoming further involved in the silly politics of the tiny islands, the physician leaves for home via his newly built boat.

After a long day's rowing, Gulliver falls asleep and awakens in the arms of a huge girl, Glumdalclich (Sherri Alberoni). She takes her toy man to the king, who informs Gulliver that he is in Brobdingnag. He is reunited with his fiancee, who was swept ashore when the ship eventually went down. Because of his curative powers, displayed when he rids the queen of an upset stomach, Gulliver is branded a witch and must fight a giant alligator for his life. Defeating the dragonlike monster, Gulliver and Elizabeth are grabbed by Glumdalclich who rushes them to the sea. Pursued by the king's men, the girl places the lovers in her basket and heaves them into the ocean. The current returns them to England where they are left to speculate

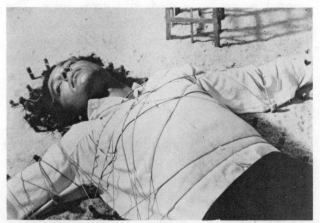

Kerwin Mathews trussed on the beaches of Lilliput for *The Three Worlds of Gulliver.*

whether their adventures had been real or imagined.

Not unlike *First Men in the Moon, Three Worlds of Gulliver* has very little stop-motion work, and there is no build to each new monster scene the way there was in the Jason or Sinbad films. Of course, what animation there is is superb. Gulliver's fight with the alligator and bout with a monster squirrel are doubly impressive since the puppets effectively mime their real-life counterparts. However, the bulk of the special effects budget went, of necessity, into making Gulliver appear large or small. These illusions came off without a hitch. Especially clever was the echoed redubbing of Mathews' voice to emphasize his giantism in Lilliput.

While the Englishman was adventuring around the world, George Pal was busy working wonders in his native land. Pal had long-wanted to film the story of Tom Thumb, a kind of movie he felt the public needed. Evidently the producer was right. Based on the Grimm Brothers' fairy tale, *Tom Thumb* was released in 1958 and became an instant success.

When a woodcutter (Alan Young) meets the Queen of the Forest (June Thorburn), the sprite promises him three wishes. Returning home, Young and his wife squander their wishes in an argument and come to regret it. The thoughtful fairy, however, fulfills their one great desire, which is to have a son. Thus, to the couple's door comes the inches-tall Tom Thumb (Russ Tamblyn). After settling in, Tom becomes involved with thiefs and, in the end, defeats them and is a hero.

One of the scenes in *Tom Thumb* that helped win the film its much-deserved special-effects Oscar was Tom's dance with the toys in his room. Tamblyn, an excellent dancer—he played Riff in the film version of *West Side Story*—joined forces with literally dozens of stop-motion playthings to march and sing a lengthy number in Tom's enormous playroom. For over five minutes, the screen is alive with the most impossible visions: in all, the kind of magic that even begrudging adults had to find delightful.

After filming *The Time Machine* and the Cinerama superproduction *The Wonderful World of the Brothers Grimm* (1962) (see chapter 8), Pal turned to a novel by Charles Finney for his next project. Published in 1935, Finney's adult fantasy *The Circus of Dr. Lao* became Pal's *Seven Faces of Dr. Lao* (1964). To make the film palpable for his younger patrons, Pal sapped the novel of its harder blows against the spurious nature of man and wiped clean its more literal sexual displays.

Into the fictitious Southwestern town of Abalone comes the mysterious Dr. Lao, a Chinaman who is many hundreds of years old. He opens a bizarre circus just outside the turn-of-the-century city. There, each of the visitors finds his inner-self personified by the attractions. A young widowed librarian (Barbara Eden) has her passion reborn by the great God Pan; a self-centered old spinster (Minerva Urecal) is humbled by the blind seer Appolonius with the forecast of a lonely future. A domineering wife is turned to stone by her mythological counterpart the Medusa, while a wealthy rancher is mimicked by a huge snake who claims to be his brother.

Between these various visitations, the film shows us the rancher's (Arthur O'Connell) attempts to buy the town from its inhabitants. Only a young newspaperman (John Erickson) demands that the citizens hold onto their homes. It is a losing battle, however, as the people care less for the value of their roots than for the quick money the sale will earn. Accordingly, Lao presents a vision in his center ring, showing the fall of the ancient empire of Wolderkand. The story woven by this ethereal presentation parallels the plight of Abalone. The populace, moved by the tale, elects not to sell their town. Defeated, and also greatly affected by the Wolderkand tale in which he had been portrayed as the villain, O'Connell admits that a railroad is coming through Abalone and will make everyone rich. Everyone is pleased, of course, except for two of O'Connell's henchmen. They had been looking forward to a piece of the railroad money. Disgruntled, they visit Lao's deserted circus and find a small fishbowl in which, the Chinaman had claimed, lives the ferocious Loch Ness Monster, which, when exposed to air, will alledgedly grow huge. The ruffians break the glass and, as Lao had warned, the slug becomes a snarling giant serpent. The monster ravages the countryside and is stopped only when Lao arrives and, with his rainmaking machine, causes a downpour that shrinks the beast. His work completed, the wizened Lao leaves for another Abalone.

Tony Randall gives a brilliant tour-de-force performance as six of the *Seven Faces of Dr. Lao*. These include Lao, Appolonius, the Medusa, Pan, Merlin the Magician, and the Abominable Snowman. The stop-motion snake and Loch Ness Monster are the work of Jim Danforth, whose efforts earned him an Oscar nomination. The award that year went to the undeserving *Mary Poppins*. On a less clinical level,

The *Seven Faces of Dr. Lao.* Moving clockwise from the horned Pan on top, we have Merlin, the Abominable Snowman, Dr. Lao, Appolonius and the Medusa. In the center is Tony Randall. Incidentally, the hair in the center picture is not Tony's. He was shaved for the part and borrowed a toupe from Gene Kelly to take the picture. Notice his pencilled-in eyebrows!

Mary Poppins **prepares to answer two children's ad for a nanny. Talking parrot umbrella is to her left. (c) Walt Disney Productions**

Together with a fun-loving chimney sweep (Dick Van Dyke), they enter cartoon and fantasy worlds partaking in all manner of strange adventures. Eventually, the childrens' father realizes he must spend more time with his kids. No longer needed, Mary takes hold of her talking umbrella and disappears into the clouds.

Julie Andrews and Dick Van Dyke—who also doubles as the aged president of the bank—are marvelous in their roles, and the Oscar-winning score by Robert and Richard Sherman is one of the catchiest and most inventive ever written for a motion picture. Indeed, the only complaint one can level against the film is that it lacks the charm and the polish of Disney's animated works. On the topic of its technical skill alone, when Mary flies into town, the wires that hold her aloft are plainly visible; the process work is shoddy; and when Mary orders a room to clean itself, the stop-motion animation is

Pal and Finney's concept of the circus being inside each one of us is effectively translated for the young by Lao's many conversations with Barbara Eden's screen son. While far-removed from the more subtle and biting presentation of this in the novel, it's a valuable lesson to children, and a worthwhile reminder to the old. In every respect, *Seven Faces of Dr. Lao* is a showpiece of which the genre can be proud. More than any other film, it illustrates what the world's greatest storytellers, from Aesop to Dickens, always knew: that fantasy is the finest means of preaching a change in the more abstract aspects of human nature.

We mentioned, several paragraphs back, Walt Disney's *Mary Poppins* as an irresponsible choice for the Best Special Effects Oscar of 1964. This is not to be construed as a condemnation of the film as a whole. Although not Disney's greatest achievement, it was certainly his most popular and lavish live-action production.

The irony of any consideration about *Mary Poppins* is the fact that Disney books based on the film have, for over a decade now, outsold the original P. L. Travers stories by a ratio of five-to-one. There is something crude about this which, just as unfairly, colors any attempt to look at the film without bias.

The story concerns a magical governess (Julie Andrews) who comes to look after the two young children (Karen Dotrice and Matthew Garber) of a banker (David Tomlinson) and his suffragette wife (Glynnis Johns) in nineteenth-century England.

Mary Poppins **descends upon London. (c) Walt Disney Productions**

Behind *Dr. Dolittle* (left) is the pushmi-pullyu; to the right is Mr. Blossom, the circus proprietor.

not up to George Pal's earliest Puppetoon work. Even the cartoon work is nowhere near the studio's best. This is hardly the kind of special-effects display one expects from a purported landmark of technical acuity.

The Disney name justified the very fanciful nature of the *Mary Poppins* story, a fate not enjoyed by a more polished film, with an equally fine cast and score, *Dr. Dolittle* (1967). Based on the dozen novels written by Hugh Lofting and published in the early 1920s, this Arthur P. Jacobs *(Planet of the Apes)* production is perhaps the most spectacular fantasy film ever made. It's the story of veterinarian Dr. Dolittle (Rex Harrison) who lives in the seaport village of Puddleby in Western England. Dolittle's specialty is that he can talk to animals. On the arrival of friends Matthew Mugg (Anthony Newley) and twelve-year-old Tommy Stubbins (William Dix), who bring the doctor a wounded duck, Dolittle is busy blowing bubbles through a straw into a goldfish bowl. Communicating with a fish, he explains, is preparation to his learning ancient shellfish, which he will need when he sets out to find the Great Pink Snail.

When a large crate arrives at the Dolittle residence, the doctor finds a two-headed llama inside, the pushmi-pullyu. It was sent by a friend of Dolittle's who suggests he sell it to raise money for the forthcoming expedition. The doctor peddles it to Mr. Blossom (Richard Attenborough), proprietor of a local circus, much to the dismay of Emma (Samantha Eggar), a young admirer of the doctor. She accuses him of being insensitive by selling the

animal into captivity, and Dolittle is hurt. Discussing the problem with Blossom's seal Sophie, he learns that she is lonely for her husband, who lives in the North Pole. Looking to repent, Dolittle dresses the animal as a baby, sneaks it away in a carriage, and tosses it, clothing and all, into the English Channel. His selfless act is misunderstood by a passerby who has Dolittle arrested for murder. The court decrees that the vet be put in an insane asylum. Under the guidance of Chee-Chee the monkey and Polynisia the parrot who, like Dolittle, can talk to other animals, police horses are instructed to drive the van with a captive Dolittle to the docks instead of the sanatorium. The officers who set off in pursuit are thrown by their mounts. Waiting in the harbor are Matthew, Emma, and Tommy onboard Dolittle's boat the *Flounder.* They set sail in search of the Great Pink Snail.

When a vicious storm arises, the *Flounder* is fortuitously smashed on the shores of the creature's legendary home, the fabulous floating Sea Star Island. After a confrontation with the native inhabitants thereof—who blame all strangers for the cold climes into which the island keeps sailing—Dolittle gets an idea. He calls on a great blue whale to push the land to a temperate zone. In so doing, the sea mammal rejoins the island with its native Africa and everyone is thrilled, except Dolittle. He had wanted to find the snail. Fortunately, as tribal leader William Shakespeare the Tenth (Geoffrey Holder) points out, legend says the mollusk will reveal itself when the floating island is once again anchored to its mother land. Sure enough, the snail appears. When Dolittle cures it of a cold, the creature offers to carry the castaways home. In England, everyone disembarks save Dolittle. Although he has been forgiven by the authorities— every animal in Puddleby went on strike after his conviction—Dolittle decides to go on a new adventure. He will seek out the legendary Giant Lunar Moth. As the film ends, the great animalitarian is seen flying over Puddleby on the back of the huge insect.

A truly delightful film, *Dr. Dolittle* was shredded by critics who found its innocence and matchless sense of discovery too simple for their lofty tastes. While some of the film's Todd-AO spectacle often overwhelms its light, airy intent, *Dr. Dolittle* creates a warm feeling for its characters and the 1,200 on-screen animals. It is difficult to believe that the good veterinarian is not, in fact, "talking to the

Dick Van Dyke and one of his mad inventions in *Chitty-Chitty, Bang-Bang.*

animals," as the Oscar-winning tune suggests. Add to this enchantment some catchy musical numbers, strong, unpretentious performances, striking sets, and magnificent photography, and you have *Dr. Dolittle*, a storybook come to life.

After *Dr. Dolittle* failed to recoup its $12,000,000 expenditure, studios, as we mentioned earlier, were reluctant to finance any further big-budget musical fantasies. There were, however, several films already in production: *Chitty-Chitty, Bang-Bang* (1968) and *Finian's Rainbow* (1968). *Chitty-Chitty, Bang-Bang* was written by Ian Fleming, the creator of James Bond. It centers around the exploits of a compulsive inventor, Caractacus Potts (Dick Van Dyke) who, after failing to sell his inventions, creates an equally unmarketable flying car. However, the evil Baron Bombast (Gert Frobe) covets, then steals Chitty, and imprisons Caractacus' grandfather (Lionel Jeffries). Bombast is under the mistaken notion that it was the elder Potts who built the car, and he wants him to build another. Invading the castle disguised as lifesize puppets, Caractacus and his girlfriend Truly Scrumptious (Sally Anne

Howes) rescue the inventor's grandfather, free Chitty, and depose the evil tyrant.

Filmed by James Bond producer Albert Broccoli, the $10,000,000 film was shot in Super-Panavision on location in Europe and became yet another expensive disappointment. Despite the presence of much of the *Mary Poppins* staff—the composers Sherman, choreographers Breaux and Wood, musical supervisor Irwin Kostal, and star Dick Van Dyke—the airborne car didn't have the appeal of Disney's flying nanny. Too, the complex intrigue that was worked around the automobile story overstuffed the film with stock villains, standard henchmen, and typical plot contrivances. In all, the beautifully produced film was simply too heavy and too long.

Finian's Rainbow, on the other hand, was a strangely low-keyed adaptation of the successful Broadway play. Directed by Francis Ford Coppola (*The Godfather*), the film featured Tommy Steele as a leprechaun who turns white men black, and Fred Astaire as a miser in search of the legendary pot of gold at rainbow's end. There was great musical talent in evidence—Petula Clark co-starred with Astaire and singer-dancer Steele—but the film was musically shallow, leaning more on drama than its contemporaries. As such, it played well to an adult audience although, again, the public responded coldly.

One of the cinema's most captivating and unusual fantasies came to the screen after the dust and disappointment of these musical extravaganzas had settled. The film was *Peter Rabbit and Tales of Beatrix Potter* (1971) and it was a delightful picture danced by the Royal Ballet of England. Beatrix Potter (Erin Geraghty), who wrote the Peter Rabbit tales, is shown creating one of her stories. This particular tale is about the picnic organized by Mrs. Tittlemouse (Julie Wood), Johnny Town Mouse (Keith Martin), and their town mice friends. They hurry to the country, unaware of the drama being enacted nearby. Jemima Puddleduck (Ann Howard) is looking for a place to lay her eggs when along comes Mr. Fox (Robert Mead). The duck falls for the cunning reynard's flattery, unaware that he wants only to eat her. Fortunately, hunters' horns sound and scare the fox away. Quickly, Jemima flies to the barn where she relates this adventure to her friends. Meanwhile, back at the party, two mice— Tom Thumb (Wayne Sleep) and Hunca Munca (Lesley Collier)—have trouble with a cat, while the

Fred Astaire finds the pot of gold at rainbow's end in
Finian's Rainbow.

arrival of mischievous Squirrel Nutkin (Wayne Sleep) causes problems for the other picnickers. Nutkin pelts the party with nuts, which causes a conflagration between the town and country mice. A rainstorm ends the strife and everyone becomes friendly again after scampering for shelter. When the storm has passed, the entire ensemble turns out to dance.

If you're wondering where Peter Rabbit fits into the scheme of things, it's an odd position he holds. The story of Beatrix Potter, herself, is told by Mrs. Tiggy-Winkle (Sir Frederick Ashton, who also choreographed the film), the hedgehog washerwoman for the animals. She interrupts her chore of ironing Peter's coat to tell the story. Thus, the naked and frustrated hare must remain behind a large bush until the final production number.

Peter Rabbit and Tales of Beatrix Potter was filmed with the dancers wearing beautifully de-signed, incredibly lifelike animal masks, created by Rostislav Doboujinsky. The performers spoke not a word of dialogue throughout; only a wonderful musical score by John Lanchbery accompanied the on-screen images. In all, a fanciful delight.

Perhaps the fortunes of the fantasy musical are on the upswing. *Peter Rabbit and Tales of Beatrix Potter* and *Scrooge* did quite well, while the still-in-release *Little Prince* (1974), a big-budget adaptation of the classic Antoine de St. Exupery novel, has broken box-office records the world over. A professional pilot (Richard Kiley) has crashed in the Sahara Desert where he meets a little boy (Stephen Warner) in prince's raiment. The boy explains that he is from another planet, Asteroid B-612, and is scouring the universe to find out what is really important in life. His earlier travels, shown in flashback, had taken him to small worlds belonging to a King (Joss Ackland), a Businessman (Clive Revill), an Histo-

Mrs. Twiggy-Winkle in *Peter Rabbit and Tales of Beatrix Potter*.

as good as its enduring source material, with fine performances by the brilliant Richard Kiley and the equally talented Bob Fosse. Both sing and dance with great accomplishment. Fosse's snake ballet is of the same high caliber as his choreography in the Broadway play *Pippin* and the film version of *Cabaret*. Six-year-old Stephen Warner is, himself, a little prince in the title role.

While movies such as *The Little Prince* exude a magic that is unique to the medium of motion pictures, our next topic is magic of an entirely different sort: the magic of the sorcerer. Unlike the films in our repertoire of voodoo and the black arts, one is likely to find magic in most any locality. Ironically, the first film to which we turn is a classic not unlike those with which we've been dealing the last two chapters.

The Little Prince waters the one flower that grows on his tiny planet.

rian (Victor Spinetti), and a General (Graham Crowden), all of whom were too rapt in their own problems to help the Little Prince with his. Thusfar, on earth, he has met a Snake (Bob Fosse) and a Fox (Gene Wilder), who had nothing to offer save their own neuroses. Unfortunately, the pilot, like the others, is preoccupied with his own plight. Disconsolate, the Prince revisits the snake and allows himself to be fatally bitten. He dies, and only then does the pilot realize what innocence has here been sacrificed.

Filmed on location in Tunisia, the film is every bit

198

14
MAGIC AND BEYOND

While we have exhausted most of the screen sorcerors and witches in previous chapters, magic has a few otherwise unclassifiable entries of its own. First of all, what is magic, and how does it differ from the wizardry we have thus far encountered? Unlike voodoo or satanism, magic seldom involves the devil or a middleman such as the genie. It is, simply put, the mysterious ability that someone or something possesses that enables him to master the forces of nature. Often, as we shall see, man may be the recipient of magic rather than the practitioner; the quest for immortality or the need to be disciplined are common catalysts. Too, although the settings are largely contemporary, there are many simple reworkings or contemporizations of classic formulae, such as the Arabian Nights.

A superb example of an amulet or magical icon at work was W.W. Jacobs' short story of the very dark magic inherent in *The Monkey's Paw*. Twice-filmed during the silent era, in 1915 and 1923, it resurfaced as hour-long films in 1932 and 1948. The story concerns a preserved simian appendage that grants the holder three wishes. A couple finds it and their first wish is for great wealth. This comes to them in a fashion most unexpected: their son is mangled to death by a machine and they collect his insurance. The bereaved parents' second wish is for their son's return. They forget, however, to stipulate that they want the young man as he was *before* the accident. When he comes to the door as a butchered corpse, their final request is that everything be returned to the way it was. The success of this resolution is left to the viewer. The moral, as we shall also see in other

fantasies featuring magic, is that mystic powers must not be used for greedy purposes.

An entirely different kind of gramarye was the sort practiced by Ayisha, the heroine of H. Rider Haggard's classic novel *She*. Filmed by Merian C. Cooper in 1935, and again by Hammer in 1965, the story is of a timbre similar to the Mummy films. Explorers are mysteriously summoned to a lost city ruled by the five-hundred-year-old Queen Ayisha. One of the expedition members is a reincarnation of her long-dead lover, and she intends for him to remain by her side. In Cooper's film, the monarch (Helen Gahagan) is spurned by Randolph Scott and steps into the magic fires that first gave her immortality. Bathed in flame, she manifests her true age and perishes. In the Hammer production, Ursula Andress succeeds in coaxing John Richardson to remain behind. They live through eternity, and even into *The Vengeance of She* (1967). In this sequel, Richardson is shown to be the lone master of the Kallikrates after the interim death of Ms. Andress. Olinka Berova is her reincarnation, however, and Richardson calls her to the lost Egyptian city. When Ms. Berova refuses to join our hero as an immortal, he steps into the fires and dies. "She" flees, and the city blows up behind her.

As we indicated earlier, the realm of magic is a piecemeal one, assembled from bits and slices of themes that are sometimes murdered in the translation. Examples of bastardized motifs are *Where Do We Go From Here?* (1945), *The Genie* (1953), *The Brass Bottle* (1964). In *Where Do We Go From Here?*, Fred MacMurray finds Aladdin's lamp and

Ursula Andress proves to John Richardson that *She* is immortal, while Christopher Lee looks on.

A reluctant queen: *The Vengeance of She*.

asks genie Gene Sheldon to get him into the army. The hapless djinn tries hard but accidentally sends the would-be hero back in time, as one of George Washington's soldiers. In *The Genie*, Douglas Fairbanks Jr. once again plays with his father's fire. This time he's the genie of Aladdin's lamp, at long last granted the painful joy of mortality. He remains in human form until his magic is needed, at which time he makes the supreme sacrifice and returns, forever, to being a djinn. In *The Brass Bottle*, Tony Randall finds a large metal cannister that houses the less altruistic Burl Ives. While Randall uses magic to build his own confidence, Ives' assistant Kamala Devi makes life difficult for Randall's girlfriend Barbara Eden. Even moreso than *The Genie*, *The Brass Bottle* is naggingly anachronistic. Both, however, lack the swash of a period piece.

More traditional forms of magic have also had brief exposure on the screen. Barely seen have been amulets and talismans, limited to exposure in the films *One Wish Too Many* (1956) and *Zotz!* (1962). The former had a boy discover wish-granting marbles, while in *Zotz!*, professor Tom Poston discovers an ancient mystic coin. However, the most

Tom Poston destroys toy battleships in his bathtub using a magic coin and the word *Zotz!*

effective and original film of this type was *Miracle in Milan* (1951), produced and directed by the great Italian filmmaker Vittorio de Sica. It's the story of an angel who gives a boy a dove, which when stroked enables him to work magic. Along similar but more comical lines was H. G. Wells' *The Man Who Could Work Miracles* (1936), produced by Alexander Korda from a screenplay by Wells. In it, mild-mannered department-store salesman Roland Young is empowered by the Gods to do things simply by thinking them. In the end, Young stops the world from rotating, causing mass devestation, and the deities are forced to intercede. If nothing else, Young proved that magic is best left in the hands of the pros. Speaking of which, magicians have had a sprawling film history. As we have seen, they span the globe from England's Pendragon in *Jack the Giant Killer* to Abalone's Merlin in *Seven Faces of Dr. Lao*. Of course, there have been others. The most irritable, nastiest man in all the world, Peter Ustinov, met one of them. In *The Man Who Wagged His Tail* (1957), a writer of fairy tales turns Ustinov into a dog. He is doomed to remain in this story state until told by someone that they love him. When the mongrel saves a little boy's life, the lad embraces the dog and a reformed Ustinov materializes. Less allegorical than this Dickensesque fantasy is *Bedknobs and Broomsticks* (1971), the Disney organization's expensive and unsuccessful attempt to repeat the triumph of *Mary Poppins*. The film stars Angela Lansbury as a kindly witch who takes her family on a strange, magical voyage beneath the sea, and summons forth apparitions to

Barbara Eden and Tony Randall watch Burl Ives emerge from *The Brass Bottle*.

Magic afoot in *Bedknobs and Broomsticks*.

combat Nazis in prewar England. While the special effects are better than those in *Mary Poppins*, the film, as a whole, is not. Similar adventures awaited Charles Herbert, a young boy sent by genie Joseph Turkel to Blackbeard's ship in Bert I. Gordon's *The Boy and the Pirates* (1960).

In an entirely different vein was the blacker magic of *The Raven* (1962) and *Equinox* (1967). *The Raven*, a loose, comical adaptation of Poe's immortal poem, featured Peter Lorre as the black bird, Jack Nicholson as his dullard son, Vincent Price as the good magician Craven, and Boris Karloff as the mighty sorceror Scarabus. Throughout, Karloff tries to wrest from Price the secret of his powers: this culminates in a deadly and climactic duel of magic. Seated in the largest hall of Karloff's castle, the magicians fire spells at one another, which causes lightning, fireballs, confetti, spears, and other projectiles to fly about the room. The wicked Karloff is finally defeated when the ceiling collapses, crushing him beneath tons of debris. In *Equinox*, a young geologist (Edward Connell) finds an ancient book of magic that opens the barrier between our world and the occult. As a result, the expedition is beset by monsters from the netherworld with stop-motion work courtesy of Jim Danforth and long-time collaborator David Allen. With a film like Equinox, we are clearly straddling the fence between magic and our previous study of the occult in film.

Most of these pictures, as we have seen, take place primarily in modern settings with ordinary citizens living the enchantments. This is still the case as we

shade from hard magic to impossible events, people, and beings. Animals, for example, represent a large portion of the fantasy film cast, what with such efforts as *Dr. Dolittle* and the man-to-dog transformations in *Man Who Wagged His Tail*, Korda's *Thief of Bagdad*, and *Jack the Giant Killer*. Other animal efforts are of a more curious nature. In *The Enchanted Forest* (1945), old Edmund Lowe taught young Billy Severn about life by showing him how to converse with animals, trees, and even the weather. Cary Grant was the proud owner of a dancing caterpillar—who eventually becomes a moth and flies away—in *Once Upon a Time* (1943), while in *Everything's Ducky* (1961), sailors Buddy Hackett and Mickey Rooney discover a talking duck. Then there was the lovable Mr. Dowd (James Stewart) who insisted that his best friend and constant companion was a six-foot-tall invisible rabbit known as *Harvey* (1950). Whether the so-called "pookah" was real or imagined is up to the viewer. Finally, we had two more "transformation" films, *The Shaggy Dog* (1959) and *The Two Little Bears* (1961). One of Disney's better low-budget live-action films, *The Shaggy Dog* stars Tommy Kirk as a teenager who finds a magic ring that turns him into a sheepdog. He can still articulate and drive a car, however, and thwarts a gang of spies before the film has ended. In *The Two Little Bears*, a gypsy (Nancy Kulp) shows young Butch Patrick and Donnie Carter how to turn themselves into bear cubs.

In addition to bizarre animals, the genre has also seen some strange people. And while the magic

Boris Karloff and Vincent Price in a publicity still for *The Raven*.

The Shaggy Dog. (c) Walt Disney Productions.

involved is not of the "hocuspocus" sort, it is certainly far beyond the range of mortal comprehension. Through it, we will see such amazing sights as Santa Claus in a padded cell and a maniacal music teacher.

Miracle on 34th Street (1947) featured Edmund

Edmund Lowe and friend in a publicity still for *The Enchanted Forest.*

Gwenn claiming to be the real Kris Kringle. He is put on trial to determine the truth or falsity of his allegation. The result of court proceedings and a psychiatric examination prove that he is, in fact, Father Christmas, and everything ends happily. The film was remade in 1956 as *Meet Mr. Kringle*. Less satisfying is a tale of the strange love shared by a meek department-store executive (Robert Walker) and his art gallery's statue of Venus (Ava Gardner), the latter come-to-life in *One Touch of Venus* (1948). Despite the interesting premise, it's all very banal material ultimately frustrating as Miss Gardner returns to her petrified state. Finally, the

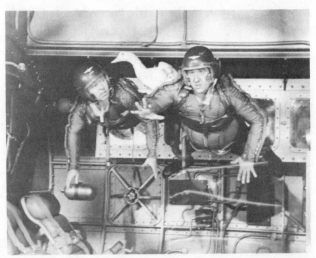

Mickey Rooney, Buddy Hackett, and their pet duck try out for the space program in *Everything's Ducky.*

maniacal music teacher of whom we spoke belonged to the nightmares of a young boy in the Stanley Kramer-Dr. Seuss collaboration *The Five Thousand Fingers of Dr. T.* (1953). The boy (Tommy Rettig) dreams that his piano teacher, Mr. Terwilliker (Hans Conreid), keeps five-hundred children locked in a huge castle where they are duty bound to perpetual practice on the world's largest piano. Fine sets, a good script, and remarkable imagery highlight this thoroughly entertaining tale. All of which leads us to the last stop in our look at magical happenings: strange events. Movies in which the fantasy is not in the people, but in their surroundings.

Artist Winsor McKay's *Dreams of the Rarebit Fiend* was a popular comic strip of the early 1900s, and the film version (1906) by E. S. Porter *(The*

A Spanish version of the classic *Puss N' Boots* (1963).

Edmund Gwenn is given psychiatric tests to determine whether or not he is the real Santa Claus. From *Miracle on 34th Street*.

Great Train Robbery, made in 1903 and the first film to tell a cohesive narrative story) is a short fantasy classic. The plot is nothing more than a series of nightmares dreamed by a man (John Brawn) who has overindulged in Welsh rabbit. His food—lifesized with hands and feet—comes to life and chases him from floor to wall to ceiling; the bed takes to the air and carries him over New York; and sundry little devils come forth to haunt the indigested hero. the film is notable for its superb special effects and has many technical "firsts" to its credit. One such innovation is the personified food sequence. In actuality, although it appears to be a mad chase about the bedroom, the man and meal were simply running in place. It was the room and the camera that revolved. This same technique was later used by Stanley Kubrick to enable his *2001: A Space*

Odyssey waitress to walk down the aisle of a spaceship, step onto a wall, and pass through a door in the ceiling.

Dreams of the Rarebit Fiend was surreal, but it remained for the uncontested king of that mode, Salvador Dali, to team with French filmmaker Louis

A Spanish version of *The Golden Goose* (1965).

Ava Gardner poses with the studio craftsman responsible for her heavenly likeness in *One Touch of Venus*.

Bunel and create what has to be the most unusual film ever made: *Un Chien Andalou* (1928), literally *The Andalusian Dog*. With the admitted intent of using this new artistic medium as a vehicle for outrageous expression, the producers made a very visual film that hasn't a sensible narrative. The picture opens with a young man (Bunel) stropping a razor blade. There is a girl sitting by his side. Bunel moves to her and, very casually and in an extreme closeup, slits her eyeball horizontally, the liquid therein spilling about her face. The eye was, in fact,

Dreams of the Rarebit Fiend. (Museum of Modern Art Film Stills Archive).

that of a cow. Not being in possession of this information, however, can leave a viewer numb. This is followed by sometimes gentle, sometimes brutal visions—a man caressing a woman's breasts; ants devouring a human hand in the gutter—that give the movie great power despite its *apparently* random assembly. The intent, of course, was to gain impact through a new and innovative use of film and fantasy.

In a more conventional vein, Leslie Howard—who died after completing his role of Ashley in *Gone With the Wind* (1939)—portrayed an American who finds himself transported to eighteenth-century London's *Berkley Square* (1933). There, he falls in love with a beautiful girl (Heather Angel) whose reincarnation he meets upon returning to the twentieth century. The picture was remade in 1957 as *I'll Never Forget You* with Tyrone Power in the

Howard role. Both pictures have the romantic quality of *Wuthering Heights* with the fantasy element adding an extra wisp of delicacy.

A strange newspaper handed to Dick Powell by an even stranger man is the basis for *It Happened Tomorrow* (1945), about a tabloid that tells the next day's news. Using it to win a fortune at the racetrack, Powell is content until he reads his own obituary. He panics and tries desperately to avoid his fate. It's all a misinterpretation of the item, however, and the frightened newspaperman learns never to tamper with things beyond his ken. Meanwhile, beyond everyone's understanding was *The Next Voice You Hear* (1950), in which God addressed mankind via radio, and a strange crop that appeared in the garden of Irene Dunne when *It Grows on Trees* (1952). After much to-do about that bush which sprouts money instead of leaves, the growth dries out and the greenery goes brown. Fortunately, Hollywood had a solution to the sorrow fostered by this great loss. A toucan infected by a strange virus gets loose in New York and causes an epidemic of happiness in *What's So Bad About*

Tyrone Power and ancestor in *I'll Never Forget You.*

Dick Powell indulges in a spot of chain-smoking while seeking a means to escape his fate in *It Happened Tomorrow*.

Thus, with a grab bag of odds and ends, we end our survey of the live action, feature-length fantasy film. But it is far from the end of our look at the genre. Following our next chapter, a history of the animated fantasy cartoon, we will examine two additional breeding grounds for imagination: amazing anthologies and fantasy on television.

James Whitmore listens to the voice of God in *The Next Voice You Hear . . .*

Feeling Good (1968). A novel idea, one can only take so much glee from stars George Peppard, Mary Tyler Moore, and Dom de Louise before the film becomes grating and the novelty wears thin.

15
FANTASY ANIMATION

It's impossible to say which filmmaker was the first to create a series of progressive drawings and record them on film. However, James Blackton is widely considered to have made the first *popular* animated movie, *Humorous Phases of Funny Faces* (1906) featuring the leers of old men and the smiles of a clown. Each picture, or *frame* of the short film, was drawn on a blackboard and then erased between exposures. This, of course, left mounting layers of chalk dust on the slate, which all but obliterated the final images. Nonetheless, the film was a success and inspired Blackton, a staff artist of *The New York World,* to form the Vitagraph Corporation, which made the artist and his partners millionaires. The company was bought in 1925 by the Warner Brothers, and Blackton stayed on as a technical consultant.

A contemporary of Blackton's was Emile Cohl, a French jeweler and amateur cartoonist, who made Europe's first commercial animated film, *Mr. Stop* (1907). The picture was shot in the backroom of his store and told of a man who could halt the movements of any animated object. This film was followed by *Phantasmagoria* (1908), a plotless series of changing shapes. These minute-long productions were exhibited in theatres and enjoyed great success.

Advertising films were also popular animated subjects, since cartoons were distinctive and caught the eye. These were displayed between twenty-minute live-action films, much to the public's enjoyment. Newspaper syndicates followed this lead and, to promote their daily strips, made them into short animated films. Seeing one such effort, *Maggie and Jiggs* (1906), comic strip genius Winsor

McCay decided to make a few movies of his own. He shot a three-minute, four-thousand-frame version of his popular *Little Nemo* serial (1906) followed by *How a Mosquito Operates* (1906), and finally *Gertie the Dinosaur* (1906). Gertie is McCay's classic, a brontosaur whose screen appearance embellished an on-stage performance by McCay. The animator would stand next to the screen and order his monster about; Gertie would "obey," as if by magic. The most impressive gimmick in the film was worked around the dinosaur's feeding. McCay would toss a clump of food at the screen, behind it, just as its animated counterpart flew into the dinosaur's mouth.

These independent efforts were largely novelties, of course, and it remained for animation to be incorporated, much as Blackton had done. One particularly successful studio was Bray and Hurd, whose staff worked from a small office on New York's Forty-second street. Among their contributions to the art of animation was the clear-cel, a process in which the foreground figure was painted on a clear transparency, placed against a static background, and photographed. The next cel was then placed in position and filmed. Before this development in 1913, background scenes had to be redrawn for each individual frame. Eventually, due to competition from the new crop of animators in Hollywood—such as Bray and Hurd alumni Walter Lantz (*Woody Woodpecker*) and Max Fleischer (*Popeye*), along with the pre-Mickey Mouse Walt Disney—Bray and Hurd folded, Hurd eventually joining the Disney staff.

Meanwhile, characters were being developed, and

Bambi meets GODZILLA

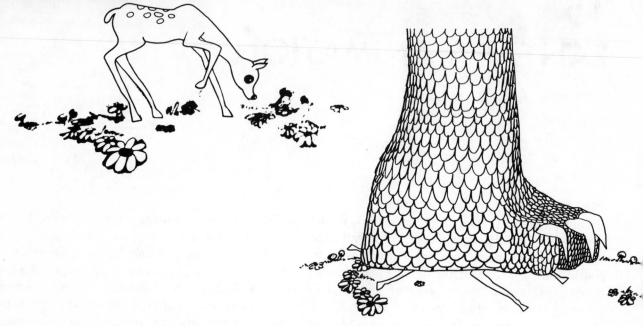

Windsor McCay's *Gertie the Dinosaur* has eaten a tree and is crying for further sustenance. (Museum of Modern Art Film Stills Archive.)

The witch prepares a poison apple for _Snow White_. (c) Walt Disney Productions

audiences clamored for their return. Thus, _Felix the Cat_ by Pat Sullivan and _Koko the Clown_ from Max Fleischer made the animated cartoons a draw in and of themselves. In this manner, too, did Disney get his start. Walt, who had come near-penniless to California from Kansas and setup shop in an uncle's garage, built a small staff by producing the adventures of _Alice in Cartoonland,_ a live girl in an animated environment, and _Oswald the Rabbit._ When Walt's New York-based distributor-producer cut the latter's production costs to increase his own profit, he expected Disney to accept the

offer. Disney did not. Instead, he and his top animator, Ub Iwerks, created _Mickey Mouse._ Walt was always very much impressed with technology and saw potential in the process of talking motion pictures. Thus, Mickey's second adventure, _Steamboat Willie_ (1928), was the first sound cartoon. It sent the mouse well on his way to becoming the most popular fictional character of this century. From these West Coast animators the short subjects kept on coming, new characters were continually being added, and even color was tried. Then in 1938, the first feature-length cartoon was released, Disney's _Snow White._ [17]

The fantasy elements in _Snow White_ are meager: the enchanted mirror—"Mirror, mirror on the wall . . ."—and the witch who feeds our heroine a poisoned apple. The film is of historical value simply because fantasy is a catalyst in this monumental milestone of cinema history. Imaginative elements played a larger part in the world's second feature-length cartoon, the largely forgotten _Gulliver's Travels_ (1939). This Max Fleischer film is, in many ways, superior to _Snow White._ The colors and animation are as good as Disney's, but in its favor is the fact that the human Gulliver is not nearly as stylized as Snow White or her Prince. As a result, Gulliver plays well against the caricatured Lilliputians. Certainly it is a far less saccharin effort than _Snow White._ In many ways, Fleischer's career paralleled that of Disney. His _Betty Boop_ shorts had

Two views of the marvelous Max Fleischer _Superman_ from the forties.

been a success since 1929, although she quickly faded when the more popular comic strip character *Popeye* made his screen debut in 1932. It should come as no surprise, then, that *Gulliver's Travels* was a great success. Strangely, Fleischer's second feature, *Mr. Bug Goes to Town* (1941), failed at the box office due to the outbreak of war and direct competition from Disney's *Dumbo* (1941). Although Fleischer made several other short series— among them, the remarkable *Superman* cartoons—unlike Disney, he did not own his productions. Eventually, Max gave up the pressure of running his own shop and dealing with the major studios for money and distribution. He went to work for a film subsidiary of General Motors, while his firm continued as Famous Studios, producing *Popeye, Little Lulu, Herman and Catnip,* and *Casper the Friendly Ghost* cartoons.

After *Snow White* took the nation by storm, Disney released *Pinocchio* (1940). Pinocchio is a wooden puppet led from the straight and narrow of his creator's shop by a fox and a cat. He is eventually spirited away to Pleasure Island where wicked little boys are turned into donkeys; he escapes, and is swallowed by the giant whale Monstro. He, his creator Geppetto, and his consort Jiminy Cricket flee the monster's gullet and, in the end, Pinocchio is turned into a real boy by a gracious guardian fairy.

In both *Snow White* and *Pinocchio*, the segments of fantasy are their most arresting assets, and in each film there is a transformation from human to monster. In *Snow White*, the beautiful witch drinks a magic potion and metamorphoses into a wretched old crone. Her transformation is done in shadow amidst bubbling vials of formulae that would put to shame any Frankenstein laboratory the screen has

Infuriated by their escape, Monstro the whale pursues the raft of Gepetto, *Pinocchio*, and Jiminy Cricket. (c) Walt Disney Productions.

A preproduction sketch showing the tyrannosaur-stegosaur fight from the *Rite of Spring* segment of *Fantasia*. (c) Walt Disney Productions

ever seen. In *Pinocchio*, the puppet's allegedly streetwise buddy Lampwick becomes a mule, while Pinocchio looks on in horror. Indeed, this segment has been accurately labeled the most frightening scene ever filmed. As Lampwick and Pinocchio eat, smoke, and shoot pool, the boy starts to change. His initial panic, which consists of running about the room, is replaced by a donkey's kicking hooves; his yells of terror become high-pitched whinneys. When he has become a mule, Limpwick is carted away to be ground into glue. Pinocchio himself undergoes only a partial transformation and is thus able to escape.

Pinocchio was not nearly as well received as its predecessor, due in great part to the loss of the foreign market with the coming of World War II. As

well, critics were generally agreed that the picture lacked the charm of *Snow White*. Hindsight has corrected this misjudgment and the relentless, brooding, and heavily moralistic *Pinocchio* is acknowledged to be one of Disney's great productions.

Hard on the heels of *Pinocchio* came an even greater disappointment for Walt, the failure of his ambitious *Fantasia* (1940). Using another technical gimmick—stereophonic sound—Disney's high-minded intent was to bring the public classical music in a popular, palatable form. In the process, he would use animation to create various moods instead of a story. Once again, the critics responded negatively: they found *Fantasia* pretentious, which it was, and boring, which it was not. Only in the

The Sorcerer's Apprentice feels the burning wrath of his mentor in *Fantasia*. (c) Walt Disney Productions

1960s did the film first find an audience that appreciated the kind of audio-visual experience that *Fantasia* represented.

Fantasia is not the ultimate masterwork its acolytes have built it to be. Without a doubt, it is an awesome technical achievement, but the many segments tend to disjoint and singularly impress the viewer, rather than overwhelm him as some of Disney's later films did. The picture is made up of eight musical segments, the first of which is an abstract translation of Bach's *Toccota and Fugue in A Minor*. There are lumbering masses, sprays of wash, explosions of color, and floating shapes throught the passage, capped by conductor Leopold Stokowski commanding great bursts of hue with his baton. This segment—described by narrator Deems Taylor as "absolute music"—is followed by Tchaikovsky's *Nutcracker Suite*, itself divided into several separate stories. These are looks at the sprites who bedew the morning flowers, fish who do an underwater ballet, dancing flowers, waltzing mushrooms, and the frost fairies who bring winter and sleep to the forest awakened by the morning sprites. The third segment is perhaps the most famous: Mickey Mouse as Dukas' *The Sorceror's Apprentice*. Planned as a short subject in itself, it was this sequence from which the rest of the film grew. Donning his hoary master's hat, Mickey brings to life a broom and orders it to fetch and carry water to a well. When the broom refuses to lay down its buckets, Mickey hacks at it with an axe. Each splinter becomes a water-bearing servant. Inevitably, the wizard must descend from his tower to dry up the flood, as well as his young aide's ambition. In terms of being a crowd pleaser, *The Sorceror's Apprentice* is *Fantasia's* focal point. Mickey's appearance invariably draws applause from patrons.

Igor Stravinsky's *Rite of Spring* formed the basis for the next selection, the story of life's origin on earth. The sequence begins with the formation of our planet and follows its birth pains to the appearance of small, cellular animals, to fish, to the rise and fall of the dinosaurs. Nothing more than a dramatic biology lesson, this offering is the weakest in the film. Its drama is shallow, as there is no attempt to create empathy for the suffering dinosaurs. Even the battle between a tyrannosaur and a stegosaur hasn't the power of a similar struggle from *King Kong* seven years earlier. Despite these failings, it was the next segment that became the most controversial. Beethoven's *Pastoral Symphony* was used as the background for a mythical look at centaurs, cherubs, flying horses, and the wrath of Zeus and Vulcan who rain lightning bolts from above. Certainly the most exotic cartoon in the *Fantasia* tapestry, *Pastoral Symphony* has been accused of both butchering the composer's original concept, and playing a hokey setting with too straight a face. In fact, however, the timeless, delicate world of this segment, with its soft, pastel hues, fickle gods, protective lovers and mothers, inebriated wine merchant astride his equally tipsy donkey, and hedonistic centaurs and fauns, makes it one of the most alluring sequences in the film. It is one of the few attempts the picture makes to involve the viewer in the problems of its on-screen characters. We watch the fauns prepare themselves for spring, the wooing and winning of mates, the trials and tribulations of the winged-horse family, the cherubs' joyful playing, and the making of wine. Then the Gods awaken from sleep to disrupt this tranquility with their own sadistic merriment. Unlike the death of the dinosaurs in the previous selection, this holocaust has meaning since the characters have depth. Thus, in terms of mood and dimension, the *Pastoral Symphony* is *Fantasia's* finest piece.

Ponchielli's *Dance of the Hours* was intended to be *Fantasia's* comic piece, and succeeds admirably. It is the story of a ballet enacted, improbably, by hippopotami, elephants, ostriches, and alligators, with an incredible love interest developing between the prima ballerina, a hippo, and the suave hero-

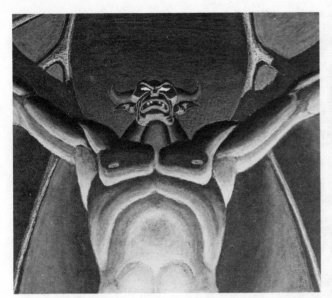

Bela Lugosi is clearly in evidence in this series of *Night on Bald Mountain* stills from *Fantasia*. (c) Walt Disney Productions

lizard who courts her. It is a perfect segment, too, in that it loosens up the audience and leaves it unprepared for the sinister nightmare that follows, *Night on Bald Mountain*. Moussorgsky's immortal composition has been transformed into a fearsome piece about the night when the huge devil Tchernobog appears on Russia's Bald Mountain and calls forth the spirits of the dead. After a mad, frenzied orgy atop the mountain, the sun rises. Tchernabog cringes at the breaking dawn and the tolling of a church bell, and is finally forced to retreat within his

The Headless Horseman greets Ichabod Crane in *The Adventures of Ichabod and Mr. Toad*. (c) Walt Disney Productions

great wings to become once more part of the mountain. Hard upon comes the final segment, the triumph of good over evil. A group of pilgrims passes through the forest near Bald Mountain chanting Shubert's *Ave Maria*. Representing a lack of conviction on Disney's part, *Ave Maria* negates the vision of ultimate evil he worked so hard to build in *Night on Bald Mountain*. In a way, this is Disney bowing to his own image, a position that decrees that light must always dispel darkness.[18]

After producing cartoons for the war effort, and continuing with his standard short subjects, Disney returned to full-length animated movies. The first supernatural production of the lot was *The Adventures of Ichabod and Mr. Toad* (1949). The film embraces two individual stories, the Mr. Toad effort hailing from Kenneth Grahame's *Wind in the Willows*. *Ichabod* is, of course, Washington Irving's *The Legend of Sleepy Hollow*. Although this latter segment is not extraordinary, with a droll narration by Bing Crosby, the climatic chase between Ichabod and the Headless Horsemen is Disney at his *Night on Bald Mountain* best.

The next feature was *Cinderella* (1951). The only amazing sequence in this otherwise routine production is when the heroine's fairy godmother appears to fashion a royal coach from a pumpkin, and transform mice into horses. Following this film was *Alice in Wonderland* (1951), a picture that, like *Fantasia*, is just now finding wide public acceptance. A misjudged interpretation of the novel, the

The caterpillar blows his smokey vowels for the bemused *Alice in Wonderland*. (c) Walt Disney Productions

film is half-Disney, half-Carroll, with neither portion being very good. For the record, Alice, following a white rabbit into its hole, finds herself too large to pursue it through a tiny door. Drinking a bottle on a table, she shrinks and enters Wonderland. There she meets the snide Cheshire Cat, the Mad Hatter, argumentative flowers, a hookah-smoking caterpillar, and the murderous Queen of Hearts and her army of playing-card henchmen. Like *The Wizard of Oz*, however, it all turns out to have been a dream.

Peter Pan (1953), like *Alice in Wonderland*, was one of Disney's less accomplished pictures. Critics carped, and rightly so, that while technically as impressive as ever, the Disney presentation was heavy-handed. The gentler fantasy of Barrie had become a driving, colorful vehicle for stock Disney characterizations. It was time for the studio to break from its rut. This it did, with Walt's next and greatest motion picture; ironically, it was also his worst box-office disaster. Still in all, the stereophonic, widescreen Technirama, multiplane[19] version of *Sleeping Beauty* (1959) is one of the great fantasy films, an achievement to rank beside Korda's *Thief of Bagdad* or Garland's *Wizard of Oz*.

The birth of Princess Aurora is a cause for celebration, and crowds of European nobility turn out for her christening. Among the well-wishers are King Hubert and his son Phillip, the latter to whom Aurora is this day betrothed. Three fairies also come to bless the child of King Stefan. Flora wishes her beauty; Fauna gives the baby the gift of song. Before Merryweather can make her offering, however, the evil sorceress Maleficent appears. For not having

Peter Pan. (c) Walt Disney Productions

Maleficent taunts the captive Prince Phillip in *Sleeping Beauty.* (c) Walt Disney Productions

The remarkable battle between Prince Phillip and the dragon in *Sleeping Beauty*. (c) Walt Disney Productions

been invited, the witch decrees that by sunset on her sixteenth birthday, Aurora shall have pricked her finger on a spinning wheel and die. In a flash of lightning, the Queen of Darkness is gone. Merryweather, unable to dispel the curse, does manage to alter it somewhat. Instead of death, the Princess shall only sleep until awakened by true love's first kiss. Nonetheless, the King decrees that all spinning wheels be burned and sends Aurora away with the fairies, into the forest, there to live for sixteen years. The sprites decide, as well, to hide their wands and live like mortals, so as not to reveal their true identities.

On the day of her sixteenth birthday, alone in the forest, Aurora meets a young man with whom she dances and falls in love. She doesn't know he is Prince Phillip; the Prince is similarly unaware that this girl is his fiancee. She invites him to visit her cottage that evening. Meanwhile, Maleficent has been searching for Aurora these sixteen years. Afraid she'll not find her before the sun has set, the witch sends forth her pet raven with orders not to return until he has found the Princess. Sailing over the forest, the bird spots a cottage with clouds of magic dust firing from the chimney. On the last day of their decade-and-a-half of abstinence, the fairies have decided to use their wands to bake a birthday cake and make their charge a beautiful dress. Maleficent now knows where to find the Princess.

Late that afternoon, the fairies tell a sobbing Aurora who she really is and lead her from the cottage. She will not be there when her handsome stranger arrives. Following her progress, Maleficent watches as the Princess is ensconced in her bedroom at the palace. There, while she awaits the royal reception, Aurora is visited by Maleficent. The witch creates an enchanted spinning wheel and, touching it, the girl falls to the floor. Finding her, the fairies put the entire kingdom to sleep that all shall lay dormant until Aurora awakens.

Elsewhere, Phillip has reached the abandoned cottage and is captured by Maleficent. Taken by her demons to the castle, he and his horse Samson are placed in irons. Simultaneously, the despondent fairies return to the cottage and find Phillip's hat. They hurry to Maleficent's castle and, avoiding an orgy of satanism and various guardian monsters, reach Phillip's dungeon. They arm him with a magic sword and shield, then set him free. Hurrying to Samson's back, Phillip fights trolls and other of Maleficent's magic until he nears King Stefan's palace. Casting spells from atop her own castle, the witch causes acres of huge, impenetrable thorn bushes to appear. Phillip's magic blade slices through the tangled limbs with ease. Furious, the witch becomes a whirling fireball and explodes on the drawbridge before Phillip. Warning that, "Now you shall deal with me and all the powers of Hell," the sorceress transforms herself into a huge, fire-breathing dragon. Setting the grounds afire, she battles Phillip toward the edge of a high cliff. When he can retreat no further, the young man hurls his blade at the dragon. It strikes her heart, and with a horrid scream, the monster tumbles from a cliff, dead. The thorn bushes vanish; Phillip finds and kisses the Princess; and everyone awakens to live happily ever after.

Produced for $6,000,000, *Sleeping Beauty* combines the visual splendor of *Fantasia* with the narrative power of *Snow White* to create the ultimate screen animation. The action is unparalleled, and the showdown between Maleficent and Phillip—with arrows turned to flowers, boulders becoming bubbles, and boiling oil stopped by invisible shields—is breathtaking. The combination of magic, monsters, flame, and the awesome battle itself, accompanied by Tchaikovsky's ballet in six-track stereo, leaves the viewer drained and swearing that Walt Disney is the greatest filmmaker in the history of the world. Ironically, this flawless and majestic work failed at the box office and has not been rereleased. Whether the film's intensity or lack of animal characters was the cause is moot; we shall never see its like again.

While such enthusiasm cannot be mustered for Disney's next fantasy, *The Sword in the Stone* (1963), it is a fine retelling of the legend of young King Arthur, with a bumbling Merlin on hand to lend a touch of magic when necessary. Unfortunately, most of the Disney cartoons since this time have been nothing more than reworkings of the format established in *The Jungle Book* (1967), with popular actors supplying the voices for animals in human roles. *Aristocats* (1970) and *Robin Hood* (1974) were direct spinoffs. These new productions, with their economy of special animation effects, have found an audience, so there is no doubt but that they will continue.

Although we have concentrated primarily on the output of Disney, he was not the only filmmaker to create animated fantasies. He was simply the best,

Young Arthur and aide from *Sword in the Stone*. (c) Walt Disney Productions

the most prolific, and the most commercial. However, other studios both here and abroad have contributed their fair share to the field, and it is to their work we now turn our attention.

In the United States and England, very few feature-length animations are created because of the time it takes for them to show a profit: if, indeed, they ever recoup their negative cost. Disney not only distributes its own films, but has a successful marketing program as well. Dolls, model kits, Colorforms, and similar merchandising products go on sale concurrent with a new release. Other studios haven't this advantage, for it is the Disney name that presells the films and toys. However, some of the more successful animated cartoons have been in the fantastic genre. They have an allure that can draw a crowd despite Disney's hold on the mode.

1001 Arabian Nights (1959) starred Mr. Magoo as Aladdin's uncle and was one of the most successful independent efforts since *Gulliver's Travels*. Subsequent fantasy animations were profitable and generally well-made, although only one was a runaway success. *The Incredible Mr. Limpet* (1963) had Don Knotts' live-action self falling into the sea, becoming a dolphin, and winning World War II for the Allies; *The Phantom Tollbooth* (1968) gives a boy a magic car that, when driven through the title enclosure, admits him to a land of magic and logic. The Beatles' fantasy-filled voyage to the land of the Blue Meanies via *Yellow Submarine* (1968) was a great success, although *Journey Back To Oz* (1971), with the gimmick of Liza Minnelli repeating her mother's role in the retelling of the original Oz story, did not reap the anticipated rewards for its producers.

Japan gave us such efforts as *Magic Boy* (1959), a

The nearsighted Mr. Magoo in *A Thousand and One Arabian Nights*.

Don Knotts and *The Incredible Mr. Limpet.*

Alakazam the Great.

A magnificently rendered scene from the Russian-made *Snow Queen.*

Toei period piece about a young samurai who befriends the forest animals while battling sea serpents and a witch; *Alakazam the Great* (1960) starring a magic monkey who also fights monsters; and *Jack and the Witch* (1967), sorcery vs. monsters fare with the mysticism tied to a crystal ball. From Russia came *Snow Maiden* (1953), a pleasant film about the daughter of Frost visiting the earth, falling in love, and melting beneath the rays of the sun; and the strangely frightening *Snow Queen* (1960), wherein the title character causes a boy to become wicked by freezing his heart. He is saved by the love of his girlfriend.

While the quality of the largely government-financed Soviet films is high, without the absolute devotion to the betterment of the art form that Disney had, the Oriental and non-Disney efforts ranged from adequate to good; nothing more. Animation is not the sort of undertaking in which a half-hearted effort can succeed. For this reason, the field has suffered greatly at the hands of its current master, television. With limited budgets and hurried production schedules, the object is to shoot a cartoon with as little animation as possible. With the inception of such catch-penny programs as *Return to the Planet of the Apes* and *Valley of the Dinosaurs*,

One of the many pseudo-animation efforts currently in public favor: television's *Return to the Planet of the Apes*. Other mediocre efforts include:

Superfriends . . .

... and *Valley of the Dinosaurs*

we have once more fostered the paradox that in seventy years of animation, our current produce is of a lesser quality than that of James Blackton and his blackboard drawings. Until the public demands an end to this "dramatic animation," as NBC described the work in their abyssmal *Return to the Planet of the Apes* series, we can expect this great art to suffer further and mounting indignities.

16
FANTASY FILM ANTHOLOGIES

There's a branch of fantasy that spans many categories that have gone before: ghosts, vampires, werewolves, magic, etc. In a way, it is unique to the genre in that these films are less a unified narrative than an attempt to create a cumulative mood.

Since horror anthologies have always been a publishing staple, it was only natural that filmmakers adopt the format to film. The first such effort was *Flesh and Fantasy* (1943) featuring a trio of fantastic tales introduced by Robert Benchley, grandfather of *Jaws* golden boy Peter. In the first story, an ugly girl (Betty Field) is made beautiful by a man's love (Robert Cummings); the second tale stars Edward G. Robinson as a man whose life is changed by a fortune teller (Thomas Mitchell); and finally, Charles Boyer is a circus star with ESP who is haunted by the ghost of Barbara Stanwyck. Despite the weight of its cast, *Flesh and Fantasy* is not a great picture. It was still too much a mainstream work, thus limiting the participation of the fantastic element. It did, however, establish a precedent for this type of motion picture. A better film was the universally acclaimed *Dead of Night* (1945), with its five ghost stories linked by a gripping sixth of the narrators gathered in an old house. This framing story, which ends where the film began, adds an ominous touch to the goings-on by suggesting that not only are the stories fiction, but the entire film may a ghastly nightmare to be relived over and over again by its participants. Contrarily, it may all, in fact, be real. This is for the audience to decide.

The stories themselves are referred to simply as *The Christmas Story, The Ventriloquist Story, The Golfing Story, The Hearse Story,* and *The Haunted Mirror*. The most celebrated of these are *The Ventriloquist Story* with Michael Redgrave as a performer who is slowly taken over by his dummy, and *The Haunted Mirror*, a looking glass that reflects a dim and deadly past it forces the new owners to relive.

The care with which *Dead of Night* was made dampered competition and did not inspire any sequels or imitations. As well, in these postwar days, audiences were turning from horror to lighter forms of entertainment, as is evidenced in the collapse of the Universal horror series. In any case, the next omnibus film was considerably more romantic then gothic. *Tales of Hoffmann* (1951) is based on the Offenbach fantasy-opera in which student Hoffmann (Robert Rounseville) tells people at an inn about his three imagined and ill-fated loves: with Olympia, a dancing doll who comes briefly to life; Giulietta, who is under a sorceror's spell; and Antonia, a girl who sings herself to death. A plush, colorful film, *Tales of Hoffmann* is strangely heavier—due to its length and melodrama—than the sum of its fanciful parts.

Ten years later, after these tentative beginnings, the amazing anthology came into its own. The Argentinian *Master of Horror* (1960) featured three stories by Edgar Allan Poe: *The Facts in the Case of M. Valdemar, The Cask of Amontillado,* and *The Tell-Tale Heart*. The example of this film, coupled with the success of his *House of Usher* (1960),

Edward G. Robinson (right) and C. Aubrey Smith (center) run through a scene of *Flesh and Fantasy* with dialogue director Don Brodie.

inspired Roger Corman to produce *Tales of Terror* (1961), a trilogy of Poe. The stories are *Morella*, about a dead mother whose spirit possesses her terminally ill daughter; *The Black Cat*—flavored with drops from *The Cask of Amontillado*—in which the feline of a man's murdered wife avenges her death; and *Facts in the Case of M. Valdemar*, the story of a hypnotist (Basil Rathbone) who puts Valdemar (Vincent Price) in a trance at the exact moment of death, suspending his soul in limbo and questioning it about the afterlife. Of the trio, only the last tale is in any way true to the author. The first story is effective and intriguing, but the Peter Lorre-Vincent Price *Black Cat* is played for laughs. It goes out of its way to be inordinately ridiculous, with such sequences as a wine-tasting test between a prissy Price and the inebriated Lorre, and a delerium tremen experience by the latter in which he sees his head being thrown around the cellar by his wife (Joyce Jameson) and Price. Despite its many flaws, compounded by a rushed shooting schedule and poor production values, the picture proved a considerable success and more anthologies followed. One such effort was used as a showcase for the

unsold television series *No. 13 Demon Street*. It became *The Devil's Messenger* (1962) with three fables showing how the devil (Lon Chaney Jr.) tries to take over the world. The first horror film to centralize its stories around a similar theme, this interesting picture was ruined by its low television-production values. Conversely, that same year also saw one of the remarkable fantasy collections, and certainly one of the most extravagant films of imagination: George Pal's Cinerama production *The Wonderful World of the Brothers Grimm*. In detailing the life story of the world's most popular tellers of fairy tales, Pal manages to relate three of these fantasies: *The Dancing Princess, The Singing Bone,* and *The Cobbler and the Elves*.

The stories are each some twenty minutes in length. The first tells of a young woodsman (Russ Tamblyn) who accepts a king's (Jim Backus) offer to find out how his daughter wears out 365 pairs of dancing shoes every year. Using a witch's cloak for invisibility, the woodsman hides atop the royal coach as it hurries off one evening to a gypsy camp. There, the lad is astonished to find that the princess (Yvette Mimieux) spends her nights dancing. Removing his cloak and donning a mask, he dances with the girl and they fall in love. The next day, the woodsman reveals the princess' secret to her father, and exposes himself as her partner from the night before. Her highness is overjoyed and they are wed.

In *The Singing Bone*, the cowardly Knight Ludwig (Terry Thomas) and his brave squire Hans (Buddy Hackett) go in search of a dragon. As the nobleman hides in a corner of the monster's cave, his underling slays the monster. To claim credit for the deed, Ludwig murders Hans. When a peasant carves a flute from one of the dead man's bones, it sings the story of what really happened. The instrument is brought before the king and, when Ludwig confesses, Hans appears, organ by organ, before the astonished court. He is given his master's title and possessions and lives happily ever after.

The finest of the three tales, however is *The Cobbler and the Elves* with Laurence Harvey—who also portrays Wilhelm Grimm—as the kindly shoemaker. It is Christmas, and the old cobbler is falling behind on his work for the king's court. This delay is due to the time he spends carving lucky elves for the local orphans. When his life is threatened should he fail to complete the monarch's order, the handyman works through the night. Unable to continue, he falls asleep; the elves come to life and

The Cobbler and the Elves sequence from *the Wonderful World of the Brothers Grimm.*

finish the job for him. Thus, everything is delivered on Christmas morning to both the king and the children.

The romanticized version of the Brothers' lives itself centers around the studious Jacob (Karl Boehem), who is concerned about earning a living, and his daydreaming brother Wilhelm, who insists on writing and collecting fairy tales. In the end, after misadventures with the local Duke (Oscar Homolka), whose family history they are supposed to be writing, Wilhelm becomes seriously ill. When his fairy-tale characters as yet unborn come to visit

The Singing Bone sequence from *The Wonderful World of the Brothers Grimm.* **Note that the lifesize replica of the dragon—used in two shots—is complete only up to the hind leg.**

the room, they inspire Wilhelm who struggles back to health. The Brothers hereafter compromise, agreeing to divide their time equally between fantasy and history. Eventually, both gain the Grimms fame and fortune.

Perhaps the most touching scene in the film comes at the end. The Brothers' historical works have earned them an appointment to the Berlin Academy. On the train to the institute, Wilhelm admits a painful truth to his brother.

"The Academy didn't even mention the fairy tales. Only the other books."

"What we did we did together," his brother responds. Nonetheless, Wilhelm is disappointed; the honor really belongs to Jacob. Their train pulls in to the station and Jacob steps forward to deliver a speech. Suddenly, from out of nowhere, hundreds of children appear and drown out his oratory. They ask for a story. Wilhelm, his voice choked with emotion, steps proudly forward and begins, "Once upon a time . . ."

The Wonderful World of the Brothers Grimm is a film geared to the nonfantasy viewer; it was made for the mass audience. Thus, its flights of fancy are simple and incorporate all the popular motifs: dragons, invisibility, elves, witches, etc. This combination of romance and timeless fantasy is certainly why Pal and MGM chose the Brothers' lives as their subject. Additionally, this was the first narrative film to use the audience participation Cinerama process, and the studio wanted a guaranteed crowd pleaser. Despite these box-office draws, however, and the impeccable quality of the production, the film did not do as well as MGM had hoped, bringing in a modest total of some $7,000,000. The film had to profit slightly more than that to break even. The next MGM-Cinerama collaboration, *How the West Was Won* (1963) did considerably better, hauling home to the ailing studio some $25,000,000 and eight Academy Award nominations. As beautifully realized as Jim Danforth and David Pal's stop-motion work was, it could not compete with John Wayne and Battle of Shiloh.

In any case, like all of Pal's lighter films, *The Wonderful World of the Brothers Grimm* was heir to a delicate, loving hand in the telling, meticulous special effects, and fine performances. In a larger sense, in its story of two men who have stirred the minds of millions, it is a strong voice for the value of imagination.

The Japanese, taking their cue from the West,

224

produced an effective collection of ghost stories called *Kwaidan* (1963). The first episode, *Kurokami (Black Hair)*, is the story of a young samurai who returns to his wife after many years of travel. Spending the night with her, he awakens to find her a skeleton. In *Yuki-Onna (Woman of the Snow)*, a man is haunted by a beautiful albino vampire who sucks the blood from freezing travelers. Not as lovely are the ghosts of *Mimihashi Hoichi (Hoichi the Earless)*. Hoichi is a blind musician who is commanded by ghosts to play for them. To protect him from harm, friends paint Hoichi with mystic symbols, forgetting his ears which the ghosts tear off. Finally, there is *Chawan No Naka (In the Cup of Tea)*, about a man who sees a stranger's reflection in his oolong. When later he meets the man, the fellow turns out to be a ghost. Visually a beautiful film, *Kwaidan* is governed by a uniquely Oriental view of ghosts and the supernatural which, to Western eyes, may seem alternately tame or sadistic. In either case, the picture never fails to captivate the viewer with its colorful images and native concepts of the occult.

Mario Bava made his contribution to macabre miscellanea with the disappointing *Black Sabbath* (1963), a film starring Boris Karloff as the host of a horror trilogy. Topping the collection is *La Goccia D'Aqua (A Drop of Water)* in which Nurse Helen Corey (Jacqueline Pierreux) steals a ring from the corpse of clairvoyant Madame Perkins. That night her apartment comes to life. Spigots drip, doors slam, and finally the spirit of the dead woman appears to claim her ring. This mildly diverting

The Illustrated Man: Rod Steiger awakens in the witch's home to find himself tatooed from head to foot.

effort was followed by the unimpressive *Il Telefono (The Telephone)*, about a call girl (Michele Mercier) who is menaced by a man she once betrayed. Finally, there is *I Wurdalak (The Wurdalak)* starring Karloff as Gorca, a form of Eastern European vampire who is driven to kill members of his own family. Not as atmospheric or evokative as Bava's other work, *Black Sabbath* is nonetheless a good vehicle for Karloff's lone portrayal of a vampire.

Dipping into the lore of Nathaniel Hawthorne, and borrowing a part of Roger Corman's stock company, United Artists produced *Twice Told Tales* (1963), an attempt to immitate American International's successful Poe films. *Dr. Heidigger's Experiment* was the film's first selection, detailing the discovery of a fluid that restores youth to a pair of aged lovers, and life to a jealous third party. In *Rappaccini's Daughter*, a man (Vincent Price) gives his daughter (Joyce Taylor) and her lover (Brett Halsey) the Midas' touch on death. And, saving the best for last, in *House of Seven Gables*, Vincent Price finds a teasure in a haunted mansion. Trying to steal the wealth, he is strangled by the owner's skeleton and the house falls to dust. Mercifully more serious and with a greater respect for source material than its Poe counterparts, *Twice Told Tales* did not stir the anticipated box-office activity and left Corman once more the unchallenged king of the classics.

Meanwhile, anticipating such future successes as *Tales from the Crypt* (1971), Hammer's English competitor Amicus made *Dr. Terror's House of Horrors* (1964) in which Death (Peter Cushing) lets

The *Mimihashi Hoichi* segment of *Kwaidan* with Hoichi covered by mystic symbols.

five men see the events that lead to their demise. These include such diverse elements as voodoo, a disembodied hand, lycanthropy, vampirism, and a murderous plant. Trying to ride on the tide of this successful film, an inexpensive American production called *Dr. Terror's Gallery of Horrors* (1967) was released, with Lon Chaney Jr. and John Carradine in tales of magic, vampirism in nineteenth-century London, the dead returning to life, and Dracula combatting a werewolf. Much better was *Torture Garden* (1967), another Amicus film with a carnival barker (Burgess Meredith)— who turns out to be the devil—showing four people their futures. *Enoch* is to be enchanted by a demon cat; in *Terror Over Hollywood*, a starlet will be kept eternally young after she is transformed into a robot. *Mr. Steinway* is the story of a jealous piano that will kill its maestro's mistress; and *The Man Who Collected Poe* will literally resurrect the author to write new stories.

For five years, the anthology was clearly a showplace for all manner of supernatural delights. Thus, the screen adaptation of Ray Bradbury's *The Illustrated Man* (1968) came as a breath of fresh air with tales of fantasy linked by the tragic history of its narrator (Rod Steiger), a man searching for the witch (Claire Bloom) who tatooed his body from head to foot. These pictures tell stories, three of which are shown in the film. *The Veldt* is about a playroom device that brings the world of a child's imagination to life; *The Long Rains* batter a planet with perpetual downpours; and *The Last Night of the World* shows how a family reacts to the coming end of life on earth. An adult, sensitive film, *The Illustrated Man* was destroyed by critics who had gone through their art-film phase several years earlier. Hopefully, future historians will correct the injustice this film has suffered.

Following this brief respite, Amicus was back with *The House That Dripped Blood* (1970), four new journeys into the bizarre. These take place within the walls of a mansion that has been cursed with misfortune. Or is it something more? Researching the disappearance of horror star Paul Henderson, a detective (John Bennet) hears the house's strange history. The first story details the efforts of a woman (Nyree Dawn Porter) and her lover (Tom Adams) to frighten her writer-husband Charles (Denholm Elliott) to death. The second tale centers around a wax figurine of Salome that decapitates owner Peter Cushing. Episode number three has a young girl (Chloe Franks) use voodoo to kill her father, John Reid (Christopher Lee), and the final piece, a comedy, tells of Henderson, who becomes a vampire after purchasing a cloak for the role.

After three anthologies, the Amicus films had, as yet, no character. They were simply a series of stories strung loosely together, often unrelated in mood or style. *Tales from the Crypt*, released the following year, changed all of that. Based on stories that appear in comic books from the early fifties, EC Publications' *(Mad Magazine)* tales were deemed by the government to be too gruesome for children. The comics were discontinued, but not forgotten.

Each tale revolves around acts of barbarism that give the film a repulsive unity. The perpetrators of these horrid deeds are on a tour of an old church where they meet a cowled stranger (Sir Ralph Richardson), who turns out to be Satan. The stories he tells justify the visitors' admission to hell. In *All Through the House*, Joan Collins murders her husband by pushing a brass poker through his head. In the end, she is herself killed by a psychotic Santa Claus. *Reflection of Death* is the vision of a skeleton seen in his rearview mirror by adulteror Ian Hendry. The shock causes Hendry to have a horrible accident from which he walks away. Arriving at his mistress' house, he finds that he has rotted away. The next tale, and the best of the bunch, is *Poetic Justice*. Peter Cushing stars in an Oscar-caliber performance as old Arthur Grimsdyke, whose wealthy neighbors, a father and son, want his property. When Grimsdyke refuses to sell, they convince the townspeople to send him nasty Valentines Day cards. Despondent, the old man hangs himself. Come February the fourteenth of the following year, he rises from the grave and, in keeping with the spirit of the day, carves out the son's heart and leaves it as a valentine for his scheming father. An adaptation of *The Monkey's Paw* follows, retitled *Wish You Were Here*. In it, a jade is the magic idol and the twist is that the deceased (Richard Greene) returns to life, as per his wife's request, but after he has already been embalmed. Though she hacks his body to pieces, still does it live, each bloody fragment pulsing with life. Finally, in *Blind Alley*, the inhabitants of a home for the blind lock their cruel landlord William Rogers (Nigel Patrick) in a room. His German Shepherd is starved in an apartment nearby. Meanwhile, the residents built a tight maze that will lead their

Peter Cushing as Arthur Grimsdyke in *Tales from the Crypt*, both before . . .

. . .and after his murder.

Death rides a motorcycle in *Tales from the Crypt*.

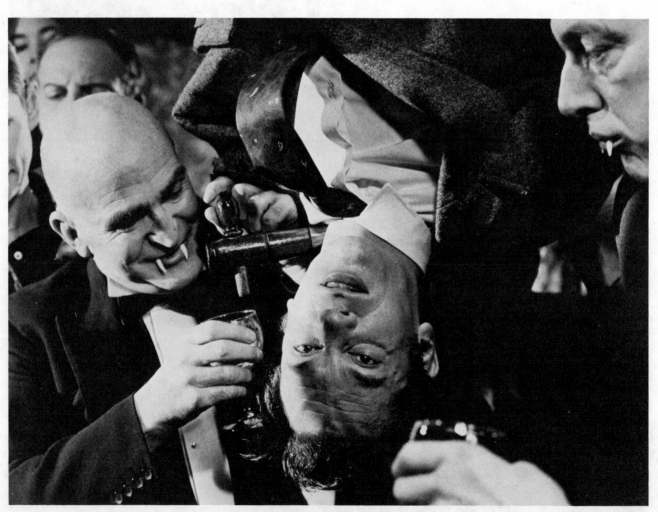

Daniel Massey is the main course at a vampire feast in
Vault of Horror.

228

captive to freedom. Unfortunately, they have lined it from floor to ceiling with razor blades. Releasing the landlord, they also set his dog loose . . . and turn out the lights.

A vivid, expensive production, *Tales from the Crypt* was a huge success and inspired another EC-adaptation *The Vault of Horror* (1972). Produced without care or polish, this awful collection is nothing more than unending displays of sadism. Unlike *Tales from the Crypt*, it is not a homage to EC and its very black humor; rather, it was an attempt to make a quick buck on the other film's reputation. Five men find themselves in an officelike room, not knowing why they are there. To pass the time, they exchange nightmares they have all had. Daniel Massey's nightmare is *Midnight Mess*, the story of how he stumbles upon a cafe for vampires and stays to become the main course. The insanely tidy Terry Thomas relates how he badgers his wife about her sloppiness in *The Neat Job* and is dismembered for his pains, placed in carefully labeled jars stacked neatly on a shelf. In *Bargain in Death*, Michael Craig sees himself buried alive to split his insurance with the man who will dig him up. Instead, grave robbers are first on the scene and when Judd jumps from his coffin, they kill him. Magician Curt Jurgens learns that *This Trick Will Kill You* when he murders an Indian girl to possess her magic rope and the cord strangles him. And, in the only well-made selection of the group, Tom Baker discovers that when portraits he has done are damaged, their subjects reflect the mishap. Thus, in *Drawn and Quartered*, he uses this power to kill his enemies. Unfortunately, Baker has already painted his own likeness. Despite great pains taken to protect the work, someone knocks turpentine on

the canvas and Baker becomes as mangled as the painting. In the end, these storytellers realize that they have all died and are doomed to come forth every night to relive their ghastly, self-imposed fates. Rising, the men head for their graves.

Amicus' next production, *Asylum* (1972) was more of the same. Each inmate in an insane asylum tells his story. One patient, Bonnie (Barbara Parkins) helped her lover Walter (Richard Todd) dismember his wife in *Frozen With Fear*. The woman's arms returned to kill her husband and chase Bonnie from the house. In *The Weird Tailor*, sartor Bruno (Barry Morse) is given a weird cloth by Mr. Smith (Peter Cushing) with which he is to make a suit for the man's son. His instructions are to work with the material only between sunset and sunrise due to its supernatural powers, which revive the dead. Charlotte Rampling was a murderous schizoid in *Lucy Comes to Stay*, and in *Mannikins of Horror*, Herbert Lom creates living dolls that exact vengeance on the people who put him in the institution.

The asylum was again used as a locale for *Tales That Witness Madness* (1973), in which Donald Pleasance tries to get the bottom of his patients' strange hallucinations. This was followed into release by *Tales from Beyond the Grave* (1973), to date the last of the Amicus series. Doubtless there will be more.

At best, the combined impact of these short-story collections is greater than a single, lengthy narrative; at worst, there is at least the variety to provide for every taste. However, as the latter Amicus films have proven, care must be taken to assign *purpose* to the mayhem, or the anthology film becomes simply an excuse to showcase excessive bad taste and gore.[20]

17
TELEVISION

The career of fantasy in television has only recently blossomed with the great abundance of horror and supernatural films being commissioned for network movie slots, and the series spawned by a few of these. Of necessity, due to stringent production demands, these films are routine efforts made with assemblyline precision to be a specific length, not overly innovative in theme or plot, and sport only straightforward camera work, performances, and set design.

Before the first TV movie in 1966, *Fame is the Name of the Game*—which became the basis for a popular weekly series—fantasy had known only an occasional series. Episodes of *Lost in Space*, *Outer Limits,* or *Twilight Zone* often bordered on the fantastic, but are known primarily for their science-fiction presentations. Dan Curtis' *Dark Shadows* was an afternoon showcase for several years, making a sex symbol of vampire Barnabas Collins (Jonathan Frid) and bringing gothic fantasy to the normally staid soap-opera crowd. Host Boris Karloff's primetime *Thriller* and *Alfred Hitchcock Presents* also spotlighted fantasy, but are generally referred to as "mystery" or "suspense" programs. This lack of serious fantasy should come as no surprise. Only comedic series have had any success; witness *I Dream of Jeannie* with genie Barbara Eden in contemporary Florida; *The Flying Nun* starring Sally Field as the airborne Sr. Bertrille; *Topper,* from the fifties, with Leo G. Carroll; and *Bewitched* with a lovely Elizabeth Montgomery as a witch in modern-day suburbia, along with its offshoot program *Tabitha* starring her preternatural daughter.

The pilot for an unsold series in the 1950s called *Superpup.* The "pups" were actors in costumes.

Shorter-lived humor series included the one-season, efforts *Ghost and Mrs. Muir* featuring Hope Lang and Edward Mulhare; *My Mother the Car* starring Ann Southern as the reincarnated 1928 Porter; *The Second Hundred Years* with nineteenth-century prospector Monte Markham frozen in ice and thawed in modern Los Angeles, where he lives with his older, middle-aged son Arthur O'Connell; and *It's About Time* with two astronauts crashing in the prehistoric world of Imogene Coca and stock footage belonging to the *Beast From Hollow Mountain*. In a more serious vein, fine anthology series also came and went: *Journey Into the Unknown*; John Newland's excellent *One Step Beyond*—which did, in fact, run three full years during the late

230

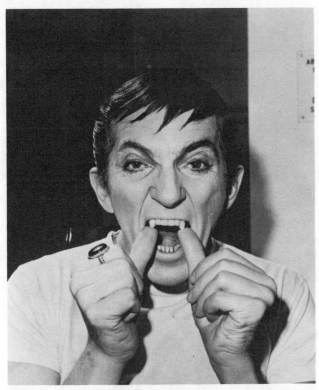

Jonathan Frid dons his fangs for a days' work on *Dark Shadows*.

Barbara Eden in *I Dream of Jeannie*.

Agnes Morehead and Elizabeth Montgomery in the television series *Bewitched*.

Darren McGavin as Kolchak, *The Night Stalker*.

The cavemen in *Korg*.

Lee Majors as one of television's fantasy-science-fiction creations, *The Six Million Dollar Man*.

Jim Nabors and Ruth Buzzi in a television abomination, *The Lost Saucer*.

Forrest Tucker (left) as Tracy, Larry Storch as Spenser, and Bob Burns as Kong, are television's *The Ghost Busters*.

Karen Black plays as embittered spinster in one of three tales of the TV movie *Trilogy of Terror*. In this story she played a teacher who uses her powers of ESP to force male students into her bed. The other tales had Karen as schizoid murderess and a victim of a voodoo doll that comes to life and eventually possesses her body.

In another television movie, Kim Novak starred as the only survivor of a shipwreck in *Satan's Triangle*, set in the Bermuda Triangle. She is rescued by Doug McClure.

fifties—and Roald Dahl's *Way Out*. More recently, the short-lived occult series have been *The Sixth Sense* and William Castle's *Ghost Story*. The best of these efforts, a pilot called *Ghost Breaker* starring Kerwin Mathews, never made it into the network lineup. For the youngsters, there have been such soggy Saturday morning entries as *Land of the Lost*, about a family stranded in earth's prehistory; the semidocumentary caveman series *Korg*; the Larry Storch, Forrest Tucker, super-gorilla team known as *The Ghost Busters*; and so forth.

The TV movies have also had their ups and downs. These ranged from the superb *Gargoyles*, about a colony of the monsters found by Cornel Wilde in the American Southwest, to Dan Curtis'

excellent *Dracula* with Jack Palance as the Count, to the allegedly comedic *Poor Devil* with Sammy Davis Jr. as the devil trying to please Satan Christopher Lee, to the ineffective *Werewolf of Washington* with the president's press agent (Dean Stockwell) as a lycanthrope who infects the Chief Executive before dying. Several TV films have fostered weekly series: *Night Gallery* and *The Night Stalker* are best known and remain in syndication after their brief runs. *Night Gallery* was disowned by its late host Rod Serling when the stories became trite; *The Night Stalker* featured Darren McGavin as Kolchak, a reporter who specialized in covering the bizarre.

It is clear, from a quick look at the above, that new directions in fantasy will not come from

Producer William Castle and a star of his film _Bug_.

television. This is especially distressing when one considers that many of the masters, such as Walt Disney and Willis O'Brien, are gone leaving relatively few serious filmmakers to continue in their stead. It remains for us to pick up the pieces and assure that the Fabulous Fantasy Films do not die. Not for the sake of the genre, but for the sake of the human race, man's imagination must not be allowed to atrophy.

Appendix 1
CAST AND CREDITS OF 500 FANTASY FILMS

Abbott and Costello Meet Frankenstein (1947). Starring: Bud Abbott, Lou Costello, Bela Lugosi, Glenn Strange, Lon Chaney Jr., Lenore Aubert. Directed by: Charles T. Barton. Produced by: Robert Arthur. Universal. 92 minutes.

Abbott and Costello Meet the Mummy (1955). Starring: Bud Abbott, Lou Costello, Marie Windsor, Michael Ansara, Eddie Parker. Directed by: Charles Lamont. Produced by Howard Christie. Universal. 79 minutes.

Abominable Snowman of the Himalayas (1957). Starring: Forrest Tucker, Peter Cushing, Maureen Connell, Richard Wattis. Directed by: Val Guest. Produced by Aubrey Baring. 20th Century Fox. 91 minutes.

Adventures of Ichabod and Mr. Toad (1949). Animated Cartoon. Produced by: Walt Disney. Walt Disney Productions. 68 minutes.

Aladdin and His Lamp (1951). Starring: Patricia Medina, Noreen Nash, John Sands. Directed by: Lew Landers. Produced by: Walter Wanger. Monogram. 67 minutes.

Alakazam the Great (1960). Animated Cartoon. Produced by: Hiroshi Okawa. Voices (dubbed): Frankie Avalon, Jonathan Winters, Arnold Stang, Sterling Holloway, Dodie Stevens. Toei. 88 minutes.

Alias Nick Beal (1949). Starring: Ray Milland, Thomas Mitchell, Audrey Totter, George Macready, Darryl Hickman. Directed by: John Farrow. Produced by: Endre Bohem. Paramount. 93 minutes.

Alice in Wonderland (1933). Starring: Charlotte Henry, Richard Arlen, Cary Cooper, W. C. Fields, Cary Grant, Sterling Holloway, Edward Everett Horton, Jack Oakie, Charlie Ruggles, Roscoe Ates, William Austin. Directed by: Norman McLeod. Produced by: Louis D. Lighton. Paramount. 90 minutes.

Alice in Wonderland (1951). Animated Cartoon. Produced by Walt Disney. Voices: Kathryn Beaumont, Ed Wynn, Sterling Holloway, Verna Felton. Walt Disney Productions. 75 minutes.

All That Money Can Buy (1940). Starring: Walter Huston, Edward Arnold, James Craig, Simone Simon, H. B. Warner. Directed by: William Dieterle. Produced by: William Dieterle. RKO. 112 minutes.

Angel Comes to Brooklyn (1945). Starring: Kaye Dowd, Robert Duke, David Street, Charles Kemper, C. Montague Shaw. Directed by: Leslie Goodwins. Produced by Armand Schaefer. Republic. 70 minutes.

Angel on My Shoulder (1946). Starring: Paul Muni, Anne Baxter, Onslow Stevens, Claude Rains, Fritz Leiber. Directed by: Archie Mayo. Produced by: Charles R. Rogers. United Artists. 102 minutes.

Angel Who Pawned Her Harp (1954). Starring: Felix Aylmer, Diane Cilento, Sheila Sweet. Directed by: Alan Bromly. Produced by: Sidney Cole. British Lion. 74 minutes.

Angels in the Outfield (1951). Starring: Paul Douglas, Janet Leigh, Keenan Wynn, Lewis Stone, Spring Byington, Bruce Bennet, Bing Crosby, Donna Corcoran. Directed by: Clarence Brown. Produced by: Clarence Brown. MGM. 99 minutes.

Animal World (1955). Stop-motion Documentary. Directed by: Irwin Allen. Produced by: Irwin Allen. Narrated by: Theodore von Eltz and John Storm. Warner Brothers. 82 minutes.

Arabian Nights (1942). Starring: Maria Montez, Jon Hall, Sabu, Shemp Howard, Turhan Bey. Directed by: John Rawlins. Produced by: Walter Wanger. Universal. 87 minutes.

Asylum (1972). Starring: Herbert Lom, Barry Morse, Peter Cushing, Britt Ekland, Patrick Magee, Barbara

Parkins, Richard Todd, Charlotte Rampling, Megs Jenkins. Directed by: Roy Ward Baker. Produced by: Milton Sobotsky and Max Rosenberg. Amicus. 98 minutes.

Atlantis, the Lost Continent (1961). Starring: Anthony Hall, Joyce Taylor, Ed Platt, Frank DeKova. Directed by: George Pal. Produced by: George Pal. MGM. 90 minutes.

Atlas in the Land of the Cyclops (1961). Starring: Mitchell Gordon, Chelo Alonso, Vira Silenti. Directed by: Antonio Leonviola. Produced by: Ermanno Donati and Luigi Carpentieri. Medallion. 96 minutes.

Attack of the Giant Leeches (1959). Starring: Ken Clark, Yvette Vickers, Michael Emmet. Directed by: Bernard L. Kowalski. Produced by: Roger Corman. American International. 62 minutes.

Attack of the Monsters (1969). Starring: Nobuhiro Najima, Miyuki Akyuama, Christopher Murphy. Directed by: Noriaki Yuass. Produced by: Hidemasa Negata. Daiei. 83 minutes.

Aztec Mummy (1957). Starring: Ramon Gay, Leslie Harrison, Steve Grant. Directed by: Rafael Lopez Portillo. Produced by: William Calderon Stell. Azteca. 85 minutes.

Babes in Toyland (1934). Starring: Stan Laurel, Oliver Hardy, Charlotte Henry, Felix Knight, Henry Kleinbach, John Downs. Directed by: Gus Meins and Charles Rogers. Produced by: Hal Roach. MGM. 77 minutes.

Babes in Toyland (1961). Starring: Annette Funicello, Ray Bolger, Tommy Sands, Ed Wynn, Tommy Kirk, Kevin Corcoran. Directed by: Jack Donohue. Produced by: Walt Disney. Walt Disney Productions. 105 minutes.

Back from the Dead (1957). Starring: Peggy Castle, Arthur Franz, Marsha Hunt. Directed by Charles Marquis Warren. Produced by: Robert Stabler. Twentieth Century Fox. 79 minutes.

Bad Lord Byron (1949). Starring: Dennis Price, Joan Greenwood, Ernest Thesiger. Directed by: David MacDonald. Produced by Aubrey Baring. International. 85 minutes.

Bambi Meets Godzilla (1969). Animated Cartoon. Produced by: Marvin Newland. Filmways. 30 seconds.

Barbarella (1967). Starring: Jane Fonda, John Phillip Law, David Hemmings, Ugo Tognazzi, Milo O'Shea, Marcel Marceau. Directed by: Roger Vadim. Produced by Dino De Laurentiis. Paramount. 98 minutes.

Baron Munchausen (1961). Starring: Milos Kopecky, Jana Brejchova. Directed by Karel Zeman. Czechoslovakian. 83 minutes.

Battle for the Planet of the Apes (1973). Starring: Roddy McDowall, Claude Akins, Natalie Trundy, John Huston. Directed by: J. Lee Thompson. Produced by: Arthur P. Jacobs. Twentieth Century Fox. 86 minutes.

Beast from Haunted Cave (1959). Starring: Michael Forest, Sheila Carol, Frank Wolff. Directed by: Monte Hellman. Produced by Roger Corman. Filmgroup. 65 minutes.

Beast from Twenty Thousand Fathoms (1953). Starring: Kenneth Tobey, Paul Christian, Cecil Kellaway, Paula Raymond, Lee Van Cleef. Directed by: Eugene Lourie. Produced by Hal Chester and Jack Dietz. Warner Brothers. 80 minutes.

Beast of Hollow Mountain (1956). Starring: Guy Madison, Carlos Rivas, Patricia Medina. Directed by: Edward Nassour and Ismael Rodriquez. Produced by: William and Edward Nassour. United Artists. 80 minutes.

Beast of the Yellow Night (1970). Starring: Eddie Garcia, John Ashley, Mary Wilcox. Directed by Eddie Romero. Produced by Roger Corman. New World. 87 minutes.

Beauty and the Beast (1946). Starring: Jean Marais, Josette Day, Marcel Andre, Mila Parely, Michel Auclair. Directed by: Jean Cocteau. Produced by: Andre Paulve and Emile Darbon. French. 90 minutes.

Beauty and the Beast (1963). Starring: Joyce Taylor, Mark Damon, Eduard Franz. Directed by: Edward Cahn. Produced by: Robert Kent. United Artists. 77 minutes.

Bedazzled (1967). Starring: Peter Cook, Dudley Moore, Eleanor Bron, Raquel Welch. Directed by: Stanley Donan. Produced by: Stanley Donan. Twentieth Century Fox. 107 minutes.

Bedknobs and Broomsticks (1971). Starring: Angela Lansbury, David Tomlinson, Roddy McDowall, Sam Jaffe. Directed by: Robert Stevenson. Produced by: Bill Walsh. Walt Disney Productions. 117 minutes.

Beginning of the End (1957). Starring: Peter Graves, Peggie Castle, Morris Ankrum. Directed by: Bert I. Gordon. Produced by: Bert I. Gordon. Republic. 74 minutes.

Bell, Book, and Candle (1958). Starring: James Stewart, Kim Novak, Jack Lemmon, Ernie Kovaks, Elsa Lanchester, Hermione Gingold. Directed by: Richard Quine. Produced by: Julian Blaustein. Columbia. 103 minutes.

Beneath the Planet of the Apes (1970). Starring: James Franciscus, Linda Harrison (Augusta Summerland), Kim Hunter, Maurice Evans, Victor Buono, Charlton Heston. Directed by: Ted Post. Produced by: Arthur P. Jacobs. Twentieth Century Fox. 95 minutes.

Berkeley Square (1933). Starring: Leslie Howard, Heather Angel, Valerie Taylor. Directed by: Frank Lloyd. Produced by: Jesse Lasky. Twentieth Century Fox. 88 minutes.

Between Two Worlds (1944). Starring: John Garfield, Paul Henreid, Sidney Greenstreet, Eleanor Parker, Edmund Gwenn. Directed by: Edward Blatt. Produced by: Mark Hellinger. Warner Brothers. 112 minutes.

Beyond Tomorrow (1940). Starring: Harry Carey, C. Aubrey Smith, Maria Ouspenskaya, Richard Carlson. Directed by: A. E. Sutherland. Produced by: Lee Garmes. RKO. 84 minutes.

Billy the Kid vs. Dracula (1965). Starring: John Carradine, Chuck Courtney, Melinda Plowman, Roy Barcroft, Harry Carey Jr. Directed by: William Beaudine Jr.

Produced by: Carroll Case. Embassy. 84 minutes.

The Birds (1963). Starring: Rod Taylor, Tippi Hedren, Suzanne Plesheete. Directed by: Aldred Hitchcock. Produced by: Alfred Hitchcock. Universal. 119 minutes.

Bishop's Wife (1947). Starring: Cary Grant, David Niven, Loretta Young, Monty Woolley, Elsa Lanchester, Regis Toomey. Directed by: Henry Koster. Produced by: Samuel Goldwyn. RKO. 109 minutes.

Black Sabbath (1963). Starring: Boris Karloff, Mark Damon, Susy Anderson, Michele Mercier, Jacqueline Pierreau. Directed by: Mario Bava. Produced by: Salvatore Billitteri. American International. 100 minutes.

Black Scorpion (1957). Starring: Richard Denning, Carlos Rivas, Mara Corday. Directed by: Edward Ludwig. Produced by: Jack Dietz and Frank Melford. Warner Brothers. 88 minutes.

Black Sunday (1960). Starring: Barbara Steele, Ivo Garrani, John Richardson, Andrea Checchi. Directed by: Mario Bava. Produced by: Massimo DeRita. American International. 83 minutes.

Blacula (1972). Starring: William Marshall, Denise Nichols, Vonetta McGee, Thalmus Rasulala, Charles Macaulay, Elisha Cooke Jr. Directed by: William Crain. Produced by: Joseph T. Naar. American International. 92 minutes.

Blackbeard's Ghost (1967). Starring: Peter Ustinov, Dean Jones, Suzanne Pleshette, Elsa Lanchester. Directed by: Robert Stevenson. Produced by: Walt Disney Productions. 107 minutes.

Blithe Spirit (1945). Rex Harrison, Constance Cummings, Kay Hammond, Margaret Rutherford. Directed by: David Lean. Produced by: Noel Coward. United Artists. 98 minutes.

The Blob (1958). Starring: Steve McQueen, Aneta Corseaut. Directed by: Irwin S. Yeaworth Jr. Produced by: Jack H. Harris, Paramount. 85 minutes.

Blood and Roses (1960). Starring: Mel Ferrer, Else Martinelli, Annette Vadim. Directed by: Roger Vadim. Produced by: Raymond Eger. Paramount. 87 minutes.

Blood Bath (1966). Starring: William Campbell, Marissa Mathes, Sandra Knight. Directed by: Jack Hill. Produced by: Jack Hill. American International. 80 minutes.

Blood of Dracula (1957). Starring: Sandra Harrison, Thomas B. Henry, Louise Lewis. Directed by: Herbert L. Strock. Produced by: Herman Cohen. American International. 69 minutes.

Blood from the Mummy's Tomb (1971). Starring: Andrew Keir, Valerie Leon, James Villiers, George Coulouris. Directed by: Seth Holt and Michael Carreras. Produced by: Howard Brandy. Hammer. 94 minutes.

Blood on Satan's Claw (1970). Starring: Patrick Wymark, Linda Hayden, Barry Andrews, Tamara Ustinov, Avice Landon. Directed by: Piers Haggard. Produced by: Tony Tenser. Tigon. 95 minutes.

Bloodsuckers (1971). Starring: Patrick Macnee, Peter Cushing. Directed by: Robert Hartford-Davis. Produced by: Peter Newbrook and Graham Harris. Chevron. 87 minutes.

Boy and the Pirates (1960). Starring: Charles Herbert, Susan Gordon, Murvyn Vye, Joseph Turkel. Directed by: Bert I. Gordon. Produced by: Bert I. Gordon. United Artists. 84 minutes.

Brass Bottle (1964). Starring: Tony Randall, Barbara Eden, Burl Ives, Kamala Devi. Directed by: Harry Keller. Produced by: Robert Arthur. Universal. 89 minutes.

Brides of Dracula (1960). Starring: Peter Cushing, David Peel, Martita Hunt, Freda Jackson, Michael Ripper, Miles Malleson. Directed by: Terence Fisher. Produced by: Michael Carreras and Anthony Hinds. Hammer. 85 minutes.

Brotherhood of Satan (1971). Starring: Strother Martin, Charles Bateman, L. Q. Jones, Anna Capri. Directed by: Bernard McEveety. Produced by: L. Q. Jones and Alvy Moore. Columbia. 92 minutes.

Burn, Witch, Burn (1961). Starring: Janet Blair, Peter Wyngarde, Margaret Johnston. Directed by: Sidney Hayers. Produced by: Albert Fennell. American International. 86 minutes.

Cabinet of Dr. Caligari (1919). Starring: Conrad Veidt, Werner Kraus, Lil Dagover. Directed by: Robert Weine. Produced by: Erich Pommer. Decla. 72 minutes.

Caltiki, the Immortal Monster (1959). Starring: John Merivale, Didi Sullivan, Gerard Herter. Directed by: Robert Hampton and Lee Kresel. Produced by: Samuel Schneider. Allied Artists. 76 minutes.

Canterville Ghost (1944). Starring: Charles Laughton, Robert Young, Margaret O'Brien, Peter Lawford, Frank Reicher. Directed by: Jules Dassin. Produced by: Arthur Fields. MGM. 96 minutes.

Captain Kronos: Vampire Hunter (1972). Starring: Horst Janson, John Carson, Shane Briant, Caroline Munro, Ian Hendry. Directed by: Brian Clemens. Produced by: Albert Fennell and Brian Clemens. Hammer. 96 minutes.

Captain Nemo and the Underwater City (1969). Starring: Robert Ryan, Chuck Conners, Nanette Newman. Directed by: James Hill. Produced by: Bertram Ostrer. MGM. 106 minutes.

Captain Sinbad (1963). Starring: Guy Williams, Heidi Bruhl, John Crawford. Directed by: Byron Haskin. Produced by: Frank and Herman King. MGM. 85 minutes.

Carousel (1956). Starring: Gordon MacRae, Shirley Jones, Cameron Mitchell, Barbara Ruick. Directed by: Henry King. Produced by: Henry Ephron. Twentieth Century Fox. 128 minutes.

Carnival of Souls (1962). Starring: Candace Hilligoss, Herk Harvey, Frances Feist. Directed by: Herk Harvey. Produced by: Herk Harvey. Herts-Lion. 80 minutes.

Cat Girl (1957). Starring: Barbara Shelley, Robert Ayres. Directed by: Alfred Saughnessy. Produced by: Peter Rogers. American International. 75 minutes.

Cat People (1942). Starring: Simone Simon, Tom Conway, Kent Smith, Jane Randolph, Alan Napier. Directed by: Jacques Tourneur. Produced by: Val Lewton. RKO. 74 minutes.

Catman of Paris (1946). Starring: Robert J. Wilke, Carl Esmond, Lenore Aubert. Directed by: Lesley Selander. Produced by: Marek Libkov. Republic. 65 minutes.

Un Chien Andalou (1928). Starring: Salvador Dali, Luis Bunuel, Simone Mareuil, Piere Batcheff. Directed by: Luis Bunuel. Produced by: Luis Bunuel. French. 23 minutes.

Chitty-Chitty, Bang-Bang (1968). Starring: Dick Van Dyke, Sally Ann Howes, Lionel Jeffries, Gert Frobe. Directed by: Ken Hughes. Produced by: Albert Broccoli. United Artists. 145 minutes.

Christmas Carol (1938). Starring: Reginald Owen, Gene Lockhart, Leo G. Carroll. Directed by: Edwin Marin. Produced by: Joseph L. Mankiewicz. MGM. 69 minutes.

Christmas Carol (1951).Starring: Alastair Sim, Mervyn Johns, Jack Warner, Miles Malleson, Ernest Thesiger, Peter Bull, Patrick MacNee. Directed by: Brian Desmon Hurst. Produced by: Brian Desmon Hurst. United Artists. 86 minutes.

Cinderella (1950). Animated Cartoon. Produced by: Walt Disney. Voices: Ilene Woods, Eleanor Audley, Verna Felton. Walt Disney Productions. 75 minutes.

Cockeyed Miracle (1946). Starring: Frank Morgan, Keenan Wynn, Cecil Kellaway, Audrey Totter, Morris Ankrum. Directed by: Sylvan Simon. Produced by: Irving Starr. MGM. 83 minutes.

Conqueror Worm (1968). Starring: Vincent Price, Ian Oglivy, Patrick Wymark, Hilary Dwyer. Directed by: Michael Reeves. Produced by: Tony Tenser. Tigon. 87 minutes.

Conquest of Mycene (1963). Starring: Gordon Scott, Genevieve Grad, Alessandra Panaro. Directed by: Giorgio Ferroni. Produced by: Bruno Turchetto. Embassy. 102 minutes.

Conquest of the Planet of the Apes (1972). Starring: Roddy McDowall, Don Murray, Natalie Trundy, Lou Wagner, Ricardo Montalban. Directed by: J. Lee Thompson. Produced by: Arthur P. Jacobs. Twentieth Century Fox. 88 minutes.

Count Yorga: Vampire (1970). Starring: Robert Quarry, Roger Perry, Michael Murphy. Directed by: Bob Kelljan. Produced by: Michael Macready. American International. 90 minutes.

Countess Dracula (1970). Starring: Ingrid Pitt, Nigel Green, Maurice Denham. Directed by: Peter Sasdy. Produced by: Alexander Paal. Hammer. 93 minutes.

Creature from the Black Lagoon (1953). Starring: Richard Denning, Julie Adams, Richard Carlson, Whit Bissell. Directed by: Jack Arnold. Produced by: William Alland. Universal. 79 minutes.

Creature of Destruction (1967). Les Tremayne, Aaron Kincaid, Pat Delany. Directed by: Larry Buchanan. Produced by: Larry Buchanan. American International. 80 minutes.

Creature Walks Among Us (1956). Starring: Jeff Morrow, Rex Reason, Leigh Snowden. Directed by: John Sherwood. Produced by: William Alland. Universal. 78 minutes.

Creatures the World Forgot (1970). Starring: Julie Ege, Brian O'Shaughnessy, Tony Bonner. Directed by: Don Chaffey. Produced by: Michael Carreras. Hammer. 95 minutes.

Creeping Flesh (1972). Starring: Peter Cushing, Christopher Lee. Directed by: Freddie Francis. Produced by: Mike Redbourn. Tigon. 90 minutes.

Crimson Cult (1968). Starring: Boris Karloff, Christopher Lee, Barbara Steele, Mark Eden, Virginia Wetherell, Michael Gough. Directed by: Vernon Sewell. Produced by: Tony Tenser and Louis Heyward. Tigon. 89 minutes.

Cry of the Banshee (1970). Starring: Vincent Price, Elisabeth Bernger, Hugh Griffith. Directed by: Gordon Hessler. Produced by: James H. Nicholson and Samuel Z. Arkoff. American International. 87 minutes.

Cry of the Werewolf (1944). Starring: Nina Foch, Stephen Crane, Fritz Leiber, Osa Massen. Directed by: Henry Levin. Produced by: Wallace MacDonald. Columbia. 65 minutes.

Curse of the Cat People (1944). Starring: Ann Carter, Simone Simon, Kent Smith, Jane Randolph. Directed by: Robert Wise. Produced by: Val Lewton. RKO. 70 minutes.

Curse of the Demon (1956). Starring: Dana Andrews, Peggy Cummins, Niall MacGinnis, Maurice Denham. Directed by: Jacques Tourneur. Produced by: Hal Chester and Frank Bevis. Columbia. 95 minutes.

Curse of the Faceless Man (1958). Starring: Richard Anderson, Bob Bryant, Elaine Edwards, Gar Moore. Directed by: Edward Cahn. Produced by: Robert Kent. United Artists. 66 minutes.

Curse of the Mummy's Tomb (1964). Starring: Dickie Owen, Terence Morgan, Fred Clark, Michael Ripper. Directed by: Michael Carreras. Produced by: Michael Carreras. Hammer. 80 minutes.

Curse of the Undead (1959). Starring: Eric Fleming, Michael Pate, Kathleen Crowley, John Hoyt. Directed by: Edward Dein. Produced by: Joseph Gershenson. Universal. 79 minutes.

Curse of the Voodoo (1964). Starring: Bryant Halliday, Dennis Price, Lisa Daniely. Directed by: Lindsay Shonteff. Produced by: Ken Rive. Allied Artists. 77 minutes.

Curse of the Werewolf (1961). Starring: Oliver Reed, Yvonne Romain, Clifford Evans, Michael Ripper. Directed by: Terence Fisher. Produced by: Michael Carreras and Anthony Hinds. Hammer. 91 minutes.

Dagora, the Space Monster (1964). Starring: Yosuke Natsuki, Yoko Fujiyama, Akiko Wakabayashi, Hiroshi Koizumi. Directed by: Inoshiro Honda. Toho. 83 minutes.

Damn Yankees (1958). Starring: Tab Hunter, Ray Walston, Gwen Verdon, Bob Fosse, Jean Stapleton. Directed by: Stanley Donen. Produced by: George Abbott. Warner Brothers. 110 minutes.

Dante's Inferno (1924). Starring: Lawson Butt, Robert Klein, Howard Gaye, Pauline Starke. Directed by: Henry Otto. Twentieth Century Fox. 60 minutes.

Dante's Inferno (1935). Starring: Spencer Tracy, Claire Trevor, Rita Hayworth. Directed by: Harry Lachman. Produced by: Sol M. Wurtzel. Twentieth Century Fox. 89 minutes.

Darby O'Gill and the Little People (1958). Starring: Albert Sharpe, Janet Munro, Sean Connery, Jimmy O'Dea, Estelle Winwood, Kieron Moore. Directed by: Robert Stevenson. Produced by: Walt Disney. Walt Disney Productions. 93 minutes.

Daughter of Dr. Jekyll (1957). Starring: Gloria Talbott, Arthur Shields, John Agar. Directed by: Edgar G. Ulmer. Produced by: Jack Pollexfen. Allied Artists. 71 minutes.

Dead Men Walk (1942). Starring: George Zucco, Dwight Frye, Mary Carlisle. Directed by: Sam Newfield. Produced by: Sigmund Neufield. PRC. 64 minutes.

Dead of Night (1945). Starring: Michael Redgrave, Sally Ann Howes, Miles Malleson, Mervyn Johns, Googie Withers. Directed by: Alberto Cavalcanti, Basil Dearden, Charles Chrichton, and Robert Hamer. Produced by: Michael Balcon. Universal. 160 minutes.

Dead One (1961). Starring: John MacKay, Linda Ormond, Clyde Kelley. Directed by: Barry Mahon. Produced by: Brandon Chase and Barry Mahon. Favorite. 71 minutes.

Deadly Mantis (1957). Starring: Craig Stevens, William Hopper. Directed by: Nathan Juran. Produced by: William Alland. Universal. 79 minutes.

Death Takes a Holiday (1934). Starring: Fredric March, Evelyn Venable, Henry Travers, Edward van Sloan, Kent Taylor. Directed by: Mitchell Leisen. Produced by: E. Lloyd Sheldon. Paramount. 78 minutes.

Death Takes a Holiday (1971). Starring: Monte Markham, Yvette Mimieux, Melvyn Douglas, Kerwin Mathews, Myrna Loy. Directed by: Robert Butler. Produced by: George Eckstein. ABC. 78 minutes.

Der Nibelungen (1923). Starring: Paul Richter, Margaret Schon, Theodor Loos, Bernhard Goetzke, Hans Adalbert von Schlettow, Hanna Ralph. Directed by: Fritz Lang. Decla. 240 minutes.

Destroy All Monsters (1968). Starring: Akira Kubo, Jun Tazaki, Kyoko Ai. Directed by: Inoshiro Honda. Produced by: Tomoyuki Tanaka. Toho. 88 minutes.

Destroy All Planets (1968). Starring: Kajiro Hongo, Toru Takatsuka, Peter Williams. Directed by: Noriaki Yuasa. Produced by: Hidemasa Nagata. Daiei. 75 minutes.

Devil's Bride (1968). Starring: Christopher Lee, Charles Gray. Directed by: Terence Fisher. Produced by: Anthony Nelson Keys. Hammer. 95 minutes.

Devil's Eye (1960). Starring: Jarl Kulle, Bibi Andersson, Stig Jarrel. Directed by: Ingmar Bergman. Produced by: Allan Ekelund. Janus. 90 minutes.

Devil's Messenger (1962). Starring: Lon Chaney Jr., John Crawford, Karen Kandler. Directed by: Herbert L. Strock and Curt Siodmak. Produced by: Ken Herts. Swedish. 75 minutes.

Devils of Darkness (1965). Starring: William Sylvester, Hubert Noel. Directed by: Lance Comfort. Produced by: Tom Blakely. Twentieth Century Fox. 88 minutes.

Devil's Own (1966). Starring: Joan Fontaine, Kay Walsh, Alec McCowan, Duncan Lamont, Martin Stephens. Directed by: Cyril Frankel. Produced by: Anthony Nelson Keys. Hammer. 91 minutes.

Devil's Partner (1958). Starring: Edwin Nelson, Edgar Buchanan, Jean Allison. Directed by: Charles R. Rondeau. Produced by: Hugh Hooker. Filmgroup. 60 minutes.

Dinosaur and the Missing Link (1917). Stop-motion Animation. Created by: Willis O'Brien. Edison. 12 minutes.

Dinosaurus (1960). Starring: Ward Ramsey, Kristina Hanson, Gregg Martell. Directed by: Irwin Yeaworth Jr. Produced by: Jack H. Harris. Universal. 85 minutes.

Disembodied (1957). Starring: Paul Burke, Allison Hayes. Directed by: Walter Grauman. Produced by: Ben Schwalb. Allied Artists. 66 minutes.

Dr. Dolittle (1967). Starring: Rex Harrison, Anthony Newley, Samantha Eggar, Richard Attenburough, Peter Bull, Geoffrey Holder, William Dix. Directed by: Richard Fleischer. Produced by: Arthur P. Jacobs. Twentieth Century Fox. 152 minutes.

Dr. Faustus (1967). Starring: Richard Burton, Andreas Teuber, Elizabeth Taylor. Directed by: Richard Burton and Nevill Coghill. Produced by: Richard Burton and Richard McWhorter. Columbia. 93 minutes.

Dr. Satan (1966). Starring: Joaquin Cordero, Alma Delia Fuentes. Directed by: Miguel Morayta. Produced by: Sidney Bruckner. Azteca. 85 minutes.

Dr. Terror's Gallery of Horrors (1967). Starring: Lon Chaney Jr., John Carradine, Rochelle Hudson. Directed by: D. L. Hewitt. Produced by: D. L. Hewitt and Ray Dorn. American General. 78 minutes.

Dr. Terror's House of Horrors (1964). Starring: Peter Cushing, Christopher Lee, Donald Sutherland. Directed by: Freddie Francis. Produced by: Milton Subotsky and Max J. Rosenbert. Amicus. 98 minutes.

Down to Earth (1947). Starring: Rita Haywork, Larry Parks, Edward Everett Horton, George Macready. Directed by: Alexander Hall. Produced by: Don Hartman. Columbia. 101 minutes.

Dracula (1930). Starring: Bela Lugosi, Edward van Sloan, Dwight Frye, Helen Chandler, David Manners. Directed by: Tod Browning. Produced by: Carl Laemmle Jr. Universal. 85 minutes.

Dracula A.D. 1972 (1971). Starring: Christopher Lee, Peter Cushing, Stephanie Beacham, Caroline Munro. Directed by: Alan Gibson. Produced by: Josephine Douglas. Hammer. 94 minutes.

Dracula Has Risen from the Grave (1968). Starring: Christopher Lee, Rupert Davies, Veronica Carlson,

Michael Ripper. Directed by: Freddie Francis. Produced by: Aida Young. Hammer. 92 minutes.

Dracula, Prince of Darkness (1965). Starring: Christopher Lee, Barbara Shelley, Andrew Keir. Directed by: Terence Fisher. Produced by: Anthony Nelson Keys. Hammer. 90 minutes.

Dracula vs. Frankenstein (1971). Starring: J. Carrol Naish, Lon Chaney Jr., Anthony Eisley, Russ Tamblyn, Zandor Vorkov, John Bloom. Directed by: Al Adamson. Produced by Mardi Rustam and Al Adamson. Independent International. 90 minutes.

Dracula's Daughter (1936). Starring: Gloria Holden, Otto Kruger, Edward van Sloan, Marguerite Churchill, Irving Pichel, Nan Grey. Directed by: Lambert Hillyer. Produced by: E. M. Asher. Universal. 72 minutes.

Dreams of the Rarebit Fiend (1906). Starring: John Brawn. Directed by: Edwin S. Porter. Produced by: Edwin S. Porter. Edison. 7 minutes.

Dunwich Horror (1969). Starring: Sam Jaffe, Sandra Dee, Dean Stockwell, Ed Begley. Directed by: Daniel Haller. Produced by: Roger Corman, James H. Nicholson, and Samuel Z. Arkoff. American International. 90 minutes.

Earthbound (1940). Starring: Warner Baxter, Henry Wilcoxen, Andrea Leeds. Directed by: Irving Pichel. Produced by: Sol Wurtzel. Twentieth Century Fox. 67 minutes.

Enchanted Forest (1945). Starring: Edmund Lowe, Brenda Joyce, Billy Severn. Directed by: Lew Landers. Produced by: Jack Schwarz. PRC. 78 minutes.

Escape from the Planet of the Apes (1971). Starring: Kim Hunter, Roddy McDowall, Bradford Dillman, Natalie Trundy, Sal Mineo, Ricardo Montalban. Directed by: Don Taylor. Produced by: Arthur P. Jacobs. Twentieth Century Fox. 97 minutes.

Equinox (1967). Starring: Edward Connell, Barbara Hewitt, Fritz Leiber. Directed by: Mark McGee. Produced by: Dennis Muren and Jack H. Harris. Tonlyn. 82 minutes. (Note: This was an amateur 16 mm film purchased for theatrical release and embellished with new scenes directed by Jack Woods.)

Everything's Ducky (1961). Starring: Buddy Hackett, Mickey Rooney, Jackie Cooper. Directed by: Don Taylor. Produced by: Red Doff. Columbia. 81 minutes.

The Exorcist (1973). Starring: Linda Blair, Jason Miller, Ellen Burstyn. Directed by: William Friedkin. Produced by: William Friedkin. Warner Brothers. 121 minutes.

Fabulous World of Jules Verne (1961). Starring: Louis Tock, Ernest Navara, Milo Holl. Directed by: Karel Zeman. Czechoslovakian. 83 minutes.

Fantasia (1940). Animated Cartoon. Narrated by: Deems Taylor. Produced by: Walt Disney. Walt Disney Productions. 126 minutes.

Fearless Vampire Killers or Pardon Me, But Your Teeth Are In My Neck (1967). Starring: Jack Mac Gowran, Sharon Tate, Ferdy Mayne, Roman Polanski. Directed by: Roman Polanski. Produced by: Gene Gutowski. MGM. 118 minutes.

Finian's Rainbow (1968). Starring: Fred Astaire, Tommy Steele, Petula Clark, Keenan Wynn, Al Freeman Jr. Directed by: Francis Ford Coppola. Produced by; Joseph Landon. Warner Brothers/Seven Arts. 145 minutes.

Five Thousand Fingers of Dr. T (1953). Starring: Hans Conried, Tommy Rettig, Peter Lind Hayes, Mary Healy. Directed by: Roy Rowland. Produced by: Stanley Kramer. Columbia. 93 minutes.

Flesh and Fantasy (1943). Starring: Edward G. Robinson, Charles Boyer, Barbara Stanwyck, Robert Benchley, Robert Cummings, Thomas Mitchell, C. Aubrey Smith. Directed by: Julian Duvivier. Produced by: Charles Boyer and Julian Duvivier. Universal. 100 minutes.

Flying Serpent (1945). Starring: George Zucco, Hope Kramer, Ralph Lewis. Directed by: Sherman Scott. Produced by: Sigmund Neufeld. PRC. 59 minutes.

For Heaven's Sake (1950). Starring: Clifton Webb, Edmund Gwenn, Joan Blondell, Tommy Rettig, Gigi Perreau, Joan Bennet, Robert Cummings. Directed by: George Seaton. Produced by: William Perlberg. Twentieth Century Fox. 92 minutes.

Four Skulls of Jonathan Drake (1959). Starring: Eduard Franz, Valerie French, Henry Daniell. Directed by: Edward L. Cahn. Produced by: Robert E. Kent. United Artists. 70 minutes.

Francis in the Haunted House (1956). Starring: Mickey Rooney, Paul Cavanagh, David Janssen, Richard Deacon. Directed by: Charles Lamont. Produced by: Robert Arthur. Universal. 80 minutes.

Frankenstein Conquers the World (1964). Starring: Nick Adams, Tadao Takashima, Kumi Mizuno, Takashi Shimura. Directed by: Inoshio Honda. Produced by: Tomoyuki Tanaka. American International/Toho. 87 minutes.

Frankenstein Meets the Wolfman (1943). Starring: Lon Chaney Jr., Bela Lugosi, Maria Ouspenskaya, Patric Knowles, Ilona Massey, Lionel Atwill, Dwight Frye. Directed by: Roy William Neill. Produced by: George Waggner. Universal. 74 minutes.

Frogs (1971). Starring: Ray Milland, Sam Elliott, Joan van Ark. Directed by: George McCowan. Produced by: Peter Thomas and George Edwards. American International. 90 minutes.

From Hell It Came (1957). Starring: Tod Andrews, Tina Carver, Linda Watkins. Directed by: Dan Milner. Produced by: Jack Milner. Allied Artists. 71 minutes.

Gamera the Invincible (1966). Starring: Eiji Funakoshi, Harumi Kirtachi, Brian Donlevy, Albert Dekker. Directed by: Noriaki Yuasa. Produced by: Yonejiro Saito. Daiei. 88 minutes.

Gamera vs. Monster X (1970). Starring: Tsutomu Takakuwa, Kelly Varis, Katherine Murphy. Directed by: Noriaki Yuasa. Produced by: Yonejiro Saito. Daiei. 83 minutes.

Gamera vs. Zigra (1971). Starring: Ken Utsui, Yusuke Kawazu. Directed by: Noriaki Yuasa. Produced by: Yonejiro Saito. Daiei. 81 minutes. (Note: Daiei went bankrupt and closed its gates shortly after the completion of this film.)

Ganja and Hess (1973). Starring: Duane Jones, Marlene Clark, Bill Gunn, Directed by: Bill Gunn, Produced by: Chiz Schultz. Kelley-Jordan. 110 minutes.

Gappa, the Triphibian Monster (1967). Starring: Tamio Kawaji, Yoko Yamamoto, Tatsuya Fuji. Directed by: Haruyasu Noguchi. Produced by: Hideo Koi. Nikkatsu/American International. 85 minutes.

The Genie (1957). Starring: Douglas Fairbanks Jr., Yvonne Furneaux, Martine Miller. Directed by: Lance Comfort. Produced by: Douglas Fairbanks Jr. British. 75 minutes.

Gertie the Dinosaur (1906). Animated Cartoon. Created by: Winsor McCay. 11 minutes.

Ghidrah, the Three-Headed Monster (1965). Starring: Yosuke Natsuki, Yuriko Hoshi, Takashi Shimura, Emi Ito, Ymi Ito. Directed by: Inoshiro Honday. Produced by: Tomoyuki Tanaka. Toho. 85 minutes.

Ghost and Mrs. Muir (1947). Starring: Gene Tierney, Rex Harrison, George Sanders, Natalie Wood. Directed by: Joseph L. Mankiewicz. Produced by: Fred Kohlmar. Twentieth Century Fox. 104 minutes.

Ghost Breakers (1940). Starring: Bob Hope, Paulette Goddard, Richard Carlson, Paul Lukas, Noble Johnson, Anthony Quinn. Directed by: George Marshall. Produced by: Arthur Hornblow Jr. Paramount. 82 minutes.

Ghost Catchers (1944). Starring: Ole Olsen, Chic Johnson, Lon Chaney Jr., Tor Johnson, Mel Torme, Gloria Jean. Directed by: Edward Cline. Produced by: Edmund Hartmann. Universal. 69 minutes.

Ghost Goes West (1936). Starring: Robert Donat, Eugene Pallette, Elsa Lanchester, Jean Parker. Directed by: Rene Clair. Produced by: Alexander Korda. United Artists. 85 minutes.

Ghost of Slumber Mountain (1919). Stop-motion Animation. Created by: Willis O'Brien. 9 minutes.

Giant Behemoth (1958). Starring: Gene Evans, Andre Morell. Directed by: Eugene Lourie. Produced by: Ted Lloyd. Allied Artists. 80 minutes.

Giant from the Unknown (1958). Starring: Edward Kemmer, Bob Steele, Morris Ankrum, Buddy Baer, Sally Fraser. Directed by: Richard Chunha. Produced by: Arthur Jacobs. Astor. 77 minutes.

Giant Gila Monster (1959). Starring: Don Sullivan, Shug Fisher, Lisa Simone. Directed by: Ray Kellogg. Produced by: Ken Curtis. McLendon. 74 minutes.

Giants of Thessaly (1960). Starring: Roland Carey, Ziva Rodann, Massimo Girotti. Directed by: Riccardo Freda. Produced by: Virgilio De Blasi. Medallion. 97 minutes.

Gigantis, the Fire Monster (1955). Starring: Hiroshi Koizumi, Yukio Kasama, Takashi Shimura. Directed by: Motoyoshi Odo. Produced by: Tomoyuki Tanaka. Toho. 82 minutes.

Gnome-Mobile (1967). Starring: Walter Brennan, Matthew Garber, Karen Dotrice, Ed Wynn, Richard Deacon. Directed by: Robert Stevenson. Produced by: James Algar. Walt Disney Productions. 93 minutes.

Godzilla (1954). Starring: Raymond Burr, Akira Takarada, Akihiko Hirata, Takashi Shimura. Directed by: Inoshio Honda. Produced by: Tomoyuki Tanaka. Toho. 98 minutes.

Godzilla vs. Gigan (1971). Starring: Hiroshi Ishikawa, Tomoko Umeda. Directed by: Jun Fukuda. Produced by: Tomoyuki Tanaka. Toho. 82 minutes.

Godzilla vs. Mechagodzilla (1975). Starring: Masaaki Daimon, Kazuya Aoyama, Reiko Tajima, Hiroshi Koizumi. Directed by: Jun Fukuda. Produced by: Tomoyuki Tanaka. Toho. 84 minutes.

Godzilla vs. Megalon (1975). Starring: Katshuhiko Sasaki, Hiroyuki Kawase, Yutaka Hayashi, Robert Dunham. Directed by: Jun Fukuda. Produced by: Tomoyuki Tanaka. Toho. 82 minutes.

Godzilla vs. the Sea Monster (1966). Starring: Akira Takarada, Toru Watanabe, Hideo Sunazuka. Directed by: Jun Fukuda. Produced by: Tomoyuki Tanaka. Toho. 87 minutes.

Godzilla vs. the Smog Monster (1971). Starring: Akira Yamauchi, Toshie Kimura, Hiroyuki Kawase. Directed by: Yoshimitsu Banno. Produced by: Tomoyuki Tanaka. Toho. 87 minutes.

Godzilla vs. the Thing (1964). Starring: Akira Takarada, Yuriko Hoshi, Emi Ito, Yumi Ito, Hiroshi Koisumi. Directed by: Inoshiro Honda. Produced by: Tomoyuki Tanaka. Toho. 94 minutes.

Godzilla's Revenge (1969). Starring: Kenji Sahara, Tomonori Yazaki. Directed by: Inoshiro Honda. Produced by: Tomoyuki Tanaka. Toho. 93 minutes.

Golden Voyage of Sinbad (1973). Starring: John Phillip Law, Caroline Munro, Tom Baker, Douglas Wilmer. Directed by: Gordon Hessler. Produced by: Charles H. Schneer. Columbia. 108 minutes.

The Golem: Monster of Fate (1914). Starring: Paul Wegener, Henrik Galeen, Albert Steinruck, Lydia Salmanova. Directed by: Paul Wegener and Henrik Galeen. German. 35 minutes (?).

The Golem: How He Came Into the World (1920). Starring: Paul Wegener, Albert Steinruck, Ernst Deutsch, Lyda Salmanove. Directed by: Paul Wegener and Carl Boese. Paramount/UFA. 71 minutes.

Goliath and the Vampires (1961). Starring: Gordon Scott, Jacques Sernas, Gianna Maria Canale, Guido Celano. Directed by: Giacomo Gentilomo and Sergio Corbucci. Produced by: Paolo Moffa and Dino De Laurentiis. American International. 92 minutes

Goliath and the Dragon (1960). Starring: Mark Forest, Broderick Crawford, Eleanora Ruffo, Gaby Andre. Directed by: Vittoria Cottafavi. Produced by: Achille Piazzi and Gianni Fuchs. American International. 91 minutes.

Gorgo (1961). Starring: Bill Travers, William Sylvester, Vincent Winter. Directed by: Eugene Lourie. Produced by: Frank and Maurice King. MGM. 78 minutes.

The Great Rupert (1949). Starring: Jimmy Durante, Terry Moore, Frank Orth. Directed by: Irving Pichel. Produced by: George Pal. Eagle-Lion. 88 minutes.

Gulliver's Travels (1939). Animated Cartoon. Directed by: Dave Fleischer. Produced by: Max Fleischer. Paramount 77 minutes.

Guy Named Joe (1943). Starring: Spencer Tracy, Van Johnson, Lionel Barrymore, Ward Bond, Irene Dunn, Esther Williams. Directed by: Victor Fleming. Produced by: Everett Riskin. MGM. 120 minutes.

Half Human (1955). Starring: John Carradine, Morris Ankrum, Akira Takarade, Kenji Sahara. Directed by: Inoshio Honda. Produced by: Tomoyuki Tanaka. Toho. 70 minutes.

Halfway House (1944). Starring: Mervyn Johns, Glynis Johns, Francoise Rosay, Tom Walls, Sally Ann Howes. Directed by: Basil Dearden. Produced by: Michael Balcon. AFE. 95 minutes.

Hand of Death (1961). Starring: John Agar, Paula Raymond, Steve Dunne. Directed by: Gene Nelson. Produced by: Eugene Ling. Twentieth Century Fox. 59 minutes.

Hands of the Ripper (1971). Starring: Eric Porter, Jane Merrow, Angharad Rees. Directed by: Peter Sasy. Produced by: Aida Young. Hammer. 85 minutes.

Harvey (1950). Starring: James Stewart, Cecil Kellaway, Josephine Hull, Charles Drake, Peggy Dow. Directed by: Henry Koster. Produced by: John Beck. Universal. 104 minutes.

Haunted Palace (1963). Starring: Vincent Price, Debra Paget, Lon Chaney Jr., Elisha Cook Jr. Directed by: Roger Corman. Produced by: Roger Corman. American International. 85 minutes.

The Haunting (1963). Starring: Julie Harris, Richard Johnson, Claire Bloom, Russ Tamblyn, Lois Maxwell. Directed by: Robert Wise. Produced by: Robert Wise. MGM. 112 minutes.

The Headless Ghost (1959). Starring: Richard Lyon, Lilliane Scottane, David Rose, Clive Revill. Directed by: Peter Scott. Produced by: Herman Cohen. American International. 63 minutes.

Heaven Can Wait (1943). Starring: Don Ameche, Gene Tierney, Laird Cregar, Spring Byington. Directed by: Ernst Lubitsch. Produced by: Ernst Lubitsch. Twentieth Century Fox. 119 minutes.

Heaven Only Knows (1947). Starring: Robert Cummings, Brian Donlevy, Marjorie Reynolds. Directed by: Albert Togell. Produced by: Seymour Nebenzal. United Artists. 98 minutes.

Hellstrom Chronicle (1971). Documentary. Narrated by: Lawrence Pressman. Directed by: Walon Green. Produced by: Walon Green. David L. Wolper. 90 minutes.

Hercules (1957). Starring: Steve Reeves, Sylva Koscina,

Gianna Maria Canale, Ivo Garrani. Directed by: Pietro Francisci. Produced by: Federico Teti. Embassy. 107 minutes.

Hercules Against the Moon Men (1955). Starring: Alan Steel, Jany Clair, Anna-Maria Polani, Nando Tamberlani. Directed by: Giacomo Gentilomo. Produced by: Luigi Mondello. Italian. 88 minutes.

Hercules Against the Sons of the Sun (1964). Starring: Mark Forest, Anna-Maria Pace, Giuliano Gemma, Angela Rhu. Directed by: Osvaldo Civirani. Produced by: Osvaldo Civirani. Italian. 89 minutes.

Hercules and the Captive Women (1961). Starring: Reg Park, Fay Spain, Ettore Manni, Luciano Marin, Laura Atlan. Directed by: Vittorio Cattafavi. Produced by: Achille Piazzi. Italian. 101 minutes.

Hercules in New York (1970). Starring: Arnold Strong, Arnold Stang. Directed by: Arthur Seidelman. United Film. 89 minutes.

Hercules in the Haunted World (1961). Starring: Reg Park, Christopher Lee, Eleanora Ruffo, Giorgio Aridsson. Directed by: Mario Bava. Produced by: Achille Piazzi. Italian. 91 minutes.

Hercules Unchained (1959). Starring: Steve Reeves, Sylva Koscina, Sylvia Lopez, Sergio Fantoni, Primo Carnera. Directed by: Pietro Francisci. Produced by: Bruno Vailati. Embassy. 101 minutes.

Here Comes Mr. Jordan (1941). Starring: Robert Montgomery, Claude Rains, Evelyn Keyes, Edward Everett Horton, James Gleason. Directed by: Alexander Hall. Produced by: Everett Riskin. Columbia. 94 minutes.

Hold That Ghost (1941). Starring: Bud Abbott, Lou Costello, Richard Carlson, Joan Davis, Mischa Auer, Evelyn Ankers, Shemp Howard, the Andrews Sisters. Directed by: Arthur Lubin. Produced by: Burt Kelly and Glenn Tryon. Universal. 86 minutes.

Horn Blows at Midnight (1945). Starring: Jack Benny, Allyn Joslyn, Dolores Moran, Reginald Gardiner, Guy Kibbee. Directed by: Raoul Walsh. Produced by: Mark Hellinger. Warner Brothers. 80 minutes.

Horror Express (1972). Starring: Christopher Lee, Peter Cushing, Telly Savalas. Directed by: Eugene Martin. Produced by: Bernard Gordon. Spanish. 87 minutes.

Horror Hotel (1960). Starring: Christopher Lee, Patricia Jessel, Betta St. John, Dennis Lotis. Directed by: John Llewellyn Moxey. Produced by: Donald Taylor. Trans-Lux. 76 minutes.

Horror of Dracula (1958). Starring: Christopher Lee, Peter Cushing, Michael Gough, John Van Eyssen, Melissa Stribling, Carol Marsh, Valerie Gaunt, Miles Malleson. Directed by: Terence Fisher. Produced by: Anthony Hinds. Hammer. 82 minutes.

Horror of Party Beach (1963). Starring: John Scott, Alice Lyon, Allen Laurel, Eulabelle Moore, The Del-Aires. Directed by: Del Tenney. Produced by: Del Tenney. Twentieth Century Fox 82 minutes.

House of Dark Shadows (1970). Starring: Jonathan Frid,

Joan Bennet, Grayson Hall, Roger Davis, Thayer David, Kathryn Leigh Scott. Directed by: Dan Curtis. Produced by: Dan Curtis. MGM. 96 minutes.

House of Dracula (1945). Starring: Onslow Stevens, Lon Chaney Jr., John Carradine, Lionel Atwill, Glenn Strange, Jane Adams. Directed by: Erle C. Kenton. Produced by: Joe Gershenson and Paul Malvern. Universal. 67 minutes.

House of Frankenstein (1944). Starring: Boris Karloff, Lon Chaney Jr., John Carradine, J. Carrol Naish, George Zucco, Glenn Strange, Lionel Atwill, Frank Reicher, Elena Verdugo. Directed by: Erle C. Kenton. Produced by: Paul Malvern. Universal. 71 minutes.

House on Haunted Hill (1958). Starring: Vincent Price, Carol Ohmart, Richard Long, Elisha Cook Jr. Directed by: William Castle. Produced by: William Castle. Allied Artists. 75 minutes.

House That Dripped Blood (1970). Starring: Christopher Lee, Peter Cushing, Denholm Elliott, Nyree Dawn Porter, Chloe Franks. Directed by: Peter Duffell. Produced by: Max J. Rosenberg and Milton Subotsky. Amicus. 102 minutes.

I Married a Witch (1942). Starring: Fredric March, Veronica Lake, Cecil Kellaway, Robert Benchley, Susan Hayward. Directed by: Rene Clair. Produced by: Rene Clair. Paramount/United Artists. 76 minutes.

I Married an Angel (1942). Starring: Nelson Eddy, Jeannette MacDonal, Reginald Owen, Anne Jeffreys, Edward Everett Horton, Binnie Barnes. Directed by: W.S. Van Dyke II. Produced by: Hunt Stromberg. MGM. 84 minutes.

I Walked with a Zombie (1943). Starring: Frances Dee, James Ellison, Tom Conway, Christine Gordon, Darby Jones, Edith Barrett. Directed by: Jacques Tourneur. Produced by: Val Lewton. RKO. 69 minutes.

I Was a Teenage Werewolf (1957). Starring: Michael Landon, Whit Bissell, Guy Williams, Yvonne Lime. Directed by: Gene Fowler Jr. Produced by: Herman Cohen. American Internation. 76 minutes.

I'll Never Forget You (1951). Starring: Tyrone Power, Ann Blyth, Michael Rennie, Dennis Price. Directed by: Roy Baker. Produced by: Sol Siegel. Twentieth Century Fox. 91 minutes.

Illustrated Man (1968). Starring: Rod Steiger, Claire Bloom, Robert Drivas, Don Dubbins, Jason Evers. Directed by: Jack Smight. Produced by: Howard Kreitsek and Ted Mann. Warner Brothers/Seven Arts. 103 minutes.

Incredible Mr. Limpet (1963). Starring: Don Knotts, Carole Cook, Jack Weston, Andrew Duggan. Directed by: Arthur Lubin. Produced by: John C. Rose. Warner Brothers. 102 minutes. (Note: The beginning and end of this film are live action. The rest is an animated cartoon.)

The Innocents (1961). Starring: Deborah Kerr, Martin Stephens, Pamela Franklin, Megs Jenkins, Michael Redgrave, Peter Wyngarde. Directed by: Jack Clayton. Produced by: Albert Fennell and Jack Clayton. Twentieth Century Fox. 94 minutes.

The Invisible Creature (1960). Starring: Tony Wright, Patricia Dainton, Dandra Dorne, Derek Aylward. Directed by: Montgomery Tully. Produced by: Maurice J. Wilson. American International. 70 minutes.

Island at the Top of the World (1974). Starring: David Hartman, Donald Sinden, Jacques Marin, Agneta Eckemyr. Directed by: Robert Stevenson. Produced by: Winston Hibler. Walt Disney Productions.

Island of the Dinosaurs (1966). Starring: Armando Sivestre, Alma Delia Fuentes, Elsa Cardenas, Jenaro Moreno. Directed by: Rafael Lopez Portillo. Produced by: G.C. Stell. Azteca. 80 minutes.

It Came from Beneath the Sea (1955). Starring: Kenneth Tobey, Donald Curtis, Faith Domergue, Ian Keith. Directed by: Robert Gordon. Produced by: Charles H. Schneer. Columbia. 77 minutes.

It Grows on Trees (1952). Starring: Irene Dunne, Dean Jagger, Joan Evers, Les Tremayne, Richard Crenna. Directed by: Arthur Lubin. Produced by: Leonard Goldstein. Universal. 84 minutes.

It Happened Tomorrow (1944). Starring: Dick Powell, Linda Darnell, Jack Oakie, Marian Martin, Edgar Kennedy, John Philliber. Directed by: Rene Clair. Produced by: Arnold Pressburger. United Artists. 84 minutes.

It's a Wonderful Life (1946). Starring: James Stewart, Donna Reed, Lionel Barrymore, Thomas Mitchell, Henry Travers, Ward Bond, Beulah Bondi, H.B. Warner, Gloria Grahame, Sheldon Leonard. Directed by: Frank Captra. Produced by: Frank Capra. RKO. 129 minutes.

I've Lived Before (1956). Starring: Jock Mahoney, Leigh Snowden, John McIntire, Ann Harding. Directed by: Richard Bartlett. Produced by: Howard Christie. Universal. 82 minutes.

Jack and the Witch (1967). Animated Cartoon. Directed by: Taiji Yabushita. Toei. 80 minutes.

Jack the Giant Killer (1962). Starring: Kerwin Mathews, Torin Thatcher, Judi Meredith, Walter Burke, Don Beddoe, Barry Kelley, Roger Mobley, Dayton Lummis, Anna Lee. Directed by: Nathan Juran. Produced by: Edward Small and Robert E. Kent. United Artists. 94 minutes.

Jason and the Argonauts (1963). Starring: Todd Armstrong, Laurence Naismith, Nancy Kovak, Gary Raymond, Nigel Green, Honor Blackman, Niall MacGinnis, John Crawford, Michael Gwynn, Douglas Wilmer. Directed by: Don Chaffey. Produced by: Charles H. Schneer. Columbia. 103 minutes.

Journey to the Beginning of Time (1954). Starring: James Lucas, Victor Betral, Peter Hermann, Charles Goldsmith. Directed by: Karel Zeman. Czechoslovakian. 93 minutes.

Journey to the Center of the Earth (1959). Starring: James Mason, Pat Boone, Arlene Dahl, Diane Baker, Thayer David, Alan Napier, Peter Ronson. Directed by: Henry Levin. Produced by: Charles Brackett. Twentieth Century Fox. 132 minutes.

King Kong (1933). Starring: Robert Armstrong, Fay

Wray, Bruce Cabot, Frank Reicher, Noble Johnson. Directed by: Merian C. Cooper and Ernest B. Schoedsack. Produced by: Merian C. Cooper and Ernest B. Schoedsack. RKO. 100 minutes.

King Kong Escapes (1967). Starring: Rhodes Reason, Mie Hama, Linda Miller, Akira Takarada. Directed by: Inoshio Honda. Produced by: Tomoyuki Tanaka. Toho. 104 minutes.

King Kong vs. Godzilla (1962). Starring: James Yagi, Mie Hama, Kenji Sahara, Akihiko Hirata, Michael Keith. Directed by: Inorhio Honda. Produced by: John Beck. Toho. 99 minutes.

King of the Zombies (1941). Starring: Dick Purcell, Joan Woodbury, Mantan Moreland, John Archer, Henrey Victor. Directed by: Jean Yarbrough. Produced by: Lindley Parsons. Monogram. 67 minutes.

Kiss of the Vampire (1963). Starring: Noel Willman, Clifford Evans, Edward de Souza, Jennifer Daniel. Directed by: Don Sharp. Produced by: Anthony Hinds. Hammer. 87 minutes.

Kwaidan (1963). Starring: Renato Mikuni, Michiyo Aratama, Tatsuya Nakadai, Keiko Kishi, Tetsuro Tamba, Katsuo Nakamura, Kanyemon Nakamura. Directed by: Masuki Kobayashi. Produced by: Shigeru Wakatsuki. Toho/Walter Reade-Sterling. 164 minutes.

Lake of Dracula (1971). Starring: Midori Fujita, Sanae Emi, Mori Kishida. Directed by: Michio Yamamoto. Produced by: Fumio Tanaka. Toho. 82 minutes.

Land Unknown (1957). Starring: Jock Mahoney, Shawn Smith, William Reynolds, Doublas Kennedy. Directed by: Virgil Vogel. Produced by: William Alland. Universal. 78 minutes.

Legend of Hell House (1973). Starring: Roddy McDowell, Pamela Franklin, Clive Revill, Gayle Hunnicut, Michael Gough. Directed by: John Hough. Produced by: James H. Nicholson and Albert Fennell. Twentieth Century Fox. 94 minutes.

Leopard Man (1943). Starring: Dennis O'Keef, Margo Jean Brooks, Isabel Jewell, James Bell. Directed by: Jacques Tourneur. Produced by: Val Lewton. RKO. 66 minutes.

Let's Live Again (1947). Starring: John Emery, Hillary Brooke, Taylor Homes, Diana Doublas. Directed by: Herbert Leeds. Produced by: Frank N. Seltzer. Twentieth Century Fox. 68 minutes.

Little Nemo (1906). Animated Cartoon. Created by: Winsor McCay.

Little Prince (1974). Starring: Richard Kiley, Stephen Warner, Bob Fosse, Gene Wilder. Directed by: Stanley Donen. Produced by: Stanley Donen. Paramount.

The Living Idol (1957). Starring: Steve Forrest, Liliane Montevecchi, James Robertson Justic, Eduardo Noriega. Directed by: Albert Lewin. Produced by: Albert Lewin and Gregorio Walterstein. MGM. 101 minutes.

Lost Continent (1951). Starring: Cesar Romero, John Hoyt, Sid Melton, Whit Bissell, Hillary Brooke, Acquanetta, Hugh Beaumont. Directed by: Samuel

Newfield. Produced by: Sigmund Neufeld and Robert L. Lippert. Lippert. 83 minutes.

Lost Horizon (1936). Starring: Ronald Colman, Sam Jaffe, Jane Wyatt, Edward Everett Horton, H.B. Warner, Thomas Mitchell, Noble Johnson. Directed by: Frank Capra. Produced by: Frank Capra. Columbia. 133 minutes.

Lost Horizon (1972). Starring: Peter Finch, Liv Ullman, Michael York, Charles Boyer, George Kennedy, Sally Kellerman, John Gielgud, Bobby Van, Olivia Hussey, Kent Smith, James Shigeta. Directed by: Charles Jarrot. Produced by: Ross Hunter. Columbia. 150 minutes.

Lost World (1925). Starring: Wallace Beery, Bessie Love, Lewis Stone, Arthur Hoyt, Bull Montana, Lloyd Hughes. Directed by: Harry Hoyt. Produced by: Earl Hudson and Watterson Rothacker. First National. 111 minutes.

Lost World (1960). Starring: Claude Rains, Michael Rennie, Jill St. John, Fernando Lamas, David Hedison, Ray Stricklyn, Richard Haydn. Directed by: Irwin Allen. Produced by: Irwin Allen. Twentieth Century Fox. 97 minutes.

Lost World of Sinbad (1963). Starring: Toshiro Mifune, Makoto Satoh, Jun Fanado. Directed by: Senkichi Taniguchi. Produced by: Yuko Tanaka. Toho. 94 minutes.

Loves of Hercules (1960). Starring: Mickey Hargitay, Massimo Serato, Jayne Mansfield, Rossella Como. Directed by: Carlo Ludovico Bragaglia. Italian. 98 minutes.

Lust for a Vampire (1970). Starring: Ralph Bates, Yutte Stensgaard, Mike Raven, Barbara Jefford, Suzanna Leigh, Michael Johnson. Directed by: Jimmy Sangster. Produced by: Harry Fine and Michael Style. Hammer. 95 minutes.

Macbeth (1948). Starring: Orson Welles, Jeanette Nolan, Roddy McDowall, Alan Napier, William Alland, Edgar Barrier. Directed by: Orson Welles. Produced by: Orson Welles and Charles Feldman. Republic. 107 minutes.

Macbeth (1971). Starring: John Finch, Francesca Annis, Martin Shaw, John Stride. Directed by: Roman Polanski. Produced by: Andrew Braunsberg and Hugh M. Hefner. Playboy/Columbia. 140 minutes.

Macumba Love (1960). Starring: Walter Reed, Ziva Rodann, June Wilkinson, William Wellman Jr. Directed by: Douglas Fowley. Produced by: Douglas Fowley. United Artists. 86 minutes.

Mad Doctor of Blood Island (1969). Starring: John Ashley, Angelique Pettyjoh, Eddie Garcia, Ronald Remy. Directed by: Eddie Romero and Gerardo de Leon. Produced by: Eddie Romero and Kane Lynn. Hemisphere. 85 minutes.

Magic Boy (1959). Animated Cartoon. Directed by: Akira Daikubara. Produced by: Hiroshi Okawa. Toei. 83 minutes.

Magic Carpet (1952). Starring: Lucille Ball, Raymond Burr, John Agar, Patricia Medina. Directed by: Lew

Landers. Produced by: Sam Katzman. Columbia. 88 minutes.

Magic Serpent (1966). Starring: Hiroki Matsukata, Tomoko Ogawa, Ryutaro Otomo, Bin Amatsu. Directed by: Tetsuy Yamauchi. Toei. 86 minutes.

Magic Sword (1962). Starring: Gary Lockwood, Basil Rathbone, Estelle Winwood, Anne Helm, Liam Sullivan, Vampira. Directed by: Bert I. Gordon. Produced by: Bert I. Gordon. United Artists. 80 minutes.

Magic Voyage of Sinbad (1952). Starring: Edward Stolar, Anne Larion. Directed by: Alexander Ptushko. Mosfilm/Filmgroup. 89 minutes.

Majin (1966). Starring: Miwa Takada, Yoshihiko Aoyama, Jun Fujimaki, Ryutaro Gomi, Tatsuo Endo. Directed by: Kimiyoshi Yasuda and Yoshiyuki Kuroda. Produced by: Masaichi Nagata. Daiei. 86 minutes.

Maltese Bippy (1969). Starring: Dan Rowan, Dick Martin, Carol Lynley, Julie Newmar, Fritz Weaver, Robert Reed, Mildred Natwick. Directed by: Norman Panama. Produced by: Everett Freeman and Robert Enders. MGM. 92 minutes.

Man Beast (1955). Starring: Rock Madison, Virginia Maynor, George Skaff. Directed by: Jerry Warren. Produced by: Jerry Warren. Favorite. 67 minutes.

Man Who Could Work Miracles (1936). Starring: Roland Young, Sir Ralph Richardson, Joan Gardner, Ernest Thesiger, George Zucco, George Sanders, Torin Thatcher. Directed by: Lothar Mendes. Produced by: Alexander Korda. United Artists. 90 minutes.

Man Who Wagged His Tail (1957). Starring: Peter Ustinov, Pablito Calva, Aroldo Tieri, Silvia Marco. Directed by: Ladislo Vajda. Produced by: Ladislo Vajda. Continental. 91 minutes.

Mary Poppins (1964). Starring: Julie Andrews, Dick Van Dyke, David Tomlinson, Glynis Johns, Karen Dotrice, Mathew Garber, Hermoine Badderly, Elsa Lanchester, Arthur Treacher, Ed Wynn, Reginald Owen. Directed by: Robert Stevenson. Produced by: Walt Disney. Walt Disney Productions. 139 minutes.

Masque of the Red Death (1964). Starring: Vincent Price, Jane Asher, Hazel Court, Patrick Magee, Nigel Green. Directed by: Roger Corman. Produced by: George Willoughby. American International. 89 minutes.

Master of Horror (1960). Starring: Narciso Ibanez Menta, Inez Moreno, Carlos Estrada, Narciso Ibanez Serrador, Mercedes Carreras. Directed by: Enrique Carreras. Produced by Nicolas Carreras and Jack H. Harris. Argentinian. 115 minutes.

Master of the World (1961). Starring: Vincent Price, Charles Bronson, Henry Hull, Mary Webster, David Frankham. Directed by: William Witney. Produced by: James H. Nicholson and Samuel Z. Arkoff. American International. 104 minutes.

Meet Mr. Kringle (1956). Starring: Thomas Mitchell, Macdonald Carey, Teresa Wright, Hans Conried. Directed by: Robert Stevenson. Produced by: Jules Bricken. Twentieth Century Fox. 56 minutes.

Mephisto Waltz (1971). Starring: Alan Alda, Jacqueline Bisset, Barbara Parkins, Bradford Dillman, Curt Jurgens, William Windom. Directed by: Paul Wendkos. Produced by: Quinn Martin. Twentieth Century Fox. 115 minutes.

A Midsummer Night's Dream (1935). Starring: Olivia de Havilland, Dick Powell, James Cagney, Joe E. Brown, Victor Jory, Mickey Rooney, Anita Louise, Arthur Treacher, Jean Muir, Hugh Herbert, Ian Hunter. Directed by: Max Reinhardt and William Dieterle. Produced by: Max Reinhardt. Warner Brothers. 132 minutes.

Mighty Gorga (1970). Starring: Anthony Eisley, Scott Brady, Megan Timothy, Kent Taylor. Directed by: David Hewitt. Produced by: David Hewitt and Robert O'Neil. Western International. 82 minutes.

Mighty Joe Young (1949). Starring: Robert Armstrong, Ben Johnson, Terry Moore, Regis Toomey, Frank McHugh, Doublas Fowley, Primo Carnera. Directed by: Ernest B. Schoedsack. Produced by: John Ford and Merian C. Cooper. RKO. 94 minutes.

The Minotaur (1960). Starring: Bob Mathias, Rosanna Schiaffino, Alberto Lup, Rik Battaglia. Directed by: Silvio Amadio. Produced by: Dino Mordini, Giorgio Agliani, and Rudolph Solmsen. United Artists. 100 minutes.

Miracle in Milan (1951). Starring: Francesco Golisano, Emma Gramatica, Paolo Stoppa, Erminio Spalla. Directed by: Vittorio de Sica. Produced by: Vittorio de Sica. Italian. 101 minutes.

Miracle on 34th Street (1947). Starring: Edmund Gwenn, Maureen O'Hara, John Payne, Natalie Wood. Directed by: George Seaton. Produced by: William Pearlberg. Twentieth Century Fox. 96 minutes.

Miranda (1948). Starring: Glynis Johns, Googie Withers, Griffith Jones, John McCallum, David Tomlinson, Margaret Rutherford. Directed by: Ken Annakin. Produced by: Betty and Sidney Box. Eagle-Lion. 80 minutes.

Mr. Peabody and the Mermaid (1948). Starring: William Powell, Ann Blyth, Irene Harvey. Directed by: Irving Pichel. Produced by: Nunnally Johnson. Universal. 89 minutes.

Mr. Stop (1907). Animated Cartoon. Created by: Emile Cohl. 1 minute.

The Mole Men Battle the Son of Hercules (1961). Starring: Mark Forest, Moira Orfie, Paul Wynter, Raffaella Carra. Directed by: Antonio Leonviola. Produced by: Elio Scardamaglia. Italian. 97 minutes.

Mole People (1956). Starring: John Agar, Hugh Beaumont, Alan Napier, Cynthia Patrick, Nestor Paiva. Directed by: Virgil Vogel. Produced by: William Alland. Universal. 78 minutes.

The Monkey's Paw (1932). Starring: C. Aubrey Smith, Ivan Simpson, Louis Carter. Directed by: Wesley Rogers. Produced by: David O. Selznick. RKO. 56 minutes.

The Monkey's Paw (1948). Starring: Milton Rosmer, Megs Jenkins, Joan Seton. Directed by: Norman Lee. Produced by: Kay Films. British. 64 minutes.

Monster that Challenged the World (1957). Starring: Tim Holt, Audrey Dalton, Hans Conried. Directed by: Arnold Laven. Produced by: Arthur Gardner and Jules Levy. United Artists. 85 minutes.

Monster of Piedras Blancas (1958). Starring: Les Tremayne, Forrest Lewis, John Harmon, Jean Carmen. Directed by: Irwin Berwick. Produced by: Jack Kevan. Filmservice. 71 minutes.

Monster Zero (1965). Starring: Nick Adams, Akira Takarada, Kumi Mizuno, Jun Tazaki. Directed by: Inoshio Honda. Produced by: Tomoyuki Tanaka. Toho. 96 minutes.

Mothra (1961). Starring: Frankie Sakai, Hiroshi Koizumi, Emi Ito, Yumi Ito, Ken Uehara. Directed by: Inoshiro Honda. Produced by: Tomoyuki Tanaka. Toho. 100 minutes.

The Mummy (1932). Starring: Boris Karloff, Zita Johann, David Manners, Edward van Sloan, Bramwell Fletcher, Henry Victor, Noble Johnson. Directed by: Karl Freund. Produced by: Stanley Bergerman and Carl Laemmle Jr. Universal. 78 minutes.

The Mummy (1959). Starring: Christopher Lee, Peter Cushing, Yvonne Furneaux, Eddie Byrne, Michael Ripper, Felix Aylmer. Directed by: Terence Fisher. Produced by: Michael Carreras and Anthony Nelson Keys. Hammer. 88 minutes.

Mummy's Curse (1944). Starring: Lon Chaney Jr., Peter Coe, Virginia Christine, Kay Harding. Directed by: Leslie Goodwins. Produced by: Ben Pivar and Oliver Drake. Universal. 62 minutes.

Mummy's Ghost (1943). Starring: Lon Chaney Jr., John Carradine, Ramsay Ames, Robert Lowery, Barton MacLane, George Zucco, Frank Reicher, Claire Whitney. Directed by: Reginald Le Borg. Produced by: Joseph Gershenson and Ben Pivar. Universal. 61 minutes.

Mummy's Hand (1940). Starring: Tom Tyler, Dick Foran, Peggy Moran, Wallace Ford, Eduardo Ciannelli, George Zucco, Cecil Kellaway. Directed by: Christy Cabanne. Produced by: Ben Pivar. Universal. 67 minutes.

Mummy's Shroud (1966). Starring: Eddie Powell, Andre Morell, John Phillips, David Buck, Elizabeth Sellars, Michael Ripper. Directed by: John Gilling. Produced by: Anthony Nelson Keys. Hammer. 84 minutes.

Mummy's Tomb (1942). Starring: Lon Chaney Jr., Turhan Bey, Dick Foran, Wallace Ford, John Hubbard, Elyse Knox, George Zucco, Glenn Strange, Frank Reicher. Directed by: Harold Young. Produced by: Ben Pivar. Universal. 61 minutes.

My Son, the Vampire (1952). Starring: Bela Lugosi, Arthur Lucan, Dora Bryan, Richard Wattis. Directed by: John Gilling. Produced by: John Gilling. Blue Chip. 74 minutes.

Mysterious Island (1960). Starring: Michael Craig, Percy Herbert, Gary Merrill, Herbert Lom, Michael Callan, Joan Greenwood, Beth Rogan. Directed by: Cy Endfield. Produced by: Charles H. Schneer. Columbia. 100 minutes.

The Next Voice You Hear . . . (1950). Starring: James Whitmore, Gary Gray, Nancy Davis, Lillian Bronson. Directed by: William Wellman. Produced by: Dore Schary. MGM. 83 minutes.

Night of Dark Shadows (1971). Starring: David Selby, Lara Parker, Kate Jackson, Grayson Hall, Thayer David. Directed by: Dan Curtis. Produced by: Dan Curtis. MGM. 97 minutes.

Night of the Living Dead (1968). Starring: Duane Jones, Judith O'Dea, Russ Streiner, Karl Hardman, Keith Wayne. Directed by: George Romero. Produced by: Karl Hardman and Russ Streiner. Walter Reade. 96 minutes.

Night of the Witches (1970). Starring: Keith Burt, Randy Stafford, Ron Taft, Kathryn Loder. Directed by: Keith Burt. Produced by: Keith Burt and Vincent Forte. Medford. 78 minutes.

Nosferatu (1922). Starring: Max Schreck, Alexander Granach, Gustav von Wangenheim, Grete Schroder. Directed by: F.W. Murnau. Film Arts Guild. 70 minutes.

Oblong Box (1969). Starring: Vincent Price, Christopher Lee, Hilary Dwyer, Peter Arne, Alastair Williamson, Rupert Davies. Directed by: Gordon Hessler. Produced by: Gordon Hessler. American International. 91 minutes.

On a Clear Day You Can See Forever (1970). Starring: Barbra Streisand, Yves Montand, Bob Newhart, Jack Nicholson, Larry Blyden, Simon Oakland, Roy Kinnear. Directed by: Vincente Minnelli. Produced by: Howard W. Koch and Alan Jay Lerner. Paramount. 129 minutes.

On Borrowed Time (1939). Starring: Lionel Barrymore, Sir Cedric Hardwicke, Beulah Bondi, Una Merkel, Henry Travers. Directed by: Harold S. Bucquet. Produced by: Sidney Franklin. MGM. 100 minutes.

Once Upon a Time (1943). Starring: Cary Grant, Janet Blair, William Demarest, Kirk Alyn, Lloyd Bridges, James Gleason. Directed by: Alexander Hall. Produced by: Louis F. Edelman. Columbia. 88 minutes.

One Million B.C. (1940). Starring: Victor Mature, Carole Landis, Lon Chaney Jr., Jon Hubbard. Directed by: D.W. Griffith, Hal Roach, and Hal Roach Jr. Produced by: Hal Roach. United Artists. 85 minutes.

One Million Years B.C. (1966). Starring: Raquel Welch, John Richardson, Percy Herbert, Robert Brown, Martine Beswick, Yvonne Horner. Directed by: Don Chaffey. Produced by: Michael Carreras. Hammer. 100 minutes.

One Touch of Venus (1948). Starring: Robert Walker, Ava Gardner, Dick Haymes, Eve Arden, Tom Conway, Arthur O'Connell. Directed by: William A. Seiter. Produced by: Lester Cowan. Universal. 82 minutes.

One Wish Too Many (1956). Starring: Anthony Richmond, Rosalind Gourgey, John Pike, Terry Cooke. Directed by: John Durst. Produced by: Basil Wright. British, 56 minutes.

The Other (1972). Starring: Chris Udvarnoky, Martin Udvarnoky, Diana Muldaur, Uta Hagen, Norma Connolly. Directed by: Robert Mulligan. Produced by: Tom Tryon and Robert Mulligan. Twentieth Century Fox. 100 minutes.

Outward Bound (1930). Starring: Leslie Howard, Douglas Fairbanks Jr., Helen Chandler, Beryl Mercer, Alec Francis, Montagu Love. Directed by: Robert Milton. Produced by: Jack L. Warner. Warner Brothers. 82 minutes.

Pandora and the Flying Dutchman (1950). Starring: James Mason, Ava Gardner, Nigel Patrick, Sheila Sim, Harold Warrender. Directed by: Albert Lewin. Produced by: Albert Lewin and Joseph Kaufman. MGM. 122 minutes.

Peter Pan (1924). Starring: Betty Bronson, Mary Brian, Ernest Torrence, Cyril Chadwick, Anna May Wong, George Ali. Directed by: Herbert Brenon. Produced by: Herbert Brenon. Paramount. 144 minutes.

Peter Pan (1953). Animated Cartoon. Produced by: Walt Disney. Walt Disney Studios. 76 minutes.

Peter Rabbit and Tales of Beatrix Potter (1971). Starring: Carole Ainsworth, Salley Ashby, Frederick Ashton, Avril Bergen, Lesley Collier, Michael Coleman, Bridget Goodricke, Graham Fletcher, Alexander Grant, Ann Howard, Robert Mead, Wayne Sleep, Brenda Last, Erin Geraghty. Directed by: Reginald Mills. Choreographed by: Frederick Ashton. Produced by: John Brabourne and Richard Goodwin. MGM. 90 minutes.

Phantasmagoria (1907). Animated Cartoon. Created by: Emile Cohl. French. 1 minute.

Phantom Speaks (1944). Starring: Richard Arlen, Lynne Roberts, Stanley Ridges, Tom Powers, Jonathan Hale. Directed by: John English. Produced by: Armand Schaefer. Republic. 69 minutes.

Phantom Tollbooth (1968). Animated Cartoon. Created by: Chuck Jones, Abe Levitow, and Les Goldman. Voices: Mel Blanc, Butch Patrick, Hans Conried, Daws Butler, June Foray, Les Tremayne, Larry Thor. MGM. 90 minutes.

Pharaoh's Curse (1956). Starring: Mark Dana, Ziva Rodann, Diane Brewster, Terence de Marney, Kurt Katch. Directed by: Lee Sholem. Produced by: Aubrey Schenk and Howard W. Koch. United Artists. 66 minutes.

Picture of Dorian Gray (1945). Starring: Hurd Hatfield, George Sanders, Angela Lansbury, Donna Reed, Peter Lawford. Directed by: Albert Lewin. Produced by: Pandro S. Berman. MGM. 111 minutes.

Pied Piper of Hamelin (1957). Starring: Van Johnson, Claude Rains, Jim Backus, Lori Nelson, Doodles Weaver. Directed by: Bretaigne Windust. Produced by: Hal Stanley. International. 78 minutes.

Pied Piper of Hamelin (1971). Starring: Donovan, Donald Pleasance, Jack Wild, Roy Kinnear, Diana Dors. Directed by: Jacques Demy. Produced by: David Puttnam and Sanford Lieberson. Paramount. 90 minutes.

Pinocchio (1940). Animated Cartoon. Produced by: Walt Disney. Voices: Cliff Edwards, Dickie Jones, Walter Catlett, Evelyn Venable. Walt Disney Productions. 88 minutes.

A Place of One's Own (1944). Starring: James Mason, Margaret Lockwood, Dennis Price, Barbata Mullen. Directed by: Bernard Knowles. Produced by: Maurice Ostrer and Bernard Knowles. Eagle-Lion. 92 minutes.

Plague of the Zombies (1965). Starring: Andre Morell, Michael Ripper, Diane Clare, Jacqueline Pearce, Brook Williams. Directed by: John Gilling. Produced by: Anthony Nelson Keys. Hammer. 91 minutes.

Planet of the Apes (1968). Starring: Charlton Heston, Kim Hunter, Roddy McDowall, Maurice Evans, James Whitmore, Linda Harrison (Augusta Summerland), Lou Wagner, James Daly. Directed by: Franklin J. Schaffner. Produced by: Arthur P. Jacobs. Twentieth Century Fox. 112 minutes.

Portrait of Jennie (1948). Starring: Joseph Cotten, Jennifer Jones, Ethel Barrymore, Cecil Kellaway, Albert Sharpe, Henry Hull, Lillian Gish. Directed by: William Dieterle. Produced by: David O. Selznick. United Artists. 86 minutes.

Possession of Joel Delany (1971). Starring: Shirley MacLaine, Perry King, Michael Hordern, Lovelady Powell, Barbara Trentham, Edmundo Rivera Alvarez. Directed by: Waris Hussein. Produced by: Martin Poll. Paramount. 105 minutes.

Prehistoric Women (1950). Starring: Laurette Luez, Alan Nixon, Tony Devlin, Mara Lynn. Directed by: Greg Tallas. Produced by: Albert Cohen and Sam Abarbanel. Eagle-Lion. 74 minutes.

Prehistoric Women (1966). Starring: Martine Beswick, Edina Ronay, Michael Latimer, Stephanie Randall. Directed by: Michael Carreras. Produced by: Michael Carreras. Hammer. 96 minutes.

The Raven (1962). Starring: Boris Karloff, Peter Lorre, Jack Nicholson, Vincent Price, Hazel Court. Directed by: Roger Corman. Produced by: Roger Corman, James H. Nicholson, and Samuel Z. Arkoff. American International. 86 minutes.

The Reptile (1966). Starring: Noel Willman, Jacqueline Pearce, Jennifer Daniel, Ray Barrett, Michael Ripper. Directed by: John Gilling. Produced by: Anthony Nelson Keys. Hammer. 91 minutes.

Reptilicus (1962). Starring: Carl Ottosen, Ann Smyrner, Mimi Heinrich, Asbojorn Andersen, Marla Behrens. Directed by: Sidney Pink. Produced by: Sidney Pink. American International. 90 minutes.

Return of Count Yorga (1971). Starring: Robert Quarry, Roger Perry, Mariette Hartley, Yvonne Wilder. Directed by: Bob Kelljan. Produced by: Michael Macready. American International. 96 minutes.

Return of Dr. Satan (1967). Starring: Joaquin Cordero, Noe Murayama, Sonia Furio. Directed by: Rogelio Gonzalez. Azteca. 83 minutes.

Return of Dracula (1957). Starring: Francis Lederer, Norma Eberhardt, Ray Stricklyn, Jimmie Baird. Directed by: Paul Landres. Produced by: Jules Levy and

Arthur Gardner. United Artists. 77 minutes.

Return of the Giant Majin (1969). Starring: Kojiro Hongo, Kichijiro Ueda, Hisayuki Abe, Reiko Kashahara. Directed by: Noriaki Yuasa. Produced by: Nagata. Daiei. 84 minutes.

Return of the Giant Monsters (1967). Starring: Kojiro Hongo, Kichijiro Ueda, Hisayuki Abe, Reiko Kashahara. Directed by: Noriaki Yuasa. Produced by: Hidemasa Nagata. Daiei. 87 minutes.

Return of the Vampire (1943). Starring: Bela Lugosi, Matt Willis, Nina Foch, Frieda Inescort, Gilbert Emery. Directed by: Lew Landers. Produced by: Sam White. Columbia. 69 minutes.

Revenge of the Creature (1954). Starring: John Agar, Lori Nelson, John Bromfield, Nestor Paiva. Directed by: Jack Arnold. Produced by: William Alland. Universal. 82 minutes.

Revenge of the Zombies (1943). Starring: John Carradine, Gale Storm, Robert Lowery, Mantan Moreland, Bob Steele, Veda Ann Borg. Directed by: Steve Sekely. Produced by: Linsley Parsons. Monogram. 61 minutes.

Revolt of the Zombies (1936). Starring: Dean Jagger, Roy D'Arcy, Dorothy Stone, Robert Noland. Directed by: Victor Halperin. Produced by: Edward Halperin. Academy. 65 minutes.

Rodan (1956). Starring: Kenji Sahara, Yumi Shirakawa, Akihiko Hirata, Akio Kobori. Directed by: Inoshio Honda. Produced by: Tomoyuki Tanaka. Toho. 79 minutes.

Rosemary's Baby (1968). Starring: Mia Farrow, John Cassavetes, Ruth Gordon, Maurice Evans, Sidney Blackmer, Ralph Bellamy, Elisha Cook Jr., Victoria Vetri, Emaline Henry, Charles Grodin, Wende Wagner, William Castle. Directed by: Roman Polanski. Produced by: William Castle. Paramount. 136 minutes.

Sabu and the Magic Ring (1957). Starring: Sabu, Daria Massey, Robert Shafto, Peter Mamakos, William Marshall. Directed by: George Blair. Produced by: Maurice Duke. Allied Artists. 61 minutes.

Saga of the Viking Women and Their Voyage to the Waters of the Great Sea Serpent (1957). Starring: Abby Dalton, Gary Conway, Susan Cabot, Betsey Jones Moreland. Brad Jackson. Directed by: Roger Corman. Produced by: Roger Corman. American International. 71 minutes.

Samson and the Seven Miracles of the World (1961). Starring: Gordon Scott, Yoko Tani, Dante de Paolo, Gabriele Antonini. Directed by: Riccardo Pallotini. Produced by: Ermanno Donati and Luigi Carpentieri. American International. 95 minutes.

Satanic Rites of Dracula (1975). Starring: Christopher Lee, Peter Cushing, Michael Coles, William Franklyn, Freddie Jones. Directed by: Alan Gibson. Produced by: Roy Skeggs and Don Houghton. Hammer. 90 minutes.

Scared Stiff (1952). Starring: Jerry Lewis, Dean Martin, Lizabeth Scott, Carmen Miranda, George Dolenz, Jack Lambert, Bing Crosby, Bob Hope, Dorothy Malone.

Directed by: George Marshall. Produced by: Hal Wallis. Paramount. 108 minutes.

Scars of Dracula (1970). Starring: Christopher Lee, Dennis Waterman, Jenny Hanley, Christopher Matthews, Patrick Troughton, Michael Gwynn, Wendy Hamilton, Michael Ripper. Directed by: Roy Ward Baker. Produced by: Aida Young. Hammer. 96 minutes.

Scream, Blacula, Scream (1973). Starring: William Marshall, Pam Grier, Don Mitchell, Michael Conrad. Directed by: Bob Kelljan. Produced by: Joseph T. Narr. American International. 95 minutes.

Scrooge (1970). Starring: Albert Finney, Dame Edith Evans, Paddy Stone, Kenneth More, Anton Rogers, Alec Guiness, Laurence Naismith, Michael Medwin. Directed by: Ronald Neame. Produced by: Robert Solo and Leslie Bricusse. National General. 118 minutes.

Search For Bridey Murphy (1956). Starring: Louis Hayward, Teresa Wright, Kenneth Tobey, Nancy Gates. Directed by: Noel Langley. Produced by: Pat Duggan. Paramount. 84 minutes.

Secret of Dorian Gray (1970). Starring: Helmut Berger, Herbert Lom, Richard Todd, Marie Lijedahl, Margaret Lee. Directed by: Massimo Dallamano. Produced by: Harry Alan Towers. American International. 93 minutes.

Seven Faces of Dr. Lao (1964). Starring: Tony Randall, John Erickson, Barbara Eden, Arthur O'Connell, Noah Beery Jr., Minerva Urecal, Douglas Fowley. Directed by: George Pal. Produced by: George Pal. MGM. 100 minutes.

Seven Footprints to Satan (1929). Starring: Thelma Todd, Creighton Hale, Sheldon Lewis, William Mong, Nora Cecil. Directed by: Benjamin Christensen. Produced by: Wid Gunning. First National. 59 minutes.

Seventh Seal (1956). Starring: Max von Sydow, Gunnar Bjornstrand, Bengt Ekerot, Bibi Andersson. Directed by: Ingmar Bergman. Produced by: Allan Ekelund. Swedish. 105 minutes.

Seventh Voyage of Sinbad (1958). Starring: Kerwin Mathews, Torin Thatcher, Kathryn Grant (Crosby), Richard Eyer, Alec Mango. Directed by: Nathan Juran. Produced by: Charles H. Schneer. Columbia. 88 minutes.

Shaggy Dog (1959). Starring: Fred MacMurray, Tommy Kirk, Annette Funicello, Cecil Kellaway, Jean Hagen, Tim Considine, Kevin Corcoran, Strother Martin. Directed by: Charles Barton. Produced by: Walt Disney. Walt Disney Productions. 104 minutes.

She (1935). Starring: Helen Gahagan, Randolph Scott, Helen Mack, Nigel Bruce, Jim Thorpe. Directed by: Irving Pichel and Lansing Holden. Produced by: Merian C. Cooper. RKO. 101 minutes.

She (1965). Starring: Ursula Andress, Peter Cushing, Christopher Lee, John Richardson, Bernard Cribbens, Andre Morell. Directed by: Robert Day. Produced by: Aida Young. Hammer. 106 minutes.

The She Creature (1956). Starring: Chester Morris, Marla English, Tom Conway, El Brendel, Paul Blaisdell.

Directed by: Edward L. Cahn. Produced by: Alex Gordon and Samuel Z. Arkoff. American International. 77 minutes.

Simon, King of the Witches (1971). Starring: Andrew Prine, Brenda Scott, George Paulsin, Norman Burton. Directed by: Bruce Kessler. Produced by: David Hammond. Fanfare. 91 minutes.

Sinbad the Sailor (1946). Starring: Douglas Fairbanks Jr., Maureen O'Hara, Anthony Quinn, Walter Slezak, Alan Napier, Sheldon Leonard, Jane Greer. Directed by: Richard Wallace. Produced by: Stephan Ames. RKO. 117 minutes.

The Skull (1965). Starring: Peter Cushing, Christopher Lee, Patrick Wymark, Nigel Green, Michael Gough, Patric, Magee, Jill Bennett. Directed by: Freddie Francis. Produced by: Milton Subotsky and Max J. Rosenberg. Amicus. 90 minutes.

Sleeping Beauty (1959). Animated Cartoon. Created by: Walt Disney. Voices: Mary Costa, Bill Shirley, Verna Felton, Barbara Luddy. Walt Disney Productions. 75 minutes.

Slime People (1963). Starring: Robert Hutton, Les Tremayne, Robert Burton, Judee Morton, Susan Hart. Directed by: Robert Hutton. Produced by Joseph F. Robertson. Hansen. 59 minutes.

Snake People (1968). Starring: Boris Karloff, Julissa Carlos East, Ralph Bertrand. Directed by: Jack Hill and Juan Ibanez. Produced by: Juan Ibanez and Luis Enrique Bergara. Azteca. 81 minutes.

Snow Creature (1954). Starring: Paul Langton, Leslie Denison, Teru Shimada, Rollin Moriyama. Directed by: W.L. Wilder. Produced by: W.W. Wilder. United Artists. 80 minutes.

Snow Maiden (1953). Animated Cartoon. Directed by: I. Ivanova-Vano. Voices: I. Maslennikova, V. Borisenko, L. Ktitorov. Mosfilm. 69 minutes.

Snow Queen (1958). Animated Cartoon. Produced by: Robert Faber (American edition). Voices (dubbed): Sandra Dee, Tommy Kirk, Paul Frees, Pat McCormack. Universal. Russian. 70 minutes.

Snow White (1938). Animated Cartoon. Created by: Walt Disney. Voices: Adriana Caselotti, Harry Stockwell, Lucille LaVerne, Eleanor Audley, Scott Mattraw, Roy Atwell, Billy Gilbert. Walt Disney Productions. 83 minutes.

Son of Dracula (1943). Starring: Lon Chaney Jr., Louise Allbritton, Evelyn Ankers, J. Edgar Bromberg, Robert Paige. Directed by: Robert Siodmak. Produced by: Jack Gross and Ford Beebe. Universal. 79 minutes.

Son of Godzilla (1968). Starring: Tadao Takashima, Akira Kubo, Akihiko Hirata, Yoshio Tsuchiya, Kenji Sahara. Directed by: Jun Fukuda. Produced by: Tomoyuki Tanaka. Toho. 86 minutes.

Son of Kong (1933). Starring: Robert Armstrong, Helen Mack, Frank Reicher, Victor Wong, John Marston, Noble Johnson. Directed by: Ernest B. Schoedsack. Produced by: Merian C. Cooper. RKO. 70 minutes.

Son of Sinbad (1953). Starring: Dale Robertson, Vincent Price, Sally Forrest. Directed by: Ted Tetzlaff. Produced by: Howard Hughes and Robert Sparks. RKO. 86 minutes.

Sorrows of Satan (1926). Starring: Adolphe Menjou, Ricardo Cortez, Carol Demptster, Lya de Putti. Directed by: D. W. Griffith. Produced by: D. W. Griffith. Paramount. 80 minutes (?).

The Spider (1958). Starring: Ed Kemmer, June Kenney, Gene Persson, Gene Roth. Directed by: Bert I. Gordon. Produced by: Bert I. Gordon. American International. 73 minutes.

Stairway to Heaven (1946). Starring: David Niven, Raymond Massey, Kim Hunter, Roger Livesey, Richard Attenborough, Abraham Sofaer, Marius Goring. Directed by: Michael Powell and Emeric Pressburger. Produced by: Michael Powell and Emeric Pressburger. Universal. 104 minutes.

Strangler of the Swamp (1945). Starring: Rosemary La Planche, Charles Middleton, Blake Edwards, Robert Barrat. Directed by: Frank Wisbar. Produced by: Raoul Pagel. PRC. 60 minutes.

Student of Prague (1926). Starring: Conrad Veidt, Werner Krauss, Agnes Esterhazy, Fredinand von Alter. Directed by: Henrik Galeen. German. 60 minutes (?).

Student of Prague (1913). Starring: Paul Wegener, Lyda Salmanova, John Gottowt, Grete Berger. Directed by: Stellan Rye. Produced by: Paul Wegener. German. 40 minutes (?).

Sugar Hill (1974). Starring: Marki Bey, Robert Quarry, Don Pedro Colley, Richard Lawson, Betty Anne Rees. Directed by: Paul Maslansky. Produced by: Elliott Schick.

Supernatural (1933). Starring: Carole Lombard, Randolph Scott, Vivienne Osborne, H. B. Warner, Alan Dinehart. Directed by: Victor Halperin. Produced by: Victor and Edward Halperin. Paramount. 64 minutes.

Sword and the Dragon (1956). Starring: Boris Andreyev, Andrei Abrikosov, Natalie Medvedeva, Alexei Shvorin, Ninel Myshkova, Sol Martinson. Directed by: Alexander Ptushko. Produced by: Alexander Ptushko. Mosfilm. 95 minutes.

Sword in the Stone (1963). Animated Cartoon. Created by: Walt Disney. Voices: Ricky Sorenson, Sebastion Cabot, Junius Matthews, Alan Napier, Karl Swenson. Walt Disney Productions. 80 minutes.

Tales from Beyond the Grave (1973). Starring: Ian Bannen, Peter Cushing, Ian Carmichael, Diana Dors, Donald Pleasence, Angela Pleasence, Margaret Leighton. Directed by: Kevin Conner. Produced by: Milton Subotsky and Max J. Rosenberg. Amicus. 94 minutes.

Tales from the Crypt (1971). Starring: Sir Ralph Richardson, Peter Cushing, Ian Hendry, Richard Greene, Patrick Magee, Robert Hutton, Joan Collins, Angie Grant, Robin Phillips, Susan Denny, Roy Dotrice, David Markham, Nigel Patrick. Directed by: Freddie Francis. Produced by: Max J. Rosenberg and Milton Subotsky. Amicus. 92 minutes.

Tales of Hoffman (1951). Starring: Robert Rounseville, Moira Shearer, Robert Helpmann, Pamela Brown, Frederick Ashton, Ludmilla Tcherina, Ann Ayars, Leonide Massine. Directed by: Michael Powell and Emeric Pressburger. Produced by: Michael Powell and Emeric Pressburger. Lippert. 138 minutes.

Tales of Terror (1961). Starring: Vincent Price, Peter Lorre, Basil Rathbone, Debra Paget, Maggie Pierce, Leona Gage, Joyce Jameson, David Frankham. Directed by: Roger Corman. Produced by: Roger Corman. American International. 90 minutes.

Tales That Witness Madness (1973). Starring: Kim Novak, Joan Collins, Jack Hawkins, Georgia Brown, Michael Jayston, Donald Pleasence, Donald Huston, Suzie Kendall, Peter McEnery. Directed by: Freddie Francis. Produced by: Norman Priggen. Paramount. 88 minutes.

The Tarantula (1955). Starring: John Agar, Mara Corday, Leo G. Carroll, Nestor Paiva, Eddie Parker. Directed by: Jack Arnold. Produced by: William Alland. Universal. 80 minutes.

Taste of Blood (1967). Starring: Bill Rogers, Elizabeth Wilkinson, Thomas Wood, Otto Schlesinger. Directed by: Herschell Gordon Lewis. Produced by: Sidney Reich and Herschell Gordon Lewis. Creative. 120 minutes.

Taste the Blood of Dracula (1970). Starring: Christopher Lee, Geoffrey Keen, Gwen Watford, Linda Hayden, Peter Sallis, Anthony Corlan, Isla Blair, John Carson, Roy Kinnear, Ralph Bates, Michael Ripper. Directed by: Peter Sasdy. Produced by: Aida Young. Hammer. 95 minutes.

Terror Creatures from the Grave (1965). Starring: Barbara Steele, Richard Garret, Walter Brandt, Marilyn Mitchell. Directed by: Ralph Zucker. Produced by: Felix Ziffer, J. R. Coolidge, and Frank Merle. International. 90 minutes.

Terror in the Crypt (1963). Starring: Christopher Lee, Audry Amber, Ursula Davis, Jose Campos, Nela Conjiu, Jose Villasante, Carla Calo. Directed by: Thomas Miller. Produced by: William Mulligan. American International. 84 minutes.

That's the Spirit (1945). Starring: Jack Oakie, Peggy Ryan, Andy Devine, June Vincent, Irene Ryan, Buster Keaton, Arthur Treacher. Directed by: Charles Lamont. Produced by: Howard Benedict, Michael Fessier, and Ernest Pagano. Universal. 93 minutes.

Thief of Bagdad (1924). Starring: Douglas Fairbanks, Snitz Edwards, Charles Belcher, Anna May Wong, Noble Johnson. Directed by: Raoul Walsh. Produced by: Douglas Fairbanks. United Artists. 85 minutes.

Thief of Bagdad (1940). Starring: Sabu, Conrad Veidt, John Justin, Rex Ingram, June Duprez, Miles Malleson. Directed by: Ludwig Berger, Michael Powell, and Tim Whelan. Produced by: Alexander Korda. United Artists. 106 minutes.

Thief of Bagdad (1960). Starring: Steve Reeves, Gerogia Moll, Edy Vessel, Arturo Dominici, Daniele Vargas.

Directed by: Arthur Lubin. Produced by: Bruno Vailati. MGM. 96 minutes.

Thing That Couldn't Die (1958). Starring: William Raynolds, Andrea Martin, Jeffrey Stone. Directed by: Will Cowan. Produced by: Will Cowan. Universal. 69 minutes.

Things Happen at Night (1948). Starring: Gordon Harker, Alfred Dayton, Robertson Hare, Gwyneth Vaughan. Directed by: Francis Searle. Produced by: A. R. Shipman and James Carter. Gordon Film Company. 79 minutes.

Thirteen Ghosts (1960). Starring: Donald Woods, Jo Morrow, Charles Herbert, Rosemary de Camp, Martin Milner, Margaret Hamilton. Directed by: William Castle. Produced by: William Castle. Columbia. 85 minutes.

Thousand and One Nights (1945). Starring: Cornel Wilde, Evelyn Keyes, Phil Silvers, Rex Ingram, Shelley Winters, Adele Jergens. Directed by: Alfred E. Green. Produced by: Samuel Bischoff. Columbia. 95 minutes.

1001 Arabian Nights (1959). Animated Cartoon. Directed by: Jack Kinney. Produced by: Stephen Bosustow. Voices: Jim Backus, Kathryn Grant (Crosby), Hans Conried, Dwayne Hickman, Herschel Bernardi. Columbia. 76 minutes.

Three Stooges Meet Hercules (1961). Starring: Moe Howard, Larry Fine, Joe de Rita, Samson Burke, Vicki Trickett, Quinn Redeker, George N. Neise. Directed by: Edward Bernds. Produced by: Norm Maurer. Columbia. 89 minutes.

Three Treasures (1958). Starring: Toshiro Mifune, Yoko Tsukasa, Kyoko Kagawa, Koji Tsuruta. Directed by: Hiroshi Inagaki. Produced by: Sanezumi Fujimoto and Tomoyuki Tanaka. Toho. 182 minutes.

Three Worlds of Gulliver (1959). Starring: Kerwin Mathews, June Thorburn, Jo Morrow, Lee Patterson, Peter Bull, Sherri Alberoni, Gregoire Aslan. Directed by: Jack Sher. Produced by: Charles H. Schneer. Columbia. 99 minutes.

Time Machine (1960). Starring: Rod Taylor, Yvette Mimieux, Alan Young, Sebastian Cabot, Whit Bissell. Directed by: George Pal. Produced by: George Pal. MGM. 103 minutes.

Time of Their Lives (1946). Starring: Bud Abbott, Lou Costello, Marjorie Reynolds, Binnie Barnes, Kirk Alyn, Jess Barker, Gale Sondergaard. Directed by: Charles Barton. Produced by: Joseph Gershenson and Val Burton. Universal. 82 minutes.

Tom Thumb (1958). Starring: Russ Tamblyn, Alan Young, Terry Thomas, Peter Sellers, June Thorburn, Peter Bull, Jessie Matthews. Directed by: George Pal. Produced by: George Pal. MGM. 98 minutes.

Tomb of Ligeia (1964). Starring: Vincent Price, Elizabeth Shepherd, John Westbrook, Derek Francis, Oliver Johnston, Richard Vernon. Directed by: Roger Corman. Produced by: Roger Corman and Pat Green. American International. 81 minutes.

Topper (1937). Starring: Roland Young, Cary Grant, Constance Bennett, Billie Burke, Hedda Hopper, Alan

Mowbray, Doodles Weaver. Directed by: Norman Z. McLeod. Produced by: Hal Roach. MGM. 97 minutes.

Topper Returns (1941). Starring: Roland Young, Joan Blondell, Carole Landis, Billie Burke, Dennis O'Keefe, H. B. Warner, George Zucco, Patsy Kelly. Directed by: Roy Del Ruth. Produced by: Hal Roach. United Artists. 89 minutes.

Topper Takes a Trip (1938). Starring: Constance Bennett, Roland Young, Billie Burke, Alan Mowbray, Irving Pichel, Verree Teasdale. Directed by: Norman Z. McLeod. Produced by: Hal Roach. United Artists. 85 minutes.

Tormented (1960). Starring: Richard Carlson, Susan Gordon, Juli Reding, Joe Turkel, Vera Marsh, Lugene Sanders. Directed by: Bert I. Gordon. Produced by: Bert I. Gordon and Joe Steinberg. Allied Artists. 75 minutes.

Torture Garden (1967). Starring: Jack Palance, Burgess Meredith, Peter Cushing, Robert Hutton, Niall McGinnis, Michael Ripper, Beverly Adams, Barbara Ewing, John Standing, Maurice Denham. Directed by: Freddie Francis. Produced by: Max J. Rosenberg and Milton Subotsky. Amicus. 93 minutes.

Touch of Melissa (1971). Starring: Michael Berry, Emby Mellay, Lee Amber, Yvonne Winslow, Jeanne Gerson. Directed by: Don Henderson. Produced by: George E. Carey. Futurama. 79 minutes.

Trog (1970). Starring: Joan Crawford, Michael Gough, Joe Cornelius, Kim Braden, Bernard Kay, David Griffith. Directed by: Freddie Francis. Produced by: Herman Cohen. Warner Brothers. 93 minutes.

Twenty Million Miles to Earth (1957). Starring: William Hopper, Joan Taylor, Frank Puglia, Thomas B. Henry, John Zaremba, Tito Vuolo, Arthur Space. Directed by: Nathan Juran. Produced by: Charles H. Schneer. Columbia. 82 minutes.

Twenty Thousand Leagues Under the Sea (1954). Starring: James Mason, Kirk Douglas, Paul Lukas, Peter Lorre, Robert Wilke, Carleton Young. Directed by: Richard Fleischer. Produced by: Walt Disney. Walt Disney Productions. 127 minutes.

Twice Told Tales (1963). Starring: Vincent Price, Sebastian Cabot, Joyce Taylor, Beverly Garland, Richard Denning, Mari Blancard. Directed by: Sidney Salkow. Produced by: Robert E. Kent. United Artists. 119 minutes.

Twins of Evil (1971). Starring: Peter Cushing, Dennis Price, Katya Wyeth, Mary Collinson, Madeleine Collinson, Isobel Black, Kathleen Byron. Directed by: John Hough. Produced by: Harry Fine and Michael Style. Hammer. 87 minutes.

Two Little Bears (1961). Starring: Eddie Albert, Jane Wyatt, Butch Patrick, Nancy Kulp, Soupy Sales, Jimmy Boyd, Donnie Carter, Brenda Lee. Directed by: Randall F. Hood. Produced by: Robert Lippert and George W. George. Twentieth Century Fox. 84 minutes.

Two Lost Worlds (1950). Starring: James Arness, Laura Elliott, Bill Kennedy, Gloria Petroff, Jane Harlan, Tom Hubbard. Directed by: Norman Dawn. Produced by:

Boris Petroff. United Artists. 62 minutes.

Ulysses (1954). Starring: Kirk Douglas, Anthony Quinn, Silvana Mangano, Rossana Podesta, Daniel Ivernel. Directed by: Mario Camerini. Produced by: Dino de Laurentiis and Carlo Ponti. Paramount. 130 minutes.

Ulysses Against the Son of Hercules (1961). Starring: Georges Marchal, Michael Lane, Alessandra Panaro, Gianni Santuccio, Yvette Leon. Directed by: Maio Caiano. Produced by: G. Pasquale and A. Fantechi. Embassy. 101 minutes.

Uncle was a Vampire (1959). Starring: Christopher Lee, Sylva Koscina, Renato Rascel, Kay Fisher. Directed by: Stefano Steno. Produced by: Mario Cecchi Gori. Embassy. 83 minutes.

The Undead (1956). Starring: Pamela Duncan, Allison Hayes, Dorothy Neumann, Richard Devon, Richard Garland, Val Dufour. Directed by: Roger Corman. Produced by: Roger Corman. American International. 71 minutes.

Undying Monster (1942). Starring: James Ellison, John Howard, Heather Angel, Bramwell Fletcher, Holmes Herbert. Directed by: John Brahm. Produced by: Bryan Foy and William Goetz. Twentieth Century Fox. 63 minutes.

The Uninvited (1944). Starring: Ray Milland, Ruth Hussey, Gail Russell, Alan Napier, Cornelia Otis Skinner. Directed by: Lewis Allen. Produced by: Charles Brackett. Paramount. 98 minutes.

Unknown Island (1948). Starring: Virginia Grey, Richard Denning, Barton MacLane, Phillip Reed. Directed by: Jack Berhard. Produced by: Albert Jay Cohen. Film Classics. 76 minutes.

Valley of Gwangi (1969). Starring: James Franciscus, Gila Golan, Laurence Naismith, Richard Carlson, Freda Jackson, Gustavo Rojo, Dennis Kilbane. Directed by: James O'Connolly. Produced by: Charles H. Schneer. Columbia 95 minutes.

Valley of the Dragons (1961). Starring: Cesare Danova, Sean McClory, Joan Staley, Danielle de Metz, Greg Martell. Directed by: Edward Bernds. Produced by: Alfred Zimbalist and Bryon Roberts. Columbia 79 minutes.

Vampira (1973). Starring: David Niven, Teresa Graves, Jennie Linden, Peter Bayliss, Nicky Henson, Freddie Jones, Bernard Brewwlaw. Directed by: Clive Donner. Produced by: Jack Wiener. Columbia. 93 minutes.

Vampire and the Ballerina (1962). Starring: Helene Remy, Maria Luisa Rolando, Tina Gloriana, Walter Brandi, Iscaro Revaioli, John Turner. Directed by: Renato Polselli. Produced by: Bruna Bolognesi. United Artists. 86 minutes.

Vampire Circus (1971). Starring: Adrienne Corri, Anthony Corlan, Laurence Payne, Thorley Walters, Robert Tayman, John Moulder Borown. Directed by: Robert Young. Produced by: Wilbur Stark. Hammer. 87 minutes.

Vampire Doll (1970). Starring: Kayo Matsuo, Akira Nakao, Artsuo Nakamura. Directed by: Michio

Yamamoto. Toho. 71 minutes.

Vampire Lovers (1970). Starring: Peter Cushing, Ingrid Pitt, Pippa Steele, Madeleine Smith, George Cole, Jon Finch, Ferdy Mayne, Dawn Addams, Douglas Wilmer. Directed by: Roy Ward Baker. Produced by: Harry Fine and Michael Style. Hammer. 91 minutes.

Vampire's Ghost (1945). Starring: John Abbot, Peggy Steward, Roy Barcroft, Charles Gordon, Grant Withers, Adel Mara. Directed by: Lesley Selander. Produced by: Arman Schaefer. Republic. 59 minutes.

Vampyr (1931). Starring: Julian West, Sybille Schmitz, Henriette Gerard, Rena Mandel. Directed by: Carl Theodore Dryer. Produced by: Carl Dryer and Nicholas de Gunzburg (Julian West). German. 65 minutes.

Varan the Unbelievable (1958). Starring: Myron Healy, Tsuruko Kobayashi, Kozo Nomura, Ayumi Sonoda, Koreya Senda. Directed by: Inoshiro Honda. Produced by: Tomoyuki Tanaka.

Vault of Horror (1972). Starring: Daniel Massey, Anna Massey, Terry Thomas, Edward Judd, Michael Craig, Tom Baker, Curt Jurgens, Dawn Addams, Glynis Johns, Denholm Elliott. Directed by: Roy Ward Baker. Produced by: Milton Subotsky and Max J. Rosenberg. Amicus. 93 minutes.

Vengeance of She (1967). Starring: John Richardson, Edward Judd, Olinka Berova, Colin Blakely, Derek Godfrey, Andre Morell. Directed by: Cliff Owen. Produced by: Aida Young. Hammer. 101 minutes.

Voodoo Island (1957). Starring: Boris Karloff, Beverly Tyler, Murvyn Vye, Elisha Cook, Rhodes Reason. Directed by: Reginald Le Borg. Produced by: Howard W. Koch and Aubrey Schenck. United Artists. 76 minutes.

Voodoo Man (1944). Starring: Bela Lugosi, John Carradine, George Zucco, Wanda McKay, Louise Currie, Michael Ames. Directed by: William Beaudine. Produced by: Sam Katzman and Jack Dietz. Monogram. 62 minutes.

War of the Gargantuas (1967). Starring: Russ Tamblyn, Kumi Mizuno, Kipp Hamilton, Kanji Sahara, Jun Tazaki. Directed by: Inoshio Honda. Produced by: Tomoyuki Tanaka. Toho. 88 minutes.

War of the Monsters (1966). Starring: Kojior Hongo, Kyoko Enami, Akira Natsuki, Koji Fujiyama. Directed by: Shigeo Tanaka. Produced by: Masaichi Nagata. Daiei. 106 minutes.

War of the Zombies (1963). Starring: John Drew Barrymore, Susi Anderson, Ettore Manni, Ida Galli, Philippe Hersent, Mino Doro, Ivano Staccioli. Directed by: Giuseppe Vari. Produced by: Ferruccio de Martino. American International. 105 minutes.

Weird Woman (1944). Starring: Lon Chaney Jr., Evelyn Ankers, Anne Gwynne, Ralph Morgan, Lois Collier, Elizabeth Russel. Directed by: Reginald le Borg. Produced by: Ben Pivar and Oliver Drake. Universal. 63 minutes.

The Werewolf (1956). Starring: Steven Ritch, Joyce Holden, Don Megowan, Eleanore Tanin, Jim Charney, Harry Lauter. Directed by: Fred F. Sears. Produced by: Sam Katzman. Columbia. 83 minutes.

Werewolf in a Girl's Dormitory (1961). Starring: Barbara Lass, Curt Lowens, Carl Schell, Maurice Marsac, Maureen O'Conner. Directed by: Richard Benson. Produced by: Guido Giambartolomi. MGM. 83 minutes.

Werewolf of London (1935). Starring: Henry Hull, Warner Oland, Valerie Hobson, Spring Byington, Lester Matthews, Ethel Griffies, Zeffie Tilbury. Directed by: Stuart Walker. Produced by: Stanley Bergerman. Universal. 75 minutes.

Werewolves on Wheels (1971). Starring: Severn Darden, Stephen Oliver, D.J. Anderson, Deuce Berry, Billy Gray, Barry McGuire, Gary Johnson, Owen Orr. Directed by: Michael Levesque. Produced by: Paul Lewis. Fanfare. 85 minutes.

What's So Bad About Feeling Good? (1968). Starring: Mary Tyler Moore, George Peppard, Dom de Louise, Susan St. James, Cleavon Little, Thelma Ritter, John McMartin, Don Stroud. Directed by: George Seaton. Produced by: George Seaton. Universal. 94 minutes.

When Dinosaurs Ruled the Earth (1970). Starring: Victoria Vetri, Robin Hawdon, Patrick Allen, Drewe Henley, Sean Caffrey, Magda Konopka. Directed by: Val Guest. Produced by: Aida Young. Hammer. 100 minutes.

When Women Had Tails (1970). Starring: Senta Berger, Giuliano Gemma, Lando Buzzanca, Frank Wolff. Directed by: Pasquale Festa Campanile. Produced by: Silvio Clementelli. Equropean International. 110 minutes.

When Women Played Ding Dong (1971). Starring: Antonio Sabato, Aldo Giuffre, Vittorio Caprioli, Nadia Cassini, Valerie Fabrizi, Howard Ross, Ello Pandolfi. Directed by: Bruno Corbucci. Produced by: Edmondo Amati. Paragon. 98 minutes.

Where Do We Go From Here? (1945). Starring: Fred MacMurray, Gene Sheldon, Joan Leslie, June Haver, Anthony Quinn, Carlos Ramirez. Directed by: Gregory Ratoff. Produced by: William Pearlberg. Twentieth Century Fox. 78 minutes.

White Pongo (1945). Starring: Richard Fraser, Maris Wrixon, Lionel Royce, Al Eben, Gordon Richards, Egon Brøcher. Directed by: Sam Newfield. Produced by: Sigmund Neufeld. PRC. 74 minutes.

White Zombie (1932). Starring: Bela Lugosi, Madge Bellamy, John Harron, Robert Frazer, Brandon Hurst, Joseph Cawthorn, Dan Crimmins. Directed by: Victor Halperin. Produced by: Edward Halperin. United Artists. 73 minutes.

The Witch (1906). Directed by: George Melies. French. 9 minutes.

Witch Without a Broom (1966). Starring: Jeffrey Hunter, Maria Perschy, Gustavo Rojo, Perla Cristal, Reginal Billam, Al Mulock. Directed by: Joe Lacy. Produced by: Stan Torchia and Sidney Pink. PRO. 86 minutes.

Willy Wonka and the Chocolate Factory (1971). Starring: Gene Wilder, Jack Albertson, Peter Ostrum, Roy Kinnear. Directed by: Mel Stuart. Produced by: Stan Margulies and David L. Wolper. Paramount. 98 minutes.

Witchcraft (1964). Starring: Lon Chaney Jr., Yvette Rees, Jack Hedley, Jill Dixon, David Weston, Marie Ney, Diane Clair. Directed by: Don Sharp. Produced by: Robert Lippert and Jack Parsons. Twentieth Century Fox. 79 minutes.

Witchcraft Through the Ages (1921). Starring: Benjamin Christensen, Elisabeth Christensen, Maren Pedersen, Clara Pontopiddan Tora Teje, Elith Pio. Directed by: Benjamin Christensen. Swedish. 83 minutes (?).

Wizard of Bagdad (1960). Starring: Dick Shawn, Diane Baker, Barry Coe, Don Beddoe, John van Dreelen, Robert Simon, Vaughn Taylor. Directed by: George Sherman. Produced by: Sam Katzman. Twentieth Century Fox. 92 minutes.

Wizard of Oz (1924). Starring: Dorothy Dwan, Oliver Hardy, Larry Semon, Mary Carr, Charlie Murray. Directed by: Larry Semon. 50 minutes (?).

Wizard of Oz (1939). Starring: Judy Garland, Ray Bolger, Margaret Hamilton, Jack Haley, Bert Lahr, Billie Burke, Charley Grapewin. Directed by: Victor Fleming. Produced by: Mervyn LeRoy and Arthur Freed. MGM. 101 minutes.

The Wolfman (1940). Starring: Lon Chaney Jr., Claude Rains, Bela Lugosi, Evelyn Ankers, Ralph Bellamy, Maria Ouspenskaya, Patrick Knowles, Warren William, Fay Helm. Directed by: George Waggner. Produced by: George Waggner. Universal. 71 minutes.

Woman Who Came Back (1945). Starring: Nancy Kelly, Otto Kruger, John Loder, Ruth Ford, J. Farrell MacDonald. Directed by: Walter Colmes. Produced by: Walter Colmes. Republic. 68 minutes.

Wonderful World of the Brothers Grimm (1962). Starring: Laurence Harvey, Karl Boehem, Claire Bloom, Barbara Eden, Oscar Homolka, Walter Slezak, Arnold Stang, Yvette Mimieux, Russ Tamblyn, Jim Backus, Terry Thomas, Buddy Hackett, Beulah Bondi. Directed

by: Henry Levin (Live Action Sequences) and George Pal (Fairy Tale Sequences). Produced by: George Pal. MGM/Cinerama. 134 minutes.

World of the Vampires (1960). Starring: Mauricio Garces, Silva Fournier, Erna Marthat Bauman, Guillermo Murray, Jose Baviera. Directed by: Alfonso Corona Blake. Produced by: Abel Salazar. American International. 83 minutes.

Yellow Submarine (1968). Animated Cartoon. Directed by: George Dunning. Produced by: Al Brodax. United Artists. 87 minutes.

Yog, the Monster from Space (1970). Starring: Akiro Kubo, Atsuko Takahashi, Kenji Sahara, Yoshio Tsuchiya, Noritake Saito. Directed by: Inoshiro Honda. Produced by: Tomoyuki Tanaka and Fumio Tanaka. Toho. 84 minutes.

Yolanda and the Thief (1945). Starring: Fred Astaire, Lucille Bremer, Frank Morgan, Leon Ames, Mildred Natwick, Mary Nash, Ghislaine Perreau. Directed by: Vincent Minnelli. Produced by: Arthur Freed. MGM. 109 minutes.

You Never Can Tell (1951). Starring: Dick Powell, Peggy Dow, Charles Drake, Albert Sharpe, Joyce Holden, Sara Taft, Will Vedder, Watson Downs. Directed by: Lou Breslow. Produced by: Leonard Goldstein. Universal. 81 minutes.

Zombies of Mora-Tau (1957). Starring: Allison Hayes, Morris Ankrum, Ray Corrigan, Gregg Palmer, Autumn Russell, Joel Ashley. Directed by: Edward Cahn. Produced by: Sam Katzman. Columbia. 70 minutes.

Zombies on Broadway (1945). Starring: Bela Lugosi, Wally Brown, Alan Carney, Anne Jeffreys, Sheldon Leonard, Darby Jones. Directed by: Gordon Douglas. Produced by: Sid Rogell and Ben Stoloff. RKO. 68 minutes.

Zotz! (1962). Starring: Tom Poston, Cecil Kellaway, Jim Backus, Julia Meade, Fred Clark, Mike Mazurki, Louis Nye. Directed by: William Castle. Produced by: William Castle. Columbia. 85 minutes.

Appendix 2
INTERVIEWS

The following interviews with people involved in fantasy films were conducted either in person (IP) or via a mailed questionnaire. Their responses do not necessarily reflect the views of the author.

George Pal
(IP)

JR: What do you see as the difference between science fiction and fantasy?

GP: This is a terribly difficult borderline to find. They blend into one another. Let's just say that science fiction is the fairy tale of this century.

JR: For what elements do you look in any potential film property?

GP: I like to produce movies which are different. Boy meets girl or a Western are stories which other producers can do better than I. I like the challenge, the pioneering spirit, of doing something that's different. If somebody says to me, "Here is something impossible," then I'm already interested. Nothing is impossible in motion pictures.

JR: Are there any fantasy filmmakers you particularly admire?

GP: Well, Ray Harryhausen is, of course brilliant. We worked together many years ago, on the Puppetoons. We've wanted to work together for a long time, but everytime I have something, he is busy; when he isn't busy, I don't have anything. Another picturemaker who comes to mind is Stanley Kubrick, who is an enormously visual director. I like his work very much. I also admire Norman Jewison.

JR: Does the contemporary vogue of placing a heavy emphasis on "messages" in fantasy films annoy you?

GP: It doesn't annoy me, but first of all, I look at the entertainment value of a picture. If you have something to say, don't say it too loud. Use it to underline the picture. Like we did in *Seven Faces of Dr. Lao* or the Puppetoons.

JR: The Puppetoons must be very special to you, since they were the first projects you did in America.

GP: Yes. Unfortunately, the Puppetoons just barely broke even. Eventually, we couldn't make them for the price theaters would pay. Short subjects are the stepchildren of the industry. The theaterowners feel that nobody comes in for the shorts. Consequently, they didn't want to pay more in 1950 than they had paid in 1940. Meantime, the costs tripled, then quadrupled, which is why limited animation came into being. But it's primitive. You're going backward instead of forward. During the Puppetoon years, however, we were actually preparing for *Tom Thumb*. At that time, we wanted to think of Tom as a little wooden puppet. When we discontinued the Puppetoons, we had the Tom Thumb screenplay and music ready to go. Still, it took three more years to get it to the screen. But a funny thing happened with that. We originally designed the part that Alan Young played for Donald O'Conner. I remember that Donald came to the house and I pushed that part to him. When I was finished showing him the storyboard sketches, I felt very stupid because he said, "I want to play Tom Thumb." I hadn't even thought of that! Unfortunately, when we took the project to MGM, they had Russ Tamblyn under contract and wanted him in the picture. But Russ was wonderful and it worked out very well. The satisfaction, of course, is that the picture is still playing matinees; it never seems to die. It's probably the most durable picture I ever made.

JR: Even moreso than *The Time Machine?*

GP: Well, *The Time Machine* was received better than any of my other films *right away*. It was a big hit all over the world. There's something about H.G. Wells: I wish he were alive today, for he would be a terrific screenwriter. Every film based on his stories has been a success. He sensed what an audience wanted.

JR: Of all your films, which was the most satisfying?

GP: I'd have to say *Seven Faces of Dr. Lao*, and I'll tell you why. Just last weekend, I was at a science-fiction film convention and I looked at *Dr. Lao* to see how it held up. It wasn't my picture anymore. I had forgotten most of it and was very much stimulated by the reaction of the audience. It got a beautiful reaction. Of course, the book was so good. Then there was Charles Beaumont, the screenwriter. He also wrote *Wonderful World of the Brothers Grimm*, which is where we got acquainted. In fact, that's how *Dr. Lao* came about. I asked Charles, as I ask all my writers, if they have any favorite stories they've been unable to sell. And he said, "Yes, the *Circus of Dr. Lao*." I asked him to let me see the book, and he said, "I'll do better than that. I'll let you have the script." It was marvelous. I put in my 2¢, and we were both very happy with the picture. Original-ly, it was designed for Peter Sellers, but Tony Randall did a wonderful job.

JR: How did you feel about losing the special effects Oscar on *Dr. Lao* to *Mary Poppins*?

GP: Well, it's not bad to lose to Walt Disney. I have very sentimental feelings about Walt, personally. When I came to this country in 1940, all I had was a bag of puppets and I called Walt Disney. He was the most courteous, most wonderful friend. He helped me along, advised me who was a good animator, and always spoke to me in great detail. I could call him any time and he came to the phone right away, or called me back very shortly. We had lunch together every two months. One thing especially shows what a great man he was. When we finished *Destination Moon* (1950), I wanted next to go instead of into space, in the other direction. Kurt Newman, a very fine director, submitted *Twenty Thousand Leagues Under the Sea* to me. He had a very fine script, but his studio, Monogram, just didn't want to go for it. I was over at Paramount working on *When Worlds Collide* and wanted very much to do *Twenty Thousand Leagues Under the Sea*. I tried to sell it to the front office but they said, "Who wants an old-fashioned submarine? Make a movie about a modern, atomic submarine." A few weeks later, Walt called and said, "George, I know you're interested in *Twenty Thousand Leagues Under the Sea*. I won't buy it unless you've decided not to take it." I told him to take Newman's script, which he did. He made the picture, did a beautiful job, and it was very successful.

JR: One of your least successful pictures was *Atlantis, the Lost Continent*. Why did it not come off as well as your other films?

GP: The problem was in the writing. We weren't ready to go with the picture because we had a poor script. But it was scheduled to shoot, a writer's strike broke out, and we couldn't get anyone to rewrite it. We had a very pedestrian script, but the studio told me not to worry. "You'll pull it out with the special effects," they said, which we did. But the story and dialogue were horrible.

Tony Randall
(IP)

JR: It's been over a decade since *Seven Faces of Dr. Lao*. How do you feel, looking back at the picture?

TR: I thought that *Seven Faces of Dr. Lao* was dreadful. I was ashamed of it, and I have precious little admiration for the kinds of special effects that appear in the film. It's all trickery. Technical trickery. Ordinarily, these should be no different than lights in a theatrical play. They should be well done and unobtrusive. You shouldn't be so damned aware of them as you are in *Dr. Lao*. Although I must admit, I liked one effect in the movie, when the Loch Ness monster picked me up. It was fun to do. I was wired like Peter Pan, and they had me lay on the ground. Suddenly, I was way up in the air. The monster was matted in later. Anyway, that's not what I'm interested in. I had read the Finney novel, and that's why the movie is so poor. The novel is really good. Now, where the movie adheres to the novel, it's good. But that's less than half the movie. The rest is simply dross, the most unimaginative padding and stuffing and wrapping. But Mr. Pal did have one really good theatrical notion, and that was that all characters in the Circus should be one man. This was good thinking, for they are all the products of Dr. Lao. They are all a part of his spell.

JR: How did you get along with Mr. Pal?

TR: Pretty well. We get along *very* well off-screen. He's a gentleman and a very nice man.

JR: Of all the characters in *Dr. Lao*, did you have a favorite?

TR: No favorite. I just loved making the picture. I never wanted it to end, and that's the only time this has ever happened. Working on and develop-ing the makeups was just so much fun. You see, an actor like me is freed by makeup. I can do anything; it's a feeling of extraordinary release. You know the fantasy that you're invisible and can go into girls' bathrooms? That's what an actor like me gets from makeup. Of course, on *Dr. Lao*, MGM did not provide funds or time for our experiements, which we did on our own. The first thing we did was shave my head and eyebrows. Then we had big Chinese teeth made that changed the shape of my mouth. They cost $400. Then we had a queue made, which glued on the back of my head and came down. Then we had me padded so I was a very ovoid man. That was George Pal's conception. We achieved all of that and fell in love with it. It looked marvelous in the makeup room. Then we did a screen test of it and it was horrible. The screen caused a different color to come through. It came out mean. Lao looked vicious, gross, and villainous. So we started all over again. We dulled my own teeth with gray finger nail polish. Then we added the wispy moustache and beard. It gave Lao a philosophical look, and an ancient look. Then there were the other characters. We achieved certain wonders with the Pan. Bill Tuttle, who is a bit of a genius, fashioned a head in water color that was a real Roman head. But when he got it on me, I thought it looked too handsome and too intelligent. I had wanted the Pan to have that animal lack of intelligence. Now, these added pieces he used are made from foam rubber. We used to do all makeups like that with papier mache or wax. These are not good, although they're good enough. That's what was used in Lon Chaney's day. The newer latex moves as your face moves. Anyway, I didn't want the Pan to resemble Don Juan. So I grabbed a hunk of mortician's wax and made the bridge of the nose come to the center of the forehead, the way a ram's does. That made the eyes stupid, automatically. It was just what I wanted. I also had several different color eyes. They were agony to wear.

JR: How long did each makeup application take?

TR: Two hours.

JR: And what about the Medusa? How were the snakes manipulated?

TR: Well, it never worked properly. They had some marvelous Chinese puppeteer. He was on a scafolding above me. The plastic snakes were wired with some electromagnetic device and he was up there with a powerful magnet, moving it around and causing the snakes to appear alive. They were just never convincing.

Robert Wise
(IP)

JR: How did you approach the various scientific and supernatural elements in *The Haunting?*

RW: I really never thought of it too much in scientific terms. It was a supernatural fantasy. I know that more and more, as time goes on, we're getting closer to feeling that there might not be quite so much difference between some of our realities and some of the nonrealities in *The Haunting.* But it was still a fantasy.

JR: This may sound a somewhat glib question, but do you believe in ghosts?

RW: I can't give you an out and out answer. I'm intrigued by the possibility. I'm not really completely convinced, although I'd *like* to believe, and I find myself being pulled towards it very much. I think that's what helps make me, from time to time, want to make this kind of a film.

JR: You worked with Val Lewton on several occasions. What was the genesis of your association?

RW: He was the first producer I work with in the capacity of a director. As a matter of fact, he was the one who gave me the opportunity to direct. I had been the editor of *Curse of the Cat People.* Gunther Fritsch, the original director of the film, got really behind, and they had warned him on several occasions to speed it up. Finally, they had to take him off the film. I had been asking for the chance to direct, so Lewton and Sid Rogell, who was head of the unit, told me on a Saturday that they wanted me to take over on Monday. I told them that I felt very awkward about it because I was working with the man. They said, "Well, look. There's going to be someone else directing that picture on Monday morning. Now it can be you, or somebody else." I'm sure that Val did everything he could to keep Gunther on. He was a man who felt for his people. He never imposed himself on a director. He was there, and gave you everything he could to help, but he didn't stand over your shoulder and second-guess you constantly. It's just a great shame he passed away as early as he did. Anyway that's how I got into it, and I was fortunate to work for Val. He was a very, very creative man, a well-meaning, erudite, articulate man, a writer, and a man of taste: all the good things! So I think the overall influence of all those qualities of his was very fortunate for me.

JR: Who came up with the idea for the Headless Horseman in *Curse of the Cat People?*

RW: That was Val's idea. He did a tremendous amount of work not only as a producer, but on the scripts as well.

JR: You worked with Boris Karloff and Bela Lugosi on *The Body Snatcher* (1945). Have you any recollections of either actor?

RW: Lugosi didn't work that much on the picture. As a matter of fact, his part was added in because the front office wanted to get those two in the film. So Val came up with the part for him. He was not a terribly well man at the time, and I can't remember much except that it was rather tedious working with him, getting the things out. But he was all right. Boris was marvelous. A marvelous gentleman and a great contrast to the figure he presented on the screen. He was gentle, very soft-spoken, a good education, good background, and very sensitive. I found him a much better actor than he has been given credit for. Of course, he wasn't well either. He had had back surgery just a few months before the picture, and I had to nurse him through a few things. But he was lovely to work with.

Ray Harryhausen

JR: Most of your films have had a hero in the very classical, very noble sense of the word. What do you feel is the role of the hero in both film and the modern world?

RH: Everything in nature has its opposites. Good and evil; truth and lie; positive and negative; black and white; hero and villain. The gradations between the extremes are tremendous. But there is a point between the balance where, for example, the hero gradually shades into the villain. He ceases to be a hero and all that it stands for, and you have the currently fashionable antihero. To me, this concept of the antihero has approached the delicate dividing line between positive and negative, which is much too close for comfort. Most countries in a state of growth have a strong set of ideals, laws, and moral values to bind them together, sets of rules which produce unity and progress. The traditional storybook hero is a personification of these ideals in his fight against the dragons and monsters of adversity. Peoples who discard these simple sets of values, on the whole, show a marked decline in their culture. The recent antipathy toward the hero reflects this. Without the example of the idealistic hero, the extreme of everyone "doing his own thing" erodes the very foundation of organization of any kind. And if we reject the freedoms that are a part of our self-imposed laws, which develop through a strong philosophic or religious concept, then we can only rely on a form of dictatorship to keep society from falling apart. It would seem there is only one possible choice.

JR: Can I also assume, from this, that you would be opposed to the use of artificial stimuli such as marijuana to achieve a creative end?

RH: An exploration into philosophy and various religious concepts must bring about a more satisfying result than any weed or alcoholic relaxation of the inhibitions, which sometimes bind creativity. In an age where there is constant seeking of shortcuts to bliss, it follows that these also bring with them a short-lived and superficial illusion of true satisfaction.

JR: Clearly, you kept this ideal in mind when you developed your Sinbad character in both *Seventh Voyage of Sinbad* and *Golden Voyage of Sinbad*.

RH: When we made *Seventh Voyage of Sinbad*, we were trying hard to avoid the cliche figure of Sinbad which had gone before. Douglas Fairbanks Jr.'s *Sinbad the Sailor, Son of Sinbad*, and the Maria Montez films with a pseudo-Arabian background all pursued the "devil-may-care" concept. We strongly felt that we wanted to try

another style of characterization. I think it worked. In *Golden Voyage of Sinbad*, we again tried an alternative which would fit the mood of the particular story we were telling. The dashing figure with smiling, gleeming teeth and carefree attitude usually goes hand-in-hand with a tongue-in-cheek approach to filmmaking. This I dislike in a fantasy tale. We made Sinbad an idealistic, classical, symbollic hero who was virtually incorruptible. Perhaps a lesser mortal, with more human failings, would also work, depending on the type of story told. Jason, for example, approaches this concept in *Jason and the Argonauts*. He actually ended up trying to steal the Golden Fleece from Colchis. Hardly a noble undertaking!

JR: Speaking of *Jason and the Argonauts* and its characterization, Nigel Green's Hercules was certainly an unusual interpretation.

RH: Of course, Green's Hercules was also a minor part. It is difficult to say if one could sustain this type of characterization in a central figure for over an hour and a half. It would depend on the cleverness of the writing and directing. Usually, in a fantasy adventure film, characterization must suffer in favor of pace, action, and visual grandeur.

JR: Why was *Gulliver's Travels* diluted in both theme and sophistication for *Three Worlds of Gulliver*?

RH: At the time *Three Worlds of Gulliver* was made, it would not have been permissible to put Jonathan Swift on the screen "to the letter." Aside from censorship problems, there would be costly production difficulties. But even in the present time, there is far too much cynicism for our own good; I find myself a victim of it many times. Cynicism is a negative quality and if overused, has a tendency to smother the more positive qualities of hope and faith. A form of supersophistication would seem to be the turning point from growth to decline.

JR: Why do you think that King Kong and Mighty Joe Young remain the most successful stop-motion characterizations in film?

RH: An animal, in films, usually tends to be a victim of circumstance. This immediately gives it a head start in the race for audience affection. Most actors today tend to underplay their parts, particularly if they are cast in straight, contemporary roles. The villain has the greater opportunity of letting himself go. Kong, as an animated villain, was able to make many melodramatic gestures which an actor would be embrassed to do. Kong could get away with it because these exaggerated movements aided in making him more alive and human. Mighty Joe Young was not so much the villain as the exploited one. A victim of man's greed. This, of course, gave him pathos and a rather heroic quality. Perhaps, on a different level, the main fascination with the two great apes of filmland comes from the realization that a bundle of metal joints and sponge rubber muscles, mixed with artificial fur and the animator's imagination, can produce an activated personality with which one can become attached. This is undoubtedly the envy of many an actor. The creation of this illusion of life, in many ways, compares with the ancient alchemists in their search for the means to produce a living homonculus. O'Brien succeeded in producing the most impressive "homonculus" of all time.

William Castle

JR: Did the gimmicks you used during the fifties help your horror films at the box office?

WC: Yes, they increased our box-office revenue. I was, by the way, the only producer doing gimmicks at the time.

JR: Have you any favorites among your repertoire?

WC: A favorite film is *Homicidal* because of its originality. It was way ahead of its time. *Time Magazine* chose it as one of the ten best pictures of that year, preferring it to Alfred Hitchcock's *Psycho*. It was the story of a transvestite, and at that time the word masquerade had to be substituted for transvestite. If it were done today, it would be a big picture.

JR; Who is your favorite among the horror actors?

WC: Vincent Price. He is, in my opinion, one of the most cooperative actors I've ever worked with, as well as the most talented. I was the one who started him on his horror-films career.

JR: *Jaws* and *Bug* were released at the same time, yet the former received far more publicity. How do you react to this injustice as a producer?

WC: Since *Bug* is my film, it is difficult for me to make a judgment. However, I feel that if *Bug* had received the same hype as *Jaws*, it would have gotten a much larger reaction than it did at the box-office.

JR: What is the unique talent involved in making a successful horror film?

WC: It is *difficult* to make a horror film. It is audience manipulation, and a few writers, producers, and directors know how to create in this genre. I've spent a lifetime working in horror films.

JR: Was there any fear that the sexual aspects of *Rosemary's Baby* might dull its chances of success?

WC: No. *Rosemary's Baby* broke the barrier to openly deal with sex. The pubic was ready for it at that time, after having had years of the cinderella stories.

JR: Have you any favorite films by other directors?

WC: Clouzot's *Diabolique*, Hitchcock's *Psycho*, Bob Wise's *The Haunting*, and Val Lewton's *The Cat People*.

Ricou Browning

JR: In many ways, *The Creature from the Black Lagoon* is a more convincing creation than the shark in *Jaws*. Do you have this same feeling?

RB: I think perhaps the reason the Creature films seen more convincing is because the Creature is a more "human-type" monster as opposed to the shark in *Jaws*. You are able to feel sorry for the Creature.

JR: In many ways, though, the Creature is also more technically convincing than *Jaws*' mechanical shark.

RB: I believe the level of craftsmanship has improved, however there is now less time to photograph because of budgets and tight schedules.

JR: What was the attitude of the crew and cast on the Creature sets?

RB: We all took the films very seriously and were all professional.

JR: Of what was the Creature suit made?

RB: The Creature suit was made of sponge rubber. It was very much like swimming with your overcoat on.

JR: You did the underwater sequences in all the Creature films, as well as playing the surface monster in *Revenge of the Creature*. How did you receive air underwater?

RB: I received air through an air hose, very similar to drinking water from a hose in your backyard, except it was air and not water. That was the only process used.

JR: How did you land the job as the Creature?

RB: I was picked as the Creature because of my unique style of underwater swimming, which is very similar to the top-water freestyle stroke. I look aback on the three Creature pictures I worked on with fondness and a great deal of satisfaction. It was hard work but it was also a lot of fun.

JR: Lastly, what have you done since the Creature films?

RB: I created *Flipper* and was responsible for the dolphin's accomplishments, directed all thirty-four episodes of the show, directed twelve *Gentle Bens*, was second unit director on *Sea Hunt* with Lloyd Bridges, was technical advisor on *Day of the Dolphin*, did stunt work on Disney's *Twenty Thousand Leagues Under the Sea*, and was the second unit director on *Thunderball* and *Lucky Lady*.

NOTES

1. Perhaps this name is an "in" joke on Matheson's part. Bela Lugosi's original Hungarian name was Bela Belasko.

2. After one day's shooting, the original Billy, Frank Sinatra, walked off the set. Since 55mm prints could be shown only in theaters equipped with the specialized projectors, every scene had to be photographed twice. The first "take" was in 55mm, and the second in normal 35mm. Angry with the additional work load, Sinatra left the picture.

3. George Melies was one of the early filmmakers, and the father of the science-fiction film. He produced hundreds of short films between 1896 and 1903, when *A Trip to the Moon* was made, and was the first filmmaker to use motion picture special effects. By 1913 he was no longer able to sell his gimmick films and closed his studio. Melies thereafter faded from the limelight, discovered in 1929 selling toys in a French railroad station.

4. Downing *The Exorcist* is not a matter of iconoclasm, as is so often the case in critical circles regarding a successful property. Quite simply, it's a shoddy, sensational, far-from-classic horror film..

5. It has been oft-recounted that so thorough was Lugosi's identification with the Dracula role that, upon his death in 1956, he was buried in the Count's cape.

6. Glenn Strange has played the Frankenstein Monster more often than any other actor, save Karloff. Both essayed the role on three separate occasions. Strange went on to play Sam the Bartender in television's *Gunsmoke* until his death in 1973.

7. There are many visual representations of the loftiness of authority in *Cabinet of Dr. Caligari*. The two most striking examples are the unusually high seat in which the town clerk sits, towering above Caligari, and the exaggerated, inordinate number of steps that lead from the street to the front door of the police station.

8. It should be pointed out that there were two "live" monsters in *One Million Years B.C.* The first dinosaur that Tumak meets is really a photographically enlarged lizard. Originally, this was to have been a brontosaur. However, the schedule and budget did not allow for the several months additional filming the stop-motion monster would have required. The second "real" performer was a huge tarantula, which menaced Tumak but briefly.

9. It has been argued that the careful reconstruction of the dinosaurs was eviscerated by the anachronistic cavemen. While the break with history was for dramatic and not archeologic reality, it should be pointed out that recent discoveries have placed the age of man at 4.5 million years. While this is a far cry from 1,000,000 years, it is farther back than the 2 million-year date believed to be accurate when the picture was made. Perhaps future discoveries will prove both *One Million* and *One Million Years B.C.* prophetic!

10. In many of the shots, Godzilla was also a hand puppet or a small, limited-action machine. These foot-tall models were used for scenes requiring longshots of the destroyed Tokyo. To have built miniatures to the mansized monster's sclae would have been far too costly.

11. American director Terry Morse was responsible for taking the original Japanese *Godzilla* film and chopping it to pieces. When the film was reassembled, Morse's made-in-America sequences of reporter Raymond Burr on assignment in Tokyo were added. The scenes intercut rather poorly with the Japanese print since the original actors were not available. Ineffective doubles had to be used in Burr's scenes with the principals.

12. Projects Unlimited, recently disbanded, was the special-effects organization of Jim Danforth, model-maker Wah Chang, David Allen, Gene Warren, and Tim Barr. They worked not only on the films of George Pal, but on television's *Outer Limits* and commercial advertisements as well.

13. Process work is the means by which an actor, on a studio sound-stage, is photographically placed in a different setting. The actor performs before a blue screen, which does not photograph, and a prefilmed background is superimposed behind him by means of an optical printer. In some cases, the more convenient back screen projection is used. This is simply the projection of a prefilmed background on a huge screen before which the actors perform. The image is projected from the rear since the camera setups and actors would cast a shadow on the screen were it to be shown from the front. In the case of stop-motion projects, the small, foot-long models are placed in front of a prefilmed background projected on a back screen. The background film is advanced one frame, the model is manipulated, one frame of the monster and the background is photographed, and the process is repeated.

14. It is interesting to specualte why the original Maciste name was never used. Perhaps American distributors thought, ironically, that it sounded too foreign? In any case, since no film released in this country ever bore the name in its title, we shall never know how it would have been received.

15. It is ironic that at least three of Wells' films have featured germs as a catalyst: the cold germs of *First Men in the Moon*, the bacteria that slaughtered the martians in *War of the Worlds*, and the germ warfare that leveled mankind in *Things to Come*.

16. A glass painting is a means of creating spectacle on a limited budget. Simply put, a detailed painting is done on a huge (often nine-yard square) clear-glass, showing buildings, terrain, or whatever locale the director requires. A clear spot is left in the illustration where it will match the constructed, lifesize set. The painting is then set before the camera and both the artwork and the actors, in the distance, are photographed simultaneously. More recently, glass paintings have been

shot on separate strips of film and combined with the actors via an optical printer.

17. It can be persuasively argued that *all* cartoons, and not just those featuring fairy tale or fantasy elements, are fantasy films. However, the above-mentioned boundary must be observed to keep the subject manageable. Further, it can be fairly stated that *all* motion pictures are fantasy, since they create an event as interpreted through a filmmaker's imagination. Remember, with the exception of a documentary, no movie is "real."

18. Another well-known Lugosi legend is that he enacted Tchernobog for the Disney artists. His movements were photographed, then traced onto cels for the cartoon.

19. Multiplane photography is one of the great cartoon animation innovations. It was developed by Ub Iwerks of the Disney studio. Instead of photographing the character cel on one flat layer of background art, there are several levels of foreground, midground, and background. These are photographed vertically with a foot between each level. This allows the camera to zoom in through the scenery, creating the illusion of depth; it also allows the characters to "perform" on several different levels creating a sense of dimension. In *Sleeping Beauty*, some scenes required as many as twelve levels. For *Pinocchio*, the first shot of the film cost Disney over $150,000. It was a slow pan into Geppetto's shop from high in the sky, as buildings, trees, and other shops passed on either side of the camera.

20. It cannot be stressed too strongly that, quite often, the director or producer has no choice but to flood the screen with blood in order to draw patrons. One of the misfortunes of the horror film in modern times is that it often plays to a drive-in crowd that demands this sort of grotesque display. The validity of overdone gore in the contemporary detective films or in *The Exorcist* is, contrarily, a matter of personal taste and the filmmaker's own sense of responsibility.

INDEX

Abbott and Costello Meet Frankenstein, 61, 76, 79
Abbott and Costello Meet the Mummy, 87
Abbott, Bud, 15, 16
Abbott, John, 62
Abby, 55
Abominable Snowman of the Himalayas, The, 90, 96
Abrikosov, Andrei, 161
Ackland, Joss, 197
Adams, Julie, 94, 95, 96
Adams, Nick, 133
Adams, Tom, 226
Adventures of Ichabod and Mr. Toad, 213
Agar, John, 98
Ainley, Anthony, 52
Aladdin and His Lamp, 142
Alakazam the Great, 219
Alberoni, Sherri, 191
Alda, Alan, 53
Alexander Nevsky, 159
Alexander, Ross, 186
Alfred Hitchcock Presents, 230
Alias Nick Beal, 45–46
Ali Baba and the Forty Thieves, 142
Ali Baba Goes to Town, 140
Alice in Cartoonland, 209
Alice in Wonderland (1933), 184
Alice in Wonderland (1951), 213
Allbritton, Louise, 60
Allen, David, 202
Allen, Irwin, 105, 108
All That Money Can Buy, 45
Amber, Audry, 33
Ameche, Don, 22, 45
Ames, Leon, 27
Ames, Ramsey, 85
Anderson, Bibi, 47
Andre, Marcel, 78
Andress, Ursula, 199
Andrews, Barry, 66
Andrews, Dana, 46, 47
Andrews, Julie, 194
Andreyev, Boris, 160
Angel Comes to Brooklyn, 27
Angel, Heather, 205
Angel On My Shoulder, 45

Angels in the Outfield, 27
Angel Who Pawned Her Harp, The, 27
Ankers, Evelyn, 35, 74
Animal World, 105–107, 108, 121, 126
Arabian Nights, The, 142
Ardisson, Giorgio, 155
Aristocats, 217
Armstrong, Robert, 112–113, 115–117, 119
Armstrong, Todd, 157, 158
Arness, James, 105
Arnold, Edward, 45
Arnold, Jack, 95
Around the World in Eighty Days, 108
Asher, Jane, 31
Ashton, Roy, 80
Ashton, Sir Frederick, 197
Astaire, Fred, 27, 196
Asylum, 229
Atlantis, The Lost Continent, 178, 256
Atlas in the Land of the Cyclops, 154
Attack of the Giant Leeches, 127
Attack of the Monsters, 136
Attenborough, Richard, 195
Aylmer, Felix, 87
Aztec Mummy, The, 87

Babes in Toyland (1903), 184
Babes in Toyland (1924), 184
Babes in Toyland (1961), 186
Bacharach, Burt, 187
Back From the Dead, 47
Backus, Jim, 223
Bad Lord Byron, 27
Baer, Buddy, 96
Baker, Rick, 99
Baker, Tom, 149, 229
Balderston, John, 56
Ball, Lucille, 144
Bambi Meets Godzilla, 135
Barbarella, 180
Baron Munchausen, 163, 176
Barr, Tim, 131
Barret, Edith, 43
Barrett, Nancy, 68
Barrett, Ray, 99
Barrie, Sir James, 184
Barrymore, John Drew, 41

Barrymore, Lionel, 30
Barthory, Elizabeth, 67
Bassett, Ronald, 38
Bateman, Charles, 53
Battle for the Planet of the Apes, 180
Baum, Frank L., 184
Bava, Mario, 36–37, 127, 155, 225
Baxter, Anne, 45
Baxter, Warner, 15
Beach Girls and the Monster, 98
Beast from the Haunted Cave, 98
Beast from Twenty Thousand Fathoms, 120, 122, 124, 127
Beast of Hollow Mountain, 119, 124, 126, 230
Beast of the Yellow Night, 52
Beatles, The, 218
Beaumont, Charles, 256
Beaumont, Hugh, 98
"Beauty and the Beast," 76, 112
Beauty and the Beast (1946), 78–79, 81
Beauty and the Beast (1963), 81
Bedazzled, 49
Beddoe, Don, 165, 167
Beery, Wallace, 101
Beginning of the End, 124
Behind the Door, 55
Bellamy, Madge, 39
Bellamy, Ralph, 74
Bell, Book and Candle, 36
Benchley, Robert, 222
Beneath the Planet of the Apes, 180
Benet, Stephen Vincent, 45
Bennet, John, 226
Bennett, Joan, 68
Benny, Jack, 25
Berger, Senta, 111
Bergman, Ingmar, 30, 47, 54
Bernger, Elizabeth, 51
Berova, Olinka, 199
Berry, Michael, 39
Beswick, Martine, 108
Betty Boop, 209–210
Between Two Worlds, 28
Bewitched, 230
Bey, Turhan, 84
Beyond Tomorrow, 25

Bierce, Ambrose, 71
Bigfoot, 99
Billy the Kid vs. Dracula, 64–65
Birds, The, 98–99
Bishop's Wife, The, 27
Bissell, Whit, 32, 94
Bjornstrand, Gunnar, 30
Blackbeard's Ghost, 18
Blackman, Honor, 157
Black Sabbath, 37, 225
Black Scorpion, The, 126
Black Sunday, 36–37
Blackton, James, 207, 221
Blacula, 69
Blair, Linda, 54, 55
Blair, Janet, 35
Blithe Spirit, 16
Blob, The, 127, 131
Bloch, Robert, 49
Blood and Black Lace, 37
Blood Bath, 33
Blood Beast, 99
Blood of Dracula, 62
Blood of Dracula's Castle, 65
Blood of the Mummy's Tomb, 88–89
Blood on Satan's Claw, The, 52
Bloodsuckers, 69
Bloom, Claire, 20, 226
Blythe, Ann, 94
Body Snatcher, The, 19, 251
Bolger, Ray, 186, 188
Boone, Pat, 174
Borgnine, Ernest, 55
Borg, Veda Ann, 40
Boy and the Pirates, The, 202
Boyer, Charles, 222
Boy Who Cried Werewolf, The, 81
Bradbury, Ray, 120, 226
Brady, Scott, 111
Brandi, Walter, 63–64
Brass Bottle, The, 199, 201
Brawn, John, 204
Bray, John, 207
Bremer, Lucille, 27
Brennan, Walter, 165
Bricusse, Leslie, 24
Bride of Frankenstein, 82
Brides of Dracula, 62
Briscoe, Donald, 68
Broccoli, Albert, 196
Bronson, Charles, 174
Brotherhood of Satan, 53
Brown, Wally, 41
Browning, Ricou, 94, 96, 259
Browning, Robert, 190
Browning, Tod, 57, 67
Bruhl, Heidi, 148
Bryant, Bob, 87
Bug, 99, 259
Builliot, Alvaro, 87
Bull, Raymond, 260
Bunel, Louis, 204–205
Burger, Gottfried, 162
Burke, Billy, 188
Burke, Samson, 155
Burn, Witch, Burn, 35

Burroughs, Edgar Rice, 111
Burstyn, Ellen, 54, 55
Burton, Richard, 49
Byron, Arthur, 82

Cabinet of Dr. Caligari, 90–91, 99, 142, 260
Cabiria, 151
Cabot, Bruce, 112–113
Cagney, James, 186
Callas, Maria, 158
Caltiki, The Immortal Monster, 127
Cameron, Ian, 180
Campbell, William, 33
Canterville Ghost, The, 15
Cantor, Eddie, 140
Capote, Truman, 19
Capra, Frank, 27, 186, 187, 188
Capri, Anna, 53
Captain Kronos, Vampire Hunter, 70
Captain Nemo and the Underwater City, 174
Captain Sinbad, 148
Carey, Roland, 156
Carlson, Richard, 22, 25, 94, 138
Carlson, Veronica, 66
"Carmilla," 56, 58, 63, 67, 68
Carnera, Primo, 153
Carney, Alan, 41
Carnival of Souls, 30–31
Carousel, 27–28
Carradine, John, 38, 40, 61, 64, 85, 96, 226
Carroll, Leo G., 230
Carroll, Lewis, 184
Carson, John, 42
Carter, Ann, 22
Carter, Donnie, 202
Carter, John, 70
Casella, Alberto, 28
Case of Charles Dexter Ward, The, 37
Casper, The Friendly Ghost, 210
Cassavetes, John, 51
Castle of Doom, 58
Castle, Peggy, 47
Castle, William, 18, 51, 234, 258
Cat Girl, The, 79
Catman of Paris, 76, 79
Cat People, The, 22, 40, 75, 76, 79, 82, 259
Cawthorn, Joseph, 39
Celano, Guido, 154
Chandler, Helen, 28, 57
Chaney, Lon Jr., 35, 37, 38, 60, 61, 62, 69, 72, 74, 75, 76, 79, 82, 84, 85, 87, 103, 222, 226
Chaney, Lon Sr., 57, 58, 82, 93, 257
Chang, Wah, 131
Chapman, Ben, 94, 96
Charley and the Angel, 28
Charlie and the Chocolate Factory, 180
Chitty Chitty Bang Bang, 180, 196
Christine, Virginia, 85
Christmas Carol, A, 22–23
Churchill, Marguerite, 60
Ciannelli, Eduardo, 84
Cilento, Diane, 27
Cinderella, 213
Circus of Dr. Lao, The, 192
Clarkee, Gage, 62

Clark, Marlene, 70
Clark, Petula, 196
Clayton, Jack, 19
Clouzot, 259
Coca, Imogene, 230
Cockeyed Miracle, 27
Cocteau, Jean, 76–79, 81
Coe, Peter, 87
Cohen, Herman, 62
Cohl, Emile, 207
Coleman, Ronald, 187
Collier, Lesley, 196
Collins, Joan, 226
Collinson, Madelaine, 68
Collinson, Mary, 68
Conjure Wife, 35
Connecticut Yankee in King Arthur's Court, A, 190
Connell, Edward, 202
Connery, Sean, 163
Conqueror Worm, The, 38, 42
Conquest of Mycene, 156
Conquest of Space, 176
Conquest of the Planet of the Apes, 180
Conreid, Hans, 203
Conway, Tom, 40, 74
Cooke, Elisha, 41
Cook, Peter, 49
Cooper, Gary, 184
Cooper, Merian C., 112, 119, 199
Cooper, Wilkie, 158
Coppola, Francis Ford, 196
Corcoran, Donna, 27
Cordero, Joaquin, 42
Corelli, Marie, 44
Corlan, Anthony, 68
Corman, Roger, 31, 33, 37, 38, 51, 98, 127, 159, 223, 225
Corneliss, Joseph, 99
Cortez, Richardo, 45
Costello, Lou, 15, 16, 61
Cotton, Joseph, 20
Count Dracula, 67
Countess Dracula, 67
Count Yorga: Vampire, 67
Coutney, Chuck, 65
Coward, Noel, 16
Craiger, Laird, 45
Craig, James, 45
Craig, Michael, 229
Crawford, Joan, 99
Crawford, John, 157
Crazies, The, 43
Creation, 112
Creature From the Black Lagoon, 90, 94, 95, 96, 98, 259
Creature From the Haunted Sea, 98
Creature of Destruction, 33
Creatures the World Forgot, 108, 110
Creature Walks Among Us, The, 95
Creeping Flesh, 100
Crimson Cult, The, 33, 52
Crosby, Bing, 190, 213
Crowden, Graham, 198
Cry of the Banshee, 51
Cry of the Werewolf, 76, 82

Cummings, Robert, 27, 222
Cummings, Peggy, 46
Curse of Frankenstein, 42, 63
Curse of the Aztec Mummy, 87
Curse of the Cat People, 21–22, 55, 75, 257
Curse of the Demon, 46–47, 158
Curse of the Faceless Man, The, 87
Curse of the Mummy's Tomb, 88
Curse of the Undead, 63
Curse of the Voodoo, 42
Curse of the Werewolf, 79–81
Curtis, Dan, 68, 230, 234
Curtis, Tony, 142
Curusico, Enzo, 156
Cushing, Peter, 49, 62, 63, 67, 68, 69, 70, 87, 88, 96, 100, 225, 226, 229

Dagora, The Space Monster, 133
Dagover, Lil, 90
Dahl, Roald, 180, 234
Dali, Salvador, 204
Damn Yankees, 47, 49
Damon, Mark, 81
Danforth, Jim, 110, 111, 131, 153, 165, 192, 202, 224, 260
Daniel, Jennifer, 99
Danova, Cesare, 108
Dante's Inferno, 44
Darby O'Gill and the Little People, 163–164
D'Arcy, Alex, 65
Dark Shadows, 68, 230
Daughter of Dr. Jekyll, The, 79
David, Hal, 187
David, Thayer, 68
Davies, Rupert, 66
Davis, Roger, 68
Davis, Sammy, Jr., 234
Davis, Ursula, 33
Dawson, Anthony, 79–80
Day, Josette, 78
Day of the Dolphin, 259
Day The Earth Stood Still, 19
Day The World Ended, 98
Deadly Mantis, 124–126
Dead Men Walk, 60
Dead of Night, 222
Dead One, The, 41
Deane, Hamilton, 56
Death Takes a Holiday, 28, 30
Dee, Frances, 40
Dee, Sandra, 51
DeHavilland, Olivia, 186
Delgado, Marcel, 101, 102, 103, 112, 119, 124, 131, 153
DeLouise, Dom, 206
DeMille, Cecil B., 45, 151
Dempster, Carol, 45
Denahm, Maurice, 46
Denison, Leslie, 96
Denning, Richard, 94, 104, 126
Der Nibelungen, 139, 159, 171
DeSica, Vittorio, 147, 201
Destination Moon, 176, 256
Destroy All Monsters, 135
Destroy All Planets, 136
Deutsch, Ernst, 92

Devi, Kamala, 201
Devil and Daniel Webster, The, 45
Devil Rides Out, The, 39
Devil's Bride, The, 39
Devil's Eye, The, 47–49
Devil's Messenger, The, 223
Devil's Own, The, 38
Devil's Partner, The, 47
Devil's Rain, The, 55
DeWitt, Louis, 126
Diabolique, 259
Diaz, Vic, 52
Dickens, Charles, 22
Dinosaur and the Missing Link, The, 102
Dinosaurs, 128–131
Disembodied, The, 41
Disney, Walt, 18, 28, 99, 107, 163, 164, 165, 172, 173, 175, 180, 184, 185, 194, 201, 207, 209, 210, 213, 214, 217, 218, 219, 235, 256
Divine Comedy, The, 44
Dixon, Glen, 41
Dix, William, 195
Doboujinsky, Rostislav, 197
Donan, Stanley, 49
Donovan, 190
Dotrice, Karen, 194
Douglas, Kirk, 151, 159, 172
Down to Earth, 27
Doyle, Sir Arthur Conan, 101, 108
Dracula (novel), 39, 56, 71
Dracula (1930), 39, 57–58, 65, 71, 74, 234
Dracula (1975), 70
"*Dracula*" (TV Film), 68
Dracula A.D., 68
Dracula Has Risen From the Grave, 66
Dracula, Prince of Darkness, 65
Dracula's Daughter, 58–60, 82
Dracula's Quest, 58
Dracula vs. Frankenstein, 69
Dr. Doolittle, 195–196, 202
Dreams in a Witch House, 33
Dreams of a Rarebit Fiend, 203–204
Dr. Faustus, 49
Dr. Jekyll and Mr. Hyde, 52, 72
Dr. Satan, 42
Dr. Terror's Gallery of Horrors, 226
Druten, John van, 36
Dryer, Carl, 58
Duel of the Titans, 154
Dumbo, 210
Dumbrille, Douglas, 76
Dunne, Irene, 205
Dunwitch Horror, 51
Duprez, June, 140
Durante, Jimmy, 176
Dwan, Dorothy, 184
Dwyer, Hilary, 51

Earthbound, 15
Earth vs. the Flying Saucers, 121
Eastman, Marilyn, 42
Eberhardt, Norma, 62
Eddy, Nelson, 25
Eden, Barbara, 192, 194, 201, 230
Eden, Mark, 33
Edmonds, Louis, 68

Edwards, Elaine, 87
Eegah!, 98
Eggar, Samantha, 195
Eisely, Anthony, 111
Elliott, Denholm, 226
Elliott, Laura, 105
Ellison, James, 41
Emery, John, 32
Enchanted Forest, The, 202
Endore, Guy, 71
English, Maria, 32
Engstrom, Jean, 41
Equinox, 202
Erikson, Leif, 142
Escape From the Planet of the Apes, 180
Evans, Clifford, 80
Evans, Dame Edith, 24
Evans, Maurice, 51
Everything's Ducky, 202
Exorcist, The, 43, 53, 54–55, 260, 261
Exorcist: Part II, The, 55
Eyer, Richard, 144
Eyre, Jane, 40

Fabulous World of Jules Verne, 176
Face the Flag, 176
"Facts in the Casse of M. Valdemar," 51
Fairbanks, Douglas, Jr., 142, 201, 258
Fairbanks, Douglas, Sr., 140, 147
Fame is the Name of the Game, 230
Fantasia, 211–212, 213, 217
Farmer, Suzan, 65
Farrow, Mia, 51
Fearless Vampire Killers, The, or Pardon Me, But Your Teeth Are in My Neck, 66
Feher, Friedrich, 90
Felix the Cat, 209
Feller, Catherine, 80
Field, Betty, 222
Field, Sally, 230
Fields, W.C., 184
Finch, Peter, 187
Finian's Rainbow, 196
Finney, Albert, 23
Finney, Charles, 192, 194
First Men on The Moon, 178, 179, 193
Fisher, Terence, 63
Five Thousand Fingers of Dr. T., The, 203
Fleischer, Max, 190, 207, 209, 210
Fleming, Ian, 196
Flesh and Fantasy, 222
Fletcher, Bramwell, 82
Flipper, 259
Flying Nun, The, 230
Flying Serpent, The, 93, 94
Foch, Nina, 76
Fonda, Jane, 180
Fontaine, Joan, 16
Foran, Dick, 84
Forbidden Planet, 172
Ford, Wallace, 84, 85
Forest, Jean Claude, 180
Forest, Mark, 153, 154, 155, 156
For Heaven's Sake, 27
Forneaux, Yvonne, 87
Fosse, Bob, 198

Four Skulls of Jonathan Drake, The, 41
Franciscus, James, 138, 180
Francis in the Haunted House, 16
Frankenstein (novel), 39, 71
Frankenstein (1931), 72, 76
Frankenstein (1957), 87
Frankenstein Conquers the World, 133
Frankenstein Meets the Mummy, 82
Frankenstein Meets the Wolfman, 76, 82, 87
Frankenstein 1970, 160
Frankenstein (3D), 70
Franks, Chloe, 226
Franlin, Pamela, 18, 20
Franz, Arthur, 47
Frazer, Robert, 39
Freund, Karl, 93
Frid, Jonathan, 68, 230
Friedkin, William, 55
Fritsch, Gunther, 257
Frobe, Gert, 196
Frogs, 99
From Hell It Came, 96
Frye, Dwight, 57, 58, 60
Fugiama, Shiho, 162
Funicello, Annette, 186
Fury, Ed, 156

Gable, Clark, 188
Gahagan, Helen, 199
Gamera, The Invincible, 136
Gamera vs. Monster X, 136
Gamera vs. Zigra, 136
Ganja and Hess, 70
Gappa: The Triphibian Monster, 135
Garber, Matthew, 194
Garces, Mauricio, 63
Garcia, Eddie, 52
Gardner, Ava, 21, 203
Garfield, John, 28
Garfield, John, Jr., 150
Gargoyles, 234
Garland, Judy, 188, 214
Garrani, Ivo, 36–37
Genesis II, 135
Genie, The, 199, 201
Gentle Ben, 259
Geraghty, Erin, 196
German, Nane, 78
Gertie the Dinosaur, 207
Ghidrah, The Three-Headed Monster, 133–
134
Ghost and Mrs. Muir, The, 16, 21
"Ghost and Mrs. Muir, The," (TV), 230
Ghost Breakers, 15, 40, 234
Ghost Busters, 234
Ghost Catchers, 15
Ghost Goes West, The, 15
Ghost of Frankenstein, 76
Ghost of Slumber Mountain, 103
Ghost Story, 234
Giant Behemoth, The, 126
Giant From the Unknown, The, 96
Giant Gila Monster, The, 127
Giants of Thessaly, 157
Gigantis, The Fire Monster, 123, 131
Girotti, Massimo, 157

Gloriani, Tina, 63
Gnome-Mobile, The, 164–165
Godfather, The, 43, 53, 115
Godzilla, 122–123, 135, 139, 162, 180, 260
Godzilla's Counter Attack (see Gigantis, The
Fire Monster)
Godzilla's Revenge, 135
Godzilla vs. Gigan, 135
Godzilla vs. Mechagodzilla, 135–136
Godzilla vs. Megalon, 135
Godzilla vs. the Sea Monster, 134–135
Godzilla vs. the Smog Monster, 135
Godzilla vs. the Thing, 133
Goetzke, Bernard, 139
Gogol, Nikolai, 36
Golden Voyage of Sinbad, The, 148–150, 258
Golem: How He Came to Be, The, 90, 92–93
Golem: The Monster of Fate, 92
Goliath Against the Giants, 154
Goliath Against the Vampires, 154
Goliath and the Barbarians, 153
Goliath and the Dragon, 153
Gordon, Bert I., 22, 124, 126, 167, 170, 202
Gordon, Christine, 40
Gordon, Frank, 156
Gordon, Mitchel, 154
Gordon, Ruth, 51
Gordon, Susan, 22
Gorgo, 127–128, 131
Grahame, Kenneth, 213
Granach, Alexander, 57
Grant, Cary, 27, 184, 202
Grant, Kathryn, 144
Grant, Lawrence, 72
Graves, Teresa, 70
Gray, Charles, 39
Gray, David, 58
Greatest Gift, The, 27
Great Rupert, The, 176
Greene, Richard, 226
Green, Nigel, 157, 158, 258
Grey, Virginia, 104
Griffies, Ethel, 72
Griffith, D. W., 44, 103, 108
Guida, Wandisa, 154
Guinness, Alex, 24
Gulliver's Travels, 190–191, 209, 210
Guy Named Joe, A, 25
Gwenn, Edmund, 27, 203
Gwillim, Jack, 157
Gwynne, Anne, 35
Gwynn, Michael, 66, 157

Hackett, Buddy, 203, 223
Haggard, H. Rider, 199
Hale, Creighton, 45
Haley, Jack, 188
Half-Human, 96
Halfway House, 16
Hall, Anthony, 178
Hall, Grayson, 68
Hall, Harvey, 68
Hall, John, 98, 142
Halperin, Brothers, 40, 45
Hama, Mei, 131, 135
Hamilton, Margaret, 188, 190

Hammerstein, Oscar, 27–28
Hand of Death, The, 98
Hands of the Ripper, 33
Hanley, Jerry, 66
Hardman, Karl, 42
Hardwicke, Sir Cedric, 30
Hardy, Oliver, 184
Hargitay, Mickey, 154
Harlow, Jean, 188
Harris, Brad, 154
Harris, Jack H., 131
Harris, Jule, 20
Harris, Richard, 24
Harrison, Rex, 16, 24, 36, 190
Harrison, Sandra, 62
Harryhausen, Ray, 105, 108, 110, 111, 119,
120, 121, 122, 126, 131, 138, 144, 148, 150,
157, 158, 165, 167, 174, 178, 179, 190, 255,
258–259
Hartley, Mariette, 67
Harvey, 202
Harvey, Laurence, 223
Haskin, Byron, 148
Hatfield, Hurd, 190
Haunted Palace, 37, 38
Haunting of Hill House, 19
Haunting, The, 19–20, 22, 54, 257, 259
Hawdon, Robin, 110
Hayden, Linda, 52
Hayworth, Rita, 27
Headless Ghost, 18
Heaven Can Wait, 45
Heaven Only Knows, 27
Hedley, Jack, 38
Hefner, Hugh, 35
Helm, Anne, 170
Helm, Fay, 74
Hellstrom Chronicle, The, 99
Hendry, Ian, 226
Henesy, David, 68
Henry, Charlotte, 184
Hephaestus Plague, The, 99
Herbert, Charles, 202
Herbert, Victor, 184
Hercules, 151–153, 157
Hercules Against the Barbarians, 156
Hercules Against the Moon Men, 156
Hercules Against the Sons of the Sun, 156
Hercules and the Captive Women, 154–155
Hercules and the Tyrants of Babylon, 156
Hercules in New York, 156
Hercules in Rome, 154
Hercules in the Haunted World, 155
Hercules in the Vale of Woe, 156
Hercules of the Desert, 156
Hercules, Prisoner of Evil, 156
Hercules, Samson and Ulysses, 156
Hercules the Invincible, 156
Hercules Unchained, 153
Hercules vs. the Giant Warriors, 156
Here Comes Mr. Jordan, 25, 45
Herrmann, Bernard, 158
Hessler, George, 51
Heston, Charlton, 108, 180
Heyer, Martha, 22
Hilligoss, Candice, 31

Hilton, James, 186, 187, 188
Hitchcock, Alfred, 55, 98, 99, 259
Hobson, Valerie, 71
Holden, Gloria, 58
Holden, Joyce, 27
Holder, Geoffrey, 195
Hold that Ghost, 15
Hollaway, Stanley, 46
Holt, Tim, 124
Homer, 151
Homicidal, 258
Homolka, Oscar, 224
Honda, Inoshira, 96
Hooper, Ewan, 66
Hope, Bob, 15, 40
"Hop Frog," 31
Horn Blows at Midnight, The, 25
Horror Hotel, 37
Horror of Dracula, 42, 62–63, 65, 79, 87, 88
Horror of Party Beach, 98
House of Black Death, 38
House of Dark Shadows, 68
House of Dracula, 61, 76
House of Frankenstein, 61, 76
House on Haunted Hill, 18
House of Usher, 222
House that Dripped Blood, The, 226
How A Mosquito Operates, 207
Howard, Leslie, 28, 205
Howard, Shemp, 142
Howe, James Wong, 184
Howes, Sally Anne, 196
How the West was Won, 224
Hubbard, John, 84
Hughes, Howard, 144
Hull, Henry, 71–72, 74, 75, 76, 82
Humorous Phases of Funny Faces, 207
Hunnicutt, Gayle, 20
Hunter, Jeffrey, 38
Hunter, Ross, 187
Hunter, Tab, 47
Hunt, Martita, 63
Hurd, Earl, 207
Hussey, Ruth, 15
Huston, Walter, 45
Hutton, Robert, 51
Hyer, Martha, 178

I Am Legend, 20
I Dream of Jennie, 38, 230
I'll Never Forget You, 205
Illusiono, 18
Illustrated Man, The, 206
I Married A Witch, 35
I Married An Angel, 25
Incredible Mr. Limpet, 218
Incredible Shrinking Man, The, 20, 95
Ingram, Rex, 141, 142
Innocents, The, 18–19, 20, 34
In Search of the Castaways, 180–183
Invisible Creature, The, 18
Invisible Woman, 82
Island At the Top of the World, 180, 183
Island of the Dinosaurs, 108
It!, 93
It Came From Beneath the Sea, 121

It Came From Outer Space, 95
It Grows on Trees, 205
It Happened Tomorrow, 205
It's About Time, 230
It's A Good Life, 27, 187
Ivan the Terrible, 159
I've Lived Before, 33
Ives, Burl, 201
I Walked with a Zombie, 40–41
I was a Teenage Werewolf, 32–33, 62
Iwerks, Ub, 99, 209, 261

Jack and the Witch, 219
Jackson, Freda, 138
Jackson, Shirley, 19
Jack the Giant Killer, 165–167, 201, 202
Jacobs, Arthur P., 195
Jacobs, W. W., 199
Jaffe, Sam, 51, 187
James, Henry, 18
James, M. R., 46
Jameson, Joyce, 223
Janson, Horst, 70
Janowitz, Hans, 90
Jason and the Argonauts, 157–158, 258, 261
Jaws, 53, 99, 115, 259
Jeffries, Lionel, 179, 196
Jenkins, Megs, 19
Jesse James Meets Frankenstein's Daughter, 65
Jewel of the Seven Stars, The, 89
Jewison, Norman, 255
Johann, Zita, 83
Johns, Glynis, 16, 94, 194
Johns, Mervyn, 16
Johnson, Ben, 119
Johnson, Margaret, 35
Johnson, Michael, 67
Johnson, Noble, 40, 83, 112
Johnson, Richard, 20
Johnson, Van, 25, 190
Johnston, Julianne, 140
Jones, Darby, 40
Jones, Dean, 18
Jones, Daine, 42, 70
Jones, Griffith, 94
Jones, Gus and Constance, 94
Jones, L. Q., 53
Journey Back to Oz, 218
Journey Into the Unknown, 230
Journey to the Beginning of Time, 110–111
Journey to the Center of the Earth, 107, 108, 173–174
Judd, Edward, 179
Jungle Book, The, 217
Jurgens, Curt, 53
Justin, John, 140

Karlen, John, 68
Karloff, Boris, 19, 33, 41, 42, 57, 58, 60, 61, 62, 72, 76, 82, 83, 88, 89, 93, 202, 225, 230, 257, 260
Kellaway, Cecil, 35
Kelley, Barry, 165
Kelley, Clyde, 41
Kelly, Nancy, 35
Kemper, Charles, 27

Kennedy, George, 187
Kerr, Deborah, 18, 19
Keyes, Evelyn, 142
Kier, Andrew, 65, 88
Kiley, Richard, 197, 198
King Kong, 40, 76, 93, 96, 103, 104, 112–115, 117, 126, 139, 142, 180, 258
King Kong Escapes, 135
King Kong vs. Godzilla, 131–133
King of Kings, 45
King of the Zombies, 40
King, Perry, 53
Kipling, Rudyard, 71
Kirk, Tommy, 202
Kishida, Mori, 68
Kiss of the Vampire, 64
Kleinbach, Henry, 184
Knotts, Don, 218
Knowles, Patrick, 76
Knox, Elyse, 84
Koko the Clown, 209
Korda, Alexander, 140, 142, 144, 147, 150, 161, 201, 202, 214
Korg, 234
Koschina, Sylvia, 152, 153
Kosleck, Martin, 87
Kostal, Irwin, 196
Kovaks, Nancy, 157
Kramer, Stanley, 203
Krauss, Werner, 90
Krimhild's Revenge, 139
Kruger, Otto, 60
Kubrick, Stanley, 204, 255
Kulle, Jarl, 49
Kulp, Nancy, 202

Lady From Shanghai, 69
La Fanu, Sheridan, 56
Lahr, Bert, 188
Lake of Dracula, 68
Lake, Veronica, 35
Lamas, Fernando, 108
La Morte In Vacanza, 28
Lanchbery, John, 197
Landis, Carole, 103, 108
Land of the Lost, 234
Landon, Michael, 32
Land that Time Forgot, The, 111
Land Unknown, 107
Lane, Michael, 156
Lang, Fritz, 90, 137
Lang, Judith, 67
Lang, Hope, 230
Langton, Paul, 96
Lansbury, Angela, 201
Lanz, Walter, 207
Laplanche, Rosemary, 20
Larsen, Keith, 39
Lasky, Jesse, Sr., 119
Last Days of Pompeii, 117, 153
Last of the Vikings, 159
Latimer, Michael, 108
Laughton, Charles, 15
Laurel, Stan, 184
Law, John Philip, 149, 180
Ledebut, Frederick, 41

Lederer, Francis, 62
Lee, Anna, 165
Lee, Christopher, 33, 37, 38, 42, 49, 62, 63, 64, 65, 66, 67, 68, 69–70, 82, 87, 88, 100, 155, 226, 234
Legend of Boggy Creek, 99
Legend of Hell House, The, 20
Legend of Sleepy Hollow, 213
Legend of the Seven Golden Vampires, 70
Leiber, Fritz, 35
Leon, Valerie, 88
Leopard Man, The, 76
Leprince, Madam of Beaumont, 76
Let's Live Again, 32
Lettinger, Rudolph, 90
Levine, Joseph E., 153
Levin, Henry, 147–148
Levin, Ira, 51
Lewis, Jerry, 16
Lewis, Sheldon, 45
Lewton, Val, 22, 40, 75, 76, 79, 257, 259
Lisistrata, 111
Little Lulu, 210
Little Nemo, 207
Little Prince, The, 197–198
Living Idol, The, 33
Lom, Herbert, 174, 190
Loch Ness Monster, The, 112
Lockwood, Gary, 170
Lofting, Hugh, 195
Lombard, Carole, 45
Loos, Theodor, 139
Lopez, Sylvia, 153
Lorre, Peter, 172, 202
Lost Continent, The, 105
Lost Horizon (1936), 186, 187
Lost Horizon (1973), 187
Lost in Space, 108, 230
Lost World of Sinbad, The, 162
Lost World, The, 101–102, 103, 105, 111, 112, 139
Lost World, The (1960), 107–108, 126
Lotis, Dennis, 37
Louise, Anita, 186
Lourie, Eugene, 127, 128
Lovecraft, H. P., 33, 37, 51
Loves of Hercules, 154
Lowe, Edmund, 202
Lowens, Curt, 79
Lowery, Robert, 85
Loyd, Richard, 156
Lubin, Arthur, 147
Lucky Lady, 259
Lugosi, Bela, 39–40, 41, 56–58, 60, 61, 62, 67, 71, 76, 74, 87, 257, 260, 261
Likas, Paul, 172
Lummis, Dayton, 165
Lust for a Vampire, 67

Macbeth (1948), 35–36
Macbeth (1971), 35–36
Maccauly, Charles, 69
MacDonald, Jeanette, 25
MacGinnis, Niall, 46, 47, 158
Maciste the Mighty, 151
Mack, Helen, 115

Maclaine, Barton, 32, 104
Maclaine, Shirley, 53
MacMurray, Fred, 28, 199
Macnee, Patrick, 69
MacRae, Gordon, 28
MacReady, Michael, 67
Macumba Love, 41
Mad About Men, 94
Mad Doctor of Blood Island, 99
Madison, Guy, 124
Madison, Rock, 96
Magic Boy, 218–219
Magic Carpet, The, 144
Magic Serpent, The, 161
Magic Sword, The, 167, 170
Magic Voyage of Sinbad, The, 159
Mahoney, Jack, 33, 107
Majin, 162
Malleson, Miles, 140
Maltese Bippy, The, 81
Man Beast, The, 96
Man Who Could Work Miracles, The, 201
Mangano, Silvana, 151
Manners, David, 83
Mansfield, Jayne, 154
Man Who Wagged His Tail, The, 201, 202
Marais, Jean, 78
March, Fredric, 28, 35
Markham, Monte, 30, 230
Marlow, Christopher, 49
Marshall, William, 69, 144
Marsh, Reginald, 24
Marston, John, 115
Martin, Dean, 16
Martin, Dick, 81
Martinelli, Elsa, 63
Martin, Keith, 196
Martin, Mary, 184
Mary Poppins, 164, 192, 194, 195, 196, 201, 202, 256
Mason, James, 21, 172, 173, 174
Masque of the Red Death, 31–32, 38, 52
Massey, Daniel, 229
Massey, Ilona, 76
Master of Horror, 222
Master of the World, 174–175
Master of the World (novel), 174–175
Matheson, Richard, 20
Mathews, Kerwin, 81, 99, 144, 165, 191, 192, 234
Mathias, Bob, 154
Matson, Norman, 35
Mature, Victor, 103
Maupassant, Guy de, 71
Maxwell, Lois, 20
Mayer, Carl, 90
Mayne, Ferdy, 66
"May We Come In?," 27
Maze, The, 94
McClure, Doug, 111
McDowall, Roddy, 20, 180
McGavin, Darren, 234
McGowran, Jack, 66
McGee, Vonetta, 69
McKay, Windsor, 203, 207
Mead, Robert, 196

Medea, 158
Medina, Patricia, 124
Meet Mr. Kringle, 203
Meet Mr. Lucifer, 46
Megowan, Don, 95, 96
Melies, George, 35, 178, 260
Menjou, Adolphe, 44
Menzies, William Cameron, 94, 184
Mephisto Waltz, 53
Mercier, Michelle, 225
Meredith, Burgess, 226
Meredith, Judi, 165
Metropolis, 139
Middleton, Charles, 20
Midsummer Night's Dream, A, 185
Mifune, Toshiro, 133, 162
Mighty Gorga, The, 111
Mighty Joe Young, 119, 258
Mighty Ursus, 156
Milland, Ray, 15, 45
Miller, Jason, 54, 55
Mills, Juliet, 55
Mimieux, Yvette, 30, 177, 223
Minnelli, Liza, 218
Minotaur, The, 154
Miracle in Milan, 201
Miracle on 34th Street, 203
Miranda, 94
Mitchell, Thomas, 45, 222
Mobley, Roger, 165
Mole Men Battle the Son of Hercules, The, 155–156
Mole People, The, 98
"Monkey's Pay, The," 199
Monster From the Ocean Floor, 98
Monster of Piedras Blancas, The, 98
Monster That Challenged the World, The, 123–124
Monster Zero, 134
Montana, Bull, 101
Montand, Yves, 33, 145
Montevecchi, Liliane, 33
Montez, Maria, 142, 258
Montgomery, Elizabeth, 230
Montgomery, Robert, 24
Monty Python and the Holy Grail, 170–171
Moore, Dudley, 49
Moore, Kieron, 163
Moore, Mary Tyler, 206
Moore, Terry, 119
Moran, Peggy, 84
More, Kenneth, 24
Morell, Andre, 88
Morgan, Frank, 27
Morgan, Henry, 28
Morgan the Pirate, 153
Morissey, Paul, 70
Morris, Kirk, 154, 156
Morrow, Jeff, 95
Morse, Barry, 229
Morse, Terry, 260
Mr. Peabody and the Mermaid, 94
Mr. Stop, 207
Muir, Jean, 186
Mulhare, Edward, 230
Mulligan, Robert, 53

Mummy's Curse, The, 85–87
Mummy's Ghost, The, 85
Mummy's Hand, The, 84, 85, 87
Mummy's Shroud, The, 88
Mummy's Tomb, The, 84–85, 87
Mummy, The (1932), 42, 63, 72, 82–84, 93
Mummy, The (1959), 82, 87–88, 144, 165, 191, 192, 294
Muni, Paul, 45
Munro, Janet, 163
Murnau, F. W., 56
Murphy, Michael, 67
My Favorite Martian, 47
My Mother the Car, 230
My Son, The Vampire, 62
Mysterious Island, 174

Naish, J. Carroll, 61, 69
Naismith, Laurence, 158
Nascimbene, Mario, 108
Nathan, Robert, 20
Neame, Christopher, 68
Nelson, Edwin, 47
Nelson, Lori, 95
Newland, John, 230
Newland, Marvin, 135
Newley, Anthony, 195
Newman, Kurt, 256
Next Voice You Hear, The, 205
Ney, Marie, 38
Nicholas, Denise, 69
Nicholson, Jack, 202
Night Gallery, 234
Night of Dark Shadows, 68
Night of the Blood Beast, 98
Night of the Living Dead, 42–43, 70
Night of the Witches, 39
Night Stalker, The, 68, 234
Niven, David, 25, 27, 70
Nosferatu, 56–57, 62, 66, 70
Novak, Kim, 36

Oakie, Jack, 25
Oblong Box, The, 42, 51
O'Brien, Willis, 101, 102, 103, 105, 107, 112, 115, 117, 119, 120, 124, 126, 133, 135, 138, 235, 259
O'Connell, Arthur, 192, 230
O'Connor, Donald, 147, 255
Octoman, 99, 100
O'Dea, Judy, 42
Off On a Comet, 108
O'Hara, Maureen, 142
O'Keefe, Dennis, 76
Oland, Warner, 71
Old Mother Riley, 62
Olson, Ole, 15
On A Clear Day You Can See Forever, 33–34
On Borrowed Time, 30
Once Upon a Time, 202
One Million B.C., 103, 105, 108, 142
One Million Years B.C., 108–110, 111, 260
One Step Beyond, 230
One Touch of Venus, 203
One Wish Too Many, 201
Osborne, Vivienne, 45

Oswald the Rabbit, 209
Other One, The, 47
Other, The, 53–54
Ouspenskaya, Maria, 74, 76
Outer Limits, 230
Outward Bound, 28
Owens, Dickie, 87

Paget, Debra, 37
Paige, Robert, 60
Palance, Jack, 68, 234
Pal, David, 224
Pal, George, 110, 176, 177, 178, 193, 194, 195, 223, 224, 255–256
Pandora and the Flying Dutchman, 21
Paradise Lost, 44
Parely, Mila, 78
Parker, Eddie, 76, 87
Parker, Eleanor, 28
Parker, Jean, 25
Parker, Reg, 154, 156
Parkins, Barbara, 229
Passionate Witch, The, 35
Pastell, George, 87
Pate, Michael, 63
Patrick, Butch, 202
Patrick, Nigel, 226
Peabody's Mermaid, 94
Pearce, Jacqueline, 99
Peel, David, 63
Peppard, George, 206
Perreau, Gigi, 27
Perry, Roger, 67
Perschy, Maria, 38
Peter Pan, 184, 214
Peter Rabbit and Tales of Beatrix Potter, 196–197
Peterson, Pete, 126
Phantasmagoria, 207
Phantom Speaks, The, 45
Phantom Toolbooth, The, 218
Pharoah's Curse, The, 87
Pichel, Irving, 60
Picture Mommy Dead, 22
Pierce, Jack, 72, 79, 81
Pied Piper of Hamelin, The (1953), 190
Pied Piper of Hamelin, The (1971), 190
Pierreux, Jacqueline, 225
Pink, Sidney, 131
Pinocchio, 172, 210–211, 261
Pit and the Pendulum, 38
Pitt, Ingrid, 67
Place of One's Own, A, 16
Plague of the Zombies, 42
Planet of the Apes, 81, 95, 180
Planet of the Vampires, 37
Pleasance, Donald, 229
Plowman, Melinda, 64
Poe, Edgar Allan, 31, 37, 38, 42, 44, 51, 52, 202, 225
Polanski, Roman, 35, 51, 65, 66
Pommer, Erich, 90
Poor Devil, 234
Popeye, 210
Porter, E.S., 203
Porter, Nyree Dawn, 226

Portrait of Dorian Gray, 190
Portrait of Jennie, 20–21
Poseidon Adventure, The, 108
Possession of Joel Delany, 53
Poston, Tom, 201
Powell, Dick 27, 186, 205
Powell, Eddie, 88
Powell, William, 94
Power, Tyrone, 205
Prehistoric Women (1950), 105
Prehistoric Women (1966), 108
Price, Dennis, 27
Price, Vincent, 18, 31, 33, 37, 38, 51, 52, 57, 174, 202, 223, 225, 259
Prine, Andrew, 39
Producers, The, 147
Puppetoons, 176, 255

Qualen, John, 142
Quarry, Robert, 67
Quinn, Anthony, 142

Rabin, Jack, 126
Rains, Claude, 25, 45, 74, 108
Ralph, Hanna, 139
Ramsey, Ward, 128
Randall, Tony, 177, 192, 201, 256–257
Randolph, Jane, 22, 75
Rascel, Renato, 63
Rasulala, Thalmus, 69
Rathbone, Basil, 170, 223
Ravaioli, Iscaro, 64
Raven, The, 84, 202
Raymond, Paula, 65
Reason, Rex, 95
Reason, Rhodes, 135
Reed, Oliver, 80–81
Reed, Philip, 104
Rees, Yvette, 38
Reeves, Steve, 147, 151, 152, 153, 154, 155, 158
Reincarnation of Peter Proud, 34
Reicher, Frank, 85, 115
Remy, Helene, 63
Rennie, Michael, 19, 108
Reptile, The, 99
Reptilicus, 131
Retik, Tommy, 27, 203
Return of Court Yorga, 67
Return of Dracula, 62
Return of Dr. Satan, The, 42
Return of the Giant Majin, 162
Return of the Giant Monsters, 126
Return of the Vampire, 60
Return to the Planet of the Apes, 219, 221
Revenge of Frankenstein, 47
Revenge of Hercules, The (see *Goliath and the Dragon*)
Revenge of the Creature, The, 94, 95, 259
Revenge of the Zombies, 40
Revill, Clive, 20, 197
Revolt of the Zombies, 40, 45
Reynolds, Marjorie, 16
Richardson, John, 36, 108, 110, 199
Richardson, Sir Ralph, 226
Rich, Steven, 79

Richter, Paul, 139
Ridley, Judy, 42
Rimsky-Korsakov, 159
Ripper, Michael, 80
Rivas, Carlo, 124, 126
Roach, Hal, 103
Robertson, Dale, 144
Robin Hood, 172, 217
Robinson, Edward G., 222
Robot vs. the Aztec Mummy, 87
Rob Roy, 172
Robur the Conqueror, 174, 175, 176
Rodan, 123
Rodgers, Richard, 25, 27–28
Rolanda, Maria Luisa, 64
Romain, Yvonne, 80
Romero, Cesar, 105
Romero, George, 42, 43
Rooney, Mickey, 186, 202
Rosemary's Baby, 49–51
Rounseville, Robert, 222
Rowen, Dan, 81
Rozsa, Miklos, 150
Ruffo, Leonora, 155
Russell, Gail, 15, 16
Rutherford, Margaret, 16
Ryan, Peggy, 25
Ryan, Robert, 174

Sabu, 140, 141, 142, 144
Sabu and the Magic Ring, 144
Sadko (see *The Magic Voyage of Sinbad*)
Saga of the Viking Women and their Voyage to the Waters of the Great Sea Serpent, 159
Salmanova, Lyda, 92
Samson and Delilah, 151
Samson and the Mighty Challenge, 156
Samson and the Seven Miracles of the World, 154
Samson in King Solomon's Mines, 156
Samson vs. the Giant King, 156
Samurai Pirate (see *The Lost World of Sinbad*)
Sands, Tommy, 186
Sarrazin, Michael, 34
Satanic Rites of Dracula, 70
Savalas, Telly, 100
Scared Stiff, 16
Scars of Dracula, 66
Schneer, Charles H., 121, 138, 174
Schreck, Max, 56–57
Schroeder, Greta, 56
Scott, Gordon, 154, 156
Scream, Blacula, Scream, 69
Scrooge, 23–24, 197
Sea Hunt, 259
Search for Bridey Murphy, The, 33
Second Hundred Years, The, 230
Secret of Dorian Gray, The, 190
Selby, David, 68
Sellers, Peter, 256
Serling, Rod, 234
Seuss, Dr., 203
Seven Faces of Dr. Lao, 110, 177, 192, 194, 201, 255, 256–257
Seven Footprints to Satan, 45
Seventh Seal, The, 30, 31, 32, 49

Seventh Voyage of Sinbad, The, 121, 144–145, 150, 165, 167, 258
Severn, Billy, 202
Seymour, Jane, 151
Shaggy Dog, The, 202
Shakespeare, William, 35
Sharpe, Albert, 163
Shawn, Dick, 147
She (1935), 199
She (1965), 199
She Creature, The, 32, 33
Sheldon, Gene, 201
Shelley, Mary, 71
Shelly, Barbara, 65, 79
Sherman, Robert and Richard, 194, 196
Shields, Arthur, 79
Shvorin, Alexi, 160
Siegfried, 139
Silvers, Phil, 142
Sim, Alistair, 24
Simon, King of the Witches, 39
Simon, Simone, 22, 75
Sinatra, Frank, 260
Sinbad and the Eye of the Tiger, 150–151
Sinbad the Sailor, 142, 258
Sixth Sense, The, 234
Skull, The, 49
Sleeping Beauty, 214–217, 261
Sleep, Wayne, 196, 197
Slime People, The, 98
Sloane, Edward van, 57, 60, 82
Small, Edward, 165
Smith, Dick, 54
Smith, Kent, 22, 75
Snake People, The, 42
Snow Creature, 96
Snowdon, Leigh, 95
Snow Maiden, 219
Snow Queen, 219
Snow White, 172, 209, 210–211, 217
Son of Ali Baba, 144
Son of Dracula, 60
Son of Godzilla, 134–135
Son of Hercules in the Land of Fire, 156
Son of Kong, 103, 115–117, 119
Son of Samson, 153–154
Son of Sinbad, 144, 258
Sorrows of Satan, The, 44–45
Sothern, Ann, 230
Spain, Fay, 154
Spider, The, 126
Spinetti, Victor, 198
Stairway to Heaven, 25–27
Stanwyck, Barbara, 222
Steamboat Willie, 209
Steele, Alan, 154, 156
Steele, Barbara, 33, 36–37
Steele, Tommy, 196
Steiger, Rod, 226
Steinrueck, Albert, 92
St. John, Jill, 108
Stensgaard, Yutte, 67
Stephens, Martin, 18
Stevens, Onslow, 61
Stevens, Rock, 156
Stewart, James, 27, 36, 202

Stockwell, Dean, 51, 234
Stoker, Bram, 56, 58, 62, 65, 67, 71, 89
Storch, Larry, 234
Strange, Glenn, 61, 62, 260
Stranger in the Night, 16
Strangler Of the Swamp, 20
Streisand, Barbra, 33
Strong, Arnold, 156
Student of Prague (1913), 44
Student of Prague (1926), 44
Sugar Hill, 42
Sullivan, Liam, 170
Sullivan, Pat, 209
Supernatural, 45
Swift, Jonathan, 190
Sword and the Dragon, 160–161, 162
Sword and the Stone, 217
Sydow, Max von, 30, 54, 55

Tabitha, 230
Talbott, Gloria, 79
Tales From Beyond the Grave, 229
Tales From the Crypt, 225, 229
Tales of Hoffmann, 222
Tales of Terror, 223
Tales That Witness Madness, 229
Tamblyn, Russ, 20, 134, 192, 223, 255
Tarantula, The, 124
Taste of Blood, 65
Taste the Blood of Dracula, 66, 68
Taylor, Elizabeth, 49
Taylor, Joyce, 81, 225
Taylor, Rod, 177
Teasdale, Veree, 186
Temple, Shirley, 188
Terror Creatures From the Grave, 42
Terror in the Crypt, 33
Thatcher, Torin, 144, 165
That's the Spirit, 25
Them!, 124
Thief of Bagdad (1924), 140
Thief of Bagdad (1940), 140–142, 144, 150, 161, 202, 214
Thief of Bagdad (1960), 145–147, 153
Thing that Couldn't Die, 47
Things Happen at Night, 16
Things to Come, 94, 142
Thirteen Ghosts, 18
Thomas, Terry, 223, 229
Thorburn, June, 191, 192
1001 Arabian Nights, 218
Thousand and One Nights, A, 142
Three Stooges Meet Hercules, The, 155
Three Treasures, 161, 162
Three Worlds of Gulliver, 190–192, 258
Thriller, 230
Thunderball, 259
Tidal Wave, 21
Tierney, Gene, 16
Time Machine, The, 176, 177–178, 192, 255–256
Time of Their Lives, 16
Tiomkin, Dimitri, 184
Todd, Richard, 229
Todd, Thelma, 45
Tomb of Ligeia, 33

270

Tomlinson, David, 194
Tom Thumb, 176, 192, 255
Topper, 15
Topper Returns, 15
Topper Takes a Trip, 15
Topper (TV), 230
Tormented, 22
Torture Garden, 226
Totter, Audrey, 45
Touch of Melissa, 39
Tourneur, Jacques, 40, 46, 47, 55, 75, 79
Towering Inferno, 108
Tracy, Spencer, 25, 44
Travers, P.L., 194
Treasure Island, 172
Trip to the Moon, A, 178–179, 260
Trog, 99
True Life Adventures, 107
Tryon, Tom, 53
Tsuburaya, Eiji, 123
Tucker, Forrest, 96, 234
Turkel, Joseph, 202
Turner, Catherine, 47
"Turn of the Screw," 18
Tuttle, William, 177, 257
Twain, Mark, 190
Twenty Million Miles to Earth, 121
Twenty Thousand Leagues Under the Sea, 108, 172–173, 174, 175, 176, 183, 256, 259
Twice Told Tales, 225
Twilight Zone, 230
Twins of Evil, 68
Two Little Bears, The, 202
Two Lost Worlds, 105
2001: A Space Odyssey, 172, 180, 204
Two Thousand Years Later, 28
Tyler, Tom, 84

Udvarnoky, Chris, 53
Udvarnoky, Martin, 53
Ulysses, 151
Ulysses Against the Son of Hercules, 156
Un Chien Andalou, 205
Uncle Was A Vampire, 63
Undead, The, 33
Undying Monster, The, 74–75
Uninvited, The, 15–16, 19
Unknown Island, 104–105, 126
Unseen, The, 16
Urecal, Minerva, 192
Ustinov, Peter, 18, 201

Vadim, Annette, 63
Vadim, Roger, 63
Vadis, Don, 156
Valley of Gwangi, 116, 119, 138
Valley of Mist, 117–119, 124, 138
Valley of the Dinosaurs, 219
Valley of the Dragons, 108
Vampira, 70
Vampire and the Ballerina, 63–64
Vampire Circus, 68–69
Vampire Doll, The, 51
Vampire Lovers, 67
Vampire's Ghost, 61
Vampyr, 58, 63, 66

Van, Bobby, 187
Van Dyke, Dick, 180, 194, 196
Vane, Sutton, 28
Van Eyssen, John, 62
Vangenheim, Gustav von, 56
Varan the Unbelievable, 126–127
Vault of Horror, The, 229
Veidt, Conrad, 44, 90, 91, 140, 141, 142
Venable, Evelyn, 28
Vengeance of She, The, 199
Verdon, Gwen, 47
Verne, Jules, 108, 172, 174, 175, 176
Vessel, Edward, 147
Vetri, Victoria, 110
Victor, Henry, 40
Vij, The, 36
Vikings, The, 159
Villiers, James, 88
Voodoo Island, 41
Voodoo Man, 41
Vorkov, Zandor, 69
Voyage to the Bottom of the Sea, 108

Walker, Robert, 203
Wallace, Inez, 40
Walsh, Edward, 67
Walsh, Kay, 38
Walston, Ray, 47
Walter, Justin, 80
Walters, Thorley, 65
War Eagles, 117–119
War of the Gargantuas, 134
War of the Monsters, 136
War of the Worlds, 176
War of the Zombies, 41–42
Warhol, Andy, 70
Warner, H. B., 45
Warner, Stephen, 197, 198
Warren, Michael, 33
Waterman, Dennis, 66
Water Witch, 47
Watson, Bobs, 30
Wayne, Keith, 42
Way Out, 234
Webb, Clifton, 27
Wegner, Paul, 44, 92, 93
Weine, Robert, 90, 91
Weird Woman, 35
Welch, Raquel, 108, 109, 110
Welles, Orson, 35, 69
Wells, H. G., 176, 178, 201, 256, 260
Wendko, Paul, 53
Werewolf in a Girl's Dormitory, 79
Werewolf of London, 71–72, 74
Werewolf of Washington, 234
Werewolf, The, 79
Werewolves on Wheels, 81
Wetherell, Virginia, 33
Wexler, Paul, 41
Whale, James, 67
What's So Bad About Feeling Good?, 205–206
Wheatley, Dennis, 39
When Dinosaurs Ruled the Earth, 108, 110
When Women Had Tails, 111
When Women Lost Their Tails, 111
When Women Played Ding Dong, 111

When Worlds Collide, 176, 256
Where Do We Go From Here?, 199–201
White Pongo, 93, 96, 45
White Zombie, 39–40, 45
Wilde, Cornel, 142
Wilde, Oscar, 190
Wilder, Gene, 180, 198
Wilding, Michael, 16
Wilkie, Robert, 76
Willman, Noel, 64
Williams, Guy, 148
"William Wilson," 44
Willis, Matt, 60
Willy Wonka and the Chocolate Factory, 180
Wilmer, Douglas, 149, 157
Wind in the Willows, 213
Winwood, Estelle, 163, 170
"Windy," 27
Wise, Robert, 19, 21–22, 55, 257–258, 259
Witchcraft, 38
Witchcraft Through the Ages, 35
Witch's Curse, The, 154
Witch, The, 35
Witch Without A Broom, 38
Withers, George, 94
Wizard of Bagdad, The, 147
Wizard of Oz (1924), 18, 184
Wizard of Oz (1937), 188–190, 214
Wolfman, The, 60, 72–73, 75, 84
Woman Who Came Back, The, 35
Wonderful World of the Brothers Grimm, 110, 192, 223–224, 256
Wonders of Aladdin, 147–148
Wong, Victor, 117
Woodbridge, George, 65
Wood, Julie, 196
Wood Painting, 30
Woods, Donald, 18
World of the Vampires, 63
Wray, Fay, 112–113
Wrestling Women vs. The Aztec Mummy, 87
Wright, Teresa, 33
Wrixon, Maris, 93
Wyeth, Katya, 68
Wyman, Jane, 187
Wymark, Patrick, 52
Wyngarde, Peter, 35

Yellow Submarine, 218
Yog, Monster From Space, 135
Yolanda and the Thief, 27
York, Michael, 187
You Never Can Tell, 27
Young, Alan, 177–178, 192, 255
Young, Loretta, 27
Young, Robert (actor), 15
Young, Robert (director), 68

Zeman, Karel, 175–176
Zimbalist, Sam, 184
Zombies of Mora-Tau, 41
Zombies on Broadway, 41
Zotz, 201
Zucco, George, 41, 60, 61, 84, 93, 94